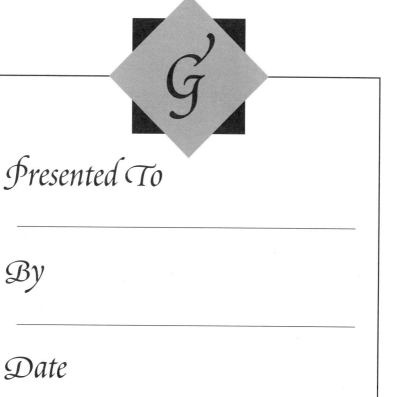

Presented To

_____

By

_____

Date

_____

Philosophy Nuggets

Ideas for building a better world

SAMOHT GIVOTANGI

■ ■ ■ ■ ■ ■ ■ ■ ■ ■

The Givotangi Company
Daytona Beach ✦ Florida

© 1994 Samoht Givotangi

The Givotangi Company
P.O. Box 120
Daytona Beach, FL 32115

Permission is granted to reprint not in excess of any two Nuggets not attributed to another party, in each and every calendar month, provided appropriate credit is given. Please send two copies of each reprint to the publisher. Printed in the USA. Smythe-sewn binding, 50% recycled acid-free paper.

Library of Congress Card Number: 94-75120
ISBN 0-9640470-8-X

10 9 8 7 6 5 4 3 2 1

Contents

"Contents" and "chapters" as normally understood are too numerous to be listed here. Check the index to locate desired subject matter. *The listing that follows is for front and back matter only.*

Contents

On the Cutting Edge of Social and Moral Theory

Philosophy Nuggets

© 1994 by Samoht Givotangi

It is good having the Johnny-one-notes looking into the *bottomless well*—after all, we do need specialists. But now and then along comes a generalist who looks out over a *limitless ocean*, mentally assimilates what he finds, and gathers in the best of what he sees to replace the worst of what he sees . . .

This snapshot does not appear in the book; it is meant only as an appetizer in a banquet of ideas. Bon appetit, my friend.

■ ■ ■

This book contains some information that has never been presented to the American people from a forum adequate to match its importance. To this add two major solutions and one explanation:

1. The moral solution (found throughout the book as the philosophy of enlightened self-interest), and

2. The economic solution (found in Nugget #186, "The Givotangi Parity Swap").

The explanation is in regards to man's climb to reach his full potential, and suggests various stages of moral evolution on the way to that end (Nugget #110-P9.29). And remember, it is always darkest before the dawn.

Credits

The individuals listed below are freelance operatives. In my view they do the best job. You decide if the results affirm the wisdom of this preference.

Carol Lawlor	*typist*
Sara Patton	*interior design & layout*
Nancy Freedom	*copy editing / indexing*

Thanks to my girlfriends . . . and a few guys, too, including cartoonists Rex F. May (Baloo) and Frank Cotham, among others.

Philosophy Nuggets
Ideas May Only Be Suppressed by Greater Ideas

Discover the fountain of truth
in a collection of thoughts with many faces,
allowing us to glimpse the star
we might someday steer by.

■ ■ ■

It is . . .   A compendious treatment of
basic principles to live by,
delving into the hidden, the
obvious, and the philosophical.

It is . . .   A potpourri of bold ideas
anchored in permanence on a
foundation of common sense.

It is . . .   A revelation of clear thinking
free of established preconceptions.

It is . . .   A disquisition of profound thoughts.

It is . . .   A melting pot of ideas distilled
from a realistic view of life.

And . . .   *It offers a secular replacement of the Bible
for those who seek alternatives.*

Dedicated to the world's eupraxophists (see glossary). May their numbers swell until the world can reclaim the grandeur that existed in Attica between 500 and 300 B.C.

Endorsement

Samoht (pen name) is a fellow checker player and a most unusual person.

— EDWARD SCHEIDT
*Chief, FBI New York City
Field Office, 1946–1952*

When I was a youngster, going to the movies was more than just the feature, you also saw at least one cartoon, a comedy, and a serial. This book in like fashion takes you back to those days when the trimmings were part of the meal, and made you feel like you were getting your money's worth. Extras that are dull and boring *should* be done away with. But if they are profound and interesting, savor them.

If the past sometimes seems better to you, it is because in many ways it really was.

Samoht Givotangi is a crossover philosopher who speaks to more than one audience.

**Enjoy the long-lasting
satisfaction of mental
thought bites.**

The Threefold Purpose of This Book,
Combining to Help Us Understand Life As It Is Today

1. To alert the public to the outrageous theft of wealth through the skimming of our country's currency (but not *yet* our coinage) by the privately owned Federal Reserve System, which is the cause of our $4-trillion national debt. The Bible says Samson pulled apart the pillars of the temple to bring it down; but they spelled the name wrong—it should have been Samoht. (The term "temple" is sometimes used when referring to the Fed.) It is not possible to reform tyranny of any stripe; it must be vanquished. (See #s 83, 110-R7, 110-R9 through X9, and others as listed in index.) Everything that is happening to us today, from our national debt to our declining standard of living, has been planned. You see, America has a cancer, and all of these other problems you can name are but a manifestation of that cancer.

2. To present some interesting observations on the slaying of JFK that have been largely overlooked. (#1)

3. And above all to offer a replacement for the Bible through a new concept of morality for mankind to live by called "enlightened self-interest" (these ideas are scattered throughout the book, with more than a few in #110), while garnering under one umbrella a litany of transgressions demanding exposure and abrogation.

Philosophy Nuggets:
Health food for the mind.

Written for people with an uncommon amount of common sense

"If you want to understand democracy, spend less time in the library with Plato and more time in the buses with people."

— SIMEON STRUNSKY

About the Author

Samoht Givotangi (a pseudonym) was born in Pennsylvania in 1931, and until this book was written his most notable achievements were a hitch in the Navy as an enlisted man during the Korean war, and a two-year proprietorship of a coffee vending machine route.

He was to spend a total of two years in three different mental hospitals on four separate occasions, and continues taking Mellaril to this day. In fact the prospect of languishing in a V.A. hospital indefinitely was a very real one until his mother secured his release in 1967.

All considered, including never having held a job paying much more than the minimum wage, Givotangi generally identifies with the man in the street although registered as a Republican (switched to Independent in December 1993). Those particulars notwithstanding, he is politically unaligned and exhorts a brand of "unity by choice" that goes beyond the pale. A secular pantheist if you will!

Our author has never been married—but has had the same girl friend since 1984 (only the third in his entire life).

Appendix

(Usually attached at the end of a piece of writing, but here contains information better known in advance.)

■ One of the first things you may notice about this book is that it is "dated." I am referring to the fact that the work began in 1984 when Communism was the great threat, and that I have chosen to allow the Nuggets relating to this subject to remain intact, even leaving on the dates they were written. While communism was an economic disaster, it has not died. Perestroika and glasnost reforms were meant to be dialectic in nature. That is to say, deception through retreating is part and parcel of their methodology, and we should never forget it.

My main regret is that those Marxists who are both sincere and idealistic do not understand the real intentions of the tiny group who are in control and hidden from view. If you need proof of this just take note of the massive suffering that has been inflicted on mankind in the name of betterment.

No, benevolence is not in their hearts. They personally have not evolved that final step upward. This is the bottom-line difference between us, notwithstanding strong similarities in our goals otherwise.

■ If we wish to peruse the most intriguing ideas, it is obligatory that we tap into a wide variety of sources. Obviously no one person has a monopoly on wisdom. Accordingly, I estimate that ⅔ of the ideas presented herein are my own product; and ⅓ have come from others (thinking them up, of course, does not necessarily make them original). By and large, proper credit was given for passages not invented here, but as a practical matter, there were numerous instances where borrowed phrases were too brief for credit to be given.

■ While I use the terms "Russia" and "USSR" inter-changeably throughout, this is not the case in #163, where Gary Kasparov uses "Russia" in its correct context meaning one of the 15 republics (the largest) which *until recently* comprised the USSR.

■ "New World Order" is certainly not a new term, and its inclusion in this work preceded the moment when we first heard it from President Bush.

■ Throughout this book I use the masculine gender almost exclusively; this is not to be mistaken as a slight against females, but is merely a grammatical convenience. No one who gives a careful reading to this work can assume that I harbor any un-warranted prejudices.

■ Inasmuch as it is not possible to avoid dual interpreta-tions of *all* one's observations, we leave it to the reader's good judgment to determine the correct meaning in its proper con-text either stated or implied by any minigram herein.

■ While most of this work and especially the philosophy are the creation of the author, use of the Givotangi credit line is unselective and limited.

Gems to Whet Your Mental Appetite
(References are to Nugget numbers, not page numbers.)

1. **The secrets of true happiness**
   (see Proem, #s 110-T4a & b, 150, 110-J7)

2. **The meaning of life**
   (comment made but do not have the answer, #110-J7)

3. **A new value system to live by**   *(see Preamble & #65)*

4. **The ultimate morality**   *(#s 110-P, 110-H4)*

5. **Rules for success**   *(#110-E5, trite but true)*

6. **The best rule for living**   *(#110-N7)*

7. **What is love?**   *(#110-Q7)*

8. **How important is money?**   *(#110-Y7)*

9. **What is the truth that shall make you free?**   *(#110-D8)*

10. **Three versions of the "New World Order"**   *(#164 DIV. 2)*

11. When will you know if you are "enlightened"?
    (#110-P9.26)

12. The progression of morality   *(#110-P9.29)*

13. How to do whatever you want and be better off for it
    (#110-P9.30)

14. Liberal "fairness," or Conservative "individualism"—which is your cup of tea?   *(#110-P9.33)*

15. When absolute power does not corrupt
    (#110-QQ & 150)

(These 15 minigrams are just a sampling of the 467 individual essays and aphorisms you will find within the pages of this book)

Three topics important enough for each to be in two parts:

1. Heaven can be found here on earth, if you know how to find it.   *(110-T4a & b)*

2. The higher the point from which you try to view a better life, the deeper your satisfaction will be upon finding it.
   (#110-R5a & b)

3. Why "interest" is public enemy #1.   *(#110-Y5a & b)*

"The mind once expanded
to the dimensions of a larger idea
never returns to its original size."
— OLIVER WENDELL HOLMES

Or as philosopher Martin Heidegger put it,
"It therefore might be helpful to us
to rid ourselves of the habit of always
hearing only what we already understand."

And then there was the prophet Hosea who said:
"My people perish for lack of knowledge."

ONE PHILOSOPHER'S JOURNEY :
I think there are some disciplines from
which a broader perspective can be gained
from figuring things out on your own, than
can be gleaned from the pronouncements
of "experts."
    In so doing you will have broken
new ground, because the route you have
selected is untraveled, and if it takes
longer to climb, it is because the mountain
you have chosen is more difficult.

Samokt Givotangi

"If we deem it appropriate to criticize others, at the very least we should not refrain from poking fun at ourselves."

– SAMOHT GIVOTANGI

Yes, I do step on some toes. Fortunately for them I wear moccasins and not jackboots.

Introduction

Within the following pages, I have put forth many ideas that are simply not politically or practically feasible for the 1990s. They are not meant to be. The vision I look to is not for the very near term. It is a world view that rejects nationalism as an outdated relic from our combative past.

The biggest stumbling block to this end is the nature of man (but not all men). The communists thought they could intervene in this regard, but their time frame to do so was too short and their efforts, although intense, were inadequate to the task.

I think the answer will come from genetic engineering and/or selective breeding, much to the horror of traditionalists—heaven forbid we should tamper with nature. But is not all medical science an exercise in tampering with nature? If we are to know, we must first look deep into our own psyche. The possibilities that lie ahead are incomprehensible to those of us living in the 1990s.

Here's to the future—it cannot be held back.

Preface

Dear Philosophy Buff:

Welcome to our world—as it is, and as it might be. This thought-provoking book addresses both, and we think it is rather special. It presents firm opinions, arrived at by starting out with an open mind, having resisted indoctrination in the early formative years, and having avoided the pitfalls of rebellion and radicalism of post-high school years. Once past those hurdles, one emerges into the fresh breezes of free thought, scanning the entire landscape unencumbered by outside vested influences. Eventually things get sorted out and opinions formed, but are always subject to reevaluation if circumstances change.

Philosophy Nuggets, then, is a potpourri of diverse yet interrelated ideas not expected to come from a single pen. We try to go to the heart of issues, without becoming mired in the superficial.

The controversial nature of many of these concepts ordains that *Philosophy Nuggets* will not be for everyone, and even if you are comfortable while reading them, it is unlikely that you will be in total agreement with everything that is offered.

Having said that, I invite you to join me on a journey from which a select few of you will never return. There is but one requirement—an open mind.

Preamble

Are you angry with the inability of our "leaders" to straighten out our problems? If you're not, you should be.

I have written Philosophy Nuggets to offer my views on how to build a better world, beginning with the foundation. As a result, I am suggesting a new value system to live by—one founded upon *enlightened* self-interest based upon enlightened common sense. It is meant also to be a secular *replacement* for the Bible, directed at those among us who reject or are wavering against superstition and fables being passed off as facts. The attempt to assemble this up-to-date machine depends on having the right parts. Fortunately, our inventory is extensive.

At the same time, I am advocating that we take the moral high ground for *practical* reasons. Those with the courage to enter this new world *might* find themselves thrust into a movement of unlimited dimensions, one that may even provide the final morality that will *ever* be needed to survive in the world of the future.

The few who are with me today will become the mentors of tomorrow's multitudes.

Proem

Here is the secret of true happiness—and it turns out to be the essence of simplicity itself:

Those who seek artificial pleasures are usually those who have missed out on natural pleasures.

The lure of a quick fix (literally and figuratively speaking) has caused them to take some wrong turns when they came to crucial forks in life's road.

So here we have it:

The greatest high comes to him who lives and acts the most sensibly.

Once you understand that, you will know the meaning of life in the way that nature surely must have intended.

Prologue

■ I have never been influenced by peer pressure, and have always chosen to go my own way. Had I allowed myself to become a part of the system, it would have prejudiced my mind and I would not today be able to see things in the same light. This, of course, is not to suggest that I am free from making errors. Being a member of a peer group is an emotional thing, giving rise to atavistic responses.

■ While most philosophical works speak to the upper class, this one is for the middle class where many more of us are, and where the greatest repository of common sense is to be found, but it *will* require you to think. I would rather be judged by the content of my ideas than by the complexity of my prose.

■ I do not aspire to pilot the plane of progress, nor do I wish to be just a passenger; what I want is to be the navigator and decide where we are going. To achieve our dreams it helps to have one who has achieved his point the way for us too.

■ Our social troubles will not abate until the right code for living is understood and applied. Enlightened self-interest be its name.

■ If you need the titillation of obscenity to spark an interest, you will not find it here. But if you delight in the stimulation of bold ideas, here is a particular mix of views that deserves attention.

Synopsis

For those who desire a fast track synopsis of this work, the summary in #56 will be helpful, as will be Gems to Whet Your Mental Appetite (pages 16–17), where a combined total of 18 points refers to concepts of special interest and where to find explanations for them.

Also, the lettered Nuggets in #110 are generally more pithy and incisive than the other numbered Nuggets. #110 is a work unto itself.

Philosophy Nuggets
Part I

For the Most Part in Chronological Order

by Samoht Givotangi

This first offering is for JFK assassination buffs whose thirst for detail is insatiable. Feel free to skip #1 if you do not include yourself in this group. Its presentation is intended to shock us awake so we can see all events by a brighter light than that provided by contemporary media candlepower.

1.   *March, 1992*

More people believe that Christ rose from the dead than believe the Warren Commission report on President Kennedy's assassination. And why not—it requires no greater leap of faith to believe the first than it does the second.

With the exception of the ending witticism and commentary, the following discourse is provided by *The Spotlight*, 300 Independence Avenue SE, Washington, D.C. 20003.

WHO KILLED JFK?
Coup d'etat in America...

On November 22, 1963 in Dealey Plaza in Dallas, the life of President John F. Kennedy came to an end. To this day the president's assassination remains one of the greatest mysteries in American history.

There have been dozens of theories advanced about "who" was behind the Kennedy assassination and "why." Hundreds of books and thousands of magazine articles have been devoted to the topic.

Two official federal "investigations" of the controversy have as yet failed to resolve the outstanding questions. Suspicions remain that the full truth has yet to be told. Thousands of pages of secret government files relating to the assassination remain locked away from public inspection.

And now a best-selling new book, *Plausible Denial*, by Mark Lane, and a blockbuster motion picture, Oliver Stone's *JFK*, have revived international interest in the circumstances surrounding the president's assassination and the subsequent cover-up.

Polls show an overwhelming majority of the American people believe there was more to the event than the official reports would have us believe and that there was, indeed, a high-level conspiracy to kill JFK.

In this special action report—containing information available nowhere else—*The Spotlight* newspaper reports on the latest controversial information linking, at the very least, the CIA to the JFK assassination and the cover-up thereafter.

Differing theories abound, but one thing's for certain: The CIA was definitely in on the murder of JFK.

Mark Lane's definitive new look at the assassination of John F. Kennedy, *Plausible Denial*, proves conclusively that the CIA had a hand in the assassination of President John F. Kennedy.

Unless somebody is, once and for all, indicted and tried for the murder of Kennedy on November 22, 1963, *Plausible Denial* may well be the last word on what has been called "the crime of the century."

This monumental book was written by the one man who sparked the search for the truth that has preoccupied perhaps millions of Americans for nearly three decades.

Here's the book that tells how the Washington-based *Spotlight* newspaper's libel trial with Watergate burglar E. Howard Hunt brought into a Florida courtroom the first hard evidence linking the CIA to the Kennedy assassination.

Lane's book picks up where his first international best-seller, *Rush to Judgment*, left off.

In *Rush to Judgment* Lane showed how it would have been absolutely impossible for a jury to convict the murdered Lee

Harvey Oswald for the killing of the president. The evidence just wasn't there.

Now, nearly thirty years later, Lane not only proves conclusively that there was a conspiracy behind the president's murder, but also a subsequent cover-up. In *Plausible Denial* the chilling tale comes full circle.

Lane agreed to serve as *The Spotlight's* defense attorney after E. Howard Hunt won a $650,000 libel judgment against the populist weekly.

In 1978, *The Spotlight* had published an article by former high-ranking CIA official Victor Marchetti which alleged that the CIA intended to frame Hunt for the Kennedy assassination.

(Until that time *The Spotlight* had cautiously avoided publishing articles delving into the Kennedy assassination controversy. Then, as today, there was such a myriad of theories and opinions about the matter that the editorial board of *The Spotlight* believed the subject was best left alone.)

Although the editors of *The Spotlight* felt Marchetti's article served, if anything, as an advance warning to Hunt about what his former employers had in mind, the ex-CIA man decided to sue, even though he admitted *The Spotlight's* story seemed plausible.

Fortunately—for *The Spotlight*—an error in the trial judge's instructions to the jury gave the populist weekly grounds for an appeal.

When the case was successfully appealed and ordered for retrial, Mark Lane stepped in for the defense.

After a heated trial, a jury came down in favor of *The Spotlight*.

Among the big names deposed during the Hunt case:
- Former CIA Director Richard Helms
- Former CIA Director Stansfield Turner

- Former CIA Chief for the Western Hemisphere
  David Atlee Phillips
- Former CIA and FBI man (and Watergate celebrity)
  G. Gordon Liddy

The most damning evidence against Hunt came, however, when attorney Lane presented the deposition of former CIA operative Marita Lorenz to the court.

Miss Lorenz testified under oath that in Dallas, Texas, just one day prior to Kennedy's assassination in that same city, she, along with a handful of other CIA figures, met not only with E. Howard Hunt, but also with nightclub operator Jack Ruby who later killed Lee Harvey Oswald, the president's alleged assassin.

According to Miss Lorenz, she was also acquainted at the same time with a CIA operative who traveled about under the name—you guessed it—Lee Harvey Oswald.

(As "assassination buffs" know all too well, there is a growing body of opinion that the real Oswald was impersonated, perhaps over a period of several years, by one or more operatives using his identity in a variety of places, both in the United States and abroad. This is just one of the many "unsolved" mysteries of the JFK murder.)

Leslie Armstrong, a Miami resident who was jury forewoman in the case, has issued a statement in conjunction with the release of Lane's written account of the trial:

"Mr. Lane was asking us [the jury] to do something very difficult. He was asking us to believe John Kennedy had been killed by our own government.

"Yet when we examined the evidence closely, we were compelled to conclude that the CIA had indeed killed President Kennedy."

Now the whole story of *The Spotlight's* pivotal role in this amazing trial is told by Mark Lane.

Following an informative introduction by retired top-ranking Pentagon official, Col. L. Fletcher Prouty, Lane describes in the opening chapters the important background regarding his entry into the controversial field of Kennedy assassination research—an arena he stumbled into, it seems, almost by accident.

An article he wrote about the mistreatment accorded Lee Harvey Oswald by the Dallas authorities and others came to the attention of Oswald's beleaguered mother.

Mrs. Oswald contacted Lane and asked him to represent her son's interests before the Warren Commission investigation (or was it a cover-up?).

The rest is history.

An important appendix to *Plausible Denial* includes the original essay Lane wrote that came to Mrs. Oswald's attention.

It is a concise, yet comprehensive overview of the flaws in the case against the alleged assassin.

An additional appendix includes an interesting review of Lane's original book *Rush to Judgment*. This review rightly says "If *Rush to Judgment* accomplishes nothing else, it will live as a classic for every serious amateur detective in America.

"Long winter nights in the farmhouse will be spent poring over the contradictions in the [Warren Commission Report] with Lane's book for a guide."

The same review is almost prophetic. It concludes: "[Lane's] work is not without a trace of that stature we call heroic. Three cheers. Because the game is not over yet."

The game was not over. Little did that reviewer know that nearly twenty years later Mark Lane would come into contact—again inadvertently—with a courageous Washington-based newspaper that had (inadvertently) found itself embroiled in the Kennedy assassination controversy.

Lane describes, in sometimes humorous, sometimes ironic

fashion how his encounter with the late Haviv Schieber, the Polish-born former Israeli who became a critic of Zionism (well known to *Spotlight* readers), led to his acquaintance with *The Spotlight*.

It was through Schieber he learned of the Hunt libel suit which, of course, had been almost totally blacked out by the Establishment media. Schieber had made it his mission to see Mark Lane come to *The Spotlight's* defense. He succeeded.

In his new book Lane quotes liberally from some of the stunning pretrial depositions he conducted in preparation of the defense.

If anything, as Lane's summations make clear, the witnesses called in Hunt's defense by the ex-CIA man's attorneys only ended up proving Hunt had more to hide than he had to admit.

As for Hunt himself, his contradictory stories about where he was situated the day before the Kennedy assassination and the day of the assassination itself become all too suspicious.

Lane takes excellent advantage of Hunt's sworn statements (in deposition and during the two trials) to show the contradictions.

These contradictions alone could have spelled Hunt's courtroom demise.

However, it was the testimony of Marita Lorenz that convinced the jury, once and for all, *The Spotlight* (and Lane himself) had a much more plausible story than Hunt. Thus, the stunning courtroom victory.

As an afterword to the Hunt trial, Lane provides his readers with some fascinating information (little publicized) which sheds some additional light onto the strange world of America's intelligence community and its connections to the Kennedy assassination.

Two separate additional appendices, along with the curiously—yet appropriately—titled epilogue "Operation Zapata" review the still-unanswered questions about yet another mystery: "Where was George Bush?"

(Is it only a coincidence that Sen. Edward M. Kennedy, brother of the slain president, repeatedly asked that question when he addressed the 1988 Democratic National Convention?

(Edward Kennedy was—or so it seemed—talking about George Bush's "absence" during the key international events of the Reagan era, including the Iran-Contra mess.

(But was Kennedy, in fact, asking "Where was George?" on the day his brother was slain in Dallas?)

Lane reviews evidence which suggests President George Bush was, in fact, an active CIA man as early as 1963—or earlier.

The president's official biography claims Bush didn't assume a position with the CIA until 1976—many years later. The evidence suggests otherwise.

As Lane's presentation reveals, it appears as though Bush not only had a key part in the infamous Bay of Pigs operation (which many believe led, in part, to Kennedy's assassination), but that he had close contacts with the anti-Castro Cuban community in Florida which has been linked (through its CIA and organized crime connections) to the JFK murder.

Is the "game over" just yet? Perhaps that is something only George Bush himself can answer.

Is it possible the alleged "October Surprise" of 1980 was only a successor to a "November Surprise" in 1963?

Lane doesn't offer any conclusions in *Plausible Denial.* He simply lays out the evidence for his readers to consider themselves.

The prestigious *Kirkus Reviews* (October 1, 1991) has already issued a highly favorable review of Lane's new blockbuster saying, "Well reasoned at every point, Lane's convincing report sounds like the last word on the assassination."

Plausible Denial can be ordered from *The Spotlight.*

You may also order the 98-minute black-and-white VHS videotape, *Rush to Judgment: The Plot to Kill the President,* co-produced by Mark Lane.

This exciting video includes original 1963 news reports, including interviews with key witnesses, law enforcement officers and others.

More importantly, however, the video includes Lane's exclusive interviews with witnesses uncovered by Lane who were ignored by the Official Warren Commission investigation. This video is a valuable supplement (and introductory preface) to *Plausible Denial.*

■ ■ ■

Did the CIA have a hand in the assassination of President John F. Kennedy? How did the CIA frame Lee Harvey Oswald for involvement in the president's murder? Did President Richard Nixon blackmail the CIA over its role in the affair? Was President George Bush working for the CIA on November 22, 1963?

These were some of the provocative topics addressed by attorney Mark Lane when he was a special guest on the October 26 and November 2, 1991 broadcasts of *Spotlight* Editor Vince Ryan's weekly radio talk forum, the *Editor's Roundtable.*

Lane is the author of *Plausible Denial* a new best-seller which describes his defense of *The Spotlight* against a libel suit brought by former CIA man E. Howard Hunt.

Following extensive litigation, *The Spotlight* prevailed. *Plausible Denial* describes the course of events leading up to the trial and its stunning resolution, in which the jury concluded that the CIA had indeed been responsible for the president's assassination.

Lane's interest in the JFK assassination is long standing. Author of the best-selling *Rush to Judgment,* the first major critique of the Warren Commission Report, Lane was the foremost pioneer in the field of research into the president's murder.

What follows is an edited transcript of Lane's two-part interview. Questions by Ryan and his colleagues are in italics. Lane's comments are in regular type.

When you first emerged as the foremost critic of the Warren Commission cover-up of the JFK assassination, there were a lot of people who didn't want to doubt the Warren Commission. Today things are very different. Could you comment?

There were so many press attacks on me, it was really incredible. At the time I was merely saying the shots had come from more than one direction. That's hardly subversive.

However, do you know what the longest article originating from the Associated Press (at least up until that time) was about? It was an attack on me.

I found out through the Freedom of Information Act years later that the CIA had directed its own "key journalists" in the news media here and around the world to attack me.

The first review of my first book on the JFK assassination, *Rush to Judgment,* was written at CIA headquarters in Langley, Virginia. I have a copy of that. They got a copy of my book from the printer before I even had a copy. The CIA reviewed the book and formulated a game plan to destroy me.

After I learned about this and spoke out, some of these people such as Jeremiah O'Leary (who now writes for the *Washington Times)* said if I ever said they worked for the CIA they would sue me.

Let me make it really plain. I don't know who pays them. If Mr. O'Leary is not being paid by the CIA, after all he's done for them, he should talk to his shop steward and not to me.

The fact is, he has carried out the government line. So has George Lardner of the *Washington Post*. So has David Burnham of the *New York Times*. These are the people who are denying the facts to the American people.

In PLAUSIBLE DENIAL you specifically address the question of whether CIA man E. Howard Hunt was in Dallas not on the day Kennedy was assassinated, but instead on the day before [November 21, 1963].

Anybody who is familiar with "popular" literature on the JFK assassination has seen the famous "tramp pictures" and at least one other as well.

It has been claimed these photos show Hunt and his fellow CIA man Frank Sturgis in Dealey Plaza moments after the president's murder.

Your book does not base its conclusions on those photos to prove your point. Could you comment on those photos?

I saw those photos many years ago. I brought those to the attention of the Dallas authorities and to the Warren Commission. I asked if three people were arrested in Dealey Plaza and who they were. We never got the answers.

Years later someone noticed one of the people looked something like Hunt and one of the others looked like Sturgis. The assertion was raised "Hunt and Sturgis were there."

David Belin of the Rockefeller Commission investigating the CIA invited Hunt and Sturgis in to talk about these photos. Then they used the testimony and the photo analysis to prove it wasn't either of them and said, "We've cleared Hunt and Sturgis."

I do not think the photos were of Hunt and Sturgis. I think the CIA cynically used this material to encourage the belief among many people that Hunt and Sturgis were there and then turned around and "cleared" them.

What the evidence does show was, Hunt was in Dallas on November 21, 1963, the day before the assassination. The testimony to this effect came during *The Spotlight's* libel trial with Hunt from Marita Lorenz, a former CIA operative.

Miss Lorenz testified she was a part of a team—a hit team of assassins—that drove from Miami to Dallas and arrived there a day before the assassination.

She traveled with Frank Sturgis, among others. She met Jack Ruby [who later killed the alleged presidential assassin, Lee Harvey Oswald] in a motel room in Dallas. Hunt came into the hotel room and paid off Sturgis. She saw the cash.

However, when she realized this was not just a usual CIA anti-Castro gun-running operation (as she first thought), she went back to Miami and then to Fort Lee, New Jersey. By then she found the president had been killed.

According to Miss Lorenz, when Sturgis later came to see her to recruit her for another CIA activity, he told her: "We killed Kennedy. That was the big one. Everything was covered. Everything was terrific." Well, it's no longer covered and it's no longer terrific, because Marita Lorenz has told her story.

Miss Lorenz said Hunt was there in Dallas and he was paying off the assassination team. That was her testimony. The jury heard that and a lot of other evidence.

This was the first time a jury in a civil case had a chance to consider the question of who killed President Kennedy.

The forewoman of the jury, Leslie Armstrong, came out and said to the news media: "Mr. Lane asked us to do something very, very difficult. We were chosen as an impartial group of men and women. We had no position on the Kennedy assassination.

"Mr. Lane wanted us to say our own government had killed

our president. We listened to the evidence very carefully. We discussed it. We concluded the CIA killed President Kennedy; and I call upon the United States government to do something about that."

What the media did, however, was black out her words, so no one ever heard what she said.

Miss Armstrong has agreed, however, to appear on radio and television with me and tell what the jury thought and why they reached their conclusion.

We are going to raise this question to the American people and hope they respond.

You don't say then, for example, that E. Howard Hunt was there in Dealey Plaza on the day of the assassination or that he was firing a gun at President Kennedy?

I doubt very much he did. Hunt's expertise, we learned, was as a paymaster for shadowy covert operations of the CIA up and down the Eastern seaboard and based primarily in Miami.

I would be very surprised to learn he did anything else other than to act as a paymaster; and Marita Lorenz says in this particular activity, Hunt paid off this operation.

Is it your opinion those people who try to use the famous tramp photos to "prove" Hunt and the CIA were involved in the JFK murder are well intentioned but doing a disservice to the overall effort to show how the CIA really was, in fact, involved?

These people are misguided. They've fallen into the CIA's trap. I have no doubt many of these people have the desire to get the truth out, but they are being misled by the CIA.

George Bush was appointed director of the CIA in the 1970s.

Yet in PLAUSIBLE DENIAL you suggest Bush was, in fact, involved in the CIA for many years before that—even as far back as November 23, 1963—the day following President Kennedy's assassination.

When Bush became director of the CIA, he testified he had never had any contact with, any position with, or any assignment from the CIA prior to that time.

In fact, at the time, some of the members of the Senate were asking why this man who had no intelligence background was being appointed to this post. The senators wondered why a career intelligence official wasn't being given the position.

I think Bush did have an intelligence background. If you are going to be the President of the United States, you should not lie to the American people about your background.

On November 29, 1963—one week to the day after the assassination of John Kennedy—then-FBI Director J. Edgar Hoover wrote a letter (a copy of which I've had for years); and the letter said someone from the FBI and from the Defense Intelligence Agency briefed "Mr. George Bush of the CIA" on November 23, 1963 about possible unauthorized activities by anti-Castro Cubans in the Miami area following the president's murder.

Hoover was saying Bush was the authority on these anti-Castro Cubans and what their authorized actions should be and that they would want to ask Bush about what other activities the Cubans might be involved in that are not authorized.

That's quite important, because in *Plausible Denial* we establish with what I think is absolute proof that it was this group within the CIA, based in Miami, utilizing anti-Castro Cubans who were in the area, who killed Kennedy.

If Bush, then, was the authority on that the day after the assassination, he was the authority on something of great significance.

I had this document for many years, having obtained it under the Freedom of Information Act, but earlier Bush was just a former congressman from Texas, and it didn't seem of great significance.

Years later, however, Joe McBride, a reporter for the *Nation* magazine, became aware of the document. By then Bush was Vice President of the United States.

McBride contacted the vice president's office and they said, "No, George Bush was not then with the CIA."

Soon afterward, the CIA issued its own statement, saying the George Bush involved [in the briefing described in Hoover's letter] was "George William Bush" who worked for the CIA at that time.

To the surprise of McBride and his editor, this was a bizarre statement. The CIA does not make public statements about who works for them. This was very strange.

McBride found George William Bush, who lives and works in the Washington area. He was working for the Social Security Administration. He had worked briefly filing photos for the CIA for a six-month period.

George William Bush responded to their inquiries, saying, "I was never briefed by the FBI or the CIA about the Kennedy assassination."

This takes us back to George Herbert Walker Bush. I think we've established he worked for the CIA at that time.

More than that, George Herbert Walker Bush (now the president) was in the New Haven, Connecticut area about the same time his fellow Yale graduate William F. Buckley Jr. (founder of *National Review* magazine) was being recruited into the CIA. Was Bush also recruited at that time? We don't know.

It was around that time, though, that Bush went down to Midland, Texas, an oil boom town.

There he met the Liedtke brothers, Hugh and Bill. They

had expertise in geology. They told Bush that if he could come back to Texas with a lot of money they could form a company.

The future president went back to Texas with all this money and they formed an oil company with Bush in the familiar starting role as vice president. They called the company Zapata Petroleum.

Bush made a lot of money from Zapata and then sold his interest. He then moved to Houston with his wife Barbara and formed Zapata Offshore Petroleum, with operations all over the Far East and Latin America.

It was around this time the CIA's so-called Bay of Pigs invasion of Cuba was being planned.

The top-secret code name for the Bay of Pigs operation known only to the Joint Chiefs of Staff and a few other people at that time—it's now certain—was "Operation Zapata."

Col. Fletcher Prouty was the individual who supplied the weapons of war for the CIA for a period of nine years. He wrote the introduction to *Plausible Denial*.

According to Prouty, he was asked, in his official capacity, to obtain the two ships which would invade Cuba during Operation Zapata.

Prouty found the ships in the Chesapeake naval facility and took them down to Elizabeth City, North Carolina to an abandoned naval base and there the naval colors were painted off and the ships were given new names; these were the only two ships used for Operation Zapata: *Barbara* and *Houston*.

There's a great deal of excitement over the publication of PLAUSIBLE DENIAL.

The book is the first book ever published (to my knowledge) which documents the role of the CIA in the assassination of John F. Kennedy.

Members of Congress have seen advance copies of the book, and there will soon be members speaking on the floor of Congress and demanding the government do something about our findings.

One member of Congress told me he is going to say the mystery of the death of President Kennedy has been solved by *Plausible Denial.*

Your book documents conclusively that two months before the president's assassination, the CIA was already laying the groundwork for framing the alleged assassin, Lee Harvey Oswald, by making it appear as though Oswald was seeking to make contact with the Soviet and Cuban embassies in Mexico City, presumably as part of his assassination plot.

Yes, but the crucial part is that the purpose of this activity by the CIA was to terrorize any potential investigation after the assassination.

Of course, the CIA did not know that after the president was killed the new president, Lyndon Johnson, would appoint an investigative commission headed by Chief Justice Earl Warren. However, they knew someone would be looking into the death of the president. Obviously it would not go unnoticed.

What the CIA did was to arrange a scenario—in advance— to frighten any investigator. This is what they did.

After the president's assassination, the CIA told Warren its investigation was complete and it had concluded that Oswald had acted alone.

The CIA went on to say, however, that it had very tragic news: Oswald, they claimed, had been in Mexico City on September 26, 1963 and remained there until October 3.

While Oswald was there, they said, he went to the Soviet Embassy at which time the CIA made photographs of him and recordings of his conversations there.

They told Warren that Oswald had a code name for some-one at the embassy, a "Comrade Kostin," and that he was heard to say: "This is Lee Harvey Oswald. Are there messages for me?"

This was to suggest an ongoing relationship.

"Comrade Kostin," the CIA told Warren, was a code name for a KGB "liquid affairs department" officer in charge of assas-sinations in the Western Hemisphere. The CIA told Warren that Oswald had seen this man less than two months before he killed the President of the United States.

Furthermore, the CIA said, Oswald then went to the Cuban Embassy in Mexico City and met with Sylvia Duran, an em-ployee there, and asked for a visa to get to Cuba from Mexico (presumably after he killed the president), and then, of course, to go on to the Soviet Union.

Warren was obviously petrified by all of this news from the CIA. The CIA did say they didn't think the Soviets or the Cubans were involved, but they did say that if the world heard this story, the third world war could break out.

Warren went to the first meeting of the staff of his com-mission—and I have the minutes of that meeting, obtained through the Freedom of Information Act. According to those minutes, Warren said: "I've just met with President [Lyndon] Johnson. Our general principles by which we have always lived, telling the truth, must be set aside. If we tell the truth, we could have World War III. Forty million people may die.

Warren bought the CIA story, and he was going to cover it up. So they covered up the facts. What happens when we look into the facts? I don't know what is more pathetic: Warren rely-ing upon the CIA for the truth or Warren deciding he would keep what he thought was the truth away from the American people for our best interests.

The fact is that the CIA's tape recording of "Oswald" asking to speak to Comrade Kostin is not a recording of Oswald. The Warren Commission never listened to the tape.

There is an FBI document from then-FBI Director J. Edgar Hoover which says the seven FBI agents who questioned Oswald after his arrest say that the voice on the CIA tape was clearly not the voice of Lee Harvey Oswald.

The photos of the person the CIA claimed were Lee Harvey Oswald in Mexico City are clearly not Oswald. It looks nothing at all like Oswald.

Yet the Warren Commission never looked into this. We also find that the Cuban Embassy employee, Sylvia Duran, when questioned by the Mexican authorities, said: "Oswald was never here. It was a short blond guy. It was someone who didn't look anything at all like him."

I have a copy of a cable from the director of the CIA to the Mexican police saying: "Arrest Sylvia Duran. Hold her incommunicado."

In essence, do whatever has to be done to make sure she changes her story and implicates Oswald.

The cable also instructed the CIA's contacts in the Mexican police not to tell the Mexican government what was going on. The CIA claimed there were "disloyal elements" in the Mexican government.

Sylvia Duran was arrested and held incommunicado. She finally agreed to say it was Oswald she had seen. So she did.

Then when she was released, she came out and told the truth, contradicting the story she had been forced to tell.

Another cable came from the CIA, ordering the arrest of Miss Duran until she [again] switched her story. So she did. However, Miss Duran is talking again, and she says it wasn't Oswald.

The whole story about Oswald meeting with the Soviets

and the Cubans in Mexico City was a charade set up by the CIA.

We're not talking about a cover-up. This was not after the president was killed—but before. We're talking about the planning stages.

This is evidence of the CIA plan to kill the president and blame it on Oswald. This was in the works almost two months before the shots were fired in Dallas.

Why would the CIA want to kill Kennedy?

Motive is important. Kennedy said—and the *New York Times* reported it—that he intended to dissolve the CIA, break it into a thousand pieces and cast it into the wind.

In *Plausible Denial* I quote written statements by E. Howard Hunt, David Atlee Phillips and other CIA officials saying that at that point, it was like a tomb in the halls of CIA headquarters at Langley, Virginia. They knew they were finished.

The Kennedy dynasty was just beginning, and the President intended to appoint his brother, then-Attorney General Robert Kennedy, to head a new super intelligence agency. The CIA was finished, without question.

What's more [John] Kennedy was beginning a rapprochement with Fidel Castro, saying to him that while he could not function as an agent of the Soviet Union, the United States would accept his socialist regime.

Kennedy was also ending the CIA's involvement in Vietnam. He intended to withdraw every single American from Vietnam.

Everything the CIA wanted, Kennedy was opposing. This was what was high on the CIA's mind when the decision was made to kill him. The Kennedy dynasty ended with those shots in Dallas.

The CIA has now elected as the President of the United States a former director of the CIA. It defeated Jimmy Carter for re-election in 1980 through the so-called October Surprise. I've learned Congress has some information about that which will be very startling to the American people.

Richard Nixon has claimed the CIA set him up at Watergate (and, of course, there's E. Howard Hunt again).

In other words, the CIA has removed president after president. Now the former CIA director is president.

Bush is, in my opinion, the most powerful single person in the history of civilization. There is no opposition. There is one person in charge of the world—the New World Order—and that is the former director of the CIA.

I believe all of this started with the shots in Dallas on November 22, 1963.

In your book you mention Nixon's fascination with the Kennedy assassination and his apparent attempt to blackmail the CIA over its involvement in the murder. Could you comment?

Nixon used what he believed to be evidence about the CIA's role in the assassination as part of an extortion attempt against the CIA.

In his book, *The Ends of Power*, H.R. Haldeman, Nixon's former White House chief of staff, describes how he was sent by Nixon to see CIA Director Richard Helms.

Nixon ordered Haldeman to tell Helms he wanted the CIA to help cover up the Watergate break-in as part of a national security matter. Nixon told Haldeman to tell Helms (if Helms refused to go along with the deal) that he knew all about the CIA and "the Bay of Pigs" and that it would all come out.

Haldeman went to Helms with the message, and Helms said, "No." Then Haldeman told Helms Nixon knew all about the CIA's role in the Bay of Pigs, and Helms went through the ceiling, pounding the table, screaming, etc.

Haldeman felt the reaction was totally inappropriate inasmuch as the truth about the CIA's activities at the Bay of Pigs invasion in Cuba was already on the public record.

After Haldeman left Helms and went back to the White House, he learned President Nixon had a code when he talked about the assassination of John F. Kennedy.

When Nixon said "Bay of Pigs," he meant the assassination of President Kennedy.

In other words, Nixon had been sending a message to the director of the CIA (through Haldeman) that he knew all about the CIA's role in the JFK assassination: Unless the CIA helped Nixon cover up Watergate, he threatened to blow things wide open.

Of course, Nixon never did. He knew what happened to Kennedy. He was removed from office, but he is still alive.

■ ■ ■

The Establishment media's attack on the new Oliver Stone film, *JFK,* was the subject of discussion on the January 11 broadcast of *Spotlight* Editor Vince Ryan's weekly radio talk forum, *Editor's Roundtable.*

Ryan's guest was Col. L. Fletcher Prouty, who was the liaison between the Pentagon and the CIA at the time of the assassination of President John F. Kennedy.

Prouty, the author of *The Secret Team,* served as primary technical adviser to Stone during the making of *JFK* and was portrayed by actor Donald Sutherland in the film.

In the discussion with Ryan, Prouty discussed the background of the making of *JFK* and commented on the Establishment's unusual critical response to the film.

Questions by Ryan and his colleagues appear in italics. Prouty's comments are in regular type.

Prior to the release of JFK, there were rumblings of criticism within the Establishment media about the film. However, as we pointed out in THE SPOTLIGHT on January 6 & 13, 1992, the very week JFK was released, there was a frenzy of media attacks. How do you account for this?

The movie is getting at very basic issues. If there's an assassination of a president and it is done by one person, then people say, "Well, he was a nut."

You don't have to think of why that person did it.

However, the minute you add a second person or a third or fourth and realize this is a conspiracy, then you ask, "Why did they conspire? Why was the president killed?"

If Oliver Stone didn't do anything else, he focused on that simple, very direct issue. People just get bowled over by the bare facts of that issue.

When people accepted Lee Harvey Oswald as the "lone assassin" all these years—and so many did—and all of a sudden someone shows very dramatically, in a magnificent movie, that it couldn't have been Oswald all by himself, they leave the theaters saying to themselves, "Well, there was a conspiracy."

In their minds is the biggest question: Why was John F. Kennedy killed?

In response, these big-time writers—not movie critics—are stepping in to see if they can't find some way to hold the barrier against the breakdown of this "lone gunman" theory so they don't have to explain "why."

We've seen writers such as Tom Wicker of the *New York Times* and George Lardner of the *Washington Post* and George Will and Ellen Goodman turning up as film critics.

Even President George Bush on his big trip to the Far East said he had no problems with the Warren Commission report. It was right, he said: one killer.

What's behind all this? The criticisms all seem to be coming from the same source. The same things keep popping up in all that's written. It's as though someone has put out instructions on what to say. Somebody is running this whole thing.

The other day Sen. Arlen Specter [R-Pa.], who was one of the counsels for the Warren Commission and who originated the "magic bullet theory," appeared on C-SPAN.

Specter's so-called magic bullet supposedly went through President Kennedy and then hit Gov. John Connally of Texas, causing several wounds, following an impossible trajectory.

Well, when Specter appeared on C-SPAN the other day, here's what he said when asked to explain to the audience what the Warren Commission was: "The Warren Commission was formed to assassinate the investigation of President Kennedy's death."

That's quite a faux pas—perhaps a Freudian slip—on Specter's part. In Specter's home town of Philadelphia film audiences are booing and hissing and laughing when Specter's name is mentioned on screen in the film.

We knew that was an important point in making the film. That's why Stone had his technicians recreate the "magic bullet charts" the Warren Commission used.

Former President Gerald Ford (who was a member of the Warren Commission) recently co-wrote a column published in the WASHINGTON POST attacking the film. He basically demanded to know: "How dare you criticize the Warren Commission?"

Well, we might as well include ex-President Lyndon Johnson himself among those [who have taken issue with the conclusions of the Warren Report].

It was, you'll recall, Johnson who said "good old Jerry Ford has trouble chewing gum and walking up the stairs at the same time."

However, I will tell you something Johnson left with us that is very important.

In 1973 Johnson was suffering from heart trouble, and he knew he would not live much longer. He brought an old friend, Leo Janos, a writer, down to his ranch in Texas. They sat there, and Johnson reminisced.

Johnson said to Janos: "Kennedy was killed as the result of a conspiracy."

That's ex-President Johnson who appointed the Warren Commission saying that. This appears in the July, 1973 issue of the *Atlantic Monthly* magazine.

The second thing he said was: "I never believed Oswald killed Kennedy alone."

The third thing he said, though, was something you could write books about. Johnson said, "We were operating a 'Murder Inc.'"

Now when Johnson said "we," he didn't mean himself and Lady Bird, his wife. What it has to mean is the U.S. government. What else can "we" mean in a context such as that?

Then, we ask, what does he mean by "Murder Inc."? In my military experience I was required to work with "Murder Inc."

We killed people—fortunately overseas. All of this was shown in Sen. Frank Church's Senate hearings in the early 1970s.

The people in this "Murder Inc." are professionals. They are called mechanics. They do other things, of course, but they can murder in very sophisticated ways. Johnson recognized that.

The interesting thing about his reference to "Murder Inc."

is the "Inc." at the end. It wasn't just being done for the JFK assassination. The process was being maintained.

So let's ask Gerald Ford and the media columnists who are criticizing the film to explain what this ex-president of the United States who created the Warren Commission meant by all this.

I'd say what Johnson said explains what happened on November 22, 1963 more than anything else I know of.

Do you have any criticisms of the film? Is there anything you would have presented differently?

That's a good question. When we finished the film we had over six hours of good film. I wish we could have shown the whole six hours to every audience.

Yet, in today's movie theaters you just can't do that. So the final version came down to three hours long. Even now the movie theaters have to sacrifice some show time because of the length of the film.

What we had to do was cut bridges between certain scenes in the film. As a consequence the audience didn't get to see the transition between those scenes. Still, it's a darned good film, considering everything.

Your own experiences involving the assassination of President Kennedy are very interesting. Movie audiences got to see those experiences as actor Donald Sutherland portrayed you—as "Col. X"— meeting with actor Kevin Costner playing New Orleans District Attorney Jim Garrison in Washington.

On the day of the assassination I was on my way back from an official military trip to the south pole. We were at a Navy base in Christ Church, New Zealand that supports south pole activities.

I was walking with a member of the U.S. Congress, and we heard a brief radio announcement President Kennedy had been shot dead in Dallas. That's all we heard.

We went into town to find a newspaper, and in short order we did. The *Christ Church Star* was printed within about two hours after the murder. So about four hours after the killing we had a copy of that newspaper in hand.

From just looking at the paper, I could see a few things that raised my eyebrows.

One thing was a complete life story of Oswald, including a picture of him wearing a business suit and necktie (which couldn't have been taken of him on the day of the assassination when he was wearing work clothes).

Now this story was a complete biography of an unknown 24-year-old whom the police had not even officially charged within that four-hour time period. They only charged him later that night.

Now also you have to take into consideration the difference in time zones. However, we figured out that that story had to have been written before the murder. That's all we knew when we were there in New Zealand.

When I arrived back in the states I had time to figure it all out carefully. There's no way that story about Oswald's life could have been in that paper so quickly unless it had been written ahead of time. Who could do that?

This is an important point about the film which shows you how meticulous Oliver Stone was in making *JFK.*

I still have that old newspaper. So Stone sent it to a printer who cleaned the paper up and reprinted it for the movie. In *JFK,* you see Sutherland walk up and buy that paper. When we saw that paper for the first time we knew it was conclusive evidence that this packaged story about Oswald had been prepared to go out even before the shots were fired.

Another thing: That newspaper also reported people on the scene in Dallas heard three rounds of automatic rifle fire.

Now the official Warren Commission version doesn't include any automatic rifle fire aimed at the president.

There could, of course, have been automatic rifles being fired, or the rapid firing of several guns, but Oswald—according to the Warren report—didn't have an automatic rifle.

I found something else interesting. In that same newspaper there was a picture of the Texas School Book Depository Building from where the fatal shots were supposedly fired. There were windows open all over the building. The picture was taken at the time of the assassination.

I had worked on presidential protection, and I knew it was against regulations to permit windows to be open in buildings near a presidential parade route. That way it's possible to ensure that no one fires from one of these open windows.

This picture was enough to tell me this whole thing was a conspiracy going right to the top.

The JFK film focused on Jim Garrison's prosecution of Clay Shaw (and the investigation of David Ferrie). It subsequently turned out both Shaw and Ferrie had been involved with the CIA—although Garrison couldn't prove it at the time.

Most of the Shaw-Ferrie story is part of the official cover story. Those people didn't do the assassination themselves.

However, they were part of the conspiracy cover-up in that they were the ones who drew the attention away from the real mechanics involved in the actual murder.

In my own experience with the military, I've sat around a table with three other people planning the overthrow of a foreign government—and it took place that night. The next day there was a new government in power.

There were four of us there at that table: two Americans (including myself) and two people from that other country.

You can't have a lot of people involved directly.

What did the pirates do in the movies when they brought their treasure to an island?

They brought two men to bury the gold, and when the pirates went back to the ship they shot the two men with the shovels. They couldn't have everybody knowing where the gold was buried.

Let's be reasonable. This is an old business. Kings are killed. So the conspiracy was a very small group as Johnson was telling us.

So Clay Shaw and David Ferrie (as shown in JFK) were utilized at one level by the top-level conspirators, but it was not something those two cooked up alone? It went much higher?

Shaw and Ferrie are essential to understanding the whole exercise. If you want to get down to the question as to where the real conspirators were and who they were—they will never be found.

■ ■ ■

New Light on JFK Murder

A top Kennedy administration official warned of a possible "CIA coup" just seven weeks before JFK was assassinated in Dallas.

EXCLUSIVE TO *THE SPOTLIGHT*
by Michael Collins Piper

Author-attorney Mark Lane has unveiled never-before-revealed information relating to the assassination of John F. Kennedy.

Lane was a special guest on the January 25 broadcast of *Spotlight* editor Vince Ryan's weekly *Editor's Roundtable* where he publicly released his findings for the first time since the publication of his new book, *Plausible Denial*, which is now No. 5 on the *New York Times* bestseller list.

Lane, whom the *Times* has acknowledged as "the dean of the critics of the Warren Commission," outlined his new research during his appearance on the *Editor's Roundtable*.

According to Lane, "One of the really interesting columns published in the *New York Times* on October 3, 1963—just a little over a month before John Kennedy was killed—was written by Arthur Krock.

"Krock was a longtime, close, personal friend of the Kennedy family. He was actually quite conservative and at that time was probably the most respected columnist in America. His column which appeared on October 3, 1963 was entitled, "The Intra-Administration War in Vietnam."

JFK-CIA War

"Krock pointed out John F. Kennedy had gone to war against the CIA. He concluded that Kennedy no longer could control the CIA.

"The columnist stated that President Kennedy sent Henry Cabot Lodge, his ambassador to Vietnam, with orders to the CIA on two separate occasions and in both cases the CIA ignored those orders, saying it was different from what the agency thought should be done.

"In other words, the CIA had decided that it—not the president—would make the decisions as to how American foreign policy should be conducted.

"Now here is what's so incredible. Here's what Krock wrote about what a high administration official had to say about all of this. [It was probably either his friend President Kennedy or perhaps Attorney General Robert Kennedy to whom he was referring.]

"This is what this unnamed official had to say—in print—about the CIA one month before the president was murdered:

"The CIA's growth was likened to a 'malignancy' which the 'very high official was not sure even the White House could control . . . any longer.'

"'If the United States ever experiences [an attempt at a coup to overthrow the government] it will come from the CIA and not the Pentagon,' [the source said]. The agency 'represents a tremendous power and total unaccountability to anyone.' "

This was John F. Kennedy sending out a message to the American people through his trusted conduit Arthur Krock. The Krock column continued:

"Whatever else these passages disclose, they most certainly establish that representatives of other Executive branches have expanded their war against the CIA from the inner government councils to the American people via the press.

"And published simultaneously are details of the agency's operations in Vietnam that can come only from the same critical official sources. This is disorderly government. And the longer the President tolerates it—the period already is considerable—the greater the real war against the Vietcong and the impression of a very indecisive Administration in Washington.

"The CIA may be guilty as charged. Since it cannot, or at any rate will not, openly defend its record in Vietnam or defend it by the same confidential press 'briefings' employed by its critics, the public is not in a position to judge . . .

"But Mr. Kennedy will have to make a judgment if the spectacle of war within the Executive branch is to be ended and the effective functioning of the CIA preserved.

"And when he makes this judgment, hopefully he also will make it public, as well as the appraisal of fault on which it is based."

(Krock himself cited a respected Scripps-Howard newspaper columnist, Richard Starnes, as a source for some of this information.)

According to Lane, this is not "new" information, but rather it has, until this time, gone unnoticed or has been deliberately ignored.

Lane points out the first thing the Warren Commission, investigating the president's assassination, should have done would be to investigate these allegations further. It was never done.

Lane is skeptical about the growing move within the Establishment to support the grassroots demand that the secret Warren Commission, House Committee and CIA files be released to the public.

"The government is now saying, 'OK, let's look at the files.' They want us to be satisfied with the opening of the files. This is not enough, however.

"Think of it this way: If there was a bank robbery and the police found out who did it, we would not be satisfied if they just opened the files so everybody could look at the files and see what happened.

"The only way to get the truth about the assassination is to appoint a special prosecutor who will bring those responsible to trial."

■ ■ ■

Releasing the secret government JFK assassination files is not enough. A special prosecutor should be appointed to reopen the case and put those responsible on trial.

The near-simultaneous release of the book *Plausible Denial* by Mark Lane and the motion picture *JFK*, raising the specter of a CIA-led conspiracy to assassinate President John F. Kennedy, has created a nationwide stir for a new investigation. Americans are writing and calling their elected representatives in the House and the Senate, urging that Congress order the release of all secret government JFK assassination files currently held in secrecy.

However, simple release of the JFK assassination files is not enough. Attorney Mark Lane has called for the appointment of a special prosecutor who will sift through all of the evidence and present that evidence to a special grand jury.

Those responsible for the JFK assassination should be brought to trial—no matter how high-ranking they may be.

Readers of *The Spotlight* and members of Liberty Lobby's Board of Policy have given an overwhelming "yes" vote in favor of the weekly newspaper, with this Washington-based populist Institution throwing its weight behind the push for the release of all files and for the appointment of a special prosecutor.

(Appointment of a special prosecutor can only be approved upon a two-thirds vote in both the House of Representatives and the Senate.)

If you agree that a special prosecutor should be appointed to reopen the JFK assassination case, you should contact your elected legislators in Congress.

You can write your representative c/o The U.S. House of Representatives, Washington, D.C. 20515 and your two senators c/o the U.S. Senate, Washington, D.C. 20510. Or call the U.S. Capitol switchboard at 202-224-3121 and ask to be connected to the office of the lawmaker you are trying to reach.

A sample letter to your representative and senators is on the next page.

■ ■ ■

Sample Letter to House and Senate Members
on JFK Assassination Files

Dear Sir:

Revelations brought forth in Oliver Stone's new film *JFK* and in Mark Lane's New York Times best-seller *Plausible Denial* as well as many other recent investigative books, suggest there was a lot more to the assassination of President John F. Kennedy than the American people have been led to believe.

It is your duty as an elected representative of the people to make certain that the truth is told. Therefore, I urge you to introduce comprehensive legislation which would do the following:

✦ Release ALL secret JFK assassination documents currently being held by all government agencies—including but not limited to, the Warren Commission files, the House Assassinations Committee files, and the FBI and CIA files.

✦ Require the appointment by Congress of a special prosecutor who would make use of all relevant JFK assassination research—including the files now held in secrecy. The special prosecutor could then convene a special grand jury if necessary and seek the indictments of those suspected of complicity.

Please let me know whether or not you are willing to introduce legislation which would provide for all of the specific needs addressed in this letter.

Sincerely,

Name & Address

Hey guys, wake up. If anyone at all controls the country and has a motive to hide things, it should be the Chase Manhattan Bank. (Now just you never mind who controls *it.*) So maybe you shouldn't be too surprised to find out that John J. McCloy, who at the time was retired after serving as chairman of the Chase Bank, was a member of the Warren Commission that provided us with the establishment's version of truth in our time.

Pretty neat, huh? Didn't Aesop have an oxymoron about that? Seems like it involved a fox—or was it a wolf—I think I forget.

Whatever, it's time we begin to unveil secrets on a nationwide scale; recognize that 80 to 90 percent of us would bite the serpent's apple if given the opportunity, and armed with that knowledge, proceed to face up to reality by suggesting that we *can* forgive past sins, may or may not forgive current sins, but should never forgive future sins.

With this testament, I will begin the process by admitting, as an amoral observer, that there but for an appreciation of the greater rewards of *enlightened* self-interest go I.

Read on, my friend; what follows are ideas galore to accept and reject, but never ignore.

2.   *December 1984*

The church is our ally, only they want to get to heaven somewhere up in the sky. I want to get to heaven here on earth. Our means may be different, but our end is the same: *universal happiness.*

3.   *December 1984 and February 20, 1985*

Exploitative capitalism is little better than Bolshevism, but can be turned into benevolent capitalism without disruption.

4. *January 17, 1985*

Everybody thinks I'm on their side, and all of them are right. It's just that some have a mistaken perception of where their own best interests lie. While I wish enlightenment for all people, I know it will come to only a very few. But there is always hope in new generations, who will seek the truths which will make them free.

5. *Late January 1985*

Long-term progress is akin to a sailing ship: It involves tacking to port one moment, to starboard the next. The journey is longer, but certainly surer, than the turbined craft which proceeds directly, only to find its fuel spent when the trip proves longer than planned.

6. *Late January 1985*

It is not enough just to be good. When wrong appears, action against it should be taken.

7. *Late January 1985*

In the real world we punish because it sets an example. In the ideal world we would punish because it's just.

8. *February 1985*

I think most bad people are really good people who don't know they're being led to where they would rather not be once they get there.

9. *February 1985*

We can't tell Father Time when we're ready; Father Time will tell us when he's ready.

"I'm not really a bad person, but I suppose I am
what you could call ethically fragile."

10. *February 1985*

While the world spins on in the real,
I prefer to think the ideal.
The puzzle that knots my hair
is getting from here to there.

11. *February 14, 1985*

Be I hated, give me anonymity; be I loved, may the whole
world know of me.

12. *February 21, 1985*

In the real world, gamble only when the odds are favorable.
In the ideal world, we would not have gambling (as opposed
to risk-taking), because whether you win or lose, it's unfair to
someone.

13.   *February 24, 1985*

I am not an altruist, nor an exploiter—but believe in enlightened self-interest, whereby the welfare of each accrues to the benefit of all.

14.   *February 24, 1985*

Might it be that there are five broad stages of overlapping social development:

1. Religions of the world (interpreted literally), not too great but better than nothing;

2. Socialism (an effort to improve, but too unproductive due to lack of incentive);

3. Benevolent capitalism, featuring the Bible as allegory;

4. Constitutional monarchy, featuring a benevolent monarch;

5. True Christian communism—the ultimate state?

The concept of God is a stepping stone to Stage Number 5, where all mankind is god-like.

15.   *February 28, 1985*

One person's win need not be another person's loss. Referring to the Iran-Iraq war, Henry Kissinger said, "Too bad they both can't lose." In fact, for the time the conflict lasted, they both *did* lose. On the other hand, you can have a *win/win* situation, such as occurs when all parties cooperate for their mutual benefit.

16. *February 28, 1985*

More than one organization with noble beginnings has found its principles corrupted and its ideas usurped by totally contrary influences. This happens more often when growth is too rapid and basic safeguards are neglected.

17. *February 28, 1985*

In referring to Nugget 14, stage 5, you may wonder how that stage can come into being after stage 4, which featured a monarch, or king. Kings are not known for their willingness to relinquish power. But this time it will be different—a benevolent monarch who, when the time is right, will *demote himself* to an equal among equals and we will ascend to stage 5. We know the true strength of a horse lies not only in how fast it can run, but also in how quickly it can stop.

18. *March 1, 1985*

Many changes that we know should be made in our world are not accomplished simply because yet not enough people see the light. But when they do, and they will, we can say the time has come.

19. *March 18, 1985*

There is a problem with cliques, groups, organizations, and even nations. Due to their very nature, they tend to look inward to their own problems and interests, rather than outward towards an overview of everyone's problems and interests. Is this not the root cause of all conflict, including war itself? I do not say there aren't good reasons for forming self-interest groups, **only that until these groups evolve to consider everyone's interests they will help perpetuate conflict.**

20.   *March 19, 1985*

The time has come to set parameters of just what we want "freedom" to mean in a free society. I say, let us be free to advance economic development and commerce, but not to evade the law, especially the laws of pragmatism and common sense. Release the powers of free enterprise, but at the same time monitor everyone via their social security numbers and— what the crooks fear most—their bank accounts. Freedom should not mean freedom to hide illicit deeds or gains from public scrutiny, nor should it mean freedom to exploit your neighbor. I firmly believe in the adage: *What are you afraid of if you've got nothing to hide?* Since large numbers of us do have something to hide, let's grant general amnesty to all but the most serious offenders, and start afresh with a combination of freedom and disclosure.

21.   *March 22, 1985*

In Nugget 20, I mentioned the need to obey the laws of pragmatism and common sense. The single biggest violation of those laws, and here I step out on a limb, is the common practice of getting interest, *any* interest, on money loaned. Most of our economic problems stem from this one practice. Yes, I believe in giving credit to worthy borrowers for specified periods of time. And of course, they should all pay their share of the associated administrative costs. But it is wrong to get something for nothing, which is what getting interest is. It causes economic pollution every bit as harmful in its own way as environmental pollution.

22.   *April 12, 1985*

Benevolent capitalism could spread its gospel throughout the world, converting all but the diehards simply by setting an example: by demonstrating what the power of free enterprise can accomplish when exercised efficiently. But to do this, it should first put its own house in order, which would mean phasing out the excess baggage of both the welfare abusers on one end, and those rentiers (on the other end) who live on interest income.

There are three ways by which an individual can get wealth— by work, by gift, and by theft. And, clearly, the reason why the workers get so little is that the beggars and thieves get so much.
— Henry George, *Social Problems*

23.   *April 12, 1985*

Those who become too successful are suppressed by others concerned for their own self-preservation. These others fear being overwhelmed by their adversaries' superiority and the unknown consequences that would result. Examples are the Jews, who excelled because they were forced to try harder in an effort to overcome barriers of prejudice, and the Japanese, who, by trying harder, overcame the harshness of their habitat. Our country is now apparently very concerned about our trade deficit with Japan. Why are we concerned if for each job lost another is created by Japanese investment in the U.S.? That's just it; we're afraid of their superior industriousness—afraid that by their increasing investments here, they will gain ever-increasing wealth and power, and who knows where it will lead? Is this also what Hitler feared (or played on others' fears) against the Jews in Germany? What, then, is the answer? Eventually the answer is assimilation of all peoples into one world government, so that parochial interests are subordinated to a greater cause.

24.   *May 13, 1985*

What would you think of a guidance counselor who advises his student to engage in criminal activity as his best bet for

**"I didn't do anything — I just took an aptitude
test and they <u>PUT</u> me here!"**

success in life? You would probably be shocked! Yet, for some,
sad to say, that might be the best advice. Of course this would
be a judgment not from society's viewpoint but solely from
that individual's point of view. This conclusion might be determined on a risk/reward ratio, much as an investment advisor
would utilize, where the reward of wrongdoing outweighs the
risk of getting caught. One candidate for such advice would
include the loser who cannot (or thinks he cannot), cope with
life in a competitive world. He is also a likely candidate for
suicide.

Verbal admonitions to be moral, as taught by the old-style
dogmatic religions with their rigid doctrines, are becoming less
palatable to an increasingly sophisticated populace. Religion is
gradually losing its effect as the opiate of the masses. People are
becoming less willing to trade real benefits here and now for
some nebulous benefits in the hereafter, which they still may
give lip service to but act as though they do not believe.

What, then, must we use to replace blind faith in obsolete religious tenets? What do we do for the loser, or for anyone inclined to commit a moment or a life of crime? To the first question: We keep everyone honest; when you play poker you must show your hand to win the pot, else you could *claim* to have a royal flush every time. Everyone must bare his financial soul—not to his Father confessor, but on the record to the general public, as Geraldine Ferraro's husband was forced to do. Hopefully, this would be met with a more forgiving spirit than he was subjected to. Past indiscretions will be mostly forgiven; future ones will not be. The evolving age of the supercomputers will make all of this feasible. The freedom to know will replace the freedom to keep from knowing—and society will be the benefactor.

To the second question: The risk/reward ratio to commit or not to commit a crime must never be allowed to favor the commission of a crime. Here I would like to address one specific and very troubling current problem. How do you make the risk outweigh the reward for a pilot who can be financially set for life if he brings in just one planeload of cocaine from Colombia? Answer: It is hard to do, but a starting point is full and universal financial disclosure as mentioned above.

If no assets could be hidden from public scrutiny, one would be forced to deal in gold, which Lenin correctly stated would some day be used to adorn public lavatories. (However, we have a while to go before that comes to pass.) At the same time Lenin was not blind to *existing* realities. He said "The Soviet Union must carefully save its gold. When living with the wolves, howl like the wolves." Marx explained it perfectly when he stated, "The first function of gold is to give the commercial world a material by which to express value, that is, to express the value of all other goods, as homonymous variables, that are qualitatively identical and quantitatively comparable."

To continue: Full and open discussion of the advantages and disadvantages of breaking laws, taking or not taking drugs, using alcohol or cigarettes, engaging in sex and waging war, should be a part of the school curricula from kindergarten through college, with a total commitment to being honest at all times. Any preconceived notions of morality or ethics must not be presumed to be correct without being subjected to the light of full and ongoing discussion. Society must then accommodate these conclusions by adopting guidelines *(instead of inflexible laws)* appropriate to the situation.

"But I passed all my <u>DRUG</u> tests!"

25.   *June 5, 1985*

What is the main attraction of left-wing thought that entices a college student? First is the allure of secular humanism, which asserts that man, without God, through reason, is master of his own fate. That's fine. Their mistake, however, is in assuming that if capitalist America is pro-religion, which they know is passe, and communism adheres to atheism, it therefore follows that communism must be superior to capitalism. Alas, this is not so. The framers of our constitution wisely kept church and state separate, and the Supreme Court has recognized and sustained this wisdom.

The second compelling attraction of the left is the egalitarian goal of a classless society. This sounds very noble, but it is difficult to realize as long as people's abilities are unequal. Moreover, this utopian dream has been subverted by the Kremlin's leaders, who have brutally suppressed all free expression of their people in order to preserve a system which bears little resemblance to its stated principles. When goals are grand and *too far ahead of their time*, successors often lack the vision to attain them. Worse yet, they often subvert them for selfish or for short-term gains.

26.   *July 5, 1985*

Why does it often seem like left-wing adherents are more dedicated to their cause than advocates of capitalism are? Especially when capitalists believe in free competition, allowing them to gain more—if not much more—of the rewards. It is because left-wing *ideology* is nobler in concept than its counterpart, and therefore arouses greater passions. Barry Goldwater said it imbues its adherents with a sense of historical mission. It is a concept of egalitarianism. Trouble is, the world is not yet ready for this kind of equality. Many of the left's supporters are well-meaning intellectuals. They see farther than most, but not as far as Simon Bolivar, who said, "Don't give the people the best form of government; give them the one most likely to succeed." Communism, if not forced upon people, would not at this point in time be the system most likely to succeed. To compound the wrong of forcing this system on people is the even greater evil of its leaders not practicing what they preach but subverting their own gospel for self-serving ends. Do not expect the masses to embrace a faith that asks of them virtues even nature has yet to conceive of.

27.   *August 3, 1985*

What is wrong with the world? Why is there so much turmoil everywhere you turn? Shouldn't the miracles of modern technology be making life easier for one and all, instead of harder for so many of us? Why is our national debt so large, and getting larger? The fundamental answer to these questions is simple: Human nature being what it is, nearly everyone wants to maximize his own advantages, yielding to others only what he has to. It seems that we act upon our desire to hurt before we act upon our desire not to hurt. The results of this mentality manifest themselves in a whole panorama of problems. Perpetual brinkmanship among competing interests is the best way to describe it. In the old days of the robber barons, the villains were easier to recognize. In time the barons would have owned everything if it hadn't been for the anti-trust laws. But they had to open their doors, and this broadened the wealth base. Today this broadened base makes remedial efforts harder to come by, as its greater numbers command greater political clout.

An example of how the "haves" bleed the "have-nots": With real interest rates (nominal rate minus inflation rate) at an excessively high 7% society is in effect subsidizing the beneficiaries of that 7% which would obviously be unsustainable for long were it not for productivity increases. As it is, the rentiers are pocketing most of the profits, while the rest of us are working to pay for it while not sharing in the increasing fruit of our own labor. Of course, if the "have-nots" become "haves" they will gladly do the same thing. The answer, I think, is to make changes so basic and fundamental as to profoundly affect the way we conduct our lives. Solutions will require a new generation of enlightened political leaders—such as the likes of the late JFK, Martin Luther King Jr., and the most underrated of all our presidents, Dwight Eisenhower—together with the support of benevolent capitalists like Sam Walton.

"Nonsense! You're not a have-not! You have me!"

28.   *August 17, 1985*

Could it be…

- That the ecology movement (which is in itself a most noble cause) has been usurped by the left for the purpose of hampering development of needed natural resources?

- That the reason the Russians don't allow Jews to emigrate more is because their talents in the underground economy help support an otherwise inefficient economic system?

72

- That seemingly constructive forces for good, such as the ACLU (which maintains a mixed basket of causes to disguise the fact that they frequently give aid to the communists by deserting conservative values) are yet one more left-wing proxy?

- And that the daily harangue against South Africa is to a large degree orchestrated by the communists (to the delight of the U.S. who also would like to control her)? Lenin reputedly once said that whoever possessed South Africa's minerals and controlled the Cape of Good Hope would control the world. Due to water peculiarities, it is the only spot on earth where one submarine can easily torpedo any passing ship and remain undetected even within a hundred yards. Do you understand why the South African navy cannot buy any more submarines and is always updating the few she has?

**These are questions for our times
that we should think about.**

29.   *September 12, 1985*

Massive buying of Treasury debt is a gigantic drain of investment capital. It should be going into wealth producing ventures, not sapping the country's monetary resources in the form of servicing this mountain of debt. The solution: First, eliminate the deficit spending that creates the need to borrow ever more. Second, reduce the existing debt itself—preferably to zero. When Jack Kemp says, "I do not worship at the altar of the balanced budget," he may find himself in the unwanted company of idolaters whose god is lacking *all* constraints.

"Awwwk! — Polly want a balanced budget
and an end to deficit spending!"

30. *September 26, 1985*

Why is Russia the only country in the world with a declining life expectancy? Is it intentional so as not to burden their society with a lot of unproductive old people? (Yes, they are tough-minded enough to do that.) And why does Russian medical care offer little or no pain alleviators? Is it to discourage the use of this care because it is costly? Here is a country so cold-blooded and calculating, so callous and uncaring for the comfort of its own citizens, that its every action is directed toward the goal of world domination. If that were to happen, would they then suddenly become the loving and caring society their ideology calls for? Does a leopard change its spots? I choose not to find out the hard way. *[Read the following sentence very carefully, as nothing I have written is more important.]* If I could be sure that their single-minded devotion towards their goal of world conquest would culminate in a new world order of benevolence towards all, I might then say: Yes, the end in this case does justify the means; it was worth all the turmoil and hardship. But think a minute! If this is really their intent, wouldn't it be better to prevail by showing benevolence *now*? To state it simply, set an example of good which would be a magnet for the rest of the world to be drawn into? The battle, then would truly rest on ideological grounds, and not in the use of military might. (Military might, which along with the risk of blowing up the world, would all be unnecessary.) Let us not gamble with the future. Let us deny them world domination. The alternative may be eternal slavery.

31.   *September 26, 1985*

Can a more ludicrous situation be imagined than for 30 years to have elapsed before it may finally be decided that firemen are no longer necessary on diesel locomotives? Multiply this behavior a thousandfold in many industries, and you can get a sense of the enormous loss of productivity occurring. Again, it is the result of self-interest groups thinking only of their own kind. For unions to make such demands and managements to acquiesce to them is a blight on both their houses. A similar conflict is the question of central control versus decentralization. Both have a role to fill. The key is cooperation among all levels and all entities. We can learn a lesson here from the Japanese, where labor, management, and government all work together. When the day comes that we can add nations to this trio, we'll be off and running.

32.   *September 28, 1985*

When Marx speaks of capitalism, I interpret this to mean exploitative capitalism. I do not think Marx (or his successors) ever considered the possibility of benevolent capitalism. I see benevolent capitalism as transcending conflict and perhaps even contradiction (which is at the very heart of dialectics), in a unifying spirit of cooperation, with most people doing the job they like and do best. The fault I find with both communist philosophy (dialectical materialism) and religions is their reliance on dogma. How can one be so sure of a tenet as to assume it should never change even though conditions change? While it is true that the dialectic of communism stresses constant change, its bedrock beliefs are stated as dogma.

33.   *October 1, 1985*

Has the U.S. become ungovernable? We think we know what has to be done with the debt, the dollar, the trade deficit, the farm problem, etc. Do we do it? No way! By the time all the politicos have their say, everything has been watered down. One person who knew what to do (and more importantly would have done it), David Stockman, quit in exasperation and disgust, and the system moved another step closer to the precipice. How do I square this sentiment with my earlier Nuggets that sang the merits of benevolent capitalism? What I said then still stands. But if we don't straighten up and fly right, we'll never get to realize our potential. While I do not know how our situation will be resolved, I believe it is possible that somehow we will muddle through. History has shown us that day follows night, and that life goes on.

34.   *October 13, 1985*

Let us think! What would it take to establish a new world order that would be run as efficiently as a Japanese auto manufacturing company; a world with no crime or unemployment, a world where compassion abounds, and a world where doctors do not interfere with the dying process unnecessarily? Consider a place where everyone must work, but the length of the work week grows shorter (for those who so desire), because of productivity increases. What would it take? Perhaps genetic engineering will be the best answer for overcoming human shortcomings. I am assuming, of course, that such a feat is scientifically possible. It is a shame that both the U.S. and Russia are so very far away from reaching their full potentials as societies. I would like to combine their faculty for making hard-headed and tough-minded decisions with our desire to allow everyone to lead the good life.

35.

In setting up a country's financial system, there is one overriding question: Who is going to control the allocation of credit in our society? That is the whole question, the long and short of it.

How then are the people to be protected? Through regulation. But if the regulators are also the bankers, you have no protection for the people's interests. And that's what has happened, and is why we have strayed into the sorry mess that is now our fate.

If we were to exercise Section 30 of the Federal Reserve Act (that gives the government the right to take back the nation's money system), some one trillion dollars could be set free between the combination of debt reduction and acquired assets. At the same time, by abolishing the Federal Reserve, all bonds held by the Federal Reserve banks would become government property, thus lowering the national debt by more billions than any knowledgeable person ever dreamed possible.

This one act by a president and congress would do more to establish public confidence in the federal government than anything done at the federal level since the Declaration of Independence.

36.   *October 25, 1985*

Why are our cities and towns unsafe, compared to the crime rate of years ago? The answer is related to the additional questions: Why is there more moonlighting than ever before? Why are there so many more women in the work force than there used to be? And why does it seem that for so many, *"getting by"* is so much harder than it used to be? The answer is that it uses more of our take home pay to make ends meet than it did before. (This, in spite of the fact that labor cost is only 20 percent of the price of an item—an all-time low, thanks to automation.) Between entitlements, defense spending, debt service, and just plain boondoggles, the squeeze is on. The higher crime rate simply reflects the greater anguish and desperation among the most disadvantaged, resulting in overcrowded jails, which even further tax the system. Investment bankers find ways to optimize returns on capital for those well-off. So while this group is largely protected, it serves to increase the burden on those who lack such cushions and widens the gap even more. All the while, numerous PAC groups are lobbying to protect their sacred cows and slow down or prevent reforms. How long

SCUD BROCKWAY
PUBLIC LIBRARY

People are trying to study. Please use your silencers.

Baloo

"But we've been living beyond our means for years —
we can't lose our nerve NOW."

can we continue on this downhill course? Where will it end? Our troubles are not merely increasing; they are increasing exponentially. Even the atheists among us must be saying: *"Let us pray."*

37.   *October 27, 1985*

How should prison inmates be handled? The answer is so obvious it screams out at us: Put them to work at productive labor, but *separate* the 5 percent hard-core incorrigibles from the rest (more on this later). Do not punish for the sake of revenge. Treat most prisoners the same as any citizen but work them longer, say 45 hours per week. Eliminate idleness. Replace iron-barred cells with barracks and housing units in a compound secured by fencing and electronics. Any schooling will be attended to after work—not in place of work. Have the women's prison within the same compound, and allow social mingling and overnight visiting of wives or girlfriends, whether they be prisoners or non-prisoners. Jobs should be rotated, so that the same people do not monopolize the more desirable jobs. Of course, if someone enjoys a job that others do not want, let him have it all the time. Discipline must be strict but fair, administered preferably by well paid "instructors" recruited from the Marine Corps and Army. Prisons should run their own commercial enterprises, paying inmates a low wage plus room and board. While output should not be priced below fair market value, pressures from vendors who don't want the competition (i.e. don't want prisoners to be producing goods for sale), need to be resisted. As we all know, government owned businesses are notorious for losing money. If this happens, so be it. But it is more important to keep the prisoners working, and even if the balance sheet is red, it's still more profitable than producing nothing at all. As Carl Icahn, chief of beleaguered TWA, says, "In a kingdom of blind men, coming out with one eye isn't so bad." And if incentives are incorporated, we may be pleasantly surprised at the outcome. The idea of

"I can tell, Fred — something's got you feeling depressed, hasn't it?"

"I got lucky. I could have gotten 200 hours of community service."

rehabilitation is *not* defunct; it *can* work in most cases if undertaken properly.

Now to the really controversial part. Deliver an ultimatum to the small percentage of hard-core incorrigibles that they must allow themselves to be used as subjects for medical experimentation or forfeit their lives. *Yes*, you heard me correctly. Subjects need to be found somewhere; what better source could there be? There are times when pragmatism is a greater virtue than compassion.

38.   *November 4, 1985*

The U.S. trade deficit is now some 150 billion dollars per year, and this is assumed to be a very bad thing. But bad for whom? True, much production is lost for us, but what about the countries exporting to us? *We* may not be producing as much, but someone else out there is. When we view the world with a single eye, how does the sum total prosperity *of all* peoples stack up? That may be all well and good for them, you say, but what about us? I must refer you here to Nuggets 19 and 23, and suggest that the broader question viewed by the one-worlders is: Are the costs of production coming down world-wide, after discounting inflation? Yes, of course they are, and this is the name of the game—reducing costs. When costs are reduced by automation, life is made easier for all. When they're lowered by "slave labor," there is no overall increase in benefits. There is, of course, an inordinate gain for the owners, offset by a less-than-adequate result for the workers. This is exploitative capitalism and is the evil which Karl Marx had in mind when he formulated his ideas. Foreign competition resulting from the former (technology) is justified, from the latter (slave labor) is not. Sometimes production is totally useless in an economic sense. By far the best example of this is military expenditures. Although necessary for security, it is all wasted effort. If the U.S. and Russia, not to mention all the other countries in the world, were to apply this production to useful items instead of arms, the world would have so much wealth that we could probably reduce the work load by five hours a week per person. And if all interest on debts were paid off, both public and private, we might knock off another three hours from the work week, assuming such interest was thereafter abolished. Now we're left with a 32-hour work week; however, this wouldn't be good news for everyone; people to whom the interest is presently owed would have to work more to make up for their loss of income.

39.   *November 15, 1985*

On August 1, 1946, the monetary authorities in Hungary declared that 400 octillion pengoe (using the American system of numeration) equaled one forint (the new currency unit). That is four followed by 29 zeroes. Could it happen here? Hardly, but it does illustrate what can happen in some times and some places under certain conditions. Complacency is dangerous. Who would have guessed that a civilized country like Germany could have spawned the extremes that we witnessed under Hitler? If history teaches us anything, eternal vigilance must be one of its more important lessons.

40.   *November 20, 1985*

Money is the fuel that runs capitalism's engine. Subjugation to authority without the incentive of monetary reward (beyond a mere subsistence level) is the driving force of communism. Are we right? Are they wrong? I would say that in today's world of imperfect mortals, money speaks louder. Am I implying that in a more perfect world, authority might be better? If that mindless authority is turned into instructive leadership with a view to universal cooperation, then I would answer *yes*, that would be better than dog-eat-dog competition for the juiciest bones. However, maturing to that point takes time, and civilization is still in its infancy. Like malaria, human nature must also run its course. Then, when the outlook is darkest, the fever breaks and a new and better world emerges from the ashes of the old.

41.   *November 25, 1985*

Russia acts, America reacts. That seems to be the pattern. As any athletic coach will tell you, the best defense is a good offense. You will not win many games if all you do is defend yourself. The Soviets apply the principles of the chessboard to their planning board, where each move along the way has one single long-range strategic purpose—to checkmate the king. When that happens, the game is over. Enroute to this goal, all sorts of moves are made that the less seasoned player does not understand. He reacts to one at a time, not appreciating their long-range significance as a single, coordinated effort to a specific end. Since Gorbachev's ascendancy to power, his reasoned oratory belies his country's increased military actions (both direct and indirect) and terrorist activities in Afghanistan, Angola, Ethiopia, Mozambique, Nicaragua, and South Africa. They seek total victory in Africa, so as to deny the free world access to its enormous mineral wealth.

We are reluctant players in this worldwide chess game. They gain advantage over us by using their grandmasters to best effect whereas our star diplomats are usually dismissed with each change of the political winds, requiring us to constantly reinvent the wheel.

42.   *November 26, 1985*

It was Lenin the misanthrope who believed "the worse the better," and Lenin the visionary who said, *"The capitalists will sell us the rope with which we will hang them."* This is not an unreasonable statement to make. Witness the current short-sightedness of Gulf Oil Corp., the Chevron Inc. unit that operates a major facility in Angola jointly with the Marxist government there. Gulf and Chevron officials are lobbying against aid to Jonas Savimbi, leader of the anti-Marxist guerilla group, saying that such aid would jeopardize American property and commerce in Angola. What do they think will happen to U.S. interests if the communists win all of Africa? This could conceivably be determined by the outcome of this one particular struggle. It is that crucial. This illustrates very well the disadvantage we suffer when confronted by a monolithic adversary with a specific coordinated strategic goal.

43.   *December 20, 1985*

Christmas is upon us, and I notice one way the U.S. and the USSR are similar, albeit for entirely different reasons. In both countries the people would like to buy more goods than they are able to. In the U.S., where we have goods and the capacity to make goods coming out of our ears, the limitation is in having enough money to buy them. In Russia, a factor even greater than lack of money is lack of merchandise (especially quality merchandise) available for sale. However, this is by design, not by accident, on their part. They are focusing their efforts and resources on higher priority areas, i.e., the military sector.

Now go to any large mall in the U.S. and you'll find half a dozen major department stores competing with one another, all of them overflowing with the same merchandise, different perhaps only in the brand names. Does all this competition keep them on their toes? Yes, but what a waste there is in all that redundancy of inventory, space, and personnel. I would rather see them consolidate their half dozen entities into a single department for each product group. This would greatly increase efficiency and simplify things for the shopper. As a substitute for the beneficial aspects of competition sacrificed by consolidation, I suggest motivating the work force in the same manner that Wal-Mart stores have done, not to mention the Japanese who also know something about motivating people. (Did you know Wal-Mart monitors store activities via ceiling TVs that beam up to Wal-Mart's own satellite? Employees—called associates—know and accept this when they sign on, creating a strong sense of mutual loyalty. They deserve to be #1.)

44.   *December 27, 1985*

Why is it that Russia and its allies have for the most part been spared from terrorist attacks? In fact, I can think of only one recent instance in which Russians were the victims of such an attack. In the first place, I believe much of the terrorism in the world is inspired by the communists themselves, using proxies, and directed against anyone and everyone who is not firmly in their camp. They believe that any disruption will ultimately, by fomenting dissatisfaction, work to their advantage. Secondly, they never allow even the appearance of submitting to any demands whatsoever, so any offenders who are logically minded know in advance that they have no chance of gaining any concessions. And, finally, they don't talk about it when something does happen. They treat misfortunes as a non-event, giving virtually no news coverage that would feed the terrorists' appetite for the publicity they thrive on (but only when it's *their* misfortune).

Along this same line, you might have noticed that the slightest incident in South Africa evokes worldwide concern while much worse atrocities are committed daily against those fighting Russian forces in Afghanistan, where disruption of an entire country goes under-reported by the liberal press who are the unwitting (or maybe witting) dupes of our adversary's cause.

45.   *Rewritten in February, 1990*

Why is it that, worldwide, there is so much animosity towards the U.S.? I think the basic answer is jealousy. But how do we account for our paramount position in the world? Is it our free enterprise system that has made us so successful or are we simply descendants of good stock? I think it is both, with the former allowing the latter to fully blossom. It was those with the greatest aspirations who migrated to this land from many lands, thus providing us with a strong genetic pool which mixed and interrelated, adding yet more strengths to the brew that came to be known as the great melting pot, but now seems to be changing into a mosaic of ethnic clusters. As for integration I say: Mixed or matched let choice be allowed, but acknowledge them all and you'll really stand tall.

What I am about to say is impossible to do without offending many sensitivities, but candor compels that we say what we

"Someplace where they don't hate Americans?
How about Nebraska?"

think. While I renounce prejudice wherever it appears, I reserve the right to have opinions that are out of sync with the mood of the moment.

While affirming that we should all enjoy equal rights—could it be that we may not all be born equal? Surely you wouldn't go into dairy farming using beef cattle. If various traits can be found in different breeds of horses, dogs, and cattle, what makes us think that man is exempt from this law of nature? As they say in veterinary school, there is only one animal kingdom, and humans are part of it.

I think statistics, let alone simple observation, will bear out the fact that blacks, especially American blacks (the slave traders selected only the healthiest, and of them only the healthiest survived the trip over) are, as a race, physically superior to whites, just as I think that blacks *as a whole*, find it difficult to compete with whites, *as a whole*, on tests requiring mental ability. (Might this be one reason it has been harder for the blacks to pull themselves up by their bootstraps the way other oppressed minorities have done?) If so, this is nothing to be ashamed of, it's just a fact of life and should be accepted as such. Genes do make a difference.

These beliefs do not make me a bigot (the cry of "bigot" is raised mostly by bigots). Neither does it make me a racist in the negative sense that the word has come to imply. But I don't think we should always tailor the facts to suit our fancy if doing so bends the truth. At the same time, I recognize that truth may be misused by some, and not dealt with objectively by others. To this extent, I support perpetuating fiction. If this sounds contradictory, I'm suggesting truth for scholars on a need-to-know basis, in much the same way the military handles secrets. This could be one of those rare times in history when the public good is furthered by having the general public believe a lie.

A new study reveals that one-fourth of all black American males in their 20s are either in prison or on prison release programs of some kind. When people are in a hopeless situation, aberrant behavior is the likely outcome. Very few are inherently bad people; most are people who turned bad because they were unable to compete legitimately, and they sensed this at a very early age. But nearly everyone has some latent talent that, if discovered and harnessed, can literally transform him (or her) into a new person. The secret is to find out what we do best, then work at doing it with support from the sidelines. A dream unnourished is an opportunity abandoned.

Another point I wish to make is that it is wrong to lower all scholastic standards so that slow students can compete. And it is also wrong not to require all youths to learn English in school as all prior immigrants had to do. If we don't watch it, the Hispanics will only speak their own language. Having a single language facilitates assimilation and has always been one of our national strengths. I have also observed that light-skinned colored people (suggesting mixed blood) more often seem to be the achievers compared to their darker brothers. In any event, the range of abilities within a group varies so greatly that the only fair way to judge people is on an individual basis. There are no absolutes for something so relative as a human life. I completely agree with the policy of publicly condemning prejudice and discrimination based on race, creed, color, or gender. But that does not cause me to distort or be blind to reality.

As for affirmative action, recipients are not helped by programs requiring quotas that are unfair in and of themselves, even though they are meant to right earlier wrongs. If your team is losing, should your pitcher be allowed to stand closer to the plate? One thing we *can* do is provide equal opportunity in the present to yield deserved benefits in the future. Those whom we intend to help and assume will benefit from affirmative action will become its victims instead due to backlash, just as all injustices invite backlash. Whites will stop resenting blacks when the blacks start to put as much into society as they take from it—not as a result of benefiting from flawed mandates, but by achievements earned in a climate of fairness for everyone. Only then will much of the ugly treatment blacks have endured begin to disappear.

The past cannot be relived outside of the context of its time. Humanity needs to forget old grievances and go forward hand in hand with our fellow man into that brave new world we have all heard about.

America is not like a blanket—one piece of unbroken cloth, the same texture, the same size. America is more like a quilt— many pieces, many colors, many sizes, all woven and held together by a common thread.

— JESSE JACKSON

46.   *January 11, 1986*

We should be neither proud nor ashamed of those things over which we have no control.

47.   *January 18, 1986*

Why is it so hard for debtors, whether they be individuals, companies, or countries, to get out of hock once they've fallen behind? I cannot overstate the importance of the two-word answer to this plight: interest payments. (Dividends are acceptable, since they are a consequence of ownership, and rise and fall with the fortunes of the company, whereas interest must be paid regardless, short of going out of business). To pay interest means that we must pay retribution for as long as the loan is in force. And what do these lenders contribute in return for their ongoing interest income? Not a thing. It is exactly what the IRS calls it—*unearned income.*

But wait, you say, shouldn't the money I've saved up be put to work earning more money? It is fine to try to earn more, but receiving interest is not earning it; it is getting something for nothing. If the subject wants this money to grow, he should assume the risks of ownership and investment accordingly (e.g. in equities). It is interesting to note that at one time the very word *interest* meant *usury.* But as interest became more acceptable, the word lost its repugnance—they had it right the first time. Ideally, worthy borrowers, and to a very limited degree governments as well, could get loans from their banks, for a specified period of time, without interest. But they would pay an administrative and processing fee to the banks. The banks would no longer earn money by charging interest, nor would they pay interest. Interest would be abolished.

While this would be a boon to the borrowers, it would also stabilize the profits of the lenders (the banks) by avoiding the perils of lending long-term at low rates with short-term borrowings at high rates. The limiting factor in extending credit—second only to the soundness of the project itself—should be the availability of qualified workers to do the job. There is nothing more senseless than having able men and women sit idle for want of financing. This has been our main failing. (As Ayn Rand put it, "If you turn down the generators, you turn down the lights.")

48.   *January 19, 1986*

What unbearable burden is gradually strangling so many countries including the U.S.? It is the continuing growth of debt caused by increasing numbers of the rich getting richer by skimming off interest wealth from our economic pie. This occurs at the expense of all. (*Important:* This is analogous to a poker game where the host skims a quarter from each pot. If the game is played long enough, guess who ends up with all the money.) At the same time increasing numbers of the poor get poorer at the expense of all of us who must pay the many welfare bills. So who do we mean by all? It must be the middle class, whose eroding membership dissolves into the other two groups. When the poorest are tapped out and bailout time rolls around, the next layer—those who are merely poorer—will be maneuvered into picking up the slack and, henceforth, carrying the heavier part of the burden on their shoulders. This is an untenable situation; how it will resolve itself remains to be seen.

49.   *January 26, 1986 & October, 1993*

Now let's talk about inflation—the justification behind it. We all know one side of it: the politician who wants to spend, spend, spend, on pork barrel projects in order to buy votes. Beneficiaries of this money know what to expect well in advance; the taxpayers who pick up the tab never seem aware until it's too late. It has always been thus. But there are also many legiti-mate expenditures for which we lack funds. Foremost among these are our military needs. To prevent the taxpayers from get-ting perturbed over the funding of these projects, deficit fi-nancing is resorted to, and, lo and behold, we have created inflation which is the product of an increasing money supply (mostly government IOUs) relative to the supply of goods and services. The fact that they might be worthy projects does not alter the consequences to the public—diluted dollars. Inflation also penalizes thrift and encourages debt—for obvious reasons.

When you consider productivity advances achieved over the years, prices (but not income) should decline, not increase (were there no inflation).

Yet another factor to consider is the change in product quality between past years and the present. Nowadays most things are made as cheaply as possible. It is a sad fact that the average worker today cannot always afford quality. My guess would be that a ten cent loaf of bread then was more nutritious than the one dollar loaf of today; it certainly had fewer chemi-cal additives in it.

While we're on this subject, have you ever wondered where the economic miracle that made possible the Renaissance came from? It all started in 1100 A.D. when Henry I became King of England, and initiated a money system based on "tallies," although silver and gold coins also circulated at the same time. This dual monetary system worked for over 600 years, but really came into its own in 1290 A.D. With an honest and convenient money system, an English working man could supply his family's needs for a year by working only 14 weeks! This left a great deal of leisure time available for intellectual, religious and charitable pursuits. This is the reason that the incredible cathedrals of England and Europe were built com-pletely with volunteer labor. Do you think that is amazing?

"To register a complaint about the high cost of living, dial 1-900-555-9318. You will be charged $3.95 for the call."

What is really amazing is how this information, essential to our freedom, has been so successfully kept concealed from us!

This tally money system continued to operate in England until 1783, when it was abolished by statute. Nevertheless, tallies continued to be used in rural areas until 1826.

Babylon Resurrected

The death knell of the tally system was sounded in 1694, when the King, William of Orange, granted a charter to William Paterson and his International Banker associates to establish the Bank of England as a fractional reserve central bank with monopoly power to issue bank notes at interest (usury). This date, 1694, is the most important date in American history, for the Bank of England has had a direct bearing on every major event in America since before our War of Independence.

50.   *January 26, 1986*

How have capitalist countries fostered terrorism? Earlier mistreatment by exploitative forces in the world laid the groundwork for rebellion against the descendants of those forces. We must now lie in the bed that they have made for us. We cannot change wrongs (whether real or imagined) committed in the past, but we can make changes in the present that will facilitate understanding among all parties in the future.

What would those changes be? A general realization that exploitation, besides being unfair, invariably leads to rebellion and conflict, both of which cast a long shadow. We can start by changing the face of capitalism from being exploitative to that of being benevolent. Not simply because of altruism, however noble that may be, but because friendship and cooperation make more sense in a world where the aggrieved party can easily acquire modern arms.

51.   *January 26, 1986*

At times there is more investment capital to lend than there are qualified people to borrow. The result is that the anxious lenders make loans with less discrimination than is prudent. This suggests to me that the rich are piling up profits faster than the market can absorb them. (Naturally, you cannot absorb investment capital if the interest costs exceed your profit margins.) Vast sums of money are being amassed at the expense of those who pay interest. By conservative estimates, the total debt in this country is $8 trillion. That means that every year, one class of people (the debtors) are paying a second class of people (the creditors) $800 billion of interest. This is tempered somewhat by the fact that most people are simultaneously debtors and creditors. You don't have to be good at math to appreciate the burdensome nature of such runaway debt.

No doubt you have noticed by now that I keep returning to this theme about the evils of charging interest. It is because I believe it to be the weak link in the free enterprise system. Interest is our economic pollution; it if were rectified, we could all breathe easier. (I have more to say on this in Nugget 52.)

And why do so many banks make all these big loans to any and all countries regardless of ability to pay back? Because in an effort to maximize their profits, they look no farther than the ends of their noses (a real case of short-term gratification). They think that countries can't go bankrupt. They're wrong. The time will come when debt from many foreign countries will have to be liquidated by repudiation. When that happens there will be disruptions.

52.   *January 28, 1986*

If people could borrow without the burden of interest payments, many more enterprises and entrepreneurs could flourish than do now. Prices would drop, reflecting the lower costs. Unemployment would go down sharply with increased job openings, adding to the total pool of wealth (GNP). Government would have added ability to function on the increased tax revenues alone (as it should), without the need for deficit financing. Am I saying that the government shouldn't sell bonds, notes, or bills? Yes, I am saying that and more. Neither should anyone else. *Investors should live off their principal,* not off interest on that principal, or if they are willing to assume the risk, they could live off the returns from some degree of ownership.

The great social equalizer that some seek in socialism could be achieved in capitalism through elimination of interest. I think it not beyond the realm of possibility that we could then have the best of both worlds (i.e., less economic disparity along with broadened free enterprise).

53. *February 2, 1986*

What I think today is not necessarily what I will think tomorrow. As conditions change, we must change in a never-ending accommodation to new realities.

54. *February 3, 1986*

It is increased world productivity that is keeping the wolf from our door. And why is the wolf even near our door? Two reasons. First, (I rate this the more important because it is the more offensive), we are siphoning off much of our national wealth to satisfy the debt monster. Second, we continue spreading our resources too thin by funding those entitlement programs which are giveaways. This is done without due regard to correcting the underlying causes for their need in the first place. Another drain, though necessary, would be rising military expenditures as a result of intense competition with the Soviet Union.

At the same time there are more millionaires and more homeless people than ever before in most western block countries, with both groups growing at faster rates than the population as a whole. How long can the productivity gain keep pace with the spending drain? As fast as the former is, the latter seems to be moving even faster. But the rubber band can only stretch so far.

Making matters even worse are Band Aid decisions such as reducing the number of IRS agents. The saving of a dime is costing us a quarter. Indiscriminate across-the-board cuts are neither wise nor cost effective. While many programs should be dropped altogether, there are some that should be expanded. In everything, each case should be judged on its own merits. Sadly, however, political jealousies often preclude the sensible approach.

55.   *February 17, 1986*

Communism preaches that to preclude the exploitation of the labor of others, only private one-man handicrafts should be allowed. The reason this is so wasteful is that the gifted individual is not able to leverage his talents by directing the work of many others under his leadership. It is true that under communism there must also be talented bosses; but the incentives are not as great for them, and the freedom to innovate and operate is likewise not nearly as great. Capitalism deals with man as he is; communism, as they hope he might be, even though at this stage of human development that "might be" may be unattainable. Since communism doesn't work very well, the Soviets force it down the throats of the citizenry, like it or not, instead of making the necessary compromises through which they could greatly improve efficiency.

56.   *February 24, 1986*

The following is a summary of the major points in this work:

1. Capitalism, at this stage of man's evolution, works better (and is therefore more productive) than socialism or communism. While the theory of communism espouses cooperation rather than competition—which is commendable in and of itself—the way it is practiced by the Soviet Union today is that of a master/slave relationship.

2. Interest charges, the bane of society, will over time polarize the "haves" and the "have-nots." Interest should be abolished.

3. Religion, once used as a moral force, is losing its influence as supernaturalism becomes less palatable in an age of science and reason.

4. Differing characteristics in people based on race *do* exist. It should be clear that there are both physical and mental differences in racial strains *when viewed as a whole*. Obfuscation of this truth is based on wishful thinking for social reasons, not on scientific reality. These differences will fade as assimilation progresses.

5. Freedom should not mean freedom to exploit your neighbor. I would recognize the proclivity of most of us to take advantage of others by unfair means if allowed to, and accordingly have the electronic equivalent of a foolproof National Identification Card that would make it very difficult to be a refugee from the law and not get caught.

6. Prison inmates should be treated with respect like other people; but they should work longer hours, producing saleable goods. Strict discipline is necessary. Education is an option limited to spare time. Overnight female visitors would be allowed, and housing in military-style barracks, with a limited number of small rooms available when privacy is called for. It is recognized that some 5 percent will be hard-core incorrigibles who must be dealt with separately.

7. *Require* virtually *everyone* to work during their productive years, but provide them with jobs and means to do so in special communities, if they cannot find employment on their own.

8. If the world survives long enough, improvement of mankind will rest on genetic engineering and producing many children from the gifted and *no* children from those not gifted. It will no longer be a *right* to breed, but a *privilege*.

9. As of July, 1989, Russia under Gorbachev appears to be making a 180-degree turnaround. While this change may have been made necessary by the inefficient nature of socialism, we should nevertheless welcome it with great enthusiasm. I do not

believe, however, that we should abandon our star wars research or let down our guard. It is always a mistake to invite temptation to do wrong, and effort should be made to eliminate opportunities for abuses by any and all factions. This is as true for nations as it is for companies or individuals. As a poker player might say, let's keep 'em honest. To ignore this basic precaution is to do so at one's peril. This truism is universal.

10. Limitations should be placed upon the amount of wealth that anyone can receive as a gift or inheritance. (He could make unlimited money himself, however.) Upon a person's death, all his surplus wealth (after the limited distributions) might best revert to a common pool used to advance science or ease the national tax burden. Everyone should make his own way in the world, but be afforded equal opportunity that would allow life's journey to begin from a level playing field without regard to race, gender or creed. All of this would bring true democracy, not just in name but also in fact.

57.   *1986, 1989, 1990*

An honest appraisal of honesty

■ Honesty is quite frequently the best policy.

■ I am honest to the extent that I perceive it to be in my best interest to be honest.

■ I'm not looking for an honest man, I'm looking for a man who's smart enough to know that, for him, honesty pays.

■ In certain circles, honesty is taken as an index of stupidity. But for the long-term, I say it is dishonesty that is more likely to be the greater stupidity.

■ *Those who try to deceive may expect to be paid in their own coin.*   – AESOP

"This is my first court appearance, Your Honor —
do I bribe you or the bailiff or both?"

■ I believe in being truthful to the extent that the listener can accept the truth.

■ When in doubt, tell the truth.

■ Do not depend on the promises of those whose interest it is to deceive you. Take what you can get when you can get it.

■ The difference between a dishonest person and an honest person is this: Allow the first one to set his own terms and he'll rob you blind, but do the same for the second, and he'll *save* you money.

■ I like to think that I can number myself among the most honest people in the world. If true, it does not mean that I'm an honest man, but merely that I'm one of the most honest persons in the world.

■ There comes a point where total honesty must be tempered by a little discretion, although in a perfect world, it would behoove everyone to be perfectly honest at all times.

58.   *May 5, 1986*

Speaking of welfare: The dole is a narcotic and has the same effect as sending domesticated animals back into the wild. Their ability to survive has for the most part been lost; they have gone the way of a pampered heiress who knows only the social graces.

59.   *May 5, 1986*

If there were no interest paid on borrowed money, it would be much easier for people to get ahead, whether they were buying a house or operating a business. In either event the economy would be expanded, thereby reducing unemployment without increasing inflation.

This seeming miracle would occur because the interest income now supporting millions of people would be put to bona fide uses. All those people who lived off interest would now have to either go to work or to live off their principal. But, you say, what would a retiree do if his money ran out and he was too old to go back to work? Prior to retirement, he should put the principal into an annuitized variable life annuity and let the actuaries determine when the proceeds would be sufficient enough to allow him to retire. After all, our ability to retire must be contingent on our having enough income to allow us to do so. Vanguard is one company that can accommodate your needs; telephone 800-522-5555.

Further, I predict that as time erodes the wealth accumulated by interest, the freer distribution of that wealth will cause prosperity to flourish for everyone to an accelerating and unprecedented degree (if the world can survive long enough).

The wealth of wise investors outside the realm of interest income, however, will not dissipate, but will increase, and deservedly so.

The author asks that this Nugget (#59) be reread until its message is understood unequivocally. I believe if its advice were taken, a dramatic change for the better would occur in all our lives and the lives of those who succeed us. Remember: It is ideas that rule the world and its events.

60.   *May 11, 1986*

Distilled to its essence, what is the purpose and meaning behind the manipulations made by the world's central banks (which includes our own Federal Reserve system)?

This much we can safely conclude: The banks are the agents of their monied patrons and attempt to optimize their profits, regardless at whose expense it may be.

They get Uncle Sam to shore up the International Monetary Fund so that it can help debtor countries meet their interest payments. This means in reality that the taxpayers are footing the bill if the actual borrowers are so tapped out they cannot fulfill their obligations. The labyrinth of ways to make the wealthy grow wealthier is awesome and endless. They even try to profit by dealing with communist regimes who have vowed to destroy them. Whether or not these same communists are the pawns of international financiers, without whose support communism would never have gotten off the ground, is something I cannot answer. I do know this much, however; Marx's economic views were entirely compatible with the views of the banking establishment in the city of London and particularly the House of Rothschild. It is no accident that Karl Marx is buried, not in Moscow, but in London. Nor is it an accident that the triumph and bloodbath of the Bolsheviks in Russia gave the Rothschilds and their associates one billion dollars in cash which the luckless Czar had deposited in their European and New York banks. Few people know that Marx had close relations with the British aristocracy through his marriage to Jenny von Westphalen. She was related to the Scottish Dukes of Argyll who had long been revolutionaries, and a mazy of other wellborns.

Going back to the original question, the central banks have learned that to optimize their profits, countries must fine tune their economies so as to extract maximum efforts from the citizenry. When worms are scarce a hen scratches harder (i.e., over half of young mothers now work—not because they want to, but because they have to). At the same time the bankers take full advantage of opportunities resulting from economic problems which they themselves have created.

Be that as it may, we may yet see the tiger turn on itself. Through complacency and greed their reach will exceed their grasp as it always does to those who never find contentment.

What, then, can we hope for? I say we should apply a more sophisticated form of self-interest, i.e., do whatever needs to be done to make it the best world possible for the *greatest number* of people. Once that happens progress will feed on itself, and the multiplying benefits to *all* will prove to be nothing short of spectacular.

■ ■ ■

Philosophy Nuggets
Part II

61. July 29, 1986

Those people who are unfortunate enough not to have a cushion of cash or other assets behind them can expect to encounter a hard time in making ends meet even at double the minimum wage. On the flip side of this coin we can see that two million dollars invested at a real rate of only 3% annual interest will yield its owner an income of $60,000 per year. The person in the first example might well labor his whole life, in effect helping to support that one millionaire who, upon his death, would still have the buying power of his original two million intact (due to growth of principal resulting from the higher nominal rate offsetting inflation) even though he and his family would never have had to do a single day's work. Is this not modern day serfdom? You be the judge.

The above passage may appear to be a denunciation of the capitalist system. It is not. Only are capitalism's faults at odds with the author's thinking, who believes that at least for the present, capitalism, if changed from the exploitative to the benevolent type, will yield results superior to alternative forms of government. And no, we do not want a welfare state; charity is not a cure for failure. Our Constitution says "promote the general welfare"—nothing about providing it.

62. *January 28, 1987*

I would think there are those who must understand the inner workings of our economic system, but they do not admit to the public that storm clouds are moving in over our country and cannot be stopped unless one major underlying problem is corrected. That is, the ever-expanding accumulation of wealth by the haves, offset by the increasing pauperism of the have-nots. This dilemma is exacerbated by the transfer of wealth through interest payments. "If you don't change your direction, you'll wind up where you're headed," says an old Chinese proverb. The charging of interest will eventually kill the goose that lays the golden egg. That goose is capitalism.

"The Philosopher's New Clothes"

I put myself in the place of the little boy in the famous Hans Christian Andersen fable, who cried out, "The emperor has no clothes on." In his innocence, he called it the way he saw it. not stopping to think how foolish he would look if he happened to be wrong. As to protesting for probity when discretion might indicate otherwise: Ships are safe in the harbor, but that's not what ships are for.

Philosophy Nuggets bares all!

These are not meant to be the final answers, but rather the starting point of new beginnings. To borrow a phrase from Bob Dylan: *"He who's not busy being born is busy dying."*

63.   *June 21, 1987*

Our problems with a financial squeeze bleeding those of us who are net debtors—either directly through personal debt, or indirectly through government debt—will continue to grow until we stop the accumulation of interest wealth from its inexorable march that transfers the wealth of those who owe to those who are owed. Pope Pius XI attacked interest in the following words in his encyclical letter "Quadragesimo Anno" in 1931: "The state which should be the supreme arbiter, ruling in kingly fashion far above all party contention, intent only upon justice and the common good, has become instead a slave, a docile instrument at the service of all passions and ambitions of interest."

Productivity gains from technological advances will ease the burden—but this is not a solution. Rapid hyperinflation would be a quick fix, but it is not the real answer either. The permanent solution is twofold: first, eliminate interest; and second, limit the amount of wealth that can be passed on to heirs. Whatever a person can accumulate in his own lifetime should be his without limits, but upon his death, it should, with reasonable exceptions, be a new ball game. John D. Rockefeller, Sr., said that a man who dies too rich has lived too poorly. He was a philanthropist whose detractors defined that term as partial restitution.

Ideally, everyone should begin life on a level playing field, thereafter progressing to where ever their efforts and abilities might lead them. Babe Ruth was once asked how he could justify being paid more than the President of the United States. He replied, "I had a better year."

"Sometimes I think it would be more merciful just to ENSLAVE them."

64.   *July 4, 1987*

Morality is nothing more than enlightened self-interest clothed in the robes of ethics and the facade of religion (which can be extremely dangerous when propelled by blind faith and dogma instead of reason and logic—witness Iran). I wonder if the ordinary citizen would appreciate the value of morality as much if its true purpose was stated as enlightened self-interest. I would like to believe that more and more people are beginning to think for themselves. Herein lie the seeds of hope for a new and better world.

65.   *July 24, 1987*

Within this series I have frequently referred to the desirability of being benevolent. Now I want to explain my reasons why, and they are totally counter to the conventional wisdom. Spiritual morality based on faith and dogma plays no role in my quest for an ideal world. That void is replaced by self-interest? You are shocked! But wait—read on. What I am talking about is enlightened self-interest (being benevolent or fair). By enlightened I mean the taking into account of the interests of all 5 billion of us, starting first with the interests of those who would be our most formidable adversaries. Would that have meant caving in to Soviet demands regardless of their merit? Of course not, but those demands should have been treated just as objectively as though coming from our allies. (While I would prefer giving equal treatment to all 5 billion immediately, this is simply not practicable. Progress takes time.)

The reasons, then, for being benevolent and for factoring the interests of others into my dealings with them are twofold and completely pragmatic: By being fair even when circumstances are such that I would not need to be (a situation that most of us would find hard to resist taking advantage of), I am at the same time avoiding their resentment and wrath toward me when it is realized that I've "done somebody wrong," and I am building trust which will lead to cooperation and be mutually beneficial both for the moment and for the future. Until man's last vestiges of ill will are eventually laid to rest, care need be taken not to ignite one set of grievances that awaken others. Former Secretary of Defense Robert McNamara has called our planet "Spaceship Earth" and proclaimed: "We must not forget that one-quarter of all the passengers on that spaceship have luxurious first-class accommodations and the remaining three-quarters are traveling in steerage. This does not make for a happy ship in space or anywhere else. All the less so when the steerage passengers realize that there are at hand the means to make the accommodations more reasonable for everyone."

To sum up: Strive to be fair not only when you're the underdog (everyone seeks fairness in that case, after all, is not the hare more likely than the hound to abhor blood sports?) but also when you have the upper hand, knowing full well that your objectivity will pay off in the long run.

Enlightened self-interest, then, (enlightened implying looking beyond just the short-term) is to understand that the reasons for doing what is "right" should be for *long-term* "selfish" reasons (such as fostering goodwill), not for "moral" reasons disassociated with practical ends.

Enlightened self-interest is all based upon enlightened common sense, which I define as simply a higher level of insight into the practical world as well as into the human condition. Living in an upper-class ivory tower does not provide the best experience for acquiring this talent.

66.   *August 11, 1987*

This is a tale of two cities. Which one is better? Both forbid interest payments; both forbid alcohol; both stand firm against corruption; both are opposed to loose morals; both are against gambling. So far, you say, they are alike—there is no way to choose between them. But what if they each had different reasons for doing these things, things which, incidentally, I concur with?

What if city A had these rules because they said it is the will of Allah (God), and the law of Islam, and cannot be questioned; while city B said that the reasons for these rules were entirely pragmatic, that they were adopted only after it was understood *why* they were in the best interests of the people?

City A, because they obey without questioning (which is okay to those for whom it works) run the risk of subverting the inherent good in their doctrine by becoming unreasoning crusaders to the point of being irrational. Have you ever noticed how many of the world's conflicts are rooted in intolerance under the banner of religion? To quote one book written a century ago, "The Spaniards, gorged with plunder and wading in blood, were at the same time, and in their own eyes, crusading soldiers of the faith." Another notable example was (depending on who's doing the counting) the 7 or 9 warlike major Christian crusades to the Holy Land extending from 1096 to 1271 A.D.

"It all started when one side said you were three people, and the other side said you were one person in three parts."

On the other hand, the inhabitants of city B can be depended upon to act in a rational manner because they know the "whys" governing their behavior, and can apply this reasoning ability to new situations as they develop. Behavior is like fortune: It can be good or bad; it can taint or enhance those touched by its manifestations; and for better or for worse, it's slowly habit-forming.

City B with its understanding citizenry is still only a dream, but one whose time is coming as mankind continues its relentless advancement (on balance) toward improvement.

September 18, 1990

AUTHOR'S NOTE: After submitting this nugget to an authority on Islam for comment, I was informed that Islam *is* in fact a totally pragmatic religion, and that Christianity would have better suited my example of city A. I admit that the reason for my choice was because I independently arrived at many of the same conclusions that the Qur'an has been advocating for over 1300 years, and preferred to think it was for different reasons. The difference is that they call it God's law, and I call it enlightened common sense. So take your pick—cola or uncola, they can both quench your thirst, but only if you drink them.

POSTSCRIPT: Here is an example of Islamic pragmatism: Could Solomon have done any better?

A Moslem workman, needing to repair the end of an overhanging crane on top of an eight-story building, lost his footing and fell. Landing on another man on the ground, the workman survived but the man he fell on did not. The victim's brother sued for damages and the case was left to the emir to decide. The emir agreed that the plaintiff had a case.

"Will you accept a financial settlement?" the emir asked.

"No," the brother replied. "Scripture demands an eye for an eye, I demand that he be executed."

The emir thought a bit, and then replied, "I will grant your wish. However, an eye for an eye is not an ear for an eye. He therefore must die in the same manner as did the victim."

Well now! Who's going to fall eight stories in order to seek retribution? So the brother declined, adding that he would settle for the money after all.

"No," said the emir. "You have already declined that option. You have therefore forfeited your claim on money. The case is closed."

67.   *August 13, 1987*

What will happen in America when the amount of wealth flowing into the pockets of the affluent becomes so burdensome on those from whom it is taken that the situation becomes untenable? I do not know the nature of the consequences that will follow, but I do not believe major changes can be instituted until, like a chronic alcoholic, we have "bottomed out" first. (The great tribulation must be past before the Millennium can come.)

Once that happens, the climate will be right for bold innovations, and will, as never before, have a receptive ear from the masses. It is at this point that new philosophies have their best chance of gaining a foothold in the public consciousness. The ideas with the most merit and appeal for that point in time will become the wave of the future. Once started, they will be hard to stop (as evidenced by history).

Whether we like them or not, drastic changes are coming just as surely as the rising sun. It is better to have imperfect progress than perfect paralysis.

We have leaders who are afraid to lead;
we have voters addicted to handouts.
It's time to leave this ill-fated convoy;
it's time to head for shore.

68. *August 23, 1987*

Economics, were it just a science, would be much like physics, where every action has an equal and opposite reaction. What if we mandated a balanced budget and stuck to it? Yes, it would help to stop inflation; but at the same time it would extract a price of similar value in another form: loss of those services that would have been available had the deficit-creating programs not been stopped. The ongoing question is, which hurts the least, one more dose of inflation or a program lost by spending cuts? The law of physics strikes again.

Think of inflation caused by deficit spending as a general tax that devalues our money across the board. If that tax yields us a total of $100 from a total of 100 people, each person has lost one dollar in buying power. In other words, the essence of

"In his press conference today, the President announced that good is bad, up is down, black is white, and the economy is improving."

inflation is an overexpansion of credit relative to available savings. Ideally, it would be better not to have any inflation at all, so that a person's money earned years ago would be worth the same today (even much more for items benefiting from technological improvements, which includes just about everything). And here is where economics as an art-form comes into play: The nature of the system is such that a maximum amount of tribute is extracted from all parties after adjusting for their varying degrees of protest, the cloth is cut according to its length. This optimizing procedure takes the form of both visible tribute (tax increases) and invisible tribute (inflation). It is all a balancing act, and will eventually collapse when the sacrifices become too great for too many to bear. The exact nature of impending chaos is unknown. An initiating impulse will be the dropping of the match; the consequences will be determined by the nature of the material with which it comes into contact.

You might be wondering how it is possible for governments to have spent and squandered all the benefits achieved through productivity gains over the years. Believe it, it's possible. It went into the military; farm subsidies (an especially illogical concept which defies common sense); entitlements; interest on the debt (which is welfare for the rich); third world "loans" (largely siphoned off by their respective oligarchies); a variety of worldwide commitments and giveaways (some good, some bad); and assorted congressional pet projects, boondoggles and white elephants.

The more things unravel, the more they're patched over without addressing the basic causes, by far the most important of which allows the transfer of wealth from those who need it most to those who need it least (via interest payments).

It is understandable and expected that this matter has not been remedied. To do so would mean to tear down the whole framework and start anew. That would be extremely traumatic; too much has been invested in the existing structure to allow a graceful change without pain. In other words, too many have a vested interest in the status quo, and they will back up their position; but "facts," like lampposts, can be used more for support than illumination. So pain will come. Will we be ready to accept the challenge of building a new order when finally it does? The abolition of interest should top the list. When H. Ross Perot says the whole system needs to be scrapped, he deserves to be listened to. Adjustments on the margin are not enough.

69.   *August 26, 1987*

To whose drummer must a politician march? In listening to the various candidates running for office, one finds it very easy to agree with almost all of them. Oh, do they sound good; they will tell you what time it is with your watch. But why is it that so much remains unchanged after they get in office? "Words are plentiful but deeds are precious," Lech Walesa has said.

Consider these two mildly offensive hypothetical examples: Mayor Botch of the city of Metropolis is asked on a call-in show why some bars in the city are open 24 hours. He replies that by law they are obliged to close at 2 a.m., repeats himself, and says no more. Case closed. The fact is that hundreds of bars in Metropolis never close. By relicensing themselves as private clubs they sidestep the 2 a.m. provision of the law. To do this it is obvious that they must know the right people. Whether with cash or otherwise, favors are being exchanged. Now, it is known by all that Mayor Botch is above reproach, he cannot be bought, he is as untouchable as Elliot Ness himself. But there are times when, to stay in office, even he must turn his back and not ask certain questions. To get along, you go along. This is understood without a word having ever been spoken.

"Porter is my speechwriter, McAllister is my legislative assistant, and Ferguson thinks up my campaign promises."

Case #2: An admiral is asked if his sailors are allowed to frequent houses of ill-repute when on liberty in a foreign city. His reply: "The cribs are off-limits," he repeats himself, and says no more. The fact is that the two "cribs" do not serve alcohol and are indeed off-limits, but the 50 odd bars where 98% of the prostitutes hang out are accepted by the Navy, which maintains a station located in the center of activity that dispenses free contraceptives and advice. This convenient accommodation between social mores and reality has a point: We need good people as our leaders, but if they try to be too good, they will distance themselves from the masses, and will lose their effectiveness. The world is still too imperfect to expect perfection of those who lead us.

My hope is that enough people of influence can come to realize the enormous advantages to all of us resulting from enlightened self-interest, and that their combined leadership will prevail when the time comes to set the most radical of new policies. To persuade the public to accept this doctrine some friendly persuasion will be necessary in the form of full financial disclosure.

Hardly a month goes by that my mail does not include a letter bemoaning the threats to our privacy—especially financial privacy. I say this sort of secrecy is the very thing that perpetuates the opportunities for abuse against our fellow man. If we can advance further by cheating, why be good? Answer: Because if we get caught, all should know that guaranteed punishment will follow. Full disclosure will substantially reduce the likelihood of not getting caught. I fully agree with Ralph Nader when he says, "Information is the currency of democracy. Its denial must always be suspect."

We need to advance to a better world one step at a time, in a planned march calculated not to move faster than the majority is able to keep pace with, unless chaos descends such as we have never known before. In that event new ground rules must be applied at once.

70.   *September 15, 1987 & October, 1993*

Having never been formally trained in economics, et al, I have been forced to rely on common sense, and thus gain insights (and no doubt make errors) that I suspect escape those properly schooled. Otherwise how is it to be explained that some of the more obvious realities as expressed in this series have been overlooked by so many for so long? For example, I deem it common sense that the Federal Reserve could be abolished and replaced by an advanced computer. But Milton Friedman, writing in the Stanford University Magazine, believes it would only require a rather simple computer for that job. Thank you, Professor, I stand corrected. (The rule of "the three threes" sums up the challenge of being a bank executive: Borrow at 3 percent. Lend at a 3-point spread. And be on the golf course by 3 p.m.)

It seems that nowadays the Fed is in a constant tug-of-war between a tight money supply that causes recession (said to be periods in which the things that went out of control during the previous boom are adjusted back to reality), yet fails to halt inflation, and an expansionary one that makes for even worse inflation. The casual observer would indeed be justified in wondering why all our options seem to offer negative results (i.e., choosing the lesser evil). Isn't any course the right one? That's a good question, and the answer is no. Our debt money system was intentionally designed to fail. And when it does, a very thin layer of the super rich, supported by those who work for them, will own us. The middle class will have disappeared. The Fascists posing as our saviors will befuddle us with rhetoric, which will be exactly the opposite of what they intend. They will see to it that any politicians with integrity do not get very far. We will learn too late that communism was their tool all along; a deception to fool and lure those disenchanted with exploitative capitalism. They will isolate or vilify any leader who poses a threat, real or potential. And yes, there is a reason

"I'm afraid the Fed is tightening up on the money supply, sir —
I can show you your money, but you can't withdraw it."

why we trade with Communist China but not with Communist Cuba. You see, not every communist country is in cahoots with the conspiracy. Cuba is not.

The world is a big place. Groups large, small, and splintered are all in competition with each other. Some are independent. Some are loose cannons. What we need to ask is: Who among them are the benevolent? Ye shall know them by their fruits . . . Matthew 7:16.

71.   *September 29, 1987*

As a country we need to face up to some unpleasant truths: We simply cannot afford to supply housing for all the homeless; to offer extensive national health insurance to all who need it; to give all the aid we would like to troubled countries around the world; to bail out the farmers, and on and on. The liberals' belief that we can be all things to all people has proven to be unrealistic. They love humanity, but don't much care for human beings. Government largess can extend only so far before it reaches a point of diminishing returns. In our effort to increase revenues for causes, however worthy they may be, care must be taken not to stifle free enterprise by oppressive taxes. And beware of the Circean spell of debt. Jefferson said he placed public debt as greatest of the dangers to be feared.

"Our job would be a lot easier if the taxpayers and the voters weren't the same darn people!"

I wish a computer could be programmed to provide us the proper balance between the funding of good causes and the point where taxing to pay for them does more harm than good.

Like enjoying anchovies, this viewpoint is, for many, an acquired taste. I am reminded of the man who said with a touch of hyperbole, "I would disown a son who was not, at least philosophically, a socialist by the age of 21, a democrat by 31, a republican by 41, and unaligned by 51."

72.   *October 29, 1987*

I am beginning to think that maybe our democracy, wherein the final arbiter of public policy is public opinion, relies too much on the whimsy of the man in the street in deciding issues of national importance. If we believe that our leaders whom we have elected are indeed men and women of superior intellect, would not we be better off to rely on their judgment, assuming we have faith in their integrity, than to opt for a referendum on matters few of us have an in-depth knowledge or understanding of? As H.L. Mencken once said, "I feel sorry for the man who, after reading the daily newspaper, goes to bed believing he knows something of what's going on in the world."

If social progress always awaits a popular majority before being implemented, it will be a watered-down version, not a leading edge state-of-the-art progress. That is one of our problems: too much democracy. What the Soviet system loses with its disincentives for the average worker, it seems to make up for with rewards for its top achievers. The classless society label does not apply when it comes to divisions based on brainpower.

May we learn from them the easy way lest we learn from them the hard way, and soon—time is running out.

73. *October 31, 1987*

As I read the papers these days (between the lines) I am becoming increasingly concerned about the inroads the communists are making against nearly every aspect of our society. I doubt that there is more than one communist (and he never acknowledges that he is one) for every 500 dissenters and protestors against nearly anything and everything. However, in many cases, he is the seed that germinates, encourages, and exploits rebellion in most of these diverse groups, until finally they take on a life of their own without any help. He tries to get his foot in every door, and if he fails in one place, moves on undaunted, until he succeeds in another. All of this is a deliberate effort to weaken our country. They have pulled out all the stops, whether it's encouraging our own homegrown big city street gangs to commit crimes, or campaigning for Congressmen sympathetic to their causes who are unwitting dupes. And if they don't think the risk too great, assassination and abduction are resorted to in some countries.

Especially disconcerting are the efforts to undermine the advancement of science, which is the fountain of most of our progress. Disruptive tactics include placing roadblocks against construction of new facilities for scientific research at our universities. This might be attempted by exploiting a legitimate concern such as protesting the use of animals used in research, which I too protest *if* there's needless suffering involved. There can be no doubt that we should always be ready to oppose the insensitiveness referred to by George Bernard Shaw when he said, "Custom will reconcile people to any atrocity. . ." But to get back to the point I was making, agitating local governments into denying building permits is also a tactic used, as is organizing individual scientists against working on certain projects such as star wars. Speaking of which some voices allegedly on our side would have us delay deployment of SDI in return for a

50% reduction in certain Soviet weaponry. Would this promote peace? Yes it would—but peace on their terms. They would be taking a giant step towards assuring their victory over us without the fear of a preemptive strike by us. For a communist the word "peace" means an absence of all opposition to communism.

We can now only hope that my fear of their leaders having been corrupted by power and having no interest in showing benevolence toward their fellow man is unfounded. Beyond that there is little else *to* hope for. AUTHOR'S NOTE: Had I had more foresight, I would have hoped for the changes that we have seen occur in 1990.

74.   *November 6, 1987*

Why doesn't America effectively address the problems of the perpetual poor and disadvantaged? Is it that we lack the will, or are we (as I believe) unable to address certain problems because realistic solutions would be too offensive to our basic democratic beliefs? That is to say we are accustomed to rules established for the majority, and are loathe to admit that just maybe we should have different rules for subcultures in our midst. Our society is driven by competition and does not offer adequate alternatives to those who find they are unable to compete (mostly because of lack of ability). We are instilled from early on with the notion that all men are created equal, and this is widely interpreted to mean that we all have an equal chance of success. A noble idea, but sorry to say, untrue. The smarter the person, the better his chances to compete in a wide spectrum of endeavors, and thus, be successful.

Slavery, for example, was indeed a dark spot on our nation's history (even though slavery has been universally practiced by man throughout recorded history). However, its abolition did not guarantee that a representative proportion of black slaves would suddenly or not so suddenly be able to compete success-fully with their white brothers in non-physical endeavors. While educated slaves are more valuable to their owners than uneducated ones the risk is that the educated are better equipped to break loose from their shackles.

I think it commendable that blacks today have doors open to them that they never had before. That speaks well for our country. But entry through those doors should be based only on merit, and not on a "fair" numerical proportion. Ability cannot be legislated, and attempting to do so results in reverse discrimination and a weakening of the system itself.

The realistic solutions I referred to earlier would include both voluntary (for some) and enforced (for others) relocation to centers that are actually towns and cities created to accommodate those (without regard to race) who would otherwise (due to their inability to compete) be jobless; in some cases homeless; and in all cases be forced to live lives of hopelessness and despair in a world that had passed them by.

"You need to improve your public image, Your Majesty —
why don't you import some slaves and free them?"

In their new locations, military style discipline would be the order of the day. Freedom as we know it would have to be earned both for their own and society's good. Responsible behavior would be the key. Those showing a willingness to learn useful skills, to cooperate, and to stay out of trouble, would lead lives similar but simpler to people outside these special centers. For example, they would lack expensive amenities such as private automobiles, which would be replaced by bus service and bicycles (mostly bicycles if terrain is flat). No street drugs, alcohol, or guns would be allowed.

Basically these enclaves would be as self-sufficient as possible, but in any event would be self-supporting, with as many amenities of life available to the people as their work efforts are able to support—but *no more*. Labor omnia vincit. [L.] Labor conquers everything.

The purpose of these Nuggets is to lay down the philosophical base upon which society can be improved. One opportunity to do this would present itself if, heaven forbid, terrorists were to detonate a nuclear device in New York City or Washington, D.C. If we prepare for that possibility now, we will know what to do afterwards should it happen. We would then need new rules to live by (meaning a less permissive society) such as monitoring the activities and curtailing the freedoms of all troublemakers in proportion to the severity of past misdeeds committed by them, and start afresh, hopefully for once and forevermore.

75.   *November 8, 1987*

In many respects the Soviets have us at a disadvantage. With absolute power to use as they see fit, the Soviet rulers can make changes easily in any and all aspects of the lives of their citizens, or the policies of their government when they think it's called for. In America, change is infinitely more difficult to effect, at times over the most trivial of matters. Can you imagine a Russian garbage scow plying the seas for months on end, as one from New York did recently, looking for a place to deposit their cargo, while each locality it visits individually deliberates the matter? How disorganized can you get? Such a hit-or-miss approach to a very real problem does not foster much confidence in inter-territorial problem solving.

Democracy works best when dealing with reasonable people. Unfortunately this quality seems to be disappearing as people become more litigious with their fellow man, and practice narrow self-interest (short-term benefits) instead of enlightened self-interest (or long-term rewards). There is a world of difference between these two approaches, the former may often be self-destructive, the latter is self-fulfilling. I think this unfortunate trend is coming from a feeling of desperation in the lives of ever more people and permeating over the land without boundaries. It is a need to worry about getting through today let alone tomorrow; of mortgaging the future—and going into

"ENLIGHTENED self-interest? But that would
take all the FUN out of it!"

"That <u>USED</u> to be the Good Humor Man."

debt is literally mortgaging the future (good when used for creating wealth; bad when used for present consumption). As is my habit, I tend to digress from one thought to related but different thoughts. Suffice it to say, the Soviet planners demonstrate a cohesiveness and singleness of purpose lacking in the United States. AUTHOR'S NOTE: While this appeared to be the Soviet case in November of '87, it is certainly no longer true in July, 1990. (Or is it?) But as General Colin Powell says, "You play the cards you're dealt at the time you're dealt 'em."

76. *November 17, 1987*

What will happen to our country if its debt load becomes too heavy to support? The same thing on a smaller scale is happening to Eastern Airlines right now. When the going got tough, Eastern found it couldn't tighten its belt anymore due to its heavy debt load. There were no notches left. So now it wants its employees to buy the company to save their jobs. They have already donated blood, but still the patient is dying, so how can the workers save the company? Simple: commit themselves to work even harder and receive less pay and, oh yes, by the way, the lucky bond holders will expect to continue to do no work with no reduction in their income as long as the company survives.

So too if our country runs out of notches on its belt, someone is going to have to work harder and get paid less, but who do you think it won't be? You guessed it; heaven forbid that the bond holders' income be penalized, that would never do. After all, they might be reluctant to loan us more in the future if we don't give them their "due" now (we should be so lucky). Let's continue doing things in the same old way that we always have. After all, there is no blood flowing in the streets at the moment.

With such rationalizations, we continue on our merry way. At this point it seems appropriate to quote Ross Perot after a 1971 foray in a brokerage firm: "There isn't enough management talent at DuPont to lead a group of monks in silent prayer." We are consuming our seed corn in order to pay off our interest debt which I call welfare for the rich, while big bear waits for us to do ourselves in, so that we'll be ripe enough to pluck with a minimum of effort.

77.   *November 22, 1987*

I think an explanation is due the readers of this work in regard to a contradiction of thoughts expressed in numbers 69 and 72. In the former I suggested that progress not outpace the majority's acceptance of it (barring of course a collapse of the whole system) and in #73 I urged a more aggressive type of progress that marched ahead of the crowd directed by leaders whose integrity we trusted. I led off by saying "I am beginning to think," and realized that I now suspect that a gradual improvement in the quality of leadership worldwide invites us to rely on the judgment of this new generation of leaders to a greater degree than had been prudent in the past. Of course this trust must be earned and not doled out indiscriminately.

To sum up: Given the current turmoil in the world, I think aggressive leadership is in order for the time being. Decades from now, when things are in better shape and order prevails, a more informed and enlightened public may better take charge of its own destiny, and the planned march referred to in #69 to an even better world will indeed be called for and accepted by the majority. As Wayne Gretsky said, "Most hockey players skate to where the puck is. I skate to where the puck is going to be."

78.   *November 28, 1987*

By now you know my feelings on "interest," and I think the time has come to sum up the situation with clarity. If you have studied economics and possess a reasonable understanding of its intricacies, you are apt to find the idea of eliminating interest totally off-the-wall. The reason for that is the different starting points from which each viewpoint has its origins: one is based on accepted tradition, with any deviations kept within certain limits; the other emanating from scratch without any inherited prejudices and based solely on the author's notion of common sense. That common sense clearly dictates that it is unfair to get something (interest) for nothing. And when continued over time, it also becomes untenable, especially when the number of beneficiaries increases exponentially as it is doing. I do *not* criticize those who accept interest, they would be foolish not to if it is allowed. It just shouldn't be allowed, that's all.

I'm sure you must be wondering if our economy could function at all without interest, since it is woven so tightly into the fabric of our society. But I can point to a precedent that is current. Sometimes car dealers offer low-interest and no-interest loans to qualified buyers. There is no reason why this same technique could not be applied to commerce in general. The key here to success is that the buyer be qualified—in other words, having the wherewithal to pay back the loan on time.

I firmly believe that the greatest insights are to be found in the simplest truths. For the eventual outcome to be satisfactory the starting premises must be sound. Our practice on receiving interest on money loaned is conveniently expedient for a while; but at some point or points in the future it will cause problems which eventually will overwhelm society's ability to correct. (We are close to that point now.) Attempts will be made to redress such problems as they occur by making adjustments and manipulations, but no matter how many bells and whistles are added they will become the Frankenstein monster that destroys its creator. I cannot overemphasize this point; nothing could be more clear.

79.   *December 6, 1987*

Adam Smith ushered in capitalism; Karl Marx, communism. What will come next? *Is* there something coming next? Yes, I think there is. Will it be an improvement over these two? If it's not, it will abort before coming to term. Need it be as ponderous to read and comprehend as were *Wealth of Nations* and *Das Kapital?* No, not at all. By what name should we refer to this new enlightenment if it comes? I would not give it a name per se, but would simply refer to it broadly as enlightened common sense. Have these ideas been formulated yet? Yes, you are reading them now. What makes me think they're so great? Simplicity of the underlying logic, untarnished by preconceived notions and established influences. Isn't it a bit conceited to presume your ideas to be so important? But I believe they are. Not to say so would be a mistake. If this is perceived as hubris I cannot help it, I am simply saying what I think without the pretensions of false modesty.

Mankind's next major advancement will be the final one necessary and will coincide with the advent of a one-world government. Assisted by a sound philosophical base, peace will have come at last, and will allow the energies that had been expended on conflict to be redirected toward the resolution of problems almost too numerous to contemplate. Martin Luther King Jr. once educed this profundity: "True peace is not merely the absence of tension, it is the presence of justice." And Adam Smith asserted, "What is wise and prudent in the affairs of individuals can scarcely be folly for nations."

80.   *December 8, 1987*

Why have the Russians gone out of their way to make a deal at this particular time with a republican president? Would they not have been able to reach an agreement more favorable to themselves by waiting until next year when a democrat with whom they would be more philosophically compatible might assume the office? The answer is that you make peace first with your toughest rival. If you can strike a deal with him (and Reagan was ripe for a deal) the rest of the opposition will fall in line quietly, where if the reverse were attempted, the ensuing clamor might possibly upstage the whole act. Incidentally, don't believe that Cap Weinberger's reason for leaving Defense was his wife's health. It was the sacrifice of a hard-liner in order to show a softer posture (which I hope was not a condition) for the General Secretary's arrival.

It is obvious that Gorbachev wants to come to terms, and we must hope that here at last they have a leader whom we can deal with. It would be a mistake for us not to pursue all avenues of opportunity to improve relations (option #1). The fact is we have no choice if we are to avoid option #2: the possibility of initiating a preemptive strike against the Soviet Union once our SDI program is on line (which I think could occur sooner than we are led to believe if we don't capitulate in the meantime). The Russians full well know this. They too are forced to the bargaining table.

The third option, of the U.S. allying itself with China, would not really be a permanent solution. Eventually the same music would have to be faced. Think how sensational it would be for the whole world if rapprochement followed by unity could some day be achieved, maybe even within the lifetime of most of us.

81. *December 20, 1987*

Not all of us who live in a capitalist society find the going easy. Unfettered capitalism can at times be brutal, taking no prisoners. Republicans lean toward the pure form; democrats prefer it modified by government tinkering when it becomes too onerous on some, whether or not through their own fault. What do I think? Just this: We come into this world with no guarantees that life will be good for us, or that it will be easy. I think the democrats' wish of bounty for all is unrealistic for

"Thank you for threatening me, sir. That was just the kind of incentive I needed."

this point in time. Those sacrificial lambs who do receive largess may enjoy the extra grass they are fed, but it never occurs to them that there must be a day of reckoning. Is dividing up the misery by replacing acute pain for some with chronic pain for all really a solution? In the end we would be considerably better off with the pure form backed up by a guaranteed work program for those who fail and desire such a program and for those who are unemployable whether they desire it or not. The Russians make parasitism illegal, and so should we.

Pure capitalism is constantly weeding out the weak, which results in hardship for them, and rewarding the efficient and industrious, who must keep on their toes lest they too be dethroned by an even more rigorous competitor. Interventions in this process such as protectionism, government subsidies, trade union excesses with inefficient work rules and featherbedding, invariably impede progress and are a disservice to us all, eventually including even those such actions were meant to help.

82. *January 2, 1988*

I am bemused by the latest Mexican debt bailout being touted as some sort of solution. It is nothing more than additional tinkering that may save face for all parties, but in reality merely distributes the pain more evenly and alleviates some of the uncertainty that heretofore prevailed. It is a non-solution dressed up to look like a solution (George Bush has said you can't put a sign on a pig and call it a horse), and fails to address the underlying fault upon which the financial structure is built. And that is, if loans do not include requirements for creating meaningful wealth, they should not be made.

What more convincing evidence could one offer against the evils of interest than to realize that just the interest alone on Mexico's external and internal debt is expected to consume about two-thirds of that country's 1988 budget?

If you still aren't convinced of the harmful nature of interest after allowing time for this sobering fact and its implications to sink in, then I pronounce you *unconvinceable*, and release you from the burden of pursuing these writings. It is the interest on debt that is bleeding the life blood from a country's citizens. Before accepting a bailout, they should know that free cheese can be found only in a mousetrap. The only thing postponing the day of reckoning is the powerful advances being made in technology and productivity.

If we were to start over from scratch with common sense principles, we could propel ourselves and the world into a near-utopia given today's technologies. But that can only come to pass after a catharsis. Such a catastrophe would be a blessing in disguise if it resulted in fundamental changes for the better.

83.   *January, 1988*

Up to this point I have freely vented my wrath against interest, but have given no hint of what I would replace it with.

I here and now admit that I do not have all the answers figured out in detail. The only thing I can provide is the bare philosophical building blocks that go into the foundation, the rest is up to others with different abilities suited to the next phase of development.

However, I *can* add a *few* more blocks and a few more thoughts. Would I retain central banks including our Federal Reserve system? Yes, but only after the Federal Reserve reverts to a government agency under congressional control (it is now privately owned, contrary to the assertion made in a new book on the subject) and submits to a full audit of its 12 banks—which it has never had in its 74-year history. Oh, what mischief privacy doth hide. Ordinarily privatization can do a job better than government but to allow it to create our national money is outrageous. Let it be known that smoke and mirrors are being used to hide secrets that cannot forever be contained. It will be quite an education for the public when the facts finally come out such as the incomprehensibly large profits made by some 300-odd holders of Federal Reserve class A stock, who accrue their vigorish through the magic of interest on money that isn't even theirs; truly an amazing feat. (The Fed holds and receives interest on the lion's share of all government bonds; the public owns only a small percentage.) The larger our national debt is, the more money they make—do you suppose this be one reason why we have so much debt? In fact, it may even be that our rollercoaster economy is caused by manipulation for the purpose of generating unseemly profit opportunities. Otherwise why wouldn't we have our act together by now after all of these years of learning? Thomas Jefferson told us: "The issuing power of money should be taken from the banks and restored to Congress and the people to whom it belongs. I sincerely believe the banking institutions having the issuing power of money are more dangerous to liberty than standing armies." (*Truth In Money Book* by Thoren and Warner.)

Would people have any incentive to deposit their money in banks if they did not get interest on it? It wouldn't matter if they did or not, but yes, they would have two of the three incentives that they have now:

1. Safety, and
2. The convenience of recordkeeping for all varieties of accounts.

The banks' only profit would now come from fees and service charges, not nearly as lucrative for them as interest, but far more stable and predictable. You seem to be saying that if we put our money in a mattress instead of the bank, it shouldn't matter in so far as the bank's ability to make loans is concerned. Yes, I believe the Fed can make compensations by juggling the

"You can't add apples and oranges, son —
only the government can do that."

eggs while seeing to it that none drop on the floor. Through creative bookkeeping they do that now. What do I think of a gold standard to back the dollar? An anachronism and a poor substitute for the real solution: the discipline of living within one's means without gold's artificial prop.

The practice of charging interest came into being because it fulfilled a need. But with it came the unhealthy excesses of wealth accumulation dividing and polarizing the borrowers from the lenders. It takes time for this to happen, but the miracle of compound interest is relentless. The medicine of interest has adverse long-term side effects for the patient. When an improved medication comes along, it is time to discontinue the old.

What will be the nature of the improvements you are anticipating? Let me preface my answer to that by first suggesting that no worthy borrower would be turned away, assuming three things:

1. His credentials give every indication that he is indeed a worthy borrower,

2. The market needs and has the capacity to absorb the product or service, and

3. There is a sufficient number of qualified workers available to fill the jobs created.

How can you accurately make these determinations? Through the improvements that I just spoke of which are the following two breakthroughs that I am anticipating:

1. A new generation of supercomputers to digest the reams of data necessary to make projections and intelligent decisions to a degree not now possible, and

2. Utilizing the emerging technology of genetic fingerprinting to identify fugitives from the law, and other deadbeats.

Critics who fear that snooping in a genetic data base could be a catastrophe, apparently don't know the difference between a catastrophe and a panacea.

I *do* feel it is necessary to give up much of our rights of privacy in the interest of public protection from rip-offs and for our personal safety. Of course, this would mean the aristocracy's underwear would be hung out to dry for all to see, also. That is why the birth of reform will likely be a cesarean delivery. Those who would abuse us need to be identified on a continual basis and isolated when called for, in the special communities I have previously referred to.

I am well aware how unpopular this notion is among freedom-loving Americans, but abuse of that freedom must be stopped. The age of permissiveness was and is a mistake. Law-abiding people should have no need for secrecy, and neither should the background and whereabouts of wrongdoers be kept secret. Once we get accustomed to full disclosure for everyone, it will be refreshing to let it all hang out. That is the only way to go in the orderly world of the future.

84. *January 10, 1988*

I sincerely believe . . . that the principle of spending money to be paid for by posterity under the name of funding, is but swindling futurity on a large scale. — THOMAS JEFFERSON

Whether consciously or otherwise, we are mortgaging our children's future by burdening them with debt that they have not incurred. I think this came about as a result of politicians currying favors for their constituents without regard for the future. But I also suspect that a reason helping it along was the rationalization that progress will make the lives of subsequent generations easier than ours were, and we should average out the load. I think there is merit in such reasoning; the bad part is that these situations are more often than not carried to an extreme. I would favor a reasonable degree of adjusting, but letting it get out of hand is as bad if not worse than no action at all. The best and certainly the fairest way we could help our seniors would be to eliminate inflation, thus preserving the purchasing power of *everyone's* savings.

"So what if your letter got here a few weeks late? We're all going to get blown up in a nuclear war anyway!"

Overall I think the world is on the path of progress, notwithstanding numerous setbacks along the way. I am less certain, however, that this long march forward is inevitable. I worry for our future, that a Hitler, Stalin, or Genghis Khan might succeed in conquering our planet and if given enough time to consolidate their position, pass on through their successors their own warped values ad infinitum. H.L. Mencken stated it bluntly: "It is a sin to think evil of others, but it is seldom a mistake."

It is clear that philosophers down through the ages have pondered this same dilemma; hence the biblical concept of God, who was shown as all-good; and Satan, who started out as an angel, but through a greed for power and apparently a sadistic proclivity, went out on his own in an effort to conquer the world and bring pain to mankind instead of joy.

This analogy is especially relevant today, in light of the fact that for the first time in history, the possibility of a one-world government is approaching. Might it be that the side that prevails initially will be in a position to perpetuate itself for all time?

I cannot say that Russia is the "evil empire," a term suggested by President Reagan and invented by one of his writers. I think that depends on who their leader is at the time. I certainly don't think the U.S. to be the fallen angel, even though as I've said before I think we are capable of initiating a preemptive strike if our defenses allow it, and if it looks like we are going to lose otherwise. I can only agree with this "better dead than Red" mentality if a full-fledged devil's advocate rules the Kremlin at the moment of showdown. If it comes to this point and Gorbachev is still in firm control, I will rub my rabbit's foot, hope for the best, and say: "better Red than dead." Like chemotherapy for a cancer patient. When it is a matter of survival, one takes the risk. I would like to add that under a truly benevolent leadership, Russia's potential for good is enormous.

SDI would preclude the Soviets from blackmailing us with a demand to capitulate or be faced with the consequences. Their sheer vehemence against it is evidence enough of its value to us.

If some of us are able to see a more distant horizon, it is only because we are standing on the shoulders of those who preceded us.

85. *January 20, 1988*

Any country not at war wherein there exists a black market for useful everyday items is not a well run country. This is so not because it cannot stop what is illegal, but because what is illegal should not be so. That's right, it is the country which is the villain, and not the black market within its borders. A true market economy reflects the real world relationships between supply and demand which should be respected, and not interfered with by the imposition of artificial restraints and controls that are applied to protect what should not be protected.

As a matter of fact, *all* trade barriers between countries should be torn down (except, of course, where used to prevent biological contaminates such as fungi or insects). A concerted effort toward that goal would well serve the interests of all people.

This idea is not new: witness free access between our 50 states. The only idea that might be new (in the sense that it is rarely practiced) is the notion to treat sovereign countries the same way as divisions within those countries. This does not mean enforced uniformity, although it will greatly expedite assimilation which can only bode well for mankind. In the long run, everyone tends to benefit when people are allowed to specialize according to their comparative advantages, thus maximizing their productivity and then exchanging their products with others who have done the same. This is what free trade is all about, and protecting any single industry from the rigors of competition ultimately lessens the total pool of wealth to all.

The efficiencies resulting from comparative advantage can be understood by a similitude: When Edison invented the light bulb, there were those who deplored the tragedy about to befall the candle industry—need I say more?

86.   *February 7, 1988*

When Paul Warburg created and Alfred Rothschild master-minded the Federal Reserve Act, Rothschild made its inner workings as complex as he could. Even to this day it is argued whether the Fed is a government or private agency. This mystification process was quite intentional, as it created a barrier to understanding, which is the first step towards explaining who the primary beneficiaries of its policies are. If we knew more, we might know why the national debt is so huge and continues to grow despite the admonishments of our leaders to rein it in. It is helpful to remember that the policies of the monarch are always those of his creditors, and it is the aim of those creditors to maximize their own profits.

If you ask me if I think it possible that an international conspiracy is in place with the aim of establishing a one-world government (which I happen to be in favor of) I would say, while not ruling it out entirely, that the world is such a big place it makes me wonder just how much influence any such entity could have. Should there *be* a grand design, the most likely vehicle for this transformation would probably be the Soviet Union. Some of the evidence I offer to support this is the fact that we allowed the Korean and Vietnam wars to end in a stalemate or worse, when it was clear that we had them both won but our generals were not allowed to complete the job. Likewise I am highly suspicious of why the neutron bomb, which would have neutralized all Soviet tanks, was never built. A look at history will show that every time bolshevism got into trouble, they were bailed out by western financiers!

If such a cabal does exist, I would oppose them only if their intentions were other than benevolence to all mankind. At this point I do not know how to make that determination, but my method of choice in dealing with the situation would be to make an effort to convert them to the philosophy of enlightened self-interest. However, it must truly be *enlightened.*

87.   *February 14, 1988*

What does "enlightened common sense" have to say about the "dumping" of goods made abroad into the U.S., the main practitioner at the moment being Japan. "Dumping" of course, is the practice of selling below cost, for the purpose of gaining market share.

My answer to this one is easy: Let them dump all they want, and if they want to give us the item in question as a gift, so much the better; let's take all we can. You see, they are just hurting themselves by this practice. The fear of the targeted country is that once its home industry is destroyed, the exporters will have the market all to themselves, and then be in a position to double and triple prices at will. Experience, however, does not always support this conclusion. You see, there is someone looking over their shoulder, an understudy waiting to take their place if the lead player stumbles, as would be the case if prices multiplied without economic justification.

Does Japan's restriction of imports from the U.S. hurt us? Yes it does, and it hurts Japan even more. Their farm production is many times less efficient than our own (a real understatement). In fact, Japanese pay up to 15 times the world price for rice, which is their basic food staple. If all countries would open their gates to all other countries (with the exception of strategic items and, as mentioned in #85—contaminants) everyone would benefit. The problem is a lack of political courage to rid themselves of uncompetitive industries, and the fear of becoming too dependent on outsiders, which is understandable. But interdependence in today's world is almost a necessity.

If Japan and/or others do not wake up to this reality, we should *not* then embark on a trade war. That would just add fuel to the fire and enlarge the problem. Enlightenment through education with patience and persistence is the treatment of choice. I think as time goes on, the benefits accruing from the elimination of protectionism will be realized, faced up to, and accepted by all. A country does not help itself by foregoing general benefit to save a few jobs temporarily by protection. Economic growth and competition will defeat no growth and protection every time.

88. *February 16, 1988*

We talk about wanting "fair" competition, and lament the "unfair" low wages paid workers in emerging countries. But what difference does it make where their leverage comes from, be it low wages, abundance of raw materials, better work habits, lower transportation costs, or more efficient factories? Competition is competition; that's what we wanted, and that's what we got. We wanted capitalism, we got capitalism. We didn't talk "fairness" when we were king-of-the-hill, so we shouldn't gripe now that the shoe's on the other foot. The fair trade argument is a delusion; what the world really needs is free trade. Nearly a century ago we closed our doors to Chinese immigration after observing that as workers they were too good. That was unfair, but it was also a mistake. Industriousness should not be penalized. We go to our government asking to be saved from the scourge of low prices, as if this is something bad. Euphemisms for restricting trade are created by those who benefit from restrictions. In the long run it is a true axiom that says: "A rising tide lifts all boats."

But, you say, cheap imports are closing our plants; our boats are not rising. To paraphrase old Charlie Wilson: What's good for production is good for the greatest number of people. There *is* a trickle-down effect without which we would be hurting even more.

Okay, so what do we do? Try to keep the plants open by any means available including repudiating any *interest* owed on debts and accepting wage cuts, providing what's left is sufficient to live on (without frills) and pay for an annuity to support oneself during one's retirement years. If this is still insufficient, work should be provided for in special communities mentioned in prior Nuggets, where fewer amenities (such as private cars) would be available. The first priority is to see everyone working, being able to compete successfully against the ablest is secondary.

89.   *March 12, 1988*

It seems you can condition people to accept anything, including being hit over the head with a hammer—but it must be done regularly.   – BARBARA KIEFER

The forces of habit are easily among the strongest in the human psyche. With this in mind, we can readily appreciate the importance of steering our children on a proper course from day one. What basic values would I choose to pass on? The following two top my list:

1. Whether you are or are not, *act* as though you are master of your own destiny; as though ultimately the bed we lie in we will have made ourselves, because the chances are that this will be so.

2. That acquiring so-called "good" habits is wise not because of some nebulous idea of morality, but because it probably favors what is in our best long-term self-interest.

Unfortunately in our present culture, this fact becomes less true as one descends the ladder of opportunity until, for many, the odds actually favor criminal behavior as being in their best short-term interest, and in some instances long-term interest as well. This is an intolerable situation for any country to be in; it is like neglecting to weed your garden. When the weeds outnumber the flowers, look out, our once lovely garden will fall into disarray, and disaster will follow.

George Orwell wrote: "We have sunk to such a depth that the restatement of the obvious has become the first duty of intelligent men."

What is obvious here is that wasted and errant lives must be given meaning and direction. It is important to provide jobs and opportunities to this underclass in special communities where the focus is on functioning at *whatever* level is *achievable*. Acceptance of these jobs will be a requirement. Multiple benefits will thus accrue to society: far less crime, far less welfare, more prosperity, and more happiness for everyone. And that is the name of the game.

90.   *March 23, 1988*

James Madison said in the Federalist Papers, 1788: *It will be of little avail to the people . . . if the laws be so voluminous that they cannot be read, or so incoherent that they cannot be understood . . . or undergo such incessant changes that no man who knows what the law is today, can guess what it will be tomorrow.*

I have been thinking about the overwhelming quantity of new laws and regulations with which government bureaucracy is inundating us. Add to this the increased burden on our courts, police, and a sea of lawyers and we have a major expenditure of both time and money. Also consider how many going businesses have been crippled and killed due to excessive, often senseless, cost-incurring codes and rules. What can we do to

"Why have a long, boring, complicated trial? I want each of you to pick a number between one and ten."

find relief? Some states are having success in using special masters and binding arbitration to secure speedier and far less expensive justice. While I heartily approve of innovations like this that work, I seek more fundamental solutions (as is to be inferred by the name "Philosophy Nuggets"). With this in mind, and with a realization that an endless stream of new laws is not the answer, but instead can be the problem as when changes in the rules of procedure make it too easy to sue, I propose the adoption of broad guidelines to replace a myriad of endless inflexible laws (but only in the higher courts) which tie a judge's hands and discourage, if not preclude, the use of discretion.

So here is the heart of my proposal:

1. Allow appellate judges to base their decisions on "common sense" rather than unbending laws, and elevate the principle of common sense to the top rung of the legal ladder.

2. Incorporate a "recall" mechanism that would weed out incompetent judges.

3. Allow all judges to levy fines on lawyers who consistently litigate cases that are frivolous or devoid of merit, and in certain cases make the losers pay the winners court costs. And as

we will have done with judges, get rid of incompetent lawyers through disbarment proceedings if they fail to measure up after fair warning.

4. Consider changing the number of jurors who must agree on a verdict, from a unanimous 12 to a majority of 11 (or 7 if we ever change to an 8-person jury). Just how often *does* a lone holdout (by being the spoiler) better serve the cause of justice?

5. Have as an ultimate goal a legal system so speedy that what now takes a year to resolve will take but two weeks. That would be justice worthy of the name.

Moderate variances in the interpretation of what constitutes common sense should be tolerated from region to region, in an effort to accommodate cultural differences. Eventually, a single set of criteria will return but this time based on a consensus that is the product of an assimilated world society. This ideal, however, will be a very long time in coming.

"I've been a burglar, and blackmailer, a mugger, and an armed robber, but by george I've never been a LAWYER!"

But getting back to the present: Are there times when a double standard is desirable? Yes there are, and here is an example which I admit is extreme, but just the same makes my point: I welcome guns in the hands of police, but I dread guns in the hands of the criminal. This double standard is common sense that few would argue with, but I know many will take issue with my next example: Might we allow polygamy to resurface among Utah's Mormon population if they desire to return to this lifestyle that they handled in a responsible way back when they did practice it? You certainly don't have to believe in their religion to envy and admire their way of life. (*Money* magazine for September 1991, selected the sister cities of Provo/Orem, Utah, as their #1 place to live for this year, and Mormons make up about 75 percent of the local population. That should tell you something.) As differences in lifestyles are charted around the country, individuals could gravitate to those regions most to their liking.

The bottom line is: Interpretations by local courts of what is common sense can be allowed to vary within certain para-

"The sentence isn't so bad, but my trial took <u>FOREVER!</u>"

meters. Let the quality of life within each locality determine how sound their particular interpretation of common sense is.

And now at last you should know about the best kept secret in the courtroom. It is the right to vote your conscience when sitting on a jury. It's unlikely the judge will tell you this. Instead, the judge will tell you that you may consider only the facts of the case and may not let your conscience, your opinion of the law, or the defendant's motives affect your decision. How do you get a fair trial if jurors are told their sense of justice doesn't count? The truth is, a lot of people don't get fair trials.

In addition to the facts, the jury is free to judge the merits of the law itself, its use in the case at hand, the motives of the accused person, and anything else necessary for it to reach what it feels is a just verdict. If juries were only supposed to judge facts, their job could be done by a computer. It is because we, the people, have feelings, opinions, wisdom, experience, and a sense of right and wrong that we depend upon jurors to judge court cases. Why don't judges tell juries about this? Today's judges generally don't appear to want ordinary citizens to make common sense decisions about the law. Judges seem to have forgotten that they are supposed to serve merely as referees of courtroom disputes, and as neutral legal advisors to the jury. We can only speculate as to why they act as they do.

Thomas Jefferson has said: "I consider the jury system as the only anchor by which a government can be held to the principles of its constitution. Juries are the judges of fact, and also *of the law when they choose*..."

This last sentence is most telling, and is evidence to the power that the jury holds. The judge should also let them know they cannot be punished for voting their conscience, even if they've sworn to follow the law as given.

The Roman historian Tacitus said it best: "The more corrupt the Republic, the more laws."

91.   *March 29, 1988*

Please refer to the first two paragraphs of #88, and treat this as an addendum.

Japan, by restricting imports from us (and others) is actually hurting itself more than it is us. Aside from this (which in reality is merely an impediment to the optimization of labor) the only complaint I have is the one-sided contribution that the U.S. provides Japan for her defense. While we thought this policy to be wise in 1945, we did not anticipate a weaker America and a stronger Japan in the years ahead. Japan (and Europe too for that matter) should now pay their fair share for the cost of providing this defense umbrella, and should realize that the tri-lateral countries are all in the same boat.

Japan's prosperity has helped this country, not hurt it. I strongly disagree with Donald Trump's notion to prohibit non-citizens from buying U.S. property. If we're going to close our doors, it should be directed against the slackers, not the industrious. And that's just common sense.

92.   *April 10, 1988*

What has happened to our once great country so that it seems no matter where we look nowadays, troubles abound? I think, as a nation, we have become soft. We are spoiled. We want luxuries, but don't want to work too hard to get them. Winning the lottery becomes a goal, never mind working and saving. When misfortune occurs, we expect and all too often receive settlements far larger than good sense or good economics would justify, even when resulting from a violation on our part. Too many of us think somehow that we are owed a living, and take the path of least resistance, which is often the least rewarding in the long run.

Much of our credibility as a just country is forfeited when we allow street gangs to terrorize our citizens; white collar crime

"They got me for contempt of court — I just
<u>COULDN'T</u> keep a straight face!"

to flourish; and all manner of rip-offs to proliferate. Also we
don't want to commit our armed forces to any action where
any of them might get killed. (What a contradiction that is;
how can any militia do its job without getting its hands dirty?)
We won't come to terms with our failing justice system, which
is laughed at by both criminals and citizens. We release wrongdoers because we say the jails are full. I say do away with jails
altogether and substitute work camps—as many as it takes—
with long sentences and 45 hour work weeks, while not allowing any room whatsoever for unruly behavior, but given civil
treatment and a social life.

They will have given up their freedom, because when they
had freedom they abused it, but in place will have self-respect
learned through the work ethic, even though it be imposed
upon them.

We hope it is not too late to salvage this country, but at
least we must act as if it were not.

93. *May 29, 1988*

Do societies carry within them the seeds of their own destruction? Are we like the alcoholic or drug addict whose first contact initiates a euphoria whose progression transcends the will to stop? If success breeds failure just what is the nature of the element that brings us to ruin, and is this process inevitable?

Let us look back to the fall of the Roman Empire for an insight into our own condition. It seems there were three major causes for Rome's fall: first, the erosion of the agricultural base evidenced by the flight from rural to urban areas where the peasantry could spend their days enjoying free entertainment at the arena instead of doing the hard work of farming; second, a heavy trade deficit caused by importing such things as the food they no longer produced for themselves, and expensive silk from China for their lavish clothing; and third, reliance on a mercenary army whose ranks held no loyalty toward Rome.

There is one common thread here: the unwillingness to earn the pleasures of life by being self-reliant; the pursuit of the good life without wanting to work. Sound familiar? It should. To quote the comic-strip character, Pogo: "We have met the enemy and he is us."

So here we have it: The nature of the element that brings us to ruin is the practice of being willing to consume more than

"The prisons are all full, so I'm sentencing you to five years in the waiting room at the Auto License Bureau."

"I want what's coming to me and I want it now!"

we are willing to produce. Is it inevitable that we destroy ourselves in this fashion? To be so inclined, yes; to be inevitable, no!

To the degree that we fail to convey the necessary disciplines on our citizenry—especially on our youth—for leading a "moral" life (having an understanding of *enlightened* self-interest) is the degree to which our nation will fail. Those who do not get this message (as determined by their brushes with the law) should have it imposed on them, by being sent to non-punitive work camps (much like the CCC camps set up by FDR in the '30s) and kept there until it is determined that henceforth they can behave in a responsible manner, however long that may take. Keep in mind that life in these camps would not be harsh as it is in our present day prison system, but would simply be subject to military style discipline. I would also convert all prisons into similar camps, with degrees of discipline in different camps commensurate with the ability of the residents to behave themselves. As many of these communities should exist as are needed, and no resident ever released before he or she is thought to be ready, regardless of the time it takes. And most important of all, every effort should be made to operate on a financially profitable basis, the result of work and production. It should not cost society, it should benefit society.

94.   *June 21, 1988*

There is one question that has always proved difficult for a nation's people to answer, namely: Whom can we most trust to lead us? If not an individual, then how large a group should the ruling body be? Our American founders deemed no one virtuous enough to be trusted with unchecked political power (the temptation to abuse it can be irresistible); hence our three branches of government evolved with their checks and balances—often diluting blunders, but just as often precluding excellence.

Is the point in history arriving when the world needs to take a chance on a faster way to put its house in order?

If a leader of most unusual ability emerged who could be trusted with autocratic powers, decisions would be made with dispatch, the administration of government would be optimized, things would happen, things would get done.

Should such a person exist, I think his country should go for the gold, as they say, and give him the power to change the world, hopefully for the better. I say hopefully because there are no guarantees. That is the ever present risk that must be taken, for without risk there can be no progress.

However, passing this great power on to a successor of lesser talents and virtues should be avoided by following the path outlined in nugget 17, which suggests a benevolent monarch who, when the time is right, will demote *himself* to an equal among equals and ascend to the ultimate state where selected principles of Christianity and communism are merged into one (all things for all people) making unnecessary thereafter the need to further risk having a single all-powerful ruler.

95. *June 30, 1988*

"May the best man win." How often have you heard that line, and how many of us really mean it when we say it? When competing for a contest, a mate, or a job, unless we actually believe that we are the best man (or woman) we *don't want* to be fair or to have justice prevail, at least not if we can help it. We don't want the next chap to beat us out just because he may be the best person. Now there are exceptions of course, a few who realize that both the person and the society he is a part of are better off when each citizen finds his own niche and strives to grow within it. Society should be structured so as to nurture a climate wherein each individual recognizes the reality of their own limitations and avoids the disillusionment that comes from biting off more than they can chew, or simply put, from unrealistic expectations.

While questioning the wisdom of trying to exceed one's reach, it is not my intention to disdain the many for acting like human beings. I only wish to make it clear what an uphill struggle lies ahead before a significant number of us can fully embrace the policy of enlightened self-interest and can appreciate its benefits in most cases.

In those remaining cases where the benefits are not clearly discernible, the risk/reward ratio in favor of the best overall course for all concerned needs to be adjusted to a point where an oddsmaker would bet on the right and sensible course.

That having been done, market forces will take their course, and common sense will prevail. Those that enlightened common sense fails to reach, when caught in an indiscretion, will be sent to newly established facilities heretofore described for indefinite periods of time, where life will not be unpleasant, but freedoms will be curtailed. Those who would abuse their freedom, will lose their freedom until such time as they can demonstrate responsible behavior.

96.   *July 22, 1988*

How should society go about implementing radical new policies that would eliminate interest, or put both prisoners and unemployed to work, each in respective camps designed for that purpose, or establish a mandatory foolproof identification system which discloses one's history (minor indiscretions excepted) or enforce full financial disclosure of everyone?

Answer: through setting up experimental proving areas in various parts of the country, starting on a small scale and gradually expanding in size as the bugs are worked out.

Overall supervision of each area should be given to bold thinkers who have demonstrated by their words, deeds, and actions the mental toughness to break new ground on a particular issue, while avoiding and correcting past mistakes through the application of a heavy dose of common sense.

We should not fear experimentation, and where it leads to dead ends, just back up and try again. As author Christopher Morley said, "Big shots are only little shots that keep shooting." Eventually, success will come and a better world will emerge.

97.   *August 20, 1988. Revised July 28, 1990*

Do I favor minimum wage laws? Let me answer that indirectly. My solution would be to reverse the dynamics of employment and create a surplus of jobs instead of a surplus of workers. When that happens, market forces would pull wages up to everyone's satisfaction (happy workers make better workers). Can we have too much of a good thing? Not if Japan's experience is a guide. They have 14 jobs for every 10 applicants, wages are now good but not burdensome to employers.

But best of all, they are being forced to increase investment in automation just to make up for the *shortage* of workers. Just as this progressive spiral of regeneration is feeding upon itself in Japan, so too the regressive vortex of degeneration feeds upon itself in Russia. For sheer magnitude there has never been a better example of the rich getting richer and the poor getting poorer. When confrontation between government, companies, and employees evolves into cooperation, and *everyone* is exposed to its effects, *all* segments should be better off; isn't that just common sense? This is my future scenario of what benevolent capitalism is to be all about.

For a machine to run smoothly, all of its separate parts must be engineered correctly. That quality has too often been lacking because various groups insist on going their own way in their efforts to seek advantage over others. When that advantage is not in harmony with the greater good, changes need to be made. Until now the free world for the most part has lacked a strategic overview, each problem has been addressed as if it were an island unto itself, and not just one part of a larger entity. The result has been a confusing patchwork that only Rube Goldberg could love. This too calls for change.

I can hear you now asking—but how can we create a surplus of jobs? I don't know the "how" of it, but I know it's doable. Putting people to work is not part of the problem, it is part of the solution. In addition to Japan's experience, another precedent for this is West Germany. They utilized guest workers from other countries during the rebuilding years of not too long ago, because their own labor pool was inadequate to meet demand. I suggest we find out how this situation came about and apply the formula to our own and other countries as well. Few things on any country's list of priorities are as important as providing jobs at a meaningful wage to *all* of its citizens. This alone would also do wonders in lowering the crime and suicide rates. We would be amazed to discover how one properly solved problem leads to the "miraculous" correcting of other problems, some of which we never even knew were related (the elimination of "interest" would bring this point home in a major way).

In addition, we need to reexamine the child labor laws which caused our country to go from one extreme to another; from overworking our youth to underworking them. Lesson: Moderation in all things. In addition, all "work" should not be lumped together. When placing limits on the number of hours that minors may work in a week, the *nature* of the job should be considered as well. Also, even the youngest children should be assigned simple tasks and learn responsibility (and discipline). A puppy dog not trained early enough, may *never* learn what you want him to as well as he might have.

Remember, the purpose of these Nuggets is simply to point us in the right direction—to set forth the basics. Detailed dissection is generally not my bag. Effort was made only to concentrate on the nub of each topic, which is an appeal to our common sense. If it fails in that, then I am not getting through in that instance to that individual. So be it. Implementation of these ideas will be left to others with their own special set of talents.

98.   *August 31, 1988*

It has occurred to me that the economies of the trilaterals (Europe, U.S., and Japan) are more alike in structure than mere chance would call for. I have in mind such things as monetary policy, rates of inflation, interest, unemployment, etc. Could it be that there are international forces at work that dictate compliance to the wishes of an unseen master? We are all playing the same board game with rules that are suspiciously similar.

The logical question that arises is: What common thread

has ensnared the free world? What legacy do we all share, like it or not?

And the answer I come up with is: A web of international banking that is usurping the life blood of the common man through (you guessed it) profiting from interest (and other ways). You might ask me how that can be, and point out that more banks are failing than ever before! To that I say, more banks are consolidating than ever before. The government (the taxpayers) pays off the debts of the weak sisters, which are absorbed by more powerful surrogates whose grip tightens slowly but surely around our pocketbooks.

Does it not seem odd to you that the average U.S. citizen is not as well off in real terms financially today as he was 15 years ago? This in spite of the fact that for the most part we have had a peacetime economy together with an explosive growth in science and technology that by any reasonable measure should have made us all better off. The fact that it has not makes me ask: Why? Who is taking our profits? Surrounding the real causes of this situation is a conspiracy of silence. When was the last time you were reminded of the enormous power of compound interest and the incomprehensible wealth it brings to the Class A stockholders of the Federal Reserve system whose existence the public is not even aware of? Even the Articles of Incorporation of the Federal Reserve at the time it was passed in 1913 are kept secret. Yes, the President of the United States does appoint the board members. No, that does not make it a government agency. No, neither the board members nor the Open Market Committee members are owners, they are merely hired managers.

I think I understand something now that I did not before—the reason for all the reckless lending to lesser developed countries. It is a ruse to extract from them every last drop of equity they may have, and when they can no longer pay back money, the banks will (when a friendly regime whom they can make a sweetheart deal with takes power) try to take their land. Land is the *real* gold, not so much the yellow metal itself, whose practical utility is limited, even though current realities still make gold our ultimate store of value. And would you like to know why it is now officially pegged at only $42.22 an ounce? It's because when they appropriate it, that is all you will get for it.

If such greed leads to a benevolent one-world government, I applaud it. If it leads to anything less, I denounce it.

99.   *September 5, 1988*

On September 3rd, the Florida lottery had its drawing and the top prize was $55 million. Besides some unjustified wealth redistribution, a portion of the proceeds goes into administering and servicing the program. It is also a drain of time and effort on both vendors and customers. The lottery offers the hope of getting something for nothing, which is not the message that people should be getting from their government.

"I find it hard to believe that we've actually won 20 million dollars when they send the letter bulk mail."

In my opinion, the only redeeming feature of gambling is the entertainment value it provides. The fact that it is being sanctioned by officialdom and is spreading is to me a sign of encroaching moral decay resulting from bankrupt government policies. I am against gambling unless there is a high degree of skill involved and only then if there is no significant skimming of the stakes.

When that distant day arrives where everyone is financially comfortable, those who wish to amuse themselves at a game of chance should have that right, but the tragedy as it now stands is that most of those who gamble are the very ones who can least afford it. It is to most players a chance to fantasize; in many instances, of escape from poverty. But their only escape is from reality by their inability to come to terms with their situation. Pursuing phantom riches via their pocketbooks is yet another shackle that keeps them weighted down.

Responsible government should not be a party to this fraud upon its people. If gains are to be made in this world they should come only from the legitimate rewards of productive labor (the means of which should as a last resort be provided by government).

I may sound like a conventional moralist, but I am really preaching the gospel of enlightened common sense.

100.   *September 21, 1988*

As much as I like to think of myself as a pragmatist, it may be that I am really more of an idealist. Here is the situation: There are signs now appearing that suggest that the productive might within the engine of modern technology is so powerful that it may come to overshadow all the inequities that I have been so concerned about. Some examples of these would be the practice of giving and receiving "interest," which includes servicing our enormous national debt; the maintenance of a costly welfare network; the tolerance shown toward featherbedding practices resulting from misguided work rules in both the public and private sectors, and all the other social burdens we find ourselves carrying.

In other words, our growing wealth may, in spite of everything, become enough that accommodation of our excesses becomes an irresistible temptation to be taken in stride. Alas, let us hope that we never get to that point. Hopefully, we will not for a minute abandon pursuit of the reforms that are called for (by bowing to political expedience), even if growing affluence allows us to sweep our problems under the rug with a golden broom, instead of seeking tougher but more lasting solutions.

We would indeed be remiss as a society if we did not make the effort to eliminate crime and strife which is largely fostered by an inability to participate in the Great American Dream (to be employed at a livable wage. No priority should be greater than that).

"I used to have the Great American Dream, but the politicians kept waking me up."

"I don't know quite when it happened, but at some point we made the transition from two-bit politicians to dime-a-dozen politicians."

The reason I now suggest of being perhaps more the idealist than the realist is that I stand by the principles of correcting what I perceive to be shortcomings, even though the road to public acceptance might be easier to travel by indulging in some gratifications, if only because we can momentarily *afford* to do so, regardless of long-term merit. This is a temptation succumbed to by many politicians (to the dismay of their constituents' descendants).

To sum up: Just because a coming prosperity might enable us to finance our faults without coming to terms with them, it does not mean that we should do so. We could become rich and still have *part* of us *hurting* badly. However, this is not to say that problems in one area should be subsidized by profits from another area. Each department should keep its own house in order.

101. *October 17, 1988*

A person's fortune, whether good or bad, carries with it the baggage of its opposite side, bringing to bear its influence to such a degree as to make its subject sometimes wonder whether his good luck was bad for him or that bad luck would have been good for him. And very often, this is exactly the case.

Given our choice, we would all opt for good fortune, but the hazards are many: We relax our guard against dangers, become lazy, or worse yet delude ourselves into a euphoric feeling of invincibility. We grow dependent on others to do our labor for us, and can become victim to predators.

On the other hand, bad luck early in life encourages us to take stock of ourselves, to set goals, to tackle our problems with fresh resolve, to strengthen our character.

The constant forces of yin and yang weaken the strong and strengthen the weak. 80% of us are caught up in this ebb and flow, elated one time, dejected the next. Then there are the others, one group of 10% who manage their luck, good and bad, in a constructive way, enabling them to avoid the negative side of the cycle. These are the long-term winners and are the most successful in any society. The remaining 10% are those born losers who for whatever reasons are never quite able to cope, and are reduced to survival without hope. Thus has it always been; need it always be?

102. *November 19, 1988*

It is said that we fought both the Revolutionary War and the Civil War to eliminate classes in our society, and here I am in 1988 suggesting that the perpetual poor are an underclass who should be relegated to their own areas. Am I not attempting to turn back the clock to an uglier period in our history? No, and here is the difference: Unlike former times, not only do I not wish to deprive *anyone* of the *opportunity* to better themselves, I wholeheartedly encourage them to do so, the passkey to such being *wealth* that is acquired legally and fairly. Crass, isn't it? Nevertheless, with all its faults, I regard wealth as being the best gauge of achievement yet invented. Materialism is what makes all the other so-called higher values possible. We must call a spade a spade, and whether we like it or not, put first things first.

Those among us who cannot support themselves in this world, should be allowed and required to relocate in friendlier surroundings that would provide work more suitable to their abilities. The practical effects of this alternate lifestyle would result in a sacrifice of some material amenities, but only ones regarded as luxuries, and only as many of them as necessary. Is this fair? Absolutely. If the ever-increasing level of skill required to produce new goods in our modern world passes by those at the end of the line who cannot keep up the pace, then they should not be entitled to share in those increased benefits to the same degree as those who *can* produce. This is where I differ with communist ideology. I do not believe in permanently subsidizing those who do not carry their own weight, not only for the rest of society's good, but for their own good as well. I do, however, believe we *should* go out of our way to help others in becoming self-sufficient. Give a man a fish and you

"I like that Maytag repairman — if I had the energy,
I'd write him a fan letter."

feed him for a day; teach him to fish and you feed him for a lifetime. By helping others to help *themselves*, we help *ourselves* threefold: directly (less financial aid is needed); indirectly (there follows less crime and other hassles); and through psychic income (the personal satisfaction that comes from helping others). And we transform a bitter, sad person into a grateful, happy person.

Those of us who are more fortunate should take care not to acquire a patronizing attitude. Remember, there but for chance go I.

In addition I quietly support point 8 of Nugget 56.

103.   *January 1, 1989*

I have just thought of an idea whose time, I think, has come. Let's privatize the jails! Thanks and no thanks to the drug problem, the crime explosion needs to be met head-on with a workable solution—like right now—not years from now. We shouldn't have to wait that long.

My idea, as already mentioned, is to send the law breakers to private work camps. Two main features would distinguish them from our present jails: (1) They would not be designed to punish the inhabitants, but to put them to work. For those who cooperate, life would be pleasurable, not harsh, with an emphasis on good food and a social life.

That's the carrot—now the stick: (2) Sentences would be much longer than at present. Release would not come easily. In fact, it may be that most would not even seek release, preferring instead the security and comfort of the life they now had compared to a life in the outside world that for whatever reasons they were not suited to compete in.

For starters, the practical approach calls for utilizing the military bases that the government is going to shut down around the country. These sites would match perfectly the needs of most (but not all) prisoners. Iron bars and small cells would be replaced by the existing inexpensive barracks dormitories. Gone would be the extremes of hard time and soft time; in their place would be good work time (required work while being treated well). While new arrivals would work a 45-hour week, those who prove they can behave would have minimal supervision, reminded of their situation only by the fact that they are "confined to base," to which has been added a double row of fencing and electronic sensors.

And yes, I did say privatize, didn't I? Private companies could lease these ex-military bases, which they would operate for profit generated by the fruits of the residents' labor. The largest share of profits, however, would go into a fund to make restitution to the victims of crime. Society would benefit in many ways, the most important of which, because of an ample supply of facilities, would permit the housing of offenders for as long as rehabilitation takes, even if that means for life. No more going free because of overcrowded prisons. If the bottom line shows a profit, as many camps should be built as it takes to meet the demand.

Chronic troublemakers who fail to produce a net gain for society, should be put to death without fuss or time delays (I am quite aware that this will not happen any time soon, if ever). I would regard it as a post-birth abortion of an incurably malicious personality. Also to receive the death penalty would be those caught dealing drugs while incarcerated. The days of mollycoddling the *hard core* offenders should give way to the days when law and order allow all of us to be substantially free from the scourge of crime. However, that does not mean to imply a deprivation of life's pleasures against those who learn to work hard and keep their noses clean. (For more on this subject see Nuggets #37 and #92.)

104.   *February 8, 1989*

What hope can we hold for the world? First, remember that progress can be made only as fast as the body politic (and the people) will allow it. Either too fast or too slow will not do. Although the face of the world is badly marred, men and women of good will everywhere are overcoming the odds. Progress is slowly but steadily holding forth.

Who would have thought just a few short years ago that a leader would emerge in the Soviet Union who could turn that nation upside down? What I thought was hostile dogma (and it was at the time) is now up for reevaluation—will wonders never cease? Or who could have guessed that the European Community would overcome their differences and unite as an economic block in the fashion that they are now doing, or that the U.S., Canada, and, it is beginning to appear, Japan, are coalescing into a cooperative unit?

It seems that just as we reach the precipice and are about to fall off, a last minute reprieve staves off disaster in a manner befitting "The Perils of Pauline." There must be an instinct in the human psyche that forces us to shape up at the last moment, like telling the birds and whales when to go south.

Yes, I am turning from pessimism to optimism about the future of our world. Instead of being overwhelmed by our problems, I think we might be able to overcome them with a little luck and a lot of effort from a majority of leaders who are good people.

105.   *March 26, 1989*

In Nugget #78, I expressed a belief that the greatest insights are to be found in the simplest truths. Let us examine this path for a moment. What do I think is the simplest, most basic of all economic truths? The answer to me is very clear: Put *everyone* who is not retired, in school, or severely disabled, to work.

You might question whether this is possible, let alone advisable. (At the McDonald's restaurant chain, even the owners are *required* to work periodically behind the counter—and there is no better-run enterprise in the world.) Look back to the World War II years, virtually everyone was working. With the proper resolve, there is no reason why the same situation could not also be made to occur in peacetime. Can you imagine the extent of prosperity there would have been had we been producing, instead of guns, tanks and bombs; homes, cars, and appliances? After the war, Japan did exactly that. In just 44 years, they progressed from being down and out, to the point where they now rule the world roost (on a per capita basis). This was not accomplished by living on interest or welfare. And if the beneficiaries of those two disparate sources of income cannot find the way to enlightenment on their own, we should help them to do so. Do not take this to mean that I am against wealth—I am only against unearned wealth. Likewise with welfare—I am only against unearned welfare, and those who do *earn* it should be paid an amount sufficient to live on while maintaining their self-respect (unlike now, where the working poor seldom enjoy this basic standard).

As long as *unearned* wealth accrues to those wealthy individuals who grow fat in their sleep, there will not be enough left to pay those working poor who I think deserve $9 per hour (in 1990 dollars) assuming work demands of the job to be normal. If my ideas prevailed, it would mean that many, many more would be working than are now. That would include a large percentage of the rich, and all of the poor.

The next apparent truth is that to the extent possible, the labor we do be constructive labor. While we have twice Japan's population, we have 20 times as many lawyers, 80% of whom would better serve society of they were engineers instead. Litigation costs the country an estimated $300 billion a year in

"Your Honor, a $100,000 settlement isn't nearly enough.
After all, my client deserves something <u>TOO</u>."

direct and indirect costs. Awards to injured parties average only 15% of the total costs of tort lawsuits.

Another simple truth that I see is the insanity of excessive paperwork imposed upon our people. I will comment on just one of countless areas in this regard, the income tax nightmare. We would all be better served were the code reduced to a single page of instructions that might read something like this: Every individual must file separately. If gross income (only a few select losses would be deductible) from *all* sources for a given year does not exceed $18,000, there is no tax. Over that amount will be a graduated rate starting at 15% to a top rate of about 22.5% for an income of $100,000 or more. To that a chart would be added showing the incremental tax increases between $18,000 and $100,000.

That's it! Period! No other exceptions! So simple that we could all do our own without an accountant. A dream? Yes, but it could come to pass if as in point 4 of Nugget #14, we found that leader who comes along once in a century whom we could entrust with the power of a monarch. It seems there is no other quick way to accomplish the things, and they are many, that need to be done. That is the reasoning I used in selecting the order of stages in #14.

"My firm is mainly dedicated to filling out federal forms, but we do try to manufacture a few carburetors on the side."

"Your return looks okay to me, but heck, what do I know?"

106. *July 14, 1989*

The problem with socialism/communism is one of lack of incentive. Those disciplines especially the latter, can be summed up with a single, devastating joke: We pretend to work, and they pretend to pay us. Another illustration of the Russian mind-set can be found in the following: How can you keep a live lobster from escaping? Answer: Put two or more lobsters in an enclosed area with a ledge around it. Lobsters cannot stand to have other lobsters above them. If one lobster begins to climb over the ledge, the others pull it down by pulling it back. They all remain prisoners. And then we have the six miracles of socialism:

- There is no unemployment, but no one works.

- No one works, but everyone gets paid.

- Everyone gets paid, but there is nothing to buy.

- No one can buy anything, but everyone owns everything.

- Everyone owns everything, but no one is satisfied.

- No one is satisfied, but 99% of the people voted for the system.

On the other hand there is a problem with free-swinging capitalism: How do you keep the best shooters from winning all the marbles? I think I have the answer.

Since great fortunes can be passed on to succeeding generations regardless of merit on the part of the recipients, de facto oligarchies create a wealthy self-perpetuating class.

Now, I have no qualms with wealth earned honestly by talented people, no matter how great it becomes. But when such fortune reaches out from beyond the grave to benefit unduly those who would not otherwise have the competence to create value, it is then that I object. (Also, power in the hands of the

"How much does this job pay, Comrade?"
"We'll pay you what you're worth, Comrade."
"I'm sorry, Comrade, but I can't afford to work that cheap."

less competent scares me.) As mentioned in a previous Nugget, I want everyone to begin life on as level a playing field as we can provide, so that achievers will largely be self-made. To do this a ceiling must be placed on how much we can pass on to whomever it may be after, or even before, we die (possibly a $500,000 total value lifetime limit in 1990 dollars to each beneficiary would be in order). Of the rest, I would give 90% to the sciences; and 10% to the arts, gradually equalizing these figures as many decades go by and the world's problems are addressed and ultimately resolved. Only then should amusements take a prominent place in our lives.

Under my controlled inheritance plan, the incompetent would be sure not to inherit the earth. Usage of this abundant source of wealth would be optimized by benefiting the general welfare.

To avoid attempts to circumvent the spirit of everyone starting with equal opportunity, total financial disclosure by all parties would be mandated. This would not be meant to restrict our freedom (as long as our actions are honorable) but only to maintain a public record of our financial activities so that unaccounted-for gains could not be easily hidden from public scrutiny. If this sounds to you like I'm advocating a police state, it is so only for those who have demonstrated a propensity for obtaining ill-gotten goods or gifts.

In other words, a permanent spotlight would shine on each of us, so that we who do behave need not have fear of those who, given a chance, would misbehave. Freedom is desirable only so long as abusing it is checked. Unlimited freedom without restraints is anarchy. Balance through common sense is the *ultimate solution.*

107.   *August 19, 1989*

The Laffer curve has proven itself correct. The government can raise more money by taxing less (the exact optimum tax probably should top out at 22.5%) than by taxing more. It has to do with added incentives and increased economic activity yielding greater pay-backs.

All this leads to a question: At what point does making the rich pay to support the poor cause the least amount of grief to both as a whole? Let's face up to the truth: Many, if not most, of the permanent poor are that way and will always be that way because they were not lucky enough to be born with

"When I promised a tax cut, I was speaking <u>METAPHORICALLY</u>."

more smarts. Communism denies this tenet. Communism is also failing. Do you suppose there's a connection?

My solution to this—one of the most difficult of all social problems—is to offer (optional to those already able to cope in the more competitive environments, but mandatory for those unable to cope) an alternate, simpler and less demanding community to live in where the main difference would be the absence of expensive materialistic baubles. Those who are proven troublemakers would be required to dwell in communities where the worst among them would be confined to grounds permanently. What is now our jails would be replaced by these more humane community living facilities. This is all ground that we have covered before.

I think that of all the ways for members of a community to be compatible, intellectual compatibility is the single most important, creates the strongest bonds, and on balance yields the greatest rewards. This is the cement I am hoping will ultimately make these communities work, although I could be wrong and reserve the right to modify this belief at some later date.

108.   *September 10, 1989*

Let's face it, in spite of the fact that the U.S. enjoys widespread affluence, we also suffer with unprecedented problems in any number of areas. How did we get in this predicament? Human nature being what it is, the rich, by and large, have lacked the incentive to help the poor, or to deal with looming problems that are easier to ignore than to solve. A "Why worry about the future when it won't affect me?" mentality exists. Well, the future is upon us, and we must do something now. The times call for a kind of leadership that we have never had before. Let us examine our options more closely. Basically, there are just two forms of government to choose from. Currently the world is leaning towards the individual freedom of capitalism as opposed to its historical rival, government-run socialism. The former features competition that unfortunately results in a tendency to polarize into the rich and the poor. The latter tends to coat everyone with a numbing mediocrity that drains ambition to a point where we equate ourselves with the least common denominator among us (why should I work hard when my gains will be given to those who, for whatever reasons, *won't* work hard?). Socialism holds out the hope that a man can quit work and be better off(?).

Until that distant day arrives when scientific intervention makes us all highly capable, must we choose between a house divided or a house demoralized? Let us hope that neither is our fate.

Okay, so what can we do? First, prepare for the worst, which would be losing New York City or Washington, D.C., to the terrorists' hydrogen bomb, in which case a full complement of major reforms could at once be implemented by our leaders. Acting under severe pressures and martial law, they would assume dictatorial powers. This would be the fast way of achieving the constitutional monarchy referred to in Nugget #14. I think if the reforms as set forth in this work were implemented all at once at that time, reactionary forces would be helpless to obstruct them. We could then proceed using as our guide the principles of enlightened common sense. Such a draconian scenario as nuking a major center would shock us into a fast fix called "instant reality," but few of us wish for trauma that extreme, regardless of its beneficial purging effects. Of all the world leaders that I am aware of, Eisenhower inspired the greatest confidence, and is the only one I would have chanced giving autocratic powers to since World War II.

Second, it is much more likely that if changes come, they will come slowly and by due process. Major reforms would start by giving incentives to the rich (both companies and individuals)

"If all this senseless violence doesn't stop, I'm going to beat the daylights out of every last one of you!"

to help the poor improve their condition, to help clean up the environment, to help raise the quality of life for everyone, along with disincentives for not so helping. We know incentive is desirable but beware, too much might lead to unconscionable gain, and can overwhelm our basic instincts of kindness, charity, and fair play—the very qualities that make up our humaneness. To act responsibly and to travel life within the speed limit will yield the greatest satisfaction.

One way to encourage responsibility is to make it fashionable. Support Greenpeace, support conservative T. Boone Pickens' United Shareholders Assn., support liberal Ralph Nader, call the communists' bluff and support peace, but on terms that are fair. Exploitative capitalism must be changed into benevolent capitalism (using the carrot and stick approach).

When the right leader appears, he should not try to become an expert at everything the way that Jimmy Carter did. This is a gross misdirection of energy. He needs instead to concentrate on determining strategic goals and selecting the right people to carry out those goals. It will require enormous discipline to avoid political patronage appointments. The best prospects will be independent-minded iconoclasts who are experts in their field and were likely to have been critics of the bureaucracy. A world-class leader need not be a workaholic. To expand on a point already touched upon, probably the most capable and effective leader we have ever had was Dwight Eisenhower, and he spent a lot of time on the golf course, because he knew how to lead, and he knew when to delegate. Ike clearly stated his philosophy during his first term when he said, "I am conservative when it comes to economic problems but liberal when it comes to human problems." I concur but only when being liberal becomes affordable, starting with a government that is debt free.

109.   *October 5, 1989*
I have not yet given an opinion about sex. Well, here it is. Prevailing thinking on the matter says that sex outside of marriage is wrong, and although that code is weakening every year, it is nevertheless ingrained in us from infancy up, and this conditioning can be a source of grave emotional problems for those who are abused against their will. However, I do not think it is *emotionally* harmful to liberated individuals who seek liaisons on their own, regardless of age. It is said that illicit sex is harmful to ⅓, neutral to ⅓ and beneficial to the other ⅓. I tend to agree with that. The original reasons for taboos against having sex outside of marriage have been lost to most, namely: disease, unwanted pregnancy and, in the case of incest, genetic weakening from inbreeding if it results in bearing offspring. These three reasons against promiscuity are still valid today, but remove them and I see no clear reason why free love or group marriages should not prevail for those who want it. The moral imperative against sex is not valid outside of practical consequences.

When that day comes which is still in our future, that the problems of disease, pregnancy and inbreeding can be resolved with a virtual 100% certainty, we will no longer need to bring up children with an unhealthy divergence between their conditioning and their biological urges. Illicit sex is like drugs, if there were no ill effects, there would be no reason not to indulge ourselves. But as long as the torment they bring outweighs the pleasures, we should discourage both, as in fact we do, but not because it's "moral," but because it's sensible.

Morality was invented to serve as an inducement to the masses who otherwise lack the discipline to do what is sensible. If a person is truly "sensible" in the spirit of enlightened common sense, he is automatically "moral," and needs neither the crutch of belief in a deity, or the baggage of religious fervor and superstition.

If the reader finds this offensive, I would just say that playing up one's beliefs, even though unpopular, is better than playing up to the crowd.

110. *Started October 24, 1989*
The following is an inventory of wisdom distilled.

110-A. Wealth is relative: If everyone was a millionaire (even in 1989 dollars), who would do the work?

110-B. There *is* honor among thieves, but only so long as such is mutually advantageous, and power among them more or less equally divided.

110-C. Private manipulation of public credit may be the bottom line result underlying the Federal Reserve system.

110-D. When countries who oppose us capture one of

our citizens and falsely accuse him of spying, it is a ploy which they later use as a bargaining chip to secure favor or to "demonstrate good will" by releasing him at virtually no cost to themselves.

110-E. Whether it's avoidance of gold confiscation or dodging taxes on bearer bonds, it seems as though there are always a few strategic loopholes left in the law (intentionally I'm sure) whereby a privileged few can hold on to their assets. For instance, when Franklin Roosevelt confiscated gold in the spring of 1933 (the fourth time in our history that this was done) there were three major loopholes you could have used to save all your gold, but not 1 in 10 people knew about them. When exotic exemptions appear in the tax laws, you can bet the reasons for them are not based on fair play. FDR was the consummate politician, so you could almost say his following remark was an ex cathedra pronouncement: "In politics nothing just happens; you can be sure it was planned that way."

110-F.

The reason I have not heretofore criticized tobacco subsidies is that the concept is so self-evidently repugnant that it seems manifestly ridiculous to take any pains even to point it out, let alone to debate the notion. "Men do not die, they kill themselves."   — SENECA, *Roman philosopher*

110-G.   When 50% of England's annual income went to service their debt in 1765, and they resorted to taxing the colonies, it resulted in the American Revolution. A few years later when 50% of France's annual income went to service her debt, it resulted in the French Revolution. Sometime in 1990, it is estimated that 40% of America's annual income will go to service its debt. Could there be a message for us somewhere in this? It is the interest on debt that is bleeding the life of its citizens. While we may muddle through anyway with this load of debt on our backs, we would be far better off in a climate of no-debt. The level of prosperity would feed on itself; it would be unprecedented. To be fair, it must be pointed out that just after World War II, the ratio of debt to income spiked up to well over 100%, with no disastrous consequences. (But only because that debt was a paper mortgage on the future, not the present.)

110-H.   My answer to the problem of unemployment is for the government to establish a few experimental communities around the country with the sole purpose of putting people to work. Initially, moving to these new towns would be entirely voluntary, and, with the assistance of Peace Corps volunteers, people would receive on-the-job training in whatever areas of work were required to build and sustain these communities. There would be little time for play, since working and learning would be the order of the day for adults and children alike, instilling all with a pioneering spirit of toil and achievement. I would envision such places as becoming self-supporting in due course.

110-I.   Hitler wrote: "Man has become great through perpetual struggle. In perpetual peace his greatness must decline."

The first part may be true. The second part, however, expresses a thought which I take strong exception to. Mussolini also expressed this line of reasoning when he said, "War alone brings up to its highest tension all human energy and puts the stamp of nobility upon the peoples who have the courage to meet it." Instead of culling out the weak through wars, I suggest it be done through sterilization and in the future through genetic engineering. Failing this, I would rather give up some greatness than have wars.

Thoughts of mandatory sterilization will shock many, but obviously the day will come when such issues must be dealt with. The number of people grows while the size of our planet remains constant. Space colonies will help only slightly, and are not a real solution in the face of this human geometric progression. It is not too soon to think of these things now, even though politically, action will not likely be taken until our head is in the lion's mouth. Paul Ehrlich and his associates of Zero Population Growth correctly admonish us to observe the obvious and ease the squeeze. They tell us that it took 4 million years for humanity to reach the 2 billion mark, only 30 years more to total 3 billion (1960), and in the 32 years since then we have grown to over 5 billion people. No wonder they call it the human race.

110-J. Eric Hoffer has said: "Our frustration is greater when we have much and want more than when we have nothing and want some. We are less dissatisfied when we lack many things than when we seem to lack but one thing." He also said: "Unless a man has the talents to make something of himself, freedom is an irksome burden." One reason people join mass movements is to escape individual responsibility, which may not be so bad if the leadership is competent and happens to believe in bettering people's lives.

110-K. The avoidance of severe and prolonged pain is far more important than the sustaining of life for its own sake.

110-L. There is a time to be principled and a time to be pragmatic.

110-M. *The discipline that comes from hardship threatens to collapse into the chaos of success.* — AUTHOR UNKNOWN

110-N. As George Orwell said: "Some ideas are so silly that only an intellectual could have thought of them."

110-O. Common sense should be the final determinant in the quest for justice, even to the point of superseding written law if indicated by circumstances. I am a firm believer in the supremacy of common sense.

110-P. The ultimate morality is to be amoral while understanding why it's advantageous to be moral, and to act accordingly.

110-Q. "God" is the adult version of Santa Claus. Both are believed in by their followers, both are well-meant, both are fictitious.

110-R. Heritage is the precursor of that which eventually becomes part of one's genetic code.

110-S. Give me understanding and I will not need knowledge.

110-T. Defend to the last man, if your opponent has already used his (last man); that is all you will need.

110-U.   Right or wrong has an alternate meaning: fair or unfair.

110-V.   Mao Tse-tung said: "Everything reactionary is the same; if you don't hit it, it won't fall. This is also like sweeping the floor; as a rule, where the broom does not reach, the dust will not vanish of itself." In my own adaptation of this, the exploitative capitalists stand as the reactionaries; the coming benevolent capitalists are the broom. *Enlightened* self-interest is the motivating force.

110-W.   If you want short-term gains, tell lies that put you in a favorable light; if you seek long-term rewards, tell the truth even though it may temporarily put you in an *unfavorable* light.

110-X.   One of history's ironies is that while a divided Europe is trying to unite, the united Soviet empire is trying to divide. The first instance illustrates the resulting benefit that comes with success; the second, the curse that accompanies incompetence. Failure is an orphan. Success has many parents.

110-Y.   Rather than ascertaining who best to play up to for purposes of self-aggrandizement, I prefer just to tell the truth and let the chips fall where they may.

110-Z.   *When government guarantees against failure, it subsidizes failure.*   – AUTHOR UNKNOWN

110-AA.   Bankers who make long-term fixed rate loans transform themselves from businessmen into crap shooters, and proceed from making comfortable returns all of the time into possibly making a lot of money or possibly losing a lot of money.

When risk is necessary it must be endured, when it is not necessary, the contented person will evaluate it dispassionately. Heed the pilot's adage: There are old pilots and there are bold pilots; but there are no old bold pilots.

110-BB. What the world needs more than a hi-tech, hi-cost trip to Mars is a billion lo-tech, lo-cost primers on 200 subjects exploring and explaining the *basics* of each.

110-CC. Josef Stalin sharply curtailed personal freedoms. Barry Goldwater would have vastly increased personal freedoms (had he become president). I would invoke Stalin's methods on suspected bad guys, and Goldwater's methods on verified good guys, sending out a loud message to the whole world that virtue pays in tangible ways. It is not a fair measure of justice for society to lump everyone together as soulmates and kindred spirits just because they're all walking the streets together.

110-DD. There is no special virtue in keeping your good deeds secret; just don't flaunt them.

110-EE. While it is true that hardship can build character, it does not follow that it is an arrangement to be sought. To ennoble ourselves *without* a catalyst is the greater achievement because it is voluntary.

110-FF. Most people would probably say that the single most important gift a person can have is good health. But I say, it's happiness. What benefit would even *perfect* health be if you're unhappy? But if you *can* be happy in spite of poor health, you are well-off indeed. It is the same story with money and power: Without happiness, all else is for naught.

110-GG. The following comes from the Libertarians: Thoreau said, "In the long run men hit only what they aim at." If you believe in truth you must speak truth. If you aim at virtue you must act virtuously. If you seek moral ends you must employ moral means. (It would be hard to state it better than that.)

110-HH. Of all people, it was Galileo who observed: "You cannot teach a man anything; you can only help him discover it within himself."

110-II. Exploitative capitalism *must* be a wonderful thing; it allows rich and poor alike the freedom to sleep under bridges. Free choice may be good, but it isn't always the whole story.

110-JJ. Arrogance is to be shunned, but humility is not what it's cracked up to be either. It saps our energies. It dulls initiative. It puts imaginary limits on our growth, and it restricts our freedom of expression. When apprised of an associate's humility, one wag remarked, "Yes, and he has much to be humble about." Charles deGaulle said, "We shall not increase our importance by humbling ourselves." No, I do not want humility unless I deserve it, and it is one thing I hope I am never deserving of.

110-KK. Squandering earned wealth is as offensive as accumulating undeserved wealth.

110-LL. Have you ever noticed how often people who are themselves guilty of a particular sin like to accuse others of the same offense? Apparently they assume that what motivates them motivates others. Saddam Hussein's accusation that the U.S. wants to control the world is simply a reflection of his *own* ambitions. While there may be two sides to every story, do not assume that both have equal merit. What a villain fears most is that if he loses, the victor might treat him the way he would have treated the victor had *he* won.

110-MM. In America's Puritan past, only luxuries were taxed heavily. (Of course, this predates our current situation. Today, the ease with which we can export such luxuries abroad complicates the equation, thus requiring us to look at a bigger picture.) A person could legally avoid taxes and keep most of his wealth by *saving* his money instead of spending it. For 300 years, six New England states provided much of the saved investment capital used to develop American industry. President John F. Kennedy understood this. His incentive tax cuts to stimulate business fueled the great boom of the '60s. Really now—common sense should be enough to tell you to do that. But I guess if you're in college learning to be a congressman nowadays, there's not much time to hone your common sense let alone to reflect on life and real solutions to our many social problems.

110-NN. It is said that what we think depends on where we sit. That being the case, let me occupy in turn *all* available seats. How else are our opinions to gain the credibility needed to be taken seriously by the rest of the world?

110-OO. Author William Tucker gives some valuable insight when he tells us: When the Mayor's Housing Program is complete, it and the other subsidy programs will have granted nearly 40% of the households in New York City some kind of property-tax exemption. The housing *solutions* of today are creating the budget crises of tomorrow. Is it any wonder New York is going bankrupt?

110-PP. 1964 Presidential nominee Barry Goldwater offered the most cogent observations ever made on farm subsidies and unions in his 1960 book, *The Conscience of a Conservative.* On unions he said in part: The time has come, not to abolish unions or deprive them of deserved gains, but to redress the balance—to restore them to their proper role in a free society. Unions perform their natural function when three conditions are observed:

1. Association with the union is voluntary,
2. The union confines its activities to collective bargaining, and
3. The bargaining is conducted with the employer of the workers concerned.

He also summed up welfare with telling effect in the following remark: "The long-range political consequences of welfarism are plain enough, the state that is able to deal with its citizens as wards and dependents has gathered unto itself unlimited political and economic power and is thus able to rule as absolutely as any old world despot."

But his greatest legacy is the military command unification and restructuring instituted as a direct result of the Goldwater-Nichols reforms. This act alone should earn the former Senator from Arizona our country's eternal gratitude.

110-QQ. Men are seldom all good or all bad, and few can rightly claim that their personal goals parallel the goals that would be best for the *universal* welfare. (And here you have the reason why absolute power corrupts almost—*but not quite necessarily*—absolutely.) However, that rare person who *can* claim the above, suffers little, *if any*, temptation to follow an uneven agenda. Now it may be that no man is perfect, but *someone* must be the closest to it relative to all the others. Let's choose him (or her) to put in charge if *otherwise capable*, and set a tone that the rest of us can strive for.

110-RR. Probably the most common fallacy that is believed in by all manner of individuals is that federal financial handouts to states and cities are somehow "free" money. Don't they stop to question where it comes from? It is taken from your right pocket, and after deducting their Washington brokerage fee, returned to your left pocket—with *strings attached.* And in return for this marvelous "gift" (now worth less than its cost) you forfeit a portion of your freedom. Some deal that is!

110-SS. The monarch must ask himself: Would *I* be happier ruling a subservient, oppressed, unhappy people, who secretly hated me; or leading a harmonious, cooperative, happy people, who genuinely loved me? The question needs no answer, that is obvious; needed only is for its *meaning* to be appreciated.

Having the goodwill of your subjects is *far* more important and rewarding than piling up booty in your vaults. That it be more fun praising someone you like than dispraising someone you don't like goes without saying. Once a base of adequate comfort is secured, no amount of excess physical wealth can begin to match the satisfaction of making the world a better place to live for *all* people. The wise man knows that wealth is more than just what goes into his bank account. Columnist Warren Brookes has written, "Wealth is not physical, but metaphysical; it is to be found not in matter, but in mind."

110-TT. Many of the changes that need to be made in society are basic, not superficial. It is folly to paint the car without first tending to the rust spots.

110-UU. We should not resent *all* rich people, just the ones who do *not* become so as a result of their own honest effort. Furthermore, we should tailor the rules of the game to exclude exceptions to this ideal. As for the truly *worthy* wealthy, they deserve our respect, support, and emulation.

110-VV. You've already heard the reasoning: A weaker dollar promotes prosperity by making our products more competitive abroad, thus reducing our trade deficit. True—in one sense, but when you look at the whole picture, it becomes utter nonsense, it defies logic. How can money that's worth more be less desirable than money that's worth less? Any competitive disadvantage a strong currency inflicts is more than offset by other advantages. If the key to national prosperity is really a

"I'm sorry, sir, but the government confiscated
all our books on economics."

weak currency, Burkina Faso would be living high off the hog! But instead, it's Japan, Germany, and now Spain with its sky-high peseta that are prosperous. Unfortunately, good sense is doled out rather sparingly; and even when it emerges as policy, there is no guarantee of continued political wisdom. If there was, the Bretton Woods monetary system that produced unprecedented world prosperity from 1945 to 1973 would never have been broken up. But unseen powers who are not *yet* enlightened value wealth in narrow relative terms for themselves rather than in broader absolute terms for everyone. The world will be a happier place to live when purchasing power parity (PPP) can be the norm. (This idea was in part inspired by an article in the *Wall Street Journal*.)

110-WW. It is not necessary or even preferable for a leader to have led a perfect life. But rather that his misdeeds were few and not particularly offensive, and that he gained something from each such experience. Minor transgressions will teach us more lessons that the lack of them ever can; will propel us to a higher level than what we might otherwise have attained; and will actually serve to help us avoid more serious pitfalls later on. The perfectionist takes pains, and gives them to others.

110-XX. Our country's interests would be far better served if the public were to put as much energy into promoting useful issues like the line item veto prerogative for the president as it puts into controversies such as school prayer, and especially into the recent inane debate over flag burning (of what practical benefit to anyone could the outcome of *that* issue be?). The ability to distinguish between what is important in our lives from what is less so or not so at all is as valuable as any single talent we may possess.

110-YY. It is possible to have an acceptable governance in which there are both winners and losers, but for this situation to remain harmonious, both must have come by their fate fairly. Beware of the person who has nothing to lose.

110-ZZ. It takes no more mental energy to effectively address major world and national issues than it takes to plan and prepare a holiday meal; all that is needed to accomplish the former is a broad perspective mixed with a healthy dose of common sense.

110-A3. How often have you heard it said that we are our own worst enemy? It seems that within the human breast there resides an alter ego who abhors too much of a good thing. But if there is no reason to punish one's self, then there should be no reason to shut out the breezes of joy that filter into our lives.

110-B3. The prophet should not himself practice *everything* he preaches if doing so alienates his potential followers. For people to accept radical changes, even when beneficial, they must be allowed sufficient time to digest them. Before we can expect a free mind to implement new concepts, its owner must first be willing to consider them as theory, which is why the teacher must have his own act together if he is to be convincing. The best way to enlist others to the cause is through personal *behavior* that does not shock sensitivities, while imparting *ideas* that do, provided they exemplify the ends we seek. The thinker can have an inner life that's very wild and an outer life that's quite dull.

110-C3. Ego is a most potent force. At one and the same time it can be either extremely powerful or extremely devastating; either our salvation, or our downfall. The difference is all in how we handle it, and how *we let it* handle us.

110-D3. When it comes to housing, far more people can benefit from being able to buy low than can benefit from being able to sell high.

110-E3. I am predictable in only one respect: I can be counted on to do what I think is the sensible thing.

110-F3. If a project is genuinely sound, it will need no touting to establish itself. That will come naturally and of its own accord through internal dynamics. The slang phrase that advises one to play it cool contains more wisdom than is apparent.

110-G3. The days of easy oil discoveries may be over. Throwing money after new finds no longer makes as much sense from economic and environmental standpoints as it once did, modern technologies notwithstanding. Concurrently, the case for alternative energies is developing fast. *The appropriate use of tax incentives* can steer our ship in the right direction. A painless little nudge early on in the form of the right tax credits is all it would take to lead us to a satisfactory outcome. It is not that difficult to do, but it does take both the vision to see things clearly and the courage to act decisively.

110-H3. In the past, if you were a politician, you proclaimed your allegiance to "the people," but in fact tended to favor either the rich or the poor. I too am for "the people," but people to me mean both the rich *and* the poor. It is the poor whose status I intend to change, but not at the expense of the rich. Abe Lincoln said, "You can't make the poor rich by making the rich poor."

110-I3.   Rational people who understand enlightened self-interest do not *have* to debate the obvious; such debate is useful only for those whose vision is unclear to begin with. I know this sounds pompous, and it probably is, but I cannot help that. The alternative is to be hypocritical, which is sometimes better, sometimes worse. This is just the way things are. Let us all accept it as such, and try to live in peace as best we can.

110-J3.   Unless your ambitions have already been realized and your position is secure, it is a mistake to be so absorbed with the business at hand that you become blinded to changes and opportunities around you, for which you must also listen; opportunity sometimes knocks very softly.

110-K3.   There seems to be no end of creative schemes when it comes to taking advantage of loopholes or quirks in tax or regulatory law. I think the advantages that would emanate from drastically simplifying these codes, instead of complicating them for the purpose of granting special privileges to special interests, would remove a burden from the back of society the likes of which can only be fully appreciated after it comes to pass.

110-L3.   One unfortunate aftereffect that survivors of any cataclysm are subject to is the damage that can be inflicted upon their psyches, and by extension, upon their descendants. Some people can emerge from the experience stronger than before, but not everyone will be so lucky, as psychological barriers may inhibit their ability to be objective. Haunting memories from the past can easily cloud their reason, their senses, and their judgment. As for our children, do not pave the road for them; provide them a road map instead.

For better or worse, our past at least influences, and often determines, our future.

110-M3. Finland's Prime Minister Harri Holkeri applies a train metaphor to the breakup of the central and eastern European socialist system. "The former East Germans are traveling in the first class section, and the ticket is paid for by their western brothers. They are the lucky ones. They know the system, they are motivated to work and the funds can be raised. In the second class but in the same train are Czechoslovakia, Poland and Hungary. Those countries still have in their national memories ideas of parliamentary democracy and what a market economy can mean. They can introduce their pre-war laws just by modernizing them. But they have to pay the ticket by themselves.

"But then the Russians. They are not in the same train. Their train is not moving. Their train stays at the station. They don't know what parliamentary democracy means. Russia has never been free. That's why it is not easy to introduce perestroika or any other form of parliamentary democracy. They are demanding a better standard of living. They have seen it on television. The new revolution is based on the modern mass media . . ."

110-N3. To be *really* successful, the trick is in knowing who to listen to, and who best to hire to do the tasks you wish to have done. Fortunately, there is no need for *you* to be as smart in each area as they are.

110-O3. *Controversy is the price of every fundamental advance.*
— THOMAS SOWELL

110-P3. Surely you've heard the old Chinese proverb(?) that says: If I could choose what to worry about, I would rather worry about how to spend my $50 million lottery winnings, than have to worry over where my next meal is coming from.

110-Q3. No, I do not place any special emphasis on holidays. To me, one moment is as valuable as any other moment, no more so and no less so. This pragmatic leveling process makes gloom a stranger that is denied entry to my house, and contentment an angel who never goes away. Being sensible generates its own rewards, just as foolishness must inevitably be self-punishing. (That's not some great discovery, it's just common sense.)

110-R3. It is a rare journey that does not at some point necessitate a walk on both sides of the street.

110-S3. Hubert Humphrey once said that a test of society is how we treat our people in the dawn of life, at the end of life, and in the shadows of life.

Until everyone is willing (and the remainder required) to carry their own weight *regardless of education* but commensurate with their abilities, and is *afforded the opportunity to do so,* Humphrey's sage thought will be only one more rhetorical pleasantry.

110-T3. A *good* history book makes the best novel, if only because it is more authentic, and therefore more useful to us as a guide for living.

110-U3. In today's world, there are very few of us so independent that we do not find the need to interrelate with other people for various reasons. Because of that, I think we have a duty to teach the young responsibility and the work ethic at the earliest practical age, including those lucky enough to be born into wealth, who could easily afford not to work. We might assume that living in freedom allows this privilege, but if it does, it *shouldn't*. Saving one from themselves might lack justification were it not that their actions can have an impact on all of society.

110-V3. When it comes time to buy a car, I'm never sure which is more patriotic: to buy a Chevrolet Caprice that gets 20 MPG but is made in America; or get a Toyota Tercel made in Japan that delivers 40 MPG and conserves our dwindling oil supplies.

110-W3. It goes without saying that buying what you *need* is prudent. But what about buying things you *don't need?* Like a fancy sports car, a pleasure boat, a mansion, or the latest fad that you think you *must* have. Even if you can afford such baubles, they will not guarantee your happiness after the initial euphoria passes. And if you can't easily afford them but buy them anyway, you are indeed foolish. When you indulge in excesses beyond what is sensible, you risk opening a Pandora's box of unknown consequences (this is equally true of governments, whose profligate ways we are witness to all the time). The wise man who understands this needs little to make himself happy, and knows that optimum satisfaction with one's lot in life depends on how well-adjusted he is as a result of *inner* choice, not *outside coercion*. The value of being well-adjusted is its own reward, and if through good fortune it becomes a habit, will be a source of lifelong contentment without the burden of cognitive dissonance (see glossary).

110-X3. As for Pete Rose being turned down for consideration into baseball's Hall of Fame, if they don't want Pete, maybe I could apply for that honor. No, I have never played baseball, but I do have impeccable moral character. After all, that *is* the principle criterion for acceptance as I now understand it, *isn't it?*

110-Y3. Risk has two faces: danger and opportunity. Most of us would prefer to avoid it if given a choice. But the secret is to master it. Controlled risk is the surest way to succeed, be it in military, corporate, or financial matters. Painless prosperity and effortless democracy are just as illusory as the ill-conceived guarantees on our bank deposits which are backed by the full faith and credit of the government (read: taxpayers). Poor oversight and accountability, traits inherent in any bureaucracy, can only result in reduced incentive and mediocre performance, a sure recipe for failure. We need a banking system that is a taker, not a shedder, of risk. And when the time comes to put our house in order, let us not refuse to bury the dead.

"The following story is true. The names have been
changed to protect the bureaucracy."

110-Z3. As Ron Chernow, author of *The House of Morgan*, says: "We must design a system that induces caution in boom times and flexibility in bad times. Most of all, we must treat the apparently separate crises of the financial industry as a *single problem.*"

110-A4. If others are critical of my views, I do not want to silence them, I want to hear their side, weigh their concerns, and listen to the alternatives that they propose. If I truly accept my behavior, I apparently do not see it as a fault. But the goal is to ferret out the truth wherever it resides, not to seek vindication for a policy merely because we may have invented it. The extent to which I can keep my emotions from interfering with my reasoning powers will determine the ease with which my mind can be changed if superior ways do emerge. As a participant in the commodity futures markets as far back as 1958, I have learned the lesson well that one should never fall in love with a position, and know that intraday monitoring of quote machines may be dangerous to your health.

110-B4. Any leader faced with a choice between losing with the crown of martyrdom on his head, or winning while carrying a victor's cross on his back, would not be worthy of his position if he did not opt for the latter.

110-C4. In 430 B.C., one year before his death, the Athenian statesman Pericles said of his society (one of the few successful democracies of early times) that when it is a question of settling private disputes, everyone is equal before the law; when it is a question of putting one person before another in positions of public responsibility, what counts is not membership of a particular class, but the actual ability which the man possesses. He also said in regard to poverty, that no one need be ashamed to admit it: The real shame is in not taking practical measures to escape from it.

That apex did not long survive Pericles, however, attesting to the critical need of self-governing societies for uncommon leadership. As Thucydides recounted the symptoms of decline, "No one was eager to deny himself for the sake of what was thought to be honorable . . . but immediate pleasure and all that contributed to it were established as both honorable and expedient. Fears of the gods or the laws of mankind restrained nobody."

This is why I believe that enlightened self-interest is more than just one of the answers—it is the *only* answer if what we're looking for is a *permanent* solution.

110-D4. Bismarck said: "If there is a revolution, we would rather make it than suffer it."

110-E4. In the future, conflicts between men, or schisms between factions, will be better understood by insights gained from playing games like chess and checkers on the highest cerebral level, than from physical anarchy on the lowest emotional level.

110-F4. To paraphrase Bernard Levine of Eugene, Oregon, who wrote a history on the subject in 1968: In the scattergun, try-anything days of the New Deal, where programs encouraging self-sufficiency were the *only* ones that hit the mark, the most notable success story was the Farm Security Administration. It helped about 1.2 million poor rural families become self-sufficient and prosperous, by offering flexible mortgage and crop financing, combined with close supervision of their farm and home practices. Over 95% remained self-sufficient without further assistance, and its loan repayment rate was better than 97%.

So what ever happened to so successful a program? I will skip the details; suffice it to say that it has become politically unacceptable for a government antipoverty program to accomplish anything, because any change in the status quo hurts entrenched interests, both liberal and conservative. Unfortunately, designing ineffective but politically safe "poverty" programs has gained respectability. The fact is, they actually perpetuate poverty—but not for everyone. Since the early 1960s, such programs have bought townhouses and Volvos for hundreds of thousands of otherwise unemployable middle-class bureaucrats handicapped by costly but worthless degrees in what was once prestigious liberal arts, but nowadays can all too often be something less than meets the eye.

110-G4. It certainly looked for a while in 1990 as if we had won the war against communism. But if this is not yet the case, it is because we have not put our own economic house in order, thereby depriving us of that ultimate persuader: the power of example.

110-H4. *If you understand this one, you understand me and what I mean by enlightened self-interest.*
To counter amoral people and nations harboring immoral intentions, you need equally amoral leaders who seek *moral* ends because *they* understand wherein their own (and others') best interests *really* lie.

110-I4. Can a simple board game (I prefer to use checkers as my example since I can claim some degree of expertise here) be an analog to life? Yes, very definitely. How so? Both can proceed on different levels and played out in a variety of styles. But because checkers, as difficult as it is (and it is that), is relatively far simpler than its complement, it makes an easier example to use when comparing the two. The opening in checkers can take any one of many paths. But soon thereafter the opportunity to embrace an individual style of play emerges. Which is the best style to adopt? Which will ultimately yield the most success? I can answer both—the *optimum* mode is not to have any one particular style at all, but to make the *best* move available depending on the circumstances at any given time. The accomplished horse does not have to carry his track with him.

Thus we can find in a game enjoyed by children and adults alike, lessons for navigating the more treacherous waters of a bigger contest—the one called life.

110-J4. It would be a mistake for me to expect that everyone might accept my views if only I could somehow enlighten them. I suggest that people are civilized in proportion to the extent they can realize their full potential, and that their well-being is optimized when mental, physical, and emotional needs are best satisfied (such as having a job, mate, religious conviction, etc. that suits them).

In essence, a person who is already totally assured in and comfortable with (for example, his religious) beliefs, would be ill-advised to turn his back on them, even if this means rejecting what may be a superior gospel that would only have the effect of overrunning his headlights.

110-K4. Payola, anyone?
Compared to tanks, journalists are cheap—and you get more for your money. — SADDAM HUSSEIN

110-L4. *When wolves are about the shepherd must guard his flock, even if he does not himself care for mutton.*
— WINSTON CHURCHILL

110-M4. If there are any financial detectives out there reading this, please contact me, I need your help in exposing the fact that private stockholders own the Federal Reserve (but not just American stockholders, and not just our own central bank), which they benefit from in many ways. (And why not? Wouldn't you?)

I found a clue in a finding by the veteran economist Robert Triffin. It seems that between 1949 and 1969, monetary reserves of central banks had climbed 75%, roughly in line with economic growth, but in the 20 years after 1969, Professor Triffin puts the rise at 13,529%. Quite obviously, this does not jibe with the lack of liquidity felt by your local businessperson.

It would appear that the wealth of nations is in fact becoming the wealth of a very select few.

110-N4. My goal is *not* to lead, it is to enlighten (see glossary under "enlightener"), so that each of us can determine our own destiny.

"This predestination is so boring — why don't you give them free will?"

110-O4. In the pursuit of goals, emotions should not be voided entirely, but only to the extent that they interfere with good business and good sense. You can be the rock of Gibralter, but nobody wants to love a stone.

110-P4. Chinese philosopher Sun-tzu summed up decoy theory 2,500 years ago in a treatise called *The Art of War.* "The supreme excellence in warfare is not to win a hundred wars on a hundred battlefields . . . but to subdue the armies of your enemies without even having to fight them."

110-Q4. When you live primarily to please others, a perverse and opposite phenomenon often occurs. One can easily become bitter, miserable, emotional and unhappy. Why is this so? I practice enlightened self-interest, which, ironically, rewards me with the very benefits that the altruist seeks with his good intentions but is denied because altruism (apart from cooperation, which is highly desirable), is unrealistic and antithetical to the nature of living things.

I suspect that exceptions like Albert Schweitzer and Mother Teresa can happen only rarely when a confluence of extraordinary belief, will, and dedication combine in some who are very far ahead of their time.

110-R4. There is less to be learned from the scrawlings of a million monkeys, than from the crayons of the plainest child. *(The deeper meaning here is simply that the superior competitor is more valuable than a legion of lesser lights. Especially is this true in mental contests.)*

110-S4. I prefer passive investments. *It is not the hunt that I savor,* but rather the surplus leisure that accrues if basic needs can be satisfied with minimal effort, thus allowing primitive survival urges to transmute into more productive uses of my time. (This is the real advantage of having work-saving devices, and is also one of several reasons why I prefer to eat out.)

110-T4a. People who are less than *totally* satisfied with their lives—and that includes most people—look forward to at least a temporary respite, or have a desire to "get away from it all" from time to time. That usually means taking a vacation.

But thanks to my beliefs (and habits), I do not desire a vacation. Why reshuffle a winning hand? After all, if you're already in heaven, anything else would be a letdown, wouldn't it? Although I don't try to force-feed my tonic on others, should they *ask* me to share it I would be glad to oblige, believing that he who seeks deserves to find.

110-T4b. At this point you must be wondering if I think that somehow I have discovered nirvana. Fair question. It *is* attainable, and yes, I have attained it. But what exactly do I mean by nirvana? First, I'll tell you what I don't mean. It is not an enchanted land up in the sky, nor is it some idyllic tropical island with fruits, fish, and willing maidens all for the asking as I once envisioned. Neither do I accept the dictionary definition: a place or state of oblivion to care, pain, or external reality. What it *is* is the intelligent handling of these inevitable tribulations, and it *is* knowing when to be satisfied once our comforts have been sufficiently met, while avoiding distasteful excesses which offer only negative returns. It is resolution of inner conflicts; and above all it is having the good fortune to possess and to exercise a generous portion of common sense.

While this kind of sagacity is fundamental to enlightened self-interest, like anything worthwhile, it is not something that comes to one overnight.

110-U4. Taxes can temper environmental damage caused by the profligate use of underpriced materials such as wood, minerals, glass and plastic, according to a study by the Worldwatch Institute, a Washington research organization.

"The single most effective incentive for source reduction, reuse and recycling would be to price materials [via taxes] to account for the real costs of their production," according to the report, "Discarding the Throwaway Society."

"Archaic laws that make public material or timber resources available at low or no cost to multinational corporations" underwrite the materials' extraction and environmental destruction, according to John E. Young, author of the report. "*Removing subsidies* and *imposing taxes* on materials would bring them closer to real costs," he said.

He also noted that higher energy taxes that are often discussed as central to averting climate change would also serve to boost the price of materials.

110-V4. Sometimes common perceptions are a more accurate gauge of reality than is the doctrine itself as believed by the faithful.

110-W4. Some people believe that it takes two to start a fight. Unfortunately, this is not necessarily so. More often than not, the bully will attack only because he perceives his victim to be vulnerable. Calls for fortress America, be it through economic barriers to free trade in the form of quotas or tariffs, undue unilateral military cutbacks, or political isolationism, may make appealing daydreams, but are actually naive, unwise, and even dangerous. More people get into trouble from allowing their aspirations and idealism to get in the way of sound judgment based on *current* realities than we will ever know.

There are two reasons that an increasingly interdependent world calls for one man's business to be every man's business: (1) to secure the safety of each, and (2) to promote the welfare of each.

110-X4. Just as you cannot make a silk purse out of a sow's ear, so you cannot have a multiple-dimensioned personality by living indefinitely on a limited, exclusive diet. Craving a particular food is the body's way of telling us what it needs; and don't exclude meat. Julia Child liked to refer to vegetarians as nutritional Nazis. It would not surprise me at all if it is discovered someday that a full range of elements obtained only by eating a full range of foods (over time) is the only way to maximize the potential of both mind and body, and consequently (but more subtly) attitudes and behavior. Hippocrates told us to "Let your food be your medicine and your medicine be your food."

To live in a medium-sized city and eat in a very busy cafeteria with a wide variety of quality food to choose from—forgive me for saying this—is actually better than dining at home.

110-Y4.   The Lemon Seeds Confession

. . . and if I'm so damned enlightened, don't I have *any* faults? What residual instincts from our savage origins still lurk in the hearts of men? Well, I have some of them, but without telling all my secrets, I'll fess up to one vestige of machismo. At the cafeteria where I like to eat six days a week, instead of paying extra for a drink, I simply take 4 to 6 free lemon wedges and convert water into lemonade. The reason is not to save money, although that's nice too, it's simply better for you than coffee or soda, and adding free sugar makes it taste good too. (I do not think a little sugar will harm a healthy person.) Now the straw will suck up lemon seeds, which I unceremoniously spit out, aiming at the tray, but usually they go bouncing off willy-nilly to lord knows where. I figure they have to clean the place up later anyway, don't they?

And you needn't look so horrified, Miss Manners; after all, I only do that when I eat alone.

"Oh, come now — surely you must be guilty of __SOMETHING__."

110-Z4. If socialism worked, there would be no United Parcel Service today. The U.S. Government Postal Service had a monopoly and didn't know what to do with it. Neither would Federal Express exist, or umpteen others like them. Opportunities like that do not come along every day, and when they do, they should be exploited, not squandered.

"No, sir, we can't guarantee that your package will arrive. The government will only guarantee our retirement benefits."

110-A5. Rather than simply putting the emphasis on getting tough with criminals, I say let's get serious about a *real* solution to the whole mess. The process should start with the elimination of the bottom rung of the economic ladder. To think it can't be done (political obstacles aside) is to deny the explosion in science and technology in the latter part of the 20th century.

110-B5. For only $1.50 you can now gain admission to a house of horrors that surely rivals a Dickens novel. It is called the New York City subway system. I would like to accompany you through it in the only safe way possible—by reading about it.

The threat of crime and harassment is pervasive. So is the squalor and disagreeableness produced by an army of transients living and sleeping there. The stench of stairwells serving as their communal urinal blends with the sight of scores of blanket-covered figures sprawled out on benches and lying underfoot wherever they find convenient.

Once seated on the train, the more aggressive panhandlers begin their solicitation by calling passengers to attention, free of interference from any authority.

Efforts to improve matters run afoul of our civil libertarians. These are the same good folks who "liberated" the mentally ill, so that now they are free to go without both the care and the antipsychotic medication most of them need.

The subways are unmanageable, even as the price of entry continues to rise in this nether region that most people would rather pay *not* to use. (The foregoing may be somewhat exaggerated, but all too many don't think so.)

Oh ye do-gooders of liberal faith, what foul plague hath ye wrought upon us? Will ye who are blinded by flawed idealism *ever* see the error of your ways? Repent! Repent!

"Nine bucks? It'd be cheaper just to take a ride on the subway!"

110-C5. It seems that most politicians are cloned from the same gene. Sometimes I wish they could also share the same cell. Paraphrasing Daniel Chaucer, Middle Village, N.Y., Henry Kissinger said that it's 90% of the politicians who give the other 10% a bad name.

110-D5. Life's puzzle can only be solved when each new piece fits correctly into the matrix. But even if an individual misses a step (and very few do not), religion can often bridge the gap. Others not so lucky will be seduced by the lure of crime or drugs. The promised land will be lost to them.

But religion is only a placebo, not a cure. When we are taught to do right but for the wrong reasons; when illusion and mystery substitute for substance and clarity; when dogma is valued above logic, how can we truly expect enlightenment to blossom?

Religion might bring temporary relief for the symptoms of our cold, but to kill the virus that caused it, and immunize us against future susceptibility, we must make all star moves (see glossary). And without first acquiring an understanding of enlightened self-interest, we might not recognize a star move when we see one. This makes it uncomfortably easy for the unwary to be led astray.

110-E5. Speaking of government: It isn't so much the two-party system that I object to, but rather the ongoing efforts by both sides to take credit for their own party, and place blame on the opposition, irrespective of the facts. This behavior is more befitting of children than adults, is not in the public interest, and is especially inconsistent with enlightened self-interest.

It is legitimate to have contrary views if they are part of one's personal beliefs; but not so if the purpose is merely an expedient for another agenda and never intended in good faith. A true statesman would not disagree with the opposing party when it is right. If Republicans say two plus two is four, Democrats are not obligated to argue that it is five.

Four good rules to follow are: Simplify; perfect the basics; keep your eye on the ball; and *be true to yourself.*

"I really appreciate your support, but now I have to go do a little time."

110-F5. It is the person who recognizes opportunity early who will be among the first to feed at the trough.

110-G5. Know thyself: If you can be offended by a put-down, you might also be beguiled by flattery.

110-H5. *When I see I am doing something wrong there is a part of me that wants to keep on doing it the same way anyway and even starts looking for reasons to justify the continuation. Don't fight a fact, deal with it.*
— HUGH PRATHER, *NOTES TO MYSELF*

110-I5. Between the vicissitudes put upon us by fate, and our own emotions, there are times when we all roll the dice. And like ingesting arsenic, life itself depends on very small amounts of it. But also like arsenic, if intake (*undue risk-taking*) is not held to the barest amount necessary, baneful consequences will likely ensue. A campfire may be a good thing, but a forest fire too much of a good thing.

110-J5. *It is easier to change one's <u>response</u> to a feeling, for which we are responsible, than to change the feeling itself, for which we are not. Emotions do not originate in compliance with the laws of logic.*
— HUGH PRATHER

110-K5. I'm sorry, but there's something I don't understand. If the rules of algebra remain the same year after year, why is it that the textbooks change so often? Would it not be a tremendous advantage if page 26 in Algebra I was the same in California as it was in Georgia year in and year out? Surely it couldn't be a plot to sell books, could it? No, of course not. Responsible educators would never allow such a thing to happen, would they? Certainly with all the attention education is receiving lately, any misfeasance or malfeasance would have come to light by now, don't you think?

In the military they rotate personnel periodically for the same reason they made me mop the floor every day: It keeps the schemers and the roaches from establishing a fiefdom.

Maybe *now* I'm beginning to understand why new societies grow in their early stages, and begin to decline once the bureaucrats become tenured.

110-L5. Many people who were made smart by nature, have been made dumb by nurture.

110-M5. If I could change one character trait of the political loyalist, it would be his attitude that if you're not willing to be a faithful, devoted friend, you must be some kind of adversary to be held in high suspicion and not worthy of trust. In fact, you are even considered fair game to be taken advantage of. (Many Republicans especially are partial to this law of the jungle, which is fine if you happen to be the hunter and not the hunted.) But the more we sympathize with others, the less we will criticize others; the more empathy felt, the less enmity dealt. However, old values do die hard, so please don't ask the captain to go down with his ship; there are better ways of furthering your principles than by dying for them. That should be the last thing you do.

110-N5. It is a truism that you cannot teach calculus before arithmetic, so don't ask kids questions that adults do not have answers for. If we want them to be in a position to handle the Saddam Husseins of the world, help them now to evolve strategies for dealing with the little tyrant who extorts their lunch money and the kid who always wants to copy their homework. These are the problems they are engaged with and ready to consider solutions for.

Problem-solving requires a confidence that solutions can be discovered and a healthy self-esteem about one's ability to find them. These attitudes require nurturing over a long period of time, on countless small, day-to-day issues. Too much too fast can only destroy them.
— STEPHEN R.C. HICKS OF TRENTON STATE COLLEGE, N.J.

110-O5. We usually think of intuition as being antithetical to the scientific method. But in its highest form, it actually incorporates reasoning faculties with instincts; some born with us and others gleaned from and honed by experience.

The resultant insights, while of a fleeting nature, can manifest themselves as flashes of brilliance, and should not be dismissed as curiosities or happenstance.

110-P5. An active mind will not remain at rest beyond the time prescribed by nature to recharge itself.

110-Q5. I do not play bridge, but if I did the dummy hand would suit me best, as I would be able to lay my cards on the table face up for the world to see, spots and honors all, just as they are.

Richard Burton once said in a movie, which I recall only because I identify with the quote: "What I am is on my face; what I think is on my tongue."

110-R5a. The scoundrel will pursue his goals with greater vigor than the honest man, because he looks forward to the spoliation that he sees can be his for the taking. Thus it becomes clear why positions offering the greatest opportunity for abuse are peopled with the greatest proportion of scalawags. What better job to have from the fox's point of view than to be guardian of the hen house? Small wonder that the public becomes cynical, without realizing that what they see is not representative of the vast majority. Wouldn't it be nice if we could just put engineers who like to build things and solve problems in charge of the country, and assign the politicians to the pulpit, where they could make their speeches but cause no harm? (There's an old cliche: "You can tell when a politician is lying: His lips are moving.") Unfortunately, engineer types are not apt to run for office because they tend to eschew ill-gotten riches. And that is the very magnet that makes others willing to put up with the hassle. But as problems get solved, the hassle index would curve down and slowly change into an approval index that would curve back up. Now you're getting a glimpse into what makes Samoht run.

110-R5b. The culprit has yet to learn—and with the world so topsy-turvy you *almost* can't blame him—that the greatest rewards (at least once sanity reigns) will come from practicing a *higher* ethic than normal, not a lower one. However, my idea of a higher ethic is one based upon pragmatism and common sense, not religious beliefs. I agree that the latter can indeed be a higher ethic for those who buy the premise; I happen not to. And yet our goals are the same: a better life for all; there is no tenable alternative. We are related; *our* future demands that we join forces to promote the common good.

110-S5. It's not how you start out that counts, it's the way you end up.

110-T5. The subconscious is our forward patrol. It can absorb information and influence our behavior long before our conscious mind is made aware. But by that time the only additional good it may do is to give us the satisfaction of understanding something that happened in the past.

110-U5. There seems to be no conceivable reduction that can be made in government spending, to effect any sort of meaningful shrinkage in the annual deficit, as long as the principal keeps growing at a compound rate, constantly forcing up the total current interest charge.

And as for the growing federal demands for borrowed money, how much new debt paper *can* the markets absorb? At the present time, the net federal deficit is running at a rate around one billion dollars for each weekday. As long as the markets are forced to swallow this amount of new federal debt instruments, it is hard to see how—with America's low savings rate—there will be enough money left in the till to allow any kind of new spending in the private sector. If the treasury borrowing thus harms the private business economy, you could see tax receipts slip again, making the deficit still wider.

– THE FEDERAL/GLOBAL LETTER,
APRIL 24, 1991

(The good news is that they believe troubled times will be followed by a boom.)

110-V5. Those who espouse nonsense court a dismal future. The only survivors in any competition, whether the combatants be ethicists, economists, or theorists, will ultimately be the ones who steer closest to the truth appropriate for their era. And truth, as once so aptly stated, is the daughter of time.

110-W5. Some people try so hard to preserve what they already have, that they overlook ways to have even more, in which case they wouldn't *have* to try so hard to preserve what had been all they had.

Loosening a tight collar might make us less punctilious, but it will also make us a lot more comfortable.

110-X5. If you have the urge to grow things or make things, they might as well be functional. You can *learn* to gain as much satisfaction from raising vegetables as you can from flowers, and nowadays they are not even distinguishable by smell. (Admittedly, this advice is more suitable for the third world.)

110-Y5a. If a car had 50 crucial parts essential to its operation, and just one of them was faulty, it would spell big trouble—never mind that the other 49 worked fine. If likewise a student were taught 50 crucial facts about a subject, but one of them was inherently flawed, don't you think it too would have an effect on the validity of the course and be a source of consternation for its practitioners? Well, that's how I feel about economics. It seems no one questions the consequences that result from the charging of interest on money. But I have one big advantage over the field. I never went to college, so whenever I encountered what seemed to be misinformation, I felt free to question it. I never took for granted the misconception that interest is somehow desirable—let alone necessary—in conducting business. Nor was I instilled with the good sense to be intimidated by experts. Actually, it takes no great intellect to realize that perpetual skimming will only compound problems (for one thing, it's the primary *cause* of inflation), in spite of the mitigating effects of technological and productivity advances. It's time we shape up and wake up. Are you listening out there?

110-Y5b. At Socialist Labor Party meetings (not to be confused with the Socialist Workers Party) during the late 1950s in Philadelphia, I was most intrigued by then deceased founder Daniel DeLeon's concept of "surplus value," as postulated by Karl Marx, as the culprit of capitalism. I now think he was wrong in attributing it to "profits," but believe he would have been on target had he designated "interest" instead as the endless iniquity to be referred to as surplus value, which he asserted was taken from the workers, thus denying them due means to buy back the product of their own labor—which in turn lead to surpluses and unemployment. The reason interest is so insidious is that it has the practical effect of some borrowers finding themselves on an ice cube in a bowl of water. But for the lucky *lenders* this same interest is compounded, it is cumulative, and to add insult to injury, altogether too much of it can be passed on to heirs without dint of effort on their part. This is where the real damage is done.

If we were merely *maintaining* the support of those idle wealthy in the manner that we maintain the welfared poor, it would be bad enough; but no, we are bequeathing to them our blood supply—and faster than the body can replace it, filling plastic bags that are as easy to see through (if only we will look) as they are expandable—compliments of the magic of you know what. One usually thinks of a "blood bank" as gainful, but it can also be ominous. (You were close, DeLeon, you were close.) [written May 31, 1991]

110-Z5. I do not hold earthly life to be unique in the universe, but I do suggest it most likely be *far* rarer than what a single grain of sand is to all of the world's beaches. It is not the conquest of space that inspires me; it is the befriending of earth. Should science—and it could only be through science—discover eternal life for me, my dreams will be fulfilled right where I am. Our habitat is here, not on the tail of a distant comet, or in the confines of an artificial space colony, however romanticized that notion has become. Before leaving home, know where it is you want to go, and what you hope to find after you get there. Wanting to get away from our problems should not impel us to get away from the world. Rather than seek relief through escape, a better way might be to rework your situation to conform with the retreat to which you are escaping.

Often what we seek afar is really where we just now are.

110-A6. Intelligent risk-taking is the seed corn of progress.

110-B6. I gave up my religion first, and many years later I also gave up the few vices that I had. Now I realize that the only time you need religion is when you *have* vices, or stated as its corollary; if you have no vices, why do you need religion? To all of which I owe a debt of gratitude to the logic behind enlightened self-interest.

110-C6. My idea of class is to drink iced tea through a straw instead of direct from the can.

110-D6. I would like to see the bottom rung of the economic ladder permanently eliminated, which means the poorest of the poor would now become less poor. This would leave a new bottom rung to work on, with each in turn being a greater challenge. Reduction to just *one* rung may never happen, but I *do* think the fewer the merrier. And by all means, let's not shorten the ladder at the expense of the wealthy. I don't want to lower the ceiling, I want to raise the floor.

110-E6. In our endless struggle to understand, we will from time to time encounter inconsistencies between the theory and the practice of things we were taught. When that happens, what *are* we to think? Who *should* we trust? To go along with tradition might make us hidebound; but to drive faster than our guardian angel can fly could bring us grief. Dealing with contradictions before we have learned to be wise can be a daunting experience. (And in case you ever wonder: At times I make quips I don't believe in, in an effort to clarify truths I do believe in.)

110-F6. They may start out as the most sophisticated and promising members of their group, but if overly "protected" from their surroundings and the world at large, if desires are *too* easily fulfilled, if they *never* know strife or struggle, can we expect such people to feel in absentia the sting of a misdealt hand to the degree that those who do suffer it will feel? If we're going to see a rainbow, we'll need to put up with a little rain, for what we gain too cheaply, we esteem too lightly. He is most blessed who has felt the pain as well as the joy of life. If all one or the other, the difference will never be fully appreciated, and "difference" is the missing link by which *we* will know, while others will not, that the legend of paradise is true after all.

110-G6. For better or for worse, we are all the product of genes and geography; of nature and of nurture. It is within these parameters that most of us will live our entire lives. And if a chosen few can successfully escape (should that be desirable), it will be by *accepting* what cannot be changed, and *changing* what needs to be changed *if* it can be.

110-H6. All space programs are not of equal merit. Sending men to Mars may boost our nation's spirits, but is it the most sensible way to spend money we don't have? I would much prefer the peace-of-mind that a successful Star Wars deployment might provide against the wild antics of any *future* Saddam Husseins. Mars may play well to a politician's audience, but Star Wars should be the prudent businessman's choice. G.K. Chesterton observed, "We are perishing for want of wonder, not for want of wonders."

110-I6. It can be the emotional peaks attained by a basketball team on a roll, or an astronomer's flush of excitement as he makes a celestial find. But whichever—it is the same heady sense of achievement that comes with being very good in any field of endeavor. Whatever one's work or play happens to be, the better he or she can perform, the greater the potential satisfaction will be. And if it brings happiness to others too, the only world that counts will have been conquered by that expert.

110-J6. I do not classify myself as a leader. An enlightener, a philosopher, a social engineer—yes, yes, yes. But not a leader. No charisma here. Shakespeare said: "Neither a borrower nor a lender be." I like that one, and will add one of my own: "Try neither to lead nor be led, but to be master of *your* life and yours alone." A leader gives orders; an enlightener furnishes explanations and offers suggestions.

Until now, the world ran best (on balance) with a few leaders calling most of the shots. But the time has come to rethink past orthodoxies. Privatize *when advantageous*, decentralize *where indicated*, and instill within each of us the discipline to be our *own* king. Coordinators, si; dictators, no.

110-K6. You don't suppose unsuspecting investors are ever lured by "Big Bank" and "superbroker" into leveraged loans or limited partnerships set up for intentional failure down the road, do you? Oh! But why would they invite their own downfall in the process? You say you think the ultimate beneficiaries can buy up tangible assets after foreclosure for nickels on the dollar, draining equity from victims and taxpayers alike until the next cycle, which will come (as chance (!) would have it) after we are again prosperous. And you *really* think that to maximize their take they know just how many

"It's no use. No matter how much we try the rich still get richer."

can be allowed to fall through the cracks into the welfare abyss? Surely such machinations are too grand of scale to be orchestrated, don't you think? My but you *are* cynical, aren't you? Besides, even if you're right, might not the cause result more from accident than from design? And are we really being squeezed all that much? By the way, could you lend me ten until payday? . . . thanks, I'll pay you back eleven.

110-L6. Reaganomics was a success story, but don't try telling that to everyone. Trouble was its wheel of fortune was out of balance. Statistics "prove" that gains in the 1980s occurred across a wide front. Unfortunately, the distribution was uneven at best. When glowing prosperity brings with it simultaneous discontent and widespread hardship, you know *something* is amiss. It's no wonder that Congress is increasingly dividing along party lines and wasting time with petty sniping—it is simply a reflection of the frustration in the country suffered by many over not knowing where to turn for answers. Republicans generally take to Reaganomics like elephants to water, while democrats lament their wards trading in their cars for donkeys. While the rich were keeping a larger percentage of their income under Reagan, the poor were losing *their* "market share" of the *take*, but not of their numbers. The speed limit on the throughway was increased, but if your tires were worn, you weren't even allowed *on* the throughway; you had to take the back roads with all the potholes and your speed was held back as rising inflation met head-on with an abysmal wage structure for many hard-working poor who deserved better—and still do, now maybe even more than ever. Our right foot was on the accelerator, but our left foot was on the break.

I think its time we called the "share-a-ride" hotline, don't you? After which please don't be shocked if it turns out that the ride with our new companions actually becomes enjoyable as we travel *together* for the first time.

110-M6. Whether we seek personal success or a superior organization of society, the comparison with climbing a ladder is telling. There is a reason for all those rungs. Each new step on the way up is made easier by the one before it. If we feel frisky, we may try to take two at a time, but that's not very smart. To attempt three at a time would be nothing less than foolhardy.

The larger the ladder is when we first buy it, the higher we can ascend when we're ready to use it. But its cost is greater, and so is the effort of moving it about. I think we make choices on a cost/benefit basis, which in turn is decided from weighing our perceived potential for success in achieving our *ultimate* goals. I *hope* I made that clear.

110-N6. There is nothing that will protect us from life's storms more than healthy habits. If one cannot be tempted into doing wrong, he need have no fear of the devil, even if he visits Lucifer in his own den. In fact, in such a case it is the devil who should not want *you* around. A Korean proverb says: If you want to hunt a tiger, you must go where the tiger lives. I once conducted a weekly checker tournament for a group of amateurs. On the day of the final session I was to play the top two finalists simultaneously after the tournament was over. But before they signed up, I noticed that one of the players was a man I had never seen before. There are times when my instincts are very good, and on this occasion they told me this fellow was a ringer brought in specifically to embarrass me. Sure enough, when the dust had settled he came out high, thus qualifying him to play me next (along with the #2 finisher). Well, I need to tell you that in checkers, as long as you can pick out the best move available every time it's your turn (which is *not* at all easy to do), you will *never* lose. You will either win or draw, but you won't lose (this kind of justice is built into the game, which is the source of its fascination). With this determination to play one game flawlessly fortifying me, I felt invincible. On his third move he blinked, and within 15 minutes a crowd-pleasing in-and-out 3 for 2 shot by me ended his misery. Little did the spectators realize that the die was cast at that third move, but had not every subsequent move of *mine* been perfect, *he* would have won instead. Such is often the case in checkers. (Yes, I defeated #2 also.)

The moral is that good need never fear evil (or the unknown) so long as truth is left free to fight it; it is evil that should fear good, which is the whole reason for *being* good in the *first* place.

110-06. As for white establishment complaints against alleged abuses by the "political correctness" (PC) movement that is currently sweeping our campuses (especially), i.e., don't dare to do, say, or think anything that might offend minorities'

"This is Steve Pomeroy, substituting for Al Osgood, who said something illiberal on the air yesterday."

or women's sensitivities, I will center on what may be the main argument. Lack of sensitivity toward (or perhaps, not pandering to) non-whites has become a punishable offense in America. PCers contend whites progressed at the expense of other races and cultures, and did not bother to be fair along the way; so now (to get even!) minorities are asserting themselves in the same forceful manner as had been done to them.

Well, evolution is a step-by-step process. One does not progress from backwardness to enlightenment in a single leap. *Of course* the advance of Western culture *did not* take the time to apologize to those it stepped over and on in its development. The world gets out of the way of the man who knows where he is going. The very fact that now the cream of our universities is tolerant of the venting of minority emotions and grievances is evidence of their willingness to be sympathetic. But the truth is they are bending over *too far* backwards. Goodwill cannot be elicited by giving in to or exercising ill will.

If minorities wanted to play leapfrog (and if they think they *can* I sincerely wish them luck), they would better advised to: learn from the past as we do with most things; try reaching for the *next* plateau; and forget about recriminations for old injustices that were nothing more than nature's natural undergrowth before cultivation would transform it into a garden of multicolored flowers.

110-P6. What would you think if, armed with a college extension truck driving certificate paid for under the GI bill, you attempted to get such a job in 1954, but always without success? And the reasons given for these rejections were memorable for their sameness: We can't hire anyone who's not already a union member. Well, thinks me, that shouldn't be any problem, we'll just go down to Local 107 and sign up. Simple as that, eh? Guess again: You can't join the union unless you already *have* a job. That's what *they* said. So I'm wondering, how did all these other drivers get their jobs, anyway? I never knew about all of them, nor *do* I to this day, but soon found out that a "gift" of less than $400 (in convenient time payments) to the right person could make a difference.

I declined, not because I was more honest than others, but because the end I sought and still seek required me to be. Some call it morality, but I view it as simply a *deeper* self-interest. The sacrifice at the time, however, was considerable. Instead of a package of benefits worth over $12 an hour, the best non-union equivalent I could find was a postcard size benefit of $2 per hour. Something in between would have been very fair, sensible, and most welcome. But corruption does not thrive in a fair and sensible environment, so it is not in the interest of those who gain from turmoil to have either order or equity. The best disinfectant is exposure to sunlight. [written June 25, 1991]

110-Q6. To capture a man's mind and soul, first satisfy his heart and stomach. Only then should we expect a call for reason to be heard.

110-R6. "And what about forgiveness?" I was asked. "Que sera sera," I answered. Since I do not take offense, forgiveness is a moot point, although I respect the fact that others probably feel differently, hence *I* will take care *not* to offend *them*. We should not inflict hurt or pain if we can reasonably avoid it. A situation that would not bother us might easily offend another. Say what you mean, and mean what you say; but don't be mean when you say it. *Physical* and *economic* abuse call for redress; that's simple justice. But insults and slights should simply be ignored, along with emotionally charged disappointments. Even young children are taught to say "Sticks and stones will break my bones, but names will never hurt me."

Had I not been asked this question, the notion of forgiving would never have occurred to me; it's all quite unnecessary as far as I'm concerned.

110-S6. If believing an untruth can inspire a person to positive achievements or good conduct beyond what he would otherwise attain, then by all means allow him to continue in this delusory state. Learn not those things which ye would rather *not* know.

110-T6. Any deviation from optimal behavior or practices will, over time, give rise to reactions that respond reflexively to those particular situations. Thus we find that habits acquired under such conditions do not make a graceful transition when changes for the better come along, as they inevitably do.

Living right and thinking straight take on added significance when the good habits *they* inspire are factored into the equation. Oscar Wilde said that every little action of the common day makes or unmakes character. Just as "bad" feeds on itself, so too does "good" feed on *itself*—and not only for those who start the process, but often for untold future generations whom we saddle with a legacy that can be for better or worse.

110-U6. So where does the world go from here? I see *one final challenge* ahead. Not communism—that's on the wane. Not Saddam—the world is on to his tricks. I'm talking about the Japanese "mafia" (in Japan). Japan's business and financial leaders have been so successful, that they chose to buy off troublemakers time after time, rather than face up to a messy showdown. But in this instance, Peck's bad boys were positioning themselves to take over the whole store, not just the cookie jars (as in other countries). The more they are allowed to get away with, the hungrier they get. The prospect of massive wealth offers the wayward an incentive advantage (a competitor on steroids you might say) over the modest but steady wealth that an honest merchant can expect, and *enlightened* self-interest is meaningless to misfits with defective personalities.

Therefore it is most disquieting to find that in spite of major recent scandals in corporate Japan, *no one has gone to jail* (see Nietzsche's remark in #127). This fact has dire universal implications. Are the mob's tentacles there now so deep that the host is rendered comatose?

The danger is this: If the *New* World Order begets a *one* World Order, there will be no second chance to make a first impression, as the first blow will be the fatal blow. We will either be economically enslaved by bad men, or we will be economically freed by good men. And unlike former times, if the bad guys win this one, there will be no one left in the world to come to the rescue. The forces of good can only prevail if they are made aware of what they are up against in time to take action. [written July 13, 1991]

110-V6. Do not maneuver your adversary into defending the indefensible if your only purpose is to embarrass him, for if you succeed in doing so, you will also succeed in antagonizing. However insignificant this may be individually, collectively it becomes as ominous as a swarm of bees.

110-W6. Making mistakes is acceptable so long as we can learn from them the value of not repeating them.

110-X6. Reformers past and present can tirelessly wage war against all manner of social injustices. But it seems they also have one fault that they share in common.

These trailblazers usually have a number of original ideas, but fail to realize that the public, not being of the same state of mind as themselves, are not open to pondering *all* of them at one time. And to ponder is only the first step in a process that may or may not lead to accepting and putting into practice. Here is where I think most of them go astray: It is difficult enough to get even obviously needed reforms adopted. But when you aggravate your audience by *forever* rubbing your most controversial notions in their faces, belittling them for muddled thinking, and *defying convention by parading your own atypical conduct*, you can hardly expect to win friends and influence people. He who advocates radical changes will stand a better chance of being heard if he keeps his own personal behavior in line with prevailing community standards. Ergo, given a reverse twist, a noble touch of hypocrisy can win the day.

When it comes to peddling my wares, I most admire the Jewish street vendor who said to the haggler with simple eloquence, "If you don't want to buy it, you don't have to." I do not want to be a salesman, I want instead to be an order taker. If my product is superior it will sell itself to those who recognize it as such. If it is not, it deserves to fail, and I would be the first to write its epitaph.

110-Y6. "The moment the market rather than politicians decides people's economic fate, the existing political parties and their complex systems of patronage will be superfluous; the principal obstacle to reform—the complex interrelationship between political parties and civic life—will have dissolved."

Joel Bainerman is a Jerusalem-based journalist. The foregoing is an excerpt from a piece he wrote in the July 23, 1991 *Wall Street Journal* titled, "Cut off aid to Israel and watch it thrive." Its message, however, has universal application: The work ethic is the best medicine anyone can take. For your own good don't ever run out of it.

110-Z6. When I was younger, I often lamented the many rigid traffic laws that prevented me from exercising common sense tailored to the situation at hand. "After all," I reasoned, "why must I wait for the light to turn green if there is nothing coming from either direction"? Well, I now realize that there *are* valid reasons. While *I* may be a professional driver and endowed with the necessary good sense to be my own traffic cop, not *everyone* is. Heaven help us if the rules of the *public* roads were the same as those for the Daytona 500. Furthermore, a lapse in judgment or attention will befall even the most qualified driver at some time. Such uncertainties compound existing risk, since acting as your own controller is more demanding than following a prewritten script. Good habits may be very boring, but their automatic benefits serve to make our lives easier in a safe (albeit complacent) sort of way.

The alternative to habit is to think our way through every little task. For those who can, thinking *is* the superior choice, but it's a lot more work (Henry Ford once suggested that thinking was harder than physical labor, which must be why so few practice it). *Depriving* one of being a creature of habit can also be an unsettling experience for the individual so targeted. Imagine the quandary that true believers would find themselves faced with if evidence surfaced disproving beliefs they had always relied on for guidance and support. Could they then, should they then, change their ways? Nature solves this problem for us by letting the old die off and the new be free to go their separate ways, using the past as a guide and only sometimes as a mandate.

All of which proves that superior is not necessarily better, at least not to those for whom the price of change is too high. (But it is a price you *will* have to pay if you are to read this work with the attention that was intended.)

110-A7. If all I can afford is a used, financed Yugo, then I would be tempted to adhere to the modern version of the golden rule: Do unto others—and then cut out. But if on the other hand, I could *afford* a new, fully paid for *Cadillac*, I think for the same price I would rather buy *two* new Chevy Caprices (oh yes you can) and *give* one to a needy neighbor. That would leave me with a car only *marginally* inferior (sorry, but it's true) yet gain the friendship of a comrade now more apt to plan a surprise birthday party for me than to plot to steal my expensive Cadillac hubcaps, which would bring him more than *his* old Yugo, hubcaps and all.

Now it is true that not *all* neighbors will be so appreciative, but odds *are* that you know one who would be, and in life one should always go with the *true* odds.

110-B7. In their lifetime, some people will go through many stages, until finally what remains for those who stay the course is pure reason. It took me over half a century to arrive at this point, but now I am enjoying the fruits of that experience by dispensing wisdom on request. I will try to make my product widely *available*, but the impetus to buy must come from you alone. *You* will have to be the closer in any deal with me by selling to *yourself.*

110-C7.   Do not dismiss a fellow as inept simply because he fails to measure up in an area where you hold sway; he might be equally ready to write *you* off for the very same reason. Finishing last in the Preakness does not preclude winning three weeks later at Belmont. Such are life's capricious ways. And never lose respect for others because you pass them on the way up; very soon you may pass again on *their* way up. Fortunes have a way of reversing with unnerving swiftness, and burning your bridges behind you has never been a good idea anyway. Every person you meet knows something you don't; learn from them!

Each of us is a composite: folly followed by foresight, cunning commingled with compassion. In the end we are nothing more than the sum of our parts. Now we know what St. Peter's real talent is, obviously he's a master number-cruncher.

110-D7.   Do not allow rhetoric to persuade you more than reasoning.

110-E7.   It's nice to be in shape, but, how *necessary* is it? While I would not want to get into a boxing ring unless I were physically fit; neither should I exercise (and certainly not do push-ups) immediately after awakening, since that is the most likely time to have a heart attack. While this is not to say proper exercise isn't beneficial to the heart—because it is—the broader point is that so long as the shape we're in is adequate to meet the body's demands, our life span will not be *appreciably* shortened. When asked once why I *didn't* exercise, I replied that I had more sense than that (although my legs *are* in good shape due to a lifetime of walking).

This brought to mind a humorous incident based upon the obligation of Roman Catholics to attend Sunday Mass (unless they are sick). At that time, not to do so was considered a mortal sin. Thinking of all those Sunday mornings when we would rather have stayed in bed, New York City's then mayor William O'Dwyer bemoaned to his friend Cardinal Spellman regarding the Protestants (for whom attendance was *not* mandatory), "Wouldn't it be hell if it turned out they were right and we were wrong?"

Well, I don't go to church and I don't go out of my way to exercise; and I feel none the worse for either, thank you and amen.

110-F7. When a governing body selects the most talented of their group to lead them; chances are more rather than less that the end result will mirror the character of that leader. It will tend to be better if he is a good person, or worse if he is a bad person, and *either* way the more so if he is a forceful person. This will likely occur irrespective of the *motives* of those who endowed him with power in the first place. It is the head that sets the tone, for without a head the tail cannot wag. [written August 23, 1991, following the three-day Soviet coup that failed]

110-G7. Hey folks, is there something going on here that almost no one has noticed? Pay attention to this please: It is October 30, 1969, and President Nixon has signed Executive Order #11490, "Assigning Emergency Preparedness Functions to Federal Departments and Agencies," *The Federal Register.*

E.O. 11490 authorizes the Office of Emergency Planning

to put all controls into effect "in times of increased international tensions and economic or financial crisis." Takeover by government agencies includes: communications media; all electrical power, gas, petroleum fuels, and minerals; food resources and farms; all modes of transportation and control of highways, seaports, etc.; health, education, and welfare functions; airports and aircraft. Provision is also made for the mobilization of civilians into work brigades under government supervision. The order directs the Postmaster General to operate a national registration of all persons; permits the Housing and Finance Authority to relocate communities, and grants authority to the Department of Justice to enforce the plans set out in E.O. 11490, and to operate penal and correctional institutions.

To all of this I say, "Wow!" But the part that unsettles me most is that which suggests putting these controls into effect "in times of increased international tensions and *economic or financial crises.*" Could this be the coming economic/financial crises that we are being set up for? And why do I say that? The last time the invisible power structure was *genuinely* threatened—in World War II—the entire country was mobilized in miraculous fashion overnight, and we never looked back. If we could pull *that* off *50* years ago, does it make sense to you that economic and social problems since then *still* have not been solved, but are in fact rapidly getting worse?

Nor does it make sense to me, friend. Is it possible there are forces that would pauperize us first so that they could subjugate us later, and maybe grease those skids by permitting outrages that will facilitate the desired backlash when the lid does finally blow off? This would provide the needed excuse to implement Executive Order #11490.

110-H7. If one's vacation were permanent, would it still be a vacation?

110-17.   Helen Keller was one of the most remarkable persons who ever lived. In her little book, *My Key of Life,* written while a student at Radcliffe College, she writes: "Deaf, dumb and blind from my nineteenth month, I had wandered helplessly in a desolate 'No-man's-land' until I was seven. Then SHE came and took my hand and led me by untrodden paths through the silent dark back to the living ways of men."

The following excerpts are taken from this work. I have omitted her numerous references to God.

When I think of the suffering, the disease, the famine, the slaughter, all the helpless blundering and slavish acquiescence, all the travail, all the sordid aspirations of my fellowmen, I am a hundredfold afflicted. But the thought comes to me that, like the little deaf, dumb and blind child I once was, mankind is burgeoning out of the darkness of ignorance and hate into the light of a happier day.

Already the rebirth of the nations has begun. Men are finding out that ignorance is the only darkness, and that useful work is the highest form of worship. They are beginning to see that life will never be fair and square for all until each one *earns* his daily bread. They are learning that cooperation in work, trade, art, science—in all life—is the hope of the world. When this lesson is thoroughly learned, "all men will be lovers: and every calamity will be dissolved in the universal sunshine." We are still stumbling in the dark, but we are facing toward the light.

A poet once said I must be happy because I did not see the bare, cold present, but lived in a beautiful dream. The very evil which the poet supposed would be a cruel disillusionment is necessary to the fullest knowledge of joy. Only by contact with evil could I have learned to feel by contrast the beauty of truth and love and goodness.

It is a mistake always to contemplate the good and ignore the evil because by making people neglectful it lets in disaster. How many good men, prosperous and contented, looked around and saw naught but good, while millions of their fellowmen were bartered and sold like cattle! I distrust rash optimism when there are grievances that call loudly for redress. That is false optimism. Optimism that does not count the cost is like a house built on sand. A man must understand evil and be acquainted with sorrow before he can write himself an optimist and expect others to believe that he has reason for the faith that is in him.

I can say with conviction that the struggle which evil necessitates is one of the greatest blessings. It makes us strong, patient, helpful men and women. It lets us into the soul of things and teaches us that although the world is full of suffering, it is full also of the overcoming of it. My optimism, then, does not rest on the absence of evil, but on a glad belief in the preponderance of good and a willing effort always to cooperate with the good, that it may prevail. The world is sown with good; but unless I turn my glad thoughts into practical living and till my own field, I cannot reap a kernel of the good.

Doubt and mistrust are the mere panic of *timid* imagination [Einstein said that imagination was more important than knowledge], which the steadfast heart will conquer, and the large mind transcend.

It was not so long ago that Carlyle flung forth his gospel of work. To the dreamers of the Revolution, who built cloud-castles of happiness, and, when the inevitable winds rent the castles asunder, turned pessimists, he cried aloud his creed of labor—Produce! Produce! Work while it is called Today; for the Night cometh wherein no man may work. I have found out that though the ways in which I can make myself useful are few, yet the work open to me is endless.

Every optimist moves along with progress and hastens it, while every pessimist would keep the world at a standstill. The consequence of pessimism in the life of a nation is the same as in the life of the individual. Pessimism kills the instinct that urges men to struggle against poverty, ignorance and crime, and dries up all the fountains of joy in the world. In imagination I leave the country which lifts up the manhood of the poor and I visit India, the underworld of fatalism—where three hundred million human beings, scarcely men, submerged in ignorance and misery, precipitate themselves still deeper into the pit. Why are they thus? Because they have for thousands of years been the victims of their philosophy, which teaches them that men are as grass, and the grass fadeth, and there is no more greenness upon the earth. They sit in the shadow and let the circumstances they should master grip them, until they cease to be Men, and are made to dance and salaam like puppets in a play. After a little hour death comes and hurries them off to the grave, and other puppets with other "pasteboard passions and desires" take their place, and the show goes on for centuries.

Go to India and see what sort of civilization is developed when a nation lacks faith in progress and bows to the gods of darkness. Under the influence of Brahminism, genius and ambition have been suppressed. There is no one to befriend the poor or to protect the fatherless and the widow. The sick lie untended. The blind know not how to see, nor the deaf to hear, and they are left by the roadside to die. In India it is a sin to teach the blind and the deaf because their affliction is regarded as a punishment for offenses in a previous state of existence. If I had been born in the midst of these fatalistic doctrines, I should still be in darkness. [Is this the real reason we call India "the subcontinent"?]

Optimism is the faith that leads to achievement; nothing

can be done without hope. In Latin countries the court proceeds with a pessimistic bias. The prisoner is held guilty until he is proved innocent. In England and the United States there is an optimistic presumption that the accused is innocent until it is no longer possible to deny his guilt. Under our system, it is said, many criminals are acquitted; but it is surely better so, than that many innocent persons should suffer. The pessimist cries, "There is no enduring good in man! The tendency of all things is through perpetual loss to chaos in the end. If there was ever an idea of good in things evil, it was impotent, and the world rushes on to ruin." But behold, the law of the two most sober-minded, practical and law-abiding nations on earth assumes the good in man and demands a proof of the bad.

Optimism is the faith that leads to achievement. The prophets of the world have been of good heart, or their standards would have stood naked in the field without a defender. Tolstoi's strictures on America lose power because they are pessimistic. If he had seen clearly the faults of America, and still believed in her capacity to overcome them, our people might have felt the stimulation of his censure. But the world turns its back on naysayers and listens to Emerson who takes into account the best qualities of the nation and attacks only the vices which no one can defend or deny. It listens to the strong man, Lincoln, who in times of doubt, trouble and need does not falter. He sees success afar, and by strenuous hope, inspires a nation. Through the night of despair he says, "All is well," and thousands rest in his confidence. When such a man censures, and points to a fault, the nation obeys, and his words sink into the ears of men; but to the lamentations of the habitual Jeremiah the ears grow dull.

Our newspapers should remember this. The press is the pulpit of the modern world, and on the preachers who fill it much depends. If the protest of the press against unrighteous measures is to avail, then for ninety-nine days the word of the preacher should be buoyant and of good cheer, so that on the hundredth day the voice of censure may be a hundred times strong. This was Lincoln's way. He knew the people; he believed in them and rested his faith on the justice and wisdom of the great majority. When in his rough and ready way he said, "You can't fool all the people all the time," he expressed a great principle, the doctrine of faith in human nature. The ecstatic prophecies of Isaiah did far more to restore the exiles of Israel to their homes than the lamentations of Jeremiah did to deliver them from the hands of evil-doers.

Ideas are mightier than fire and sword. Noiselessly they propagate themselves from land to land, and mankind goes out and reaps the rich harvest.

As I stand in the sunshine of a sincere and earnest optimism, my imagination "paints yet more glorious triumphs on the cloudcurtain of the future." Out of the fierce struggle and turmoil of contending systems and powers, I see a brighter era slowly emerge—an era in which there shall be no England, no France, no Germany, no America, no this people or that, but one family, the human race; one law, peace; one need, harmony; one means, labor. May we draw ever nearer to the age when no man shall live at his ease while another suffers.

The test of all beliefs is their practical effect in life, as the heresy of one age becomes the orthodoxy of the next.

■ ■ ■

(Miss Keller died in 1968 at the age of 88.)

110-J7. Well, now that we've come this far, shall we take the final step? I guess you could say that the ultimate question has to be: What is the meaning of life?

The jury is still out on this one, but that may not always be the case. First, forget about Deity or other supernatural explanations. This cop-out begs the question of *their* origins, and is not worthwhile debating (as Thomas Paine said, to argue with a person who has renounced the use of reason is like administering medicine to the dead). It will be through science that the doors will unlock, and sooner than we might think. In the meantime, I'll just sit this dance out. It used to be the job of philosophers to tackle questions like the meaning of life, but science has come of age, and is destined to be the new religion whose tools should solve this final mystery, too.

So while I cannot tell you *what* the meaning of life is, I *can* tell you what gives meaning *to* life, consequently adding greatly to our happiness: Find out where you belong, then get lucky enough to have the opportunity of seeing it become your livelihood. Any society worth its salt should help us to realize these two paramount goals.

110-K7. One of my desires is to replace the Bible with its secular, evolutionary, and simplified counterpart as elucidated within this work. Should I fail to get the attention of my peers in this endeavor, I shall find solace in the awareness that a prophet is without honor in his own house.

110-L7. There are times in our life when we have urges to do wrong things. We may or may not give in to them, but if we do, it by no means necessarily makes us a bad person. For you see, the collective genes of humanity that have much to do in determining our proclivities, are now in the fermentation stage of making the transition from being savage to being civilized. And although evolution's road has many twists and turns, it *should* eventually lead us to *heaven* on earth; not to *hell* on earth.

110-M7. The truth is, people automatically resist altering notions that they learned in school.

110-N7. The best rule for living can be reduced to a single directive: Seek to maximize the happiness and/or minimize the suffering of all living things capable of feeling the difference. Do this and benefits will accrue to your own account as well.

110-O7. You ask why our children are disenfranchised: When one is taught to believe a fiction, the revelation or even the suspicion of truth, if it comes, can cause disillusionment severe enough to bring down what had been regarded as the strongest of moral pillars.

110-P7. Now, in the aftermath of the Clarence Thomas/ Anita Hill testaments, I would like to offer my version of what we may be facing here. As pure chance would have it, this same drama once played itself out in my back yard too.

I have no objections to Judge Thomas becoming Justice Thomas, but I was disappointed that he chose not to listen to Ms. Hill's allegations against him (I think judges should be mentally tough enough to endure what to most others *would* be unendurable). And his courtly vocal intonations expressed his inner agony. His pain had become evident, and we all suffered with him. Whatever did or did not happen in *this* case, the person who never harbored impure thoughts is not mortal. This fact did not go unnoticed by the public; it struck a chord in the judge's favor.

As for Ms. Hill, I do not think either she or others *purposely* concocted this tale. Yet it *could* have been fabricated out of whole cloth in the inner recesses of Professor Hill's own mind, and even embellished along the way. There is a name for such a condition and I was surprised not to hear it mentioned even once the entire time, although "fantasy" *was* suggested. "Delusional thinking" was known 100 years ago, it is nothing new.

During the hearings, Hill said, "I am not imagining the conduct to which I testified." Well, maybe and maybe not. Don't you see, if she *is* imagining it, she cannot know that she is. It is possible that Ms. Hill had been in love with Judge Thomas. Were not the little girls at Fatima who claimed to have witnessed what many believe was the Virgin Mary, so convincing that the Church has declared the incident worthy of belief (which means you may believe it or not)?

At the age of 24 I (Givotangi) accused another of relating to me an incident, but after a quarter of a century passed, I realized he never did. And I believe very few to whom this happens *ever* realize it. As one mental patient who refused to admit he was ill once said to me, "If I don't have control of my own mind, what *do* I have?" And it's quite understandable, when your very sanity comes into question, denial takes on the aura of self-preservation. But if you *do* become aware of the fact that you had a mental lapse, you have a leg up on managing it.

Again, whether all of this is applicable to what happened to me or not, one thing can be said: Delusional thinking is a very real noumenon.

110-Q7. An understanding of what "love" is would more likely be found in a chemistry class than a class on social studies. While this is especially true as it pertains to love based on sexual desires, all emotions are to a large extent probably determined at their point of origin by chemical reactions in the brain, and modified by external influences for better or for worse along the way. I *do* think that one's "first love" is usually the most emotional, simply because that is the time our body chemistry is causing the hormones to boil at a higher temperature (so to speak). But as reason gradually takes command, the tempest is tamed, and more practical considerations should take root. The wit of Benny Hill peals a ring of truth when he says in jest, "To be in love with someone who doesn't love back gives you a pain in the chest at night."

To the degree that we can substitute logic for passion in our behavior is the degree to which we will advance the cause of civilizing man. (And I might add that doesn't mean life must be dull and boring.)

110-R7. Coincidence?—Maybe! Both Lincoln and JFK were their own men. No doubt it was this quality that got them into trouble. Lincoln had the temerity to create money that the government could borrow from itself without having to pay interest on. However, Lincoln's Treasury notes, also known as "greenbacks" or United States notes, did not long survive him. And like the independent-minded Kennedy, both were assassinated by a gunman acting "alone" . . . Sure!

Howsoever, we find that periodically a *token* amount of interest-free United States notes *are* issued, no doubt as a subterfuge to muddy the waters. Maybe they keep them in the vaults; have you ever seen any?

You might find interesting what some others have had to say about money:

Allow me to control and issue the nation's money and I care not who makes its laws!

– attributed to AMSHEL ROTHSCHILD

If the American people only understood the rank injustice of our money and banking system, there would be a revolution before morning.

– ANDREW JACKSON

(In Jackson's case an assassination attempt failed. The gun misfired!)

Whoever controls the volume of money in any country is absolute master of all industry and commerce.
                    – reported to have been said by JAMES A. GARFIELD
                              (And we know what happened to him.)

If the American people ever allow private banks to control the issue of their currency, first by inflation and then by deflation, the banks and the corporations that will grow up around them will deprive the people of all property until their children wake up homeless on the continent their fathers conquered.
                                                    – THOMAS JEFFERSON

Senator Robert F. Pettigrew, in his book, *Imperial Washington*, declared tersely, "The purpose of the Federal Reserve is to rob the people."

Asked why the economy of our colonies was booming: "That is simple. In the colonies we issue our own money. It is called colonial scrip. We issue it in proper proportion to the demands of trade and industry." But beginning in 1781, banker-backed Alexander Hamilton succeeded in foisting "bank" money on us, and after a few years the prosperity under colonial scrip had vanished, and the same statesman I quoted above *now* had this to say in his autobiography: "Conditions were so reversed that the era of prosperity had ended and a depression set in to such an extent that the streets of the Colonies were filled with the unemployed!"
                              – so stated by the master himself: BEN FRANKLIN

"A disordered currency is one of the greatest political evils. It undermines the virtues necessary for the support of the social system, and encourages propensities destructive to its happiness. It wars against industry, frugality, and economy, and it fosters the evil spirits of extravagance and speculation. Of all the contrivances for cheating the laboring classes of mankind, none has been more effectual than that which deludes them with paper money." [more accurately, Federal Reserve notes]

— DANIEL WEBSTER, 1846

If the Federal Reserve system *was* a U.S. government agency as alleged, should they not be listed under that category in the phone book, instead of with other private companies such as Federal Express?

There can be no doubt that undue wealth more often than not spawns inglorious ambitions that, if left unchecked, distort both the mind and conscience of their host, until either they or their victims are ultimately destroyed.

Richard Nixon's Executive Order #11490 (see 110-G7), and later revelations in the Oliver North hearings, should give us cause for alarm. Are preparations being made for a funeral? If so let us hope the deceased will not be Freedom. The surest way to lose our freedom is to abrogate our responsibilities. Think about it, but think it to yourself for now. After all, big brother may not take kindly to individual boat rockers. Now *there's* an idea: What would happen if we all rocked the boat at once?

Truth is visible when honest men seek Her diligently. When people learn to identify the source and nature of the influences swirling around them, it is sufficient.

110-S7. What about eschatology (the branch of theology concerned with end times)? Is it just one more dose of theistic fiction; or are its didacticisms to be *allegorically* interpreted— biding time and awaiting the catalyst that unleashes forces which will change the world?

I reject any notions of the supernatural; but do allow that there have been and are unexplainable events whose nature is beyond our understanding at the present time.

110-T7. Have the "influences" gotten to you yet? If you're in government it's all but guaranteed that they have. If you can remember Ripley's "Believe It or Not" drawings, and were both attentive and discerning, you might have realized he never claimed all those bizarre happenings were factual; all he said was: "Believe it or not."

Well, if he were still around today, he would have a field day by simply revealing government actions as they occur, and the new logo could be "believe it, it's true."

Here's the latest: During a political speech in New York on November 13, 1991, President Bush urged banks to cut their credit-card interest rates. The line was inserted by the president in his speech at the last minute, and hadn't been cleared by his top economic advisers. Thank you, sir, for speaking up on your own as we want you to—without getting permission first—as the "influences" expect you to.

I know the country has lost its bearings from what happened next. On *Meet the Press* the following Sunday, Treasury Secretary Nicholas Brady, bless his heart (use those three words and you may speak your mind about a person) said that Senator Alfonse D'Amato's November 14th proposal to cap credit-card interest rates at 14% (nearly 5 points below the current average), could lead many banks to withdraw credit cards from high-risk customers (heaven forbid). White House economic adviser Michael Boskin called the measure "economically dangerous" (??)—and wouldn't you know Alan Greenspan, reasoning as only he can, showed us where he stood by suggesting the cap would aggravate the current credit crunch!

I pray that those who offer such opinions as their sincere beliefs are for reasons of state merely lying through their collective teeth, but I fear that they actually believe what they're saying. There is one thing worse than a competent crook (he at least knows where to draw the line, if only to save himself), and that is an honest person who is incompetent.

Just what is behind the effort to flood our country with everything that is mediocre and trivializing, and to assign jobs for reasons other than merit, while putting fools in charge?

The answer should be clear. If you can lower the common denominator, people are less likely to think back at you. I cannot help believing that most of our problems are contrived. Chance alone could not have led us so far astray. But who would do that? And why?

To confront the sun directly is to go blind. But knowledge gathered indirectly can become power. Share this knowledge and it is power multiplied. Add understanding to the mix and you have laid your foundation as well as it is possible to do.

Benjamin Disraeli, the 19th century Jewish prime minister of Great Britain whose disconcerting habit of telling the truth seemed more to his friends like he was spilling the beans, had this to say: "The world is governed by very different personages from what is imagined by those who are *not* behind the scenes." Disraeli knew whereof he spoke.

110-U7. Consider present day events in light of what was said by one Professor Tytler, who edited *The Encyclopedia Britannica* almost 200 years ago: "A democracy cannot exist as a permanent form of government. It can only exist until the voters discover they can vote themselves largesse (welfare) from the public treasury. From that moment on, the voters always vote for the candidates promising the most benefits from the public treasury, with the result that a democracy always collapses over loose fiscal policy, always followed by a dictatorship." A government who robs Peter to pay Paul can always depend on the support of Paul.

110-V7. My apologies to these gentlemen for quoting them.

Columbia University professor of political science Seweryn Bisler attested in 1983: "The Soviet Union is not now nor will it be during the next decade in the throes of a systemic crisis, for it boasts enormous unused reserves of political and social stability that suffice to endure the deepest difficulties."

Harvard professor John Kenneth Galbraith added in 1984: "The Soviet economy has made a great national progress in recent years." Nobel laureate and MIT economist Paul Samuelson stated in 1987: "It is a vulgar mistake to think that most people in Eastern Europe are miserable."

And MIT business school dean and popular TV personality Lester Thurow intoned in 1989: "Can economic command significantly compress and accelerate the growth process? The remarkable performance of the Soviet Union suggests that it can. In 1920, Russia was but a minor figure in the economic councils of the world. Today it is a country whose economic achievements bear comparison with those of the United States."

Ed Hewitt is a former Brookings Institution scholar and current special assistant to President Bush for national security and senior director for Soviet affairs. He predicted in his 1988 book, *Reforming the Soviet Economy:* "To be sure, real income growth rates [in the Soviet Union] are falling, but they are falling from a high level, and the general downward trend is similar to one observed throughout the world. Even in recent years per capita personal incomes have been growing between two and three percent, which is quite respectable by world standards."

On unemployment, he writes: "If the Soviet Central Administration was to collect and publish unemployment statistics in a fashion similar to that in the United States, the rate of unemployment would come out under two percent for the mid-1980s. Western countries, particularly Western workers, can only envy a society with such a consistently low level of unemployment."

And on income: "The economic security provided in the USSR today is only partly a result of the high demand for labor and the low level of unemployment. It relates to certainty concerning the worth of income in real terms, which is much higher in the Soviet Union than in Western countries."

Telling on the experts things they have said may not always be polite, and might even be disrespectful, but isn't it fun? [January 12, 1992]

110-W7. It is interesting to note that since the Korean War, whenever political revolutions have occurred in various parts of the world, two companies usually end up with all of the oil and natural gas concessions: Royal Dutch Shell Oil Corporation, and Standard Oil of New Jersey. This has been largely true in Africa, the Middle East, South America and the Far East. These are also the companies whose installations seem to be virtually off limits to the bombers in both sides of any recent war. Such evidence points up the fact that the political and economic forces of the earth are being woven into a gigantic monolith of total global power.

– from The Naked Capitalist

110-X7. If you seek perfection in a would-be friend, you'll never find a friend.

110-Y7. The three stages of money:

1. Until the necessities of life are provided for, money is the *most* important thing in the world.

2. Once we have the necessities but before we can afford whatever we want, money is a convenience and something nice to have.

3. After we have more than we will ever need, money should become the *least* important thing in the world. The marginal utility of that additional money is negligible insofar as worthwhile objectives that most of us would put it to are concerned. Money should be a tool, not a scorecard. When used unwisely, we defer to another opinion: "Money is the worst of all contraband" (William Jennings Bryan).

110-Z7. There may be times when it is proper to deceive another, but *only* (even if you mean well) if they have no control over or cannot influence the event that inspires the deception.

110-A8. Man is born with self-interest, but it is not of the enlightened variety. Only time and growth can bring that about, and for too many neither will ever come.

110-B8.

American Commercial Banks Will Be the Next Crisis

Exclusive to THE SPOTLIGHT, by David Hudson,
a freelance journalist specializing in economics & precious metals

If you thought the S&L crisis was bad, hang on to your hat. The nation's banking system is under siege, and don't look to the officials in charge to do any better putting the banking houses in order than they did with the S&Ls.

The problems of the Establishment's banking sector remain much in the news. The savings and loan industry is in the process of withering away, a victim of its own excesses and a central governing authority (its state and federal regulators) that was wholly inadequate to the task it was charged with.

The banking sector's senior component—America's commercial banks—is facing similar problems. As bad as the problems of S&Ls, and as costly as the bail-out of depositors ($500 billion and growing), the problems of commercial banks are potentially much more serious. It is this sector that is licensed by the Federal Reserve system (which is owned by the very banks it regulates) to lend money into existence, at interest.

Ironically the soundest segment of America's banking system is the system of credit unions, member-owned financial cooperatives that serve working Americans. These institutions do not lend money into existence, and have almost wholly avoided the excesses that have decimated other financial institutions—Third World lending, unsound commercial real estate loans, and the financing of the "mergers and acquisitions" insanity of the 1980s.

Banks Face Downsizing

Banks everywhere are in retreat. Megabanks are merging to achieve economies of scale and eliminate "unnecessary" branch offices, data processing systems and employees. A new buzzword is being heard throughout the banking Establishment: "downsizing."

Downsizing means a bank must realize its losses and reduce the scope of its operations to maintain an adequate capital base. This is the amount of money owners (stockholders) have at risk in the bank, money that can be lost if the bank does not at least break even. When a bank downsizes it must reduce its loan portfolio, either by selling assets (loans that earn interest), or calling in loans.

California's Security Pacific Bank, which is now being merged into the (also troubled) Bank of America, will have wholly disappeared by the end of the year. Its problems began in 1985 with the ill-considered purchase of a bank in Arizona; the $480 million purchase price is gone, along with substantial loan losses in Arizona. In December, 1990, Security Pacific set aside $850 million to cover expected losses from bad loans in Arizona, Australia and elsewhere, and a failed investment in the British brokerage house of Hoare Govett.

When all is said and done, the surviving Bank of America will be substantially smaller than the two institutions were before they announced their merger last year.

Downsizing inevitably costs jobs, and this merger will come at a cost of about 20,000 jobs to employees of the merged banks.

Financial Press Happy-Talk

Have you ever wondered why, when the price of stocks or real estate goes up, the mainstream financial press, like *Barrons, Forbes* and *Fortune* pat themselves on the back and call America's business and financial elite geniuses, but when these prices fall there is great consternation? The reason, I assure you, is not that they or their masters, the bankers, are all that concerned with the value of your home or of your investment portfolio.

Instead they are concerned with the value of the loan portfolios of America's banks. Real estate and stocks are the two major forms of collateral for loans. If the value of loan collateral is diminished, then the solvency of banks is threatened.

The value of stocks pledged as collateral can be monitored by checking with any stockbroker, but real estate is different.

It is an open secret that many—probably most—American banks have loans outstanding on commercial buildings that, in 1992, could only be sold for less than the amount owed on the first mortgage, never mind its replacement cost. If forced to "mark to market" the true value of their collateral, and thus the value of their loan portfolio, a lot more loans would have to be called in.

Money Destroyed

When a bank calls in a loan, money is destroyed. Businesses must scramble to pay off lines of credit, or face bankruptcy. Credit cards can be canceled, and the repayment of outstanding balances demanded. The economy thus shrinks.

This is happening, as this is written, in the New England states as thousands of small businesses that have never missed or been late with a loan payment are having their loans called in because the value of their collateral has declined. Thus is money, and productive enterprise, destroyed by the banks that lent money into existence.

As Rutgers University professor Paul S. Nadler wrote in *Banker's Monthly:* "To anyone who has been in banking for less than 50 years, 'downsizing' is a new experience. As late as the 1970s, virtually every bank made a profit every year unless it was the victim of fraud, utter stupidity or, in a couple of cases, extremely bad luck."

Yale professor James Tobin, winner of the 1981 Nobel Prize in economics, explained bank downsizing in a *Wall Street Journal* essay last December 16: "Banks are grossly undercapitalized," Tobin wrote. "The buffer that protects depositors or taxpayer-underwritten deposit insurance funds from loss due to bad loans is perilously thin.

"On average, only 6 percent of commercial banks' assets represent stockholder's funds. Many banks are below regulator's minimum standards. Some have negative net worth, and others would if assets were realistically valued. Big banks have lower capital ratios than small banks. Commercial banks are more highly leveraged than non-bank finance companies, although they are much more dependent on liabilities payable in short terms or on demand.

"Until the 1930s, before deposit insurance enabled bankers to shift the risk of withdrawals to the government, commercial bank capital ratios were 15 percent and higher.

"No wonder banks are under regulatory pressure to raise their capital-to-asset ratios. Given their shaky balance sheets and low or negative profits, they can hardly sell shares or debt securities. Instead, they have to shrink their assets and liabilities by charging more for loans and paying less for deposits. That is why the margins between banks' lending rates on commercial, consumer and mortgage loans and the interest they pay for deposits and federal funds are twice their normal size."

Debt Equals Assets

Remember, for a bank your mortgage, car loan and credit card balance are assets that earn interest, and your savings account, money market account or certificate of deposit are liabilities on which interest must be paid. Your mortgage may be for 30 years and your car loan for five years, but your savings account and money market account can be liquidated at any time, and your certificate of deposit may be for a term of less than one year.

This, basically, is why banks call in sound, performing loans, and let productive employees go. They do not have the capital to maintain their former size, and they have few ways to raise new capital in a depressed bank stock market. Downsizing is the only way of meeting capital-to-deposit ratios imposed under new, "risk-based" capital standards.

The real issue being faced, but not publicly or even privately admitted, is that interest is ultimately unpayable under America's system of debt money. Principal is lent into existence, but not the money to pay interest, which can only be paid out of earnings (profits in the case of a business, or wages in the case of an employee).

To get money into the hands of debtors so interest can be paid, ever larger amounts of money must be created through new loans. At some point cumulated interest becomes unpayable; and sound, new loans simply cannot be made.

■ ■ ■

As Jim Townsend, publisher of the *National Educator* puts it: "A flawed money system is an economic time bomb!" This does bring immediacy to football coach George Allen's observation, "The future is now."

Update: Federales to the rescue

Subsequent to the foregoing, and unnoticed by the general public, a massive bank bailout by the Federal Reserve has occurred. Here's how it was pulled off: In late 1989 there were rumblings that the saving-and-loan scandal would be followed by an even worse debacle among the major commercial lenders. The Fed apparently thought so too. It discreetly began to lower both the so-called discount rate and the Fed funds rate; that is, the level of interest banks pay when they borrow from the central bank, or from each other.

Simultaneously, Greenspan launched a campaign of ever-larger long-term borrowing by the treasury. The payoff soon became evident: In effect, the government and the Fed were putting money into circulation at around 3 percent and then borrowing it back through treasury bond sales at about 8 percent interest. For the banking industry, it was like a license to print money.

With the sudden prosperity, the financial institutions experienced unprecedented change, says New York business writer John Crudele. By mid-1992, for the first time in history U.S. banks had more government bonds on their books than business loans, making them more like taxpayer-supported mutual funds than traditional commercial lenders.

But while the 100 biggest banks began to report record profits earlier this year (1993), the rest of the American economy was badly hurt by the Fed's audacious financial maneuver.

"No one appears fully aware yet how badly the air has been poisoned for middle-market borrowers (midsize and smaller firms) by this policy," says Christopher Snyder, president of a highly respected firm of money-market monitors. Roger Thompson, managing director of a major Wall Street firm, confirmed that "We are in a credit squeeze, and that's bad for the whole economy."

In the consensus of these knowledgeable sources, the Fed's policy of making the banks whole (in fact, prosperous) with what are, in effect, hundreds of billions in subsidized funds, has dried up the traditional sources of commercial credit: Why make a potentially risky loan to a private business when you can clean up by investing in largely risk-free government securities?

What we really have here is the swindling of futurity on a large scale.

110-C8. Justice is always to be sought, but even that noble goal has its limits. If the choice be a bloodbath that may or may not beget atonement from the offender, better to excise the tumor immediately with one swift act of amnesty in an effort to put the matter behind us and get on with the business of rebirth.

110-D8. We are approaching a moral watershed for the world-at-large, and all for pragmatic reasons. Say what you will about the motives of David Duke, his campaign for the U.S. Senate in 1990 and his Louisiana gubernatorial campaign in 1991 brought him worldwide attention. Duke's early break-away from orthodox politicking was perhaps the major event which produced the present array of anti-Establishment candidates. People are getting fed up with the old ways of governing and the widespread corruption permeating throughout all levels of society. They're getting mad as hell, they're getting wise, and they're not going to take it much longer.

Change is coming, and when it does come, it will be founded upon this precept: The best way of doing for ourselves is to do right by others. And we will do so not to please an unknown Deity, but because we dread the loss of heaven and the pains of hell, allegorically speaking, or course (see #14, point 3, and glossary). Or put another way, because it's the sensible thing to do.

We shall know this truth as enlightened self-interest, and it is *this* truth that shall make us free.

110-E8. Merely to be alive is far less important than how we conduct ourselves while we are alive. We can bring grief or happiness; joy or sorrow, both to ourselves and others. The choice *should* be obvious, but for many it is not. Why is that?

If you can only view your happiness as relative to that of others, you will be jealous anytime they seem better off than you. With negative incentives like that to deal with, your flower garden will never flourish. But measure your own happiness in absolute terms, and you are on your way to emotional health. (To modify Pericles' remark in #110-C4, the only shame is to accept your unhappiness without trying to change it.)

This homogenizing (indexing happiness) is why *socialism* has always ended in misery for those who came under its spell, and is not unlike the fad diet that will only work by having you restrain yourself: It will not likely endure because it is not a natural state.

110-F8. Treat every encounter as if it were a railroad crossing and you were a bus: *Stop, look, and listen.*

110-G8. Be wary of pledges and promises. Well-intentioned though they may be at the time they are given, any such covenants if they are to endure must be consistent and in total harmony with the *ultimate* goals of the one making them, else slippage will surely occur at some point.

There is a lesson here: Do not challenge Mother Nature, or place your faith or your treasure with those who presume to think themselves exempted from Her laws.

110-H8. The multitudes of good people who desire change should realize that action without knowledge is just as useless as knowledge without action.

110-I8. The ideal state is to have no proclivities. They serve only to cloud our judgment by burdening it with a prejudicial spin that inhibits our objectivity, and hence our ability to exercise the optimum course of action in a given situation.

110-J8. From a *Reason* magazine promotional mailing:

Who Owns You?

Do you own your future—or do *THEY?* Imagine if one day in the near future you were informed that over *half* your paycheck would be *confiscated* to support a large, affluent, politically powerful group of people *who do not work at all* . . .

Imagine if you became sick and your doctor told you that, sorry, our once-potent antibiotics simply *no longer work*, and no new ones have been approved to take their place . . .

Imagine if one day America's pollution problem began to gradually *disappear* and you and your children could look forward to an era of clean air and sparkling waters . . .

Sound intriguing? It is subjects like these that *Reason* magazine covers—a source of insight and intelligence most of our leaders and policy shapers would like to keep out of your hands forever . . .

Consider:

> . . . that our obsession with legislating a totally safe, risk-free society is choking innovation and sapping America's energy and spirit.

> . . . that America's foreign trade imbalance is actually a sign of economic *strength.*

> . . . that hostile takeovers are often *beneficial* to stockholders and the economy.

> . . . that our federal farm programs are in fact helping to *destroy* family farms.

What two things do these hypothetical "statements" have in common? (1) They are *true,* and (2) no president would *dare* utter any one of them—not without risking political suicide.

But there *is* a voice that dares to speak these truths, an astonishing, outspoken, unpredictable voice that speaks not for the Right, not for the Left . . . but for *honesty.* Welcome to *Reason*—the magazine whose motto is "free minds and free markets," the magazine that dares to bring you a new, startling vision of America!

Reason has the audacity to challenge the conventional wisdom . . . the courage to declare that today's most influential "thinkers" in most cases really aren't thinking at all!

Born to every generation, we believe, are men and women with a rare kind of eye . . . and an unerring instinct for perceiving the sham, the lies, and the hypocrisy all around them.

America functions best when it allows individuals to shape their own identities and carve out their own areas of opportunity.

Do you have an uneasy feeling that the "planners" and "social engineers" are trying to smother the American spirit with a soft, choking smog of small, complicated ultimately deadly regulations?

Do you believe that individual freedom—not some "master plan"—is the force that elevates the human spirit and enables men and women to realize their maximum potential—all of us being as different as we are?

Every so often something comes into our lives that brings with it a shock of recognition . . . the sudden realization that, NO, you are not alone . . . you are *not* the only one on earth who sees the issues and events of our day the way you do.

Here is a sampling challenging the planners' orthodoxy:

The planners say: "Mass transit is good—because it gets people out of cars and into trains and buses."

Reason says: "Mass transit is a *disaster*. Every such system in America is failing—because there are no markets for bus and rail systems in the decentralized cities of today and tomorrow!" [I fully agree.]

The planners say: "Immigration is bad—it's choking the future of America."

Reason says: "Immigration is our *best* hope for revitalizing our urban centers. There's nothing wrong with New York that a million Chinese couldn't cure!" [I *really* like that one.]

Reason is *not* the magazine you turn to when you want your conservative preconceptions *or* your liberal biases confirmed.

Reason is the one you turn to when you're grown-up enough to face the truth—when you want to know where America is really headed—when you're tired of the same conventional pieties served up endlessly by the same tired minds.

With clear, level-headed thinking, *Reason* gives you a glimpse of American society and its leadership that most policy shapers pray you'll never get to see.

Reason is not for everyone. It's certainly *not* for those who are frightened by individual freedom and the choices and challenges it offers. But the fact that you're still reading these words is evidence that it is *right for you.*

110-K8. And in case you're wondering—temptation does visit me occasionally, maybe once in every 2,000 time segments . . . at which times simple willpower is more than adequate to defend the ramparts. That is to say, if defending is called for.

110-L8. The secret of politics is to convince enough people that you know what you're talking about, and hope that the ones you can't don't take you seriously enough to regard you as a menace.

110-M8. Where do I stand on immigration? Let's damn the torpedoes and jump head first into this imbroglio. First, I do not value all potential immigrants equally. What? Are you a fascist? No—because I value each human being to such degree as they can be called a mentsch—fascists do not share this view. (Mentsch in Yiddish means "a decent person.")

However, I do not favor open and unrestricted immigration for a more compelling second reason: It is essential that *everyone* be able to carry their own weight. A Haitian boatperson certainly has the same right to life, liberty, and the pursuit of happiness as an unemployed Russian rocket scientist or a Mexican farm worker, but if the Haitian boatperson is without skills or the prospect of acquiring them, I am not prepared to expend means and energies in their behalf that can be more productively applied elsewhere. Is the optimum situation really to spare *every* spotted owl and snail darter from nature's laws, or need we also consider the attendant costs? The question should answer itself.

The dichotomy between idealism and realism can best be reconciled through initiatives based upon enlightened self-interest, starting always by correcting root causes. I *would* allow entry to that Russian scientist and that eager-to-work Mexican (but not if they had the HIV virus). Between them they would help to enrich us all. However, efforts to improve the conditions that drove them here should be undertaken, so that if ever they choose to, they can go home again.

If our country be our family, let the world be considered our extended family. To help the greatest number of our brethren everywhere, we need to give aid where it will do the most good.

110-N8. *In the short run, you can get chewed up if you pay all of your attention to the long run.* — GARY NORTH, Ph.D.

110-O8. *Permitting your life to be taken over by another person is like letting the waiter eat your dinner.*
— VERNON HOWARD

110-P8.

Social Security Shown to Be
Largest Economic Fiasco In History

Total Trust Fund Deficit Added Up For the First Time: $18 Trillion

Future of Fund Now Seen As Doubtful

by James Henry, Feature Writer

FT. WORTH—Are you counting on Social Security to "get you through"? If so, you can stop counting. It's broke, and there is no way to fix it.

That's the word from here, where government watchdog Dr. Gary North blew the whistle today on the oft-repaired federal retirement and disability program. Catching the administration establishment by surprise, his announcement seems sure to shock the public and anger officials, who have worked hard through the years to convey the idea that the Social Security and Medicare trust funds carry a large surplus.

"Not so," says North, the prolific author of over thirty books. "The various funds, including military and civil service pensions, have been systematically looted by every president since Lyndon Johnson in 1965. In fact, by law the Social Security Administration now is bound to turn over all unspent funds to the U.S. Treasury's general fund in exchange for a series of nearly worthless, non-negotiable IOUs from the Treasury Department. Treasury immediately spends these funds. So instead of a fat surplus, there is now a fat deficit that dwarfs any deficit in world history."

In the weeks and months ahead, two main scandals now appear likely to rock the Washington scene. First is the long running cover-up of the fund's plight, which has created near-total ignorance of the situation even at the highest levels of government. The second is the sheer size of the deficit, which has never been revealed until today.

The Cover-Up

Few U.S. representatives and senators are aware that the Social Security "surplus" is actually a gigantic future liability. Their staff, whose jobs depend on being familiar with the nuts and bolts of government, are usually better informed.

One former staffer, economist Louis Gasper, now relates a not-so-amusing story from his days with the Senate Finance Committee. A certain senator, it seems, could never fathom his staffers' casual references to the Social Security deficit. "Why do you keep trying to call a surplus a deficit?" he demanded over and over. "It's a surplus!" Repeated explanations never pierced the distinguished gentleman's intellect.

The Hidden Numbers Game

How is it possible to conceal such a vast problem from the citizens of an open country?

The answer lies in party rivalry. Democrats regard Social Security as the "crown jewel" of their social legislation. If it were attacked, their jewel would dim. And they would find it harder to launch more big-ticket programs.

And Republicans, as keepers of the administrative flame, do not wish to admit that the pillaging of America's retirement fund took place on their watch.

Consequently, the true numbers have never been added up clearly for mass publication. In fact, out of the thousands of federal publications issued each year, there are only three places where the Social Security fund gets reported *as a debt, not an asset:*

- Table 6D of the U.S. Treasury's *Monthly Treasury Statement of Receipts and Outlays.*

- *Winter Treasury Bulletin.* The 1989 edition covers fiscal 1988. Liabilities are on page 165.

- *Statement of Liabilities and Other Financial Commitments of the United States Government.* This is the fullest, most accurate report. By law, it must be published yearly; but to ensure that it remains virtually unread, it is not even typeset. In the past, it has been produced on a typewriter, then photostatted down to an illegible size and printed with no explanation of how to interpret it!

Although it is delivered to the entire Congress, probably only twenty or thirty people in Washington are really conversant with this report. *Yet even here the numbers are not tallied.* Each year it restates the startling disclaimer, "Because the various annuity programs have been computed on different actuarial bases and at varying valuation dates, a total has not been computed."

And therein lies the uniqueness of North's clarification of the total fund picture. Although he admits that his summing-up of the disparate figures may cause enough distortion to upset purists, he states flatly, with grim humor, "It's close enough for government work."

$18,000,000,000,000,000.00, Give or Take a Trillion

North claims to have added the numbers with all the fairness he can muster. The result is slightly over $18 trillion in future obligations: $15+ trillion for Social Security plus $3 trillion for the Civil Service Retirement program, Medicare/Medicaid, and the various military retirement programs.

This counts the official $2.8 trillion federal debt, but not the $8 trillion non-federal (state, etc.) debt or the huge personal and corporate debt figures.

Clearly, we have come a long way since 1965, when Lyndon Johnson made the decision to mix Social Security with the general fund in order to keep the Vietnam war and Great Society expenses from sending his budget deeply into the red.

These numbers are, of course, a far cry from any commonly discussed numbers in the media. As of today, the most loudly discussed fiscal figure in Washington is the $14 billion that Congress is desperately struggling to cut from the budget in order to meet the Gramm-Rudman-Hollings limits.

Hollings: "I want a divorce."

In the light of North's newly released book, *Social Security: The Coming Implosion*, the Gramm-Rudman-Hollings limits are also shown to be hollow at best, fraudulent at worst. Senator Hollings' recent reaction to the perversion of the landmark law that bears his name is, "I want a divorce!" In other words, he now decries the bookkeeping rules that allow budget limits to be evaded simply by mixing in the Social Security surplus with the general fund deficit.

He is not alone in his regrets. U.S. Comptroller General Charles A. Bowsher has said, "The rosy projections are not real numbers any more. The situation with the deficit is much worse than is being portrayed. We are adding $1 trillion every five years to the total deficit, and are digging a huge hole that will be very hard to get out of." [Since Bowsher spoke these words, the situation has deteriorated. We are now adding $1 trillion every three and one-half years.]

Mr. Bowsher is also head of the Government Accounting Office, which is the closest thing we have to a watchdog agency for expenditures. It does not bite, of course, but now and then it growls a little. In an hour-long interview with *The New York Times*, Bowsher scoffed at the Bush administration promise to hold the deficit to under $100 billion in fiscal 1990. The true figure, he says, will be around $263 billion. The difference? Mostly the annual "loan" from Social Security. "Everyone knows the numbers are fudged and that they never reflect reality," he said.

The secret of Bowsher's courage: His appointment as the head of GAO has a decade to run. He can't be fired.

After The Cover-Up: The Scandal

Every year, statisticians tally up the official Gramm-Rudman deficit estimate to the penny.

But every year, statisticians secretly *pre-shrink* that estimate by the billions Social Security lends to the Treasury Department. *In other words, Social Security is now an income-producing branch of the government.*

The Social Security fund gets left with a vast future obligation and no real assets to pay it off. Most people would call that a "debt," but the government and the media prefer to call it a "surplus."

At the same time, Treasury's IOUs (actually non-negotiable, interest-bearing bonds) never add a cent to the official national debt.

It's the bureaucrat's version of cold fusion, the perfect money machine. The Congressional pork barrel gets filled from the general fund, the general fund gets fed by Social Security, and Social Security gets fed by the taxpayers, who think they're building up a retirement fund for themselves when it's actually going down the Washington drain at hurricane speed.

What we have here, it is now clear, is the world's largest chain letter, or the world's largest Ponzi scheme, or the world's largest felony. Certainly if any corporation head were to siphon off the pension fund to pay current bills, he would go to jail. But in Washington, they don't go to jail; instead, they give themselves salary raises for a job well done.

Will this massive fiasco be the next major scandal? Not unless grandma and granddad stop getting their checks or Congress has to raise the FICA taxes again. But the latter could happen very soon if a recession strikes.

In any Ponzi scheme, the early investors get paid by funds from later investors, and the sham becomes harder and harder to disguise. In the Social Security scheme, Jimmy Carter had to raise the S.S. tax in 1977 when S.S. began to run in the red. He promised this would keep the monster quiet till the end of the century. But just six years later, it had to be fed again. Another "emergency" tax increase came in 1983. The widely anticipated next recession could easily shrink S.S. income to the point where the S.S. tax needs to be raised again. Fortunately for the administration, the public has less resistance to S.S. hikes than regular tax rate hikes simply because it doesn't view "Social Security contributions" as a tax.

Ordinarily, American voters are docile. They believe what the media and the government tell them. But some members of Congress are now beginning to admit the fraud. North says: "They want another tax hike. By moving Social Security off-budget, they may get it."

Can The System Live?

Everyone agrees that the alleged Social Security nest egg will need to be disbursed when the baby boom generation starts to retire in a few years. There is a huge lump in the worker pool that is working its way toward retirement like a pig going through a boa constrictor.

If we reach that point, what then? According to North, there are technically six options, but they boil down to two: default and massive inflation. And of course, massive inflation would be just an indirect form of default.

Even before inflation/default, however, the Social Security tax will have to be raised again. Economist Aldana Robbins has published a study based on the government's middle-of-the-road scenario (*not* their pessimistic scenario). She estimates that *total* S.S. taxes (employee plus employer) will have to hit 45% to keep the system going. That is on top of federal and state taxes.

Outlandish? No. Consider the railroad retirement system's pension fund. This older system (born in 1934) presages the problems soon to hit Social Security. After repeated Congressional bailouts and rate hikes, it now collects 36.1% of every railroad payroll dollar. And it's still going under. The American Association of Railroads now estimates it will need a hike to the 50% level. So Robbins' 45% may be quite reasonable.

Unfortunately, says North, the system won't last till 2010, when the boomers start retiring. "Recessions are a fact of life," he states. "And when they hit, government income drops like a rock while its expenses soar. Right now—at the tail end of a long boom—we're running a true deficit of $250 billion a year. So in the coming recession, that will likely jump to over $500 billion. And if the recession collapses into a depression, count on yearly deficits of over a trillion."

Naturally, neither American nor foreign investors would buy bonds from any government with a trillion-dollar yearly deficit. Far more likely would be a rush to gold and ultra-safe staple commodities. The government would thus be left with no way to pay its enormous bills, and a taxpayers' "revolt" would be the most likely scenario.

Now that this matter is out in the open, what will the authorities in the Capital say? Probably as little as possible. As usual, investors and taxpayers are on their own. North foresees "millions of older people reviving the ancient custom of moving in with the kids after retirement."

He promises to present an ongoing series of defensive strategies for investors in his monthly newsletter, *Remnant Review*, P.O. Box 84906, Phoenix, AZ 85071.

Excerpt From A 1976 Congressional Hearing

Senator William Proxmire: There are 37 million people, is that right, that get Social Security benefits?

Social Security Commissioner James Cardwell: Today, between 32 and 34 million.

Proxmire: I am a little high; 32 to 34 million people. Almost all of them, or many of them, are voters. In my state, I figure there are 600,000 voters that receive Social Security. Can you imagine a senator or congressman under those circumstances saying, "We are going to repudiate that high a proportion of the electorate"? No.

Furthermore, we have the capacity under the Constitution, the Congress does, to coin money, as well as to regulate the value thereof. And therefore we have the power to provide that money. And we are going to do it. It may not be worth anything when the recipient gets it, but he is going to get his benefits paid.

Cardwell: I tend to agree.

■ ■ ■

As the late Senator Everett Dirksen might have said, "A trillion here, a trillion there; pretty soon you're talking about big money."

110-Q8. I have learned not to dismiss out of hand those who give bad advice at times, or who harbor notions contrary to my own. The trick is to differentiate between sense and nonsense, and since we can all lay claim to a degree of both, it behooves the wise man to discern the difference so that his quiver is rendered replete with straight arrows.

110-R8. When you leapfrog over your opponent to get ahead, it does not mean that you can then rest on your laurels; just remember that he will not long stand still, but rather seek to respond in kind, and you have just given him the reason needed for doing so.

110-S8. *When you work in a fish factory you don't know it stinks.* – former governor JERRY BROWN

110-T8. When you intend sarcasm, be sure your audience understands it as such.

110-U8. The more potential you have, the longer it takes to fulfill it.

110-V8. I do not necessarily rely on other people's behavior as a guide to my own.

110-W8. Among other things . . . the public is clamoring for more affordable health care. My friends, the politicians will pretend to give it to you. And they sincerely *want* to give it to you, but how can they? The wherewithal to do so is simply *not there*. It is not there mainly for the reasons explained in the last seven lettered Nuggets (110-R9 through 110-X9). If this disease is not corrected, all the tinkering in the world will not solve anything.

In the 1960s in Philadelphia, the Horn & Hardart restaurant chain went out of business. But long before they did so, they stashed away big profits by keeping the unions out (even the prospect of a "sweetheart" contract was not sufficiently tempting). They did this by promising their employees unbelievably large retirement benefits (which they never intended to honor), while paying them slave wages in the meantime. Needless to say the "help" was left high and dry in the end. When our government resorts to hyperinflation, scores of millions will likewise be left high and dry.

A few years earlier Lee Tires of Conshohocken (near Philadelphia) sold out. But the new owners refused to honor all preexisting pension obligations. The former management was shocked by this abandonment—sure they were!

The politicians will express the same shock—as if it could be otherwise when the national *debt* compounds faster than the gross national *product!*

You say I am an alarmist, but does not the Bible (I Cor. 14:8) say: "If the trumpet give an uncertain sound, who shall prepare himself for the battle?" Someone once said that a manager does things right, while a leader does the right thing. America needs both. Right now it has neither.

As the shadows gather, I cannot help but reiterate #67: The great tribulation must be past before the Millennium can come.

110-X8. *It is all too easy for the intellectually arrogant to forget that whatever superiority they may possess is by dint of a genetic accident.* — Givotangi

110-Y8. For every man there's a woman; for every woman there's a man, provided she's willing to double up.

110-Z8. Let the grandstander beware: The dynamics that served to amuse the spectators will return to befool the performer.

110-A9. *Use reason in place of emotion, and hate will be the first casualty.* — Givotangi

110-B9. *Be especially careful not to absorb unto yourself those traits which you battled to eradicate in others.*
— Givotangi

110-C9. We would be better off *without* laws than in having to put up with *bad* laws; but we are clearly advantaged by good law (whatever its merit, the mere fact of enactment gives a law clout).

However, not even good law can surpass the value of "common sense" when properly applied. For those who do apply it and otherwise have a favorable profile, laws would serve better as recommendations than as mandates. I would readily support the spirit of such an intent, codified or not.

Hold on, you might say, this sounds like preferential treatment for a privileged class who tout common sense. Right you are—and we make no apologies for it. When competing rights are balanced, they need to be weighted according to their relative values. It is this degree of latitude in the judgmental process that will set the behavioral bounds.

110-D9a. The following comes from Thomas Sowell, who is a senior fellow at the Hoover Institution on War, Revolution, and Peace.

There is a story, which I hope is apocryphal, that the French police were chasing a criminal who fled into a building in Paris. Their first thought was that they would surround the building. But then they realized that the building was so large, and had so many exits, that they didn't have enough policemen on the scene to do that. So they surrounded the building next door, which was smaller and had fewer exits.

Dr. Sowell says that this pattern of reasoning is not unusual in academic research in the social sciences.

110-D9b. Regarding the sluggish economy, conservative economist Paul McCracken, who was an adviser to President Nixon, says: "We can't admit that our hands are tied and we can't do anything. That would mean our notions of managing the economy are all wrong." . . . good heavens, Paul, don't even think of such a thing. I mean—what would happen if the public ever got wise to our dishonest money system, which is causing most of our grief? You might have to call out the troops to maintain *order* . . . or at least surround the building next door, as we have been wont to do this century.

110-E9. You will know you have awakened to reality when you stop believing in flying saucers. So put to rest those dreams of little aliens and lightning airfoils. They may be seen as nothing more than wishful thinking.

Sorry if I punctured your own airfoil, but at least now you can come down from the clouds and plant your feet on solid ground.

110-F9. Sometimes a lie can lead to a better outcome than the truth, but be careful, it doesn't happen often.

110-G9. Some lawyers like to expound farfetched hypotheses in court for the sole purpose of justifying their position. No argument is too bizarre if it passes their litmus test; never mind that the litmus was a leftover party favor. Claims can be so silly, that even if true they should not be believed. Taking the low road is not the way to high ground. And when the methodology is flawed, you can count on one thing: garbage in; garbage out, and to hell with reason.

110-H9. Let's take a look into the recent Tailhook scandal wherein female Navy personnel were made to walk a gauntlet of pawing, grabbing sailors.

When I was stationed at the Guantanamo Bay, Cuba, Naval Air Station in 1953, off-base liberty consisted of essentially one option; a short boat ride to Caimanera. Then you had a choice, either walk on the sidewalk or walk in the street. The sidewalk left you vulnerable to being grabbed wherever by local ladies who were there for that purpose. But the *street* was off-limits to them. The mistake of the Tailhook convention was there was no "street" provided, no safe harbor to duck into for those who wanted it. You say Tailhook was demeaning to women! I would rather call it freedom of choice for both genders. Now don't be so horrified, ladies, I'm really on your side, but please realize that the civilizing process (of Homo sapiens) takes time, and besides, wouldn't changing human nature before its time be undesirable if it wasn't impossible?

I thought free choice is what the battle of the sexes was all about, didn't you?

110-I9.   In the same manner that doing wrong can grow by feeding on itself, so too will doing good spill beyond its borders, touching a widening circle of lives.

If wrongdoing is now in ascendancy, it is probably due to the difficulty in making ends meet financially. What we can't get one way, we'll get another.

Now consider a different life, one *without* the greed of an exploiting class pauperizing the unsuspecting masses. To live without shackles would find one and all feasting on milk, honey, and affordable furnishings with little reason for folks to misbehave. Happy people have discovered their own lives are bettered when those around them are happy too. This is the way it could be; the pity of it is that it's not yet a reality.

110-J9.   Defend not against imaginary demons. It is enough to contend with real ones.

110-K9.   Any gain that comes from changes made simply for the sake of change deserves no accolades; it is therefore that this benefit loses significance by becoming a stepchild of caprice rather than the godchild of design.

110-L9.   *Good habits are of greatest value where good sense is in shortest supply.*   — GIVOTANGI

110-M9.   *He who discovers for himself what others know only from having been taught, will come to possess an insuperable advantage in that field.*   — GIVOTANGI

110-N9. When there's dirt in the well, it takes more than painting the pump to cleanse the water.

110-O9. *Sometimes our actions are a result of things we have in our head that we don't even know are there.*
— GIVOTANGI

110-P9. Where opportunities for gainful activity are absent, can we not expect strife and despair to metastasize, while vengefully we rail against an unseen enemy?

110-P9.1. To those of us who think we are clever by investing in foreign currencies and securities with their high returns, be prepared for a return of the "interest equalization tax." The last time around it was 11.5% (in the 70s). When times are uncertain, I simply buy junk silver bags (pre-1965) of half dollars. We won't get super rich that way, but will always get a good night's sleep. (as of March, 1993)

110-P9.2. *Bad morals eventually produce bad results. The question is: How bad must the results be before men change their minds?*
— DR. GARY NORTH

110-P9.3. Social Security would be proper if it were administered according to sound actuarial and accounting principles. But in fact it has not been, mutating instead into a chain letter and subject to the statistical reality of a chain letter. Shades of Ponzi, you know what that means!

110-P9.4. Those who dare to dabble in intrigue must be prepared to accept its consequences.

110-P9.5   It is possible to win through attrition; we can advance by merely surviving.

110-P9.6.   According to K.B. Clark: "Pragmatic men of power have had no time or inclination to deal with . . . social morality." But to best facilitate the common good, one can be neither too pragmatic nor too idealistic, which only goes to support once more the validity of the golden mean.

110-P9.7.   The establishment bombards us with issues that are emotionally charged but intellectually diminished. The only purpose for doing this that I can see is to distract our attention from the things that really matter.

110-P9.8.   In Philippians 4:11, Paul writes, ". . . for I have learned, in whatsoever state I am, therewith to be content."

110-P9.9.   Charles Colson, former special counsel to President Richard Nixon, says: "If you want to make a small fortune, let me tell you how. You take a large fortune and put it in a blind trust."

110-P9.10.   Centralized control *could* be preferable to de-centralization, if the one running the show had more than a modicum of good sense and a surfeit of integrity (that's the tough part). For whatever form a governance might take, its success must ultimately reside in the character of those who administer it.

110-P9.11.   He who makes a few million by dint of his work and ability, can rightly be held innocent until proven guilty. But if he makes a few *billion*, it might be more fitting to hold him guilty until proven innocent.

110-P9.12.   Money is a measure of value, whether real or perceived.

110-P9.13.   *DEJA VU: The following is excerpted from a speech by W.H. Harvey, a popular writer on financial matters at the time, delivered in Nashville, Tennessee on December 9, 1895. Harvey's description of the money monopoly and the methods it uses to attain its stranglehold on the republic were prophetic.*

The most vulnerable point of attack in a republic is its finances. Through it the prosperity of a nation may be destroyed. And yet it is the least understood of all political questions by the people.

It may be so manipulated as to destroy the values of your property, to paralyze commerce and industry and to place you in the position of bonded slave to the money power. This statement I have made is an admitted truth by all students of finance, and the least educated man among us in the last two years has begun to realize the truth of it for himself. And yet those who are in a general way the most educated among the people are just entering upon the study of this subject.

Money is the lifeblood of society. All the producers, manufacturers and wage workers of the nation are measuring their property and services in it and using it again to buy other things.

One of the rules that should be applied to any necessity is that there be a normal quantity of it. There is a necessity for so much bread. There is also a necessity for a normal supply of money. If there were laws encouraging the hoarding of wheat that operated to store it away in elevators while people suffered for the want of it, you would be in favor of repealing those laws.

If we have laws that encourage the hoarding of money, the greatest of necessities, and diverting it from the channels of trade, by which the people and the nation are made to suffer for it, and to pay blackmail in order to get it, you should demand the repeal of those laws. And if there is not enough money to answer the normal requirement, you should see that more is made.

You should not leave it to a selfish class of money dealers to say what these laws should be. A cattle man in Kansas who owns 10,000 head of cattle knows that if one-half the other cattle in the nation were wiped out of existence, his 10,000 head of cattle would be worth far more to him after that calamity happened than they are worth now. The money dealer knows this principle and he applies it to his business. It would be a great temptation to the cattle man if he had the power to destroy half the cattle of the world. The temptation has been too great for the money dealers to resist.

Be warned in time that the downfall of all republics was preceded by a refusal to recognize existing evils.

110-P9.14. *The following is based on a 1959 speech by the Hon. Donald Fleming, Canadian Federal Minister of Finance at the time. It is a condensed reprint from MICHAEL JOURNAL, Quebec, Canada.*

If one wants a sound money, it must be linked to sound bases, and not to the changing decisions of the money creators and traffickers. Could money be sound when the conditions for obtaining it are subject to change from one week to the other, according to the auction sale of federal treasury bonds by the government every Thursday?

The monetary system must be linked to the productive capacity of our country, and then it will be as solid as this productive capacity. Access to credit (modern money) must be put automatically *at the service* of productive capacity, and not control it. Then one will no longer hear about depressions or recessions. Money must be issued in relation to the production made, and then it will be the end of fluctuations, the end of the instability that poisons the whole economic life, and that imposes privations of offered goods and services.

At all times, one must see to it that the consumers as a whole may have the capacity to pay for what production can supply them with, and that this purchasing power be distributed so that each one may at least have a sufficient share to purchase the basic necessities; then one will have a sound economy. It will be the consumers as a whole—each consumer according to his share of purchasing power—who will guide the production of the country.

One will have an economy based on needs, and not an economy of exploitation for the benefit of the controllers of money.

110-P9.15. We were warned about Big Brother by the Father of our Country, George Washington, who cautioned, "Government is not reason; it is not eloquence; It is force! Like fire, it is a dangerous servant and a fearful master."

110-P9.16. Our eyesight is not the best when trying to see our own faults; but when it comes to our neighbor's shortcomings, it inexplicably sharpens to 20/20.

110-P9.17. To be dishonest for a just cause is risky, if only for the troublesome habits of mind that we become infixed to.

110-P9.18.   Tomorrow Forever
a poem by Givotangi
Act like you're going to live forever,
and you'll be fine no matter what;
But to act as though there were no tomorrow,
will all but ensure that for you there will not.

110-P9.19.   If you believe in a position, defend it regardless of whence it comes. Should you disagree, stand your ground no matter what others do. Make no pledges that are insincere, cut no deals that are not fair to both. Commit not to the unknown, and do not accept the bad with the good.

110-P9.20.   If a choice had to be made, it would be better to have relief from pain than to have an equivalent dose of pleasure. It is less satisfying to do a job because you like it, than to do it because there is nothing about it that you dislike.

110-P9.21.   I am an amoral person who freely chooses to act in a moral way for pragmatic reasons—so much so that reversion is now out of the question. By rejecting iniquitous behavior my own well-being is unfailingly enhanced.

110-P9.22.   Can you believe that we (through our U.N. surrogates) are now spending more to arm Somalia's combatants that we provide their people in humanitarian relief? It's an old story. My mother used to tell me how we were asked to save the starving Armenians, and before you could say "You're welcome," we were involved in the Great War (World War I).

We need a new emancipation proclamation in this country; emancipate us from supplying the world with arms. Only then can the town crier shout: "America, free at last."

110-P9.23.   *Money is only of value if it doesn't cost you your integrity. There is nothing that I covet so greatly that I would dishonor myself to obtain it.*   – GIVOTANGI

110-P9.24.   Some people say that life is sacred. I say it is simply an event of nature, and a neutral event at that. Deciding whether it is to be or not to be, or altered for whatever reason or purpose, is best determined by circumstances as they exist at the time of decision.

110-P9.25. We are unchurched, but know the church is our friend; we support all peoples, but know that eugenics need not be an evil; we know that rules should be for the unruly, for otherwise they become our baggage, and above all we know it is only through exercising good sense that we can hope to stay free.

110-P9.26. You will know you are "enlightened" when you would reject any ill-gotten goods or monies, even if certain that you will never be caught, and that no one will be the wiser. Although such virtue should not be expected of those who are impoverished, we find that moral habits, be they good or bad, have a momentum of their own. Still, an act of survival is legitimate; an act of greed is not.

110-P9.27. It is a sad truth that to succeed in business today a person must often take advantage of the unwary in order to remain competitive. And how often will being up front land you a decent job? It is who you know or who do I need to see? If you're too straitlaced for that there is no room for you at the inn. It's become every man for himself. And the boss (unless self-employed), is more concerned with not wanting to know about irregularities than he is with the irregularities themselves.

It is when the honest run out of allies that they too will be compromised. Someday the battered underpinnings will not support the bridge when the train crosses over it. And when do we stop riding the train? It is better to be a year too early than five minutes too late.

110-P9.28. Words have no value if their source has no integrity. Take the motto of the Bolshevist Revolution for example. It was not the discreditable "The dictatorship of the proletariat. Down with democracy!" as we have been led to believe. In fact, it was the exact contrary: "Long live democracy and down with dictatorship." But they don't want us to know that, lest we catch on to the same rhetorical deception that is used today.

Just remember that the words of a knave are as questionable as his character.

110-P9.29. The progression of morality:

1. The masses. Unthinking robots who are morally adrift or fanatically inclined and subject to herd instincts. (The most numerous segment.)

2. Moral Believers who care, are well-meaning and for the most part responsible individuals. (The next most numerous group who, if allied with #3, have the potential between them to overcome #1 and their recondite manipulators, #4.)

3. The secular humanists are viewed as a nontheistic religion antagonistic to traditional religion but who, like #2, also care, are well-meaning and for the most part responsible individuals. (In numbers they run a distant third.)

4. The next step up is actually a step backwards, and therein lies the problem, which is that certain men of dangerous brilliance at the pinnacles of power throughout the world (prelates included) have only developed this far. The world is corrupt because those in control have not reached stage 5, the final step in human development.

Stage 4 is comprised of these misguided unbelievers whose vision is limited to the belief that their happiness can best come without regard to or at the expense of the happiness of others. (Those who would rule the world for their own perceived benefit only, are the clear and present danger of our time and of all time.)

What makes this group so intimidating and different from group 1 is that they know what they're doing, they have no scruples or compunctions, and they are highly intelligent. (Their numbers are fewer still than #3.)

5. Then we have the last stage of moral evolution, and the rarest breed of all: Total unbelievers as #4, but amoral rather than immoral, and not antagonistic to traditional religion as is #3. But more significantly they realize that our own happiness can be best achieved when we help others to be happy too. We call this condition enlightened self-interest that so far has come to only a chosen few, although now that it has been discovered, the way is open to all who would accept it. Now we can lead them to where they can see the light for themselves.

In all of the above, there is one obvious question that begs to be answered... If a person's attainment of stage 4 is actually advancement which comes to those of superior intellect, why has it become a regressive development relative to their behavior toward others?

Here it is: These people have lost their Belief in what their culture had inculcated them with. In true reactionary fashion they therefore also rejected the good parts of that belief as well, erroneously lumping all elements together and in effect throwing out the baby with the bath water. The bath water is supernaturalism and the trappings that go with it.

But—and here's the punch line—the bath water served a purpose. Without it the job of cleansing the baby was not possible. The barbarians would have captured our souls for all time. An intermediate stage of Belief was needed to buy time, time to allow vulnerable children to mature into self-reliant adults able to choose their own destinies. The "bath water" turns out to be holy water, cleansing neosapiens of the inherited original sin of self-interest.

Enter enlightened self-interest, the process now germinating which will allow us to be born again, this time under the secular banner of reason, and win out in the end. In this uncertain world, our country and our civilization must keep reaching higher in order to survive.

Look out world, stage 5 is about to spread its wings, and in the adopted words of Dr. Martin Luther King Jr.: "We shall overcome."

110-P9.30. I eat what I want, and I do what I want, but unlike with today's lawless renegades, I am the better for it, and so is society. In other words, I live now the way that you've been told you will live when you get to heaven. Well, friends, the only heaven you can ever know will have an earthly boundary. Now I suspect you're just dying to learn my little secret (pun intended) . . . so here it is. And it's so simple it seems odd that no one has discovered it before. ***Train yourself to want only those things that are good for you*** (while bearing in mind the enlightened self-interest concept: We best please ourselves when we please others). Do this and you can safely give in to all your desires, for you will *only* be desiring those things that are good for you in a lasting way.

So noble an idea, and yet so easy to do once you've learned the knack. Master this and you too will have found heaven on earth. [January 4, 1994]

110-P9.31. I am not a prisoner of enforced morality. Rather, I have chosen moral behavior as a consequence of free will, and hence shall retain my virtue even as others, due to uncertainty and disillusionment, are abandoning theirs.

110-P9.32. My mentor in the game of checkers, Chief Bassett, was once asked how he planned to defeat his opponent. He replied, "I don't know; he will show me."

110-P9.33. How does one choose between the Liberals' philosophy which is based on the idea of "fairness," and the conservatives' doctrine which advocates "individualism?" Obviously the masses will favor the former, while achievers prefer the latter—if you'll allow me to make a generalization. Whichever group prevails at the moment, the all too human nature which both are heir to takes over and the "in" group oversteps the line to take advantage of the "outs." The answer to the question can be sidestepped by combining enlightened self-interest with the Givotangi Parity Swap described in #186. This would lay to rest many issues that now divide, and unite us as a free people in harmony. Now read on.

What has actually come to pass is this: The "achievers" at the very top, never satisfied with what they already have, long ago realized they were vastly outnumbered, so they conspired to fool the masses by pretending to be part of them. Their big chance came when they funded communism in Russia by backing the likes of Lenin whose catch phrase "Peace; land for the peasants" (90% were then peasants) was the ultimate hypocrisy. You hear much the same doubletalk from our politicians today. If the manipulators could control movements that were ostensibly set up to help the common people, they could eventually reign supreme. This could hardly be done in a world comprised of individualists, which explains why the hidden hierarchy is moving us towards Socialism, big government, and dependency, and why they would spend $3 million to entrap a white separatist in Idaho. His defense attorney Gerry Spence said: "What happened to Randy Weaver can happen to anybody in this country." Then we suffered through the Waco, Texas, holocaust. This is someone's way of sending out a message to those who might dare to safeguard their liberties with force when the showdown comes.

Maybe you didn't know that the money kings also funded

Hitler initially (to cover all bets), but when they saw he could not be controlled and wanted to be fuhrer all by himself, they plotted America's entry into World War II, goading Hitler into declaring war on us first (this caused it to *be* a World War). Overnight America miraculously found jobs for everyone in the country. (You mean to tell me we couldn't do the same thing in peacetime making consumer goods instead of weapons of war?) People forgot that the great pontificator, Franklin Roosevelt, had assured us that no American boys would be sent to fight in foreign wars. I believe his words were: "I have said it before and I will say it again and again and again . . ." Nothing ever changes.

Cryptic Nugget #177 begins: Left is right . . . By this I mean that most leftist movements today are controlled by fascists (but not realized by the many sincere supporters who would be horrified if they knew) who can enslave humanity only if they can dupe the multitudes into believing that the Trojan horse is really a white horse ridden by a knight (of their choosing). To see things as they are we need to open our eyes.

In the beginning of a change, the patriot is a scarce man, and brave, and hated and scorned. When his cause succeeds, the timid join him, for then it costs nothing to be a patriot.

– MARK TWAIN

110-P9.34. Until you've discovered reasons to violate the rules, it's best to follow them.

110-P9.35. Now that Russia—at least for the moment—has dropped out of the game, who is the big meddler in the world today? Why, it's the U.S., the self-declared paragon of moral rectitude. The hypocrisy of the "we are on God's side" propaganda before each armed intrusion is so blatant that it cannot withstand even the most cursory examination, as we prepare to make the world safe for democracy again. Or is that safe for the internationalists and the overseers of the Global Plantation?

Well, don't worry about it. Clinton says it's the right thing to do, and we know he is motivated only by the highest of moral principles. He told us so himself.

110-Q9. When the cosmos deviates from the predictable, the astronomer knows there must be a reason for it. And I know that having inflation and debt almost every year for the past 90 years is not the result of biblical injunction, nor is it natural—there must be a reason for this too.

If you read the remainder of #110, you will acquaint yourself with a point of view regarding this aberration.

110-R9.
We can be free if we can identify the enemy.

Not one to mince words, Senator Louis T. McFadden, for 22 years Chairman, United States Banking and Currency Commission, made this rather remarkable statement: "The Federal Reserve system is one of the most corrupt institutions the world has ever seen."

And how about this: "The modern banking system manufactures money out of nothing. The process is perhaps the most astounding piece of sleight of hand that was ever invented." Major L.B. Angus said that.

Here's one I especially like: "Bankers own the earth. Take it away from them but leave them the power to create money, and, with a flick of the pen, they will create enough money to buy it back again. Take this great power away from them and all great fortunes like mine will disappear and they ought to disappear, for then this would be a better and happier world to live in. But, if you want to continue to be the slaves of the bankers and pay the cost of your own slavery, then let bankers continue to create money and control credit." So said Sir Josiah Stamp, President, Bank of England.

What is it that makes these men so indignant? Perpetual skimming. Thomas A. Edison's rhetorical question sums it up: "The people are the basis for government credit. Why, then, cannot the people have benefit of their own gilt-edge credit by receiving non-interest bearing currency (United States notes) instead of bankers receiving the benefit of the people's credit in interest-bearing bonds?" Edison also said: "If our Nation can issue a dollar bond it can issue a dollar bill. The element that makes the bond good makes the bill good also. It is absurd to say that our country can issue $30 million in bonds and not $30 million in currency. Both are promises to pay, but one promise fattens the usurers, and the other helps the people." Common sense cannot be defined any better than that; please read it again.

Then understand this: As long as we use Federal Reserve notes as our currency it is mathematically impossible to balance the budget. Also, it is impossible to have lasting relief from taxes as long as we use Federal Reserve notes for our currency. The only thing that Federal Reserve notes guarantee is inflation.

Federal Reserve notes are bank notes, and the piper must be paid. With our entire population paying unnecessary interest it is no surprise our nation is suffering recession, unemployment and crushing taxation. The way we finance political campaigns bribes Congress to use Federal Reserve notes as America's medium of exchange. So our Democracy is shot full of holes by interest-charging bank notes.

The one thing Congress absolutely will not touch, except for Henry Gonzalez of Texas and one or two others, is our deceptive money system. For 78 years Congress has prevented the Government Accounting Office from auditing the Federal Reserve system. Congress is bloated with contributions from the money men who forbid any consideration of abolishing Federal Reserve notes and replacing them with United States notes.

Humans require water, economies require a medium of exchange—money. The *source* of money is all-important. Whoever controls the source, controls the nation. Any government worth two cents would guard the source of money with its last drop of blood. Just like the colonists did in the American Revolution. The silly governments in this so-called civilized world of ours flop on their bellies and give away the *source* of money to money pirates called central bankers. In order to fool the people they are supposed to protect, all the government officials go through the "government bonds for banker's money and print the money so it looks like government money" charade. The privately owned Federal Reserve has control over our economic water supply: currency. A defective money system assures a defective economy.

Why are so very few aware of all this? Big money can buy almost anything. They can and do influence the media. Big money men suppress what they don't want us to know and they hire economists and propaganda experts to put into our minds what they want us to believe. To get the unvarnished truth, one must refer to "non-establishment" sources.

It does seem unbelievable that what is going on is really going on. For 40 years, Congressman Wright Patman tried to tell us these things, but we just didn't understand. Echoes of the warnings coming from whistle-blowers were purposely muted, and since the official attitude was (and is) that misleading us is okay but telling us the truth isn't, we never listened to the voice of reason. [distilled from a work from Colonel Howle, Box 31053#161, Laguna Hills, California]

110-S9. Let me go on: Nelson Aldrich was a banker who bought a senate seat to promote the big, big bankers of New York City to Central Bankers for the USA. Ah, money . . . the sins committed for thee! We should consider this. Central bankers are human beings just like you and me. We all do the best we can for ourselves. It so happens that the best for central bankers is the worst for people who work at useful jobs.

Paul Warburg was one of those Germans who come to this country and speak in thick German accents. Following is the gist of what he said in 1910 when he told Senator Aldrich and the other secret plotters on Jekyle Island, "Fellow conspirators, we got big trouble. More Americans think than I realized. To set them up for shearing, we've got to lie to them. We must convince them they need a central bank. Face facts. Hamilton's central bank was allowed to die and the Americans said, 'Good riddance.' Nicholas Biddle's central bank was starved to death by President Andrew Jackson after he called Biddle a viper."

Warburg drew a deep breath and continued, "So to make our plot work, we've got to call our proposed central bank by another name. We'll call it The Federal Reserve system and establish 12 branch banks all over the nation. Clever, what? Federal makes it sound like part of the federal government and by legal puffery we will disguise that we are the owners. Reserve and system are more words that will fool the people. We won't explain system means the systematic removal of money from working people in such a devious way that they'll never know what is going on. Of course, the money will come to us and we'll share it with the politicians so they will support us."

Another deep breath, "The so-called branches are a stroke of genius on my part. What senator will pass up a Federal Reserve Bank built in his state? As you know we will run everything from New York through the Federal Reserve Bank there."

It took three more years and a heckuva lot of money for the plotters to foist the third central bank on the United States. Jefferson, Lincoln, Jackson! Oh, how we needed you in 1913.

The Toll on Our Currency: The money the federal government pays out for interest is, in effect, a toll on our medium of exchange. Specifically, the toll is on dollars entitled FEDERAL RESERVE NOTE. This toll on the paper we are using as our national currency acts as a hidden tax on transactions forcing prices ever upward. The government should pay no interest, the government should borrow no money.

The Toll on U.S. Bonds and other Securities: This is an old reference and I apologize for that, but knowing how the partnership of Congress-Federal Reserve works the situation is probably worse today.

As of 1964, Congressman Wright Patman reported that a law enacted by Congress "takes money from the taxpayer and gives it to these dealers. It forces the government to pay a toll for borrowing money. It makes it impossible for one agency of the government to buy U.S. government securities from another without paying tribute to these 21 dealers, overwhelmingly located on Wall Street."

We taxpayers are paying tribute to the money pirates of Wall Street, also known as the Federal Reserve Oligarchy.

Fortunately, Thomas Jefferson told us how to protect ourselves: Bar the U.S. government from borrowing money. Then it would never print another bond or interest-paying security.

Backing for Money: Money does not require backing by a precious metal. Precious metals are valuable but not money unless used as such. Money does require backing to hold its value. The amount of money a government spends or loans out must later be balanced by money paid back in.

Distribution of Money: We have maldistribution of money in the USA. The super-rich have too much *and the lower third of our population* has too little. Congress writes our laws, that is to say, Congress writes the rules by which all of us try to fit ourselves into our economy. Citizens are homeless because of those rules. Citizens are jobless because of those rules. We have Americans who are smart enough to put men on the moon. Perhaps Congress should ask their help' to revise and improve the laws that govern our economy.

Congress, of course, will ignore this: "The government (the U.S. Treasury, *not* the Federal Reserve Banks) should create, issue and circulate all the currency and credit needed to satisfy the spending power of the Government and the buying power of consumers . . . By the adoption of these principles . . . Money will cease to be master and become the servant of humanity." Says who? The wisest of men, Abraham Lincoln, that's who.

We have two money problems:

1. Who is to own the national currency of the United States? Please visualize dollar bills rolling off the printing press. I say the United States Treasury should own those dollar bills and *not* a private bank named the Federal Reserve system. As of this date, The Federal Reserve is the owner of the national currency of the U.S. I say this is wrong.

2. Should we permit banks to work the "old goldsmith's scam"? In ye old days of the goldsmiths, citizens passed from hand to hand some cash (gold coins) but mostly they used the convenience of pieces of paper i.e. the goldsmith's receipts. Today we citizens pass from hand to hand some cash (Federal Reserve notes) but mostly we use the convenience of pieces of paper called checks which are written orders directing the payment of money by the bank named on the check.

The goldsmiths wrote about nine receipts for each gold coin they had in their vaults. Do you think that it was okay for a goldsmith to loan nine dollars when he had only one?

Should our bankers be required to keep in their vaults the amount of cash (Federal Reserve notes) that their loans represent? Or, should they be permitted to loan nine "bank credit" dollars for each dollar they actually have? If it is okay for bankers to loan the eight dollars they don't have, do you think it fair that they can and the rest of us can't? Somehow, it doesn't sound like a 100% democracy at work.

The Fed pays back its profits gimmick:

Apologists for the Federal Reserve point out that every year the Fed pays back to the U.S. Treasury its "profits" which it calls interest on Federal Reserve notes. This is an accounting gimmick. For each $100 the Fed steals from us with its left hand it gives back one dollar with its right hand. Margaret Thoren, in *Figuring Out the Fed,* gives the facts. For 1983, the U.S. debt, which is created by the Federal Reserve money system, had increased to $1.4 trillion. The Fed paid back to the Treasury $14 billion. Subtract $14 billion from $1.4 trillion. This "payback" reduced our debt from $1,400,000,000,000.00 to $1,386,000,000,000.00.

You can depend on this. For every dollar the Fed pays back to the Treasury your nation owes about $100 more. And you, my friend, are paying interest on the whole thing.

It is utterly stupid for the government to give away its monopoly power to create its own money, and then after creation by a private bank, borrow it back and pay interest on it. That is so asinine that I can hardly believe it is true, although I know it is. How can persons sane enough to head governments do such a crazy thing? Do not be misled, a democracy must own its own money, or else those who do own it will eventually own all the rest of us.

It is tragic beyond description that political pressures prevent the United States from having an honest money system.

But this injustice will not stand forever. Reformer Ron Carey upset the old Teamsters apple cart. Will a shackled Samson (or Samoht) likewise be a key to the mighty Fed's demise and bring down the temple along with its moneylenders?

The Song of the Red Taped Horsey Cart

We sing this song to make us all smart,
This song of the red taped horsey cart.

Though money doesn't grow on trees,
It's manufactured with great ease,

So it does seem strange,
That our government did arrange,

To manufacture our money, the cart before the horse.
It really is a farce,

Instead of creating money and buying what we need,
Our silly government prints bonds with interest growing
    like a weed,

Bonds buy only one thing, they buy the Federal Reserve's
    bank notes,
Which profit the bankers whose contributions buy our
    votes.

Buying bank notes is a cinch bet,
All you are buying is debt, debt, debt,

As every day the interest we owe on bonds compounds,
The deeper in debt we sink, senators and congressmen this
    astounds,

They cry borrow more, raise more taxes! We cry get smart!
Put the horse before the cart.

Do not think! It would endanger our political leaders.

"The stork brought you." Thinking people know that storks can't create human beings.

Thinking people, were they to think about it, would realize that only the power of government can create currency. Money creation is a power of government. Bankers *do not have the power* to create money—*unless* it is stolen from the people and given to bankers by the politicians who gain control of a government.

Do not think! If you do you will realize that Uncle Sam should create his own currency instead of creating IOU's.

Do not think! If you do, you will throw the Federal Reserve into the garbage where it belongs.

Do not think! By gritting your teeth, you can learn to accept recession, unemployment and crushing taxation brought to you courtesy of the Congress-Federal Reserve Bankers Partnership.

110-T9.   The Trenchant Trilogy . . .

First, a fable for our time:
Banker Box in Gumboland

J. Martindale Exeter Box, the central banker, was on vacation. Falling asleep flying to South Africa, he was rudely awakened, handed a parachute and shoved out the door. "We found out you are a central banker," the shovers yelled after him.

Box fell 40,000 feet, landing in the garden of Chief Gumbo's palace. Gumbo invited Box to lunch. "Lucky break for me," said Gumbo. "I've been watching the wars on TV and the democracies have the best airplanes, tanks, bombs and the most atomic bonds in reserve. So I want democracy for Gumboland. With our old-time socialism all we got are these spears cut from trees. As you are a central banker, you surely must be an outstanding example of the finest virtues of democracy at its shining best."

Box said, "I've never heard a central banker described in just that way before."

Gumbo said, "Don't be modest. I want you to tell me how to convert to democracy and start ordering tanks and things. You can do that for me, can't you?"

"Well, uh, yes," said Box. "You bet I can. I can fix you up with democracy, free enterprise, capitalism, free trade, a mountain of debt and a Republican Party. If you prefer a Democrat Party, I'll fix you up with one of those. Actually, there's no difference between Democrats and Republicans so you'd just as well have a one party system."

Gumbo said, "No frills, please. Just the Simple Stuff."

A man with a necklace of bones came in. Gumbo said, "This is Whiz, our medicine man and witch doctor. In his spare time, between spells and incantations, he is my treasurer. Please explain democracy to him and tell him how to order airplanes, smart bombs and things."

Box said, "How do, Whiz. Gumboland is in debt how much?"

"We have no debt, we use Abraham Lincoln's money system. We use only $1 bills up through $100, but I enjoy looking at this picture of a Lincoln $10,000 United States note."

Crisis! All members of the International Brotherhood of Central Bankers swear to murder their own mothers before they will allow any nation to employ Abraham Lincoln's money system. It does not matter if the system is called a tallies system or a New York Colony system, no nation is to be allowed to use it. If one nation used an honest money system, other nations would be sure to follow. Box thought fast. He must convince Whiz to change to a borrowed money system. Otherwise the Brotherhood would be forced to order the president to send in the marines and destroy Gumboland for its own good.

Box said, "Whiz, Chief Gumbo wants a democracy. Now I ask you, what is the most successful democracy on earth?"

"Switzerland."

"No, no. It's the United States. What nation has the most debt?"

"The United States."

"Correct, and there's your answer. The more debt you have, the more democracy you have. Let me read you the timeless words of Alexander Hamilton, first Secretary of the Treasury and the man who led the United States into endless debt. 'A national debt, if it is not excessive, will be a national blessing; a powerful cement of union; a necessity for keeping up taxation, and a spur to industry.' Understand?"

"Sounds like a man trying to start a central bank."

Box said, "You hit the nail on the head. That's exactly what happened. Hamilton bribed congressmen and fathered the United States' first central bank. The ungrateful people killed it, and the second one, but the third one is thriving."

Whiz said, "Debt is good?"

"Yes, yes. As Hamilton said, it is a national blessing. The bigger the debt, the bigger the blessing. Debt is wonderful. The more debt you have, the more money you can owe. Do you know what a bond is?"

"Certainly, I'm a Yale man. A bond is a debt instrument."

Box said, "To get started, we need an engraver."

Whiz called in Elstinko, who was the outdoor plumbing specialist but did a little engraving on the side. "Call him El for short."

Box said, "El, engrave some Gumboland currency and some Gumboland Bonds. The bonds will pay 6%, uh, 10%. It's easier to figure 10% interest than 6%."

The next day the engraving was finished and Box printed ten million dollars in currency and instructed Whiz to print ten million dollars in bonds.

Box put the money in one stack and told Whiz to put the bonds in a second stack. Then he said, "As your central banker the money is mine and as treasurer of Gumboland the bonds are yours. Now, I have good news for you. We modern central bankers do as Hamilton did. You do as I say and the political rewards for you and the Chief will be very, very nice indeed."

Whiz gagged which Box took as acquiescence. Box said, "Take a look at this dollar bill on top of my stack of money. See, in large letters it says GUMBOLAND CURRENCY, and in small letters, FEDERAL RESERVE NOTE. I'm calling my central bank 'Federal Reserve,' same as in the USA."

Whiz said, "Why bother to print the name of your central bank on Gumboland currency?"

"So that everybody will know that your dollar bills are genuine bank notes."

There was a slight pause. Then, Box said, "Whiz, Chief Gumbo wants to buy modern armament of all kinds. That takes tons of money. As your central banker I will take care of you. I'll provide you with all the money you want by buying your bonds. Any time you want more money, all you have to do is print more bonds. One of your big advantages in having a central bank is that my money is limitless, I can always print more for just the cost of printing. Well, it's time now for your first sale. Here is my ten million dollars, give me your ten million in bonds."

They exchanged the stacks of paper. Box now had the pieces of paper named bonds and Whiz had the pieces of paper named money. Box said, "You have now borrowed ten million dollars from my central bank. At the end of a year, you will owe me $10,000,000.00 plus $1,000,000.00 in interest for a total of $11,000,000.00. See how smoothly my Federal Reserve system works?"

Whiz said, "Very clearly. This Federal Reserve system of yours means debt for the government and interest charges for the people."

Box said, "Whiz, you've got it! Government debt always means interest charges for the people to pay with their taxes and that's the key to efficient government. I quoted Alexander Hamilton a moment ago. You may have missed this. He said debt is good because it is, 'a necessity for keeping up taxation.' Think on that. You can keep your citizens in line with taxes. Tax them enough and they will eat out of your hand and lick your boots for just a promise of relief. In the USA, congressmen and senators adore the system and spend half their time thinking up new ways to stomp the people down with a greater tax load. They call raising taxes cutting taxes. This fools voters long enough for these political liars to get reelected."

Whiz said, "Well, I'll tell the chief what you said."

"Very good. Be sure to quote Alexander Hamilton saying that government debt is a national blessing. Then tell him that I calculate that eleven million dollars is about all the blessing you can handle the first year, but fortunately our Federal Reserve system has an escalation feature. Automatically, your blessing will be greater every year the rest of your life. And this may be too good to believe! Your children are included in our plan. Actually, some of them may be overblessed."

Satisfied that he had done a good day's work, Box celebrated in the local night spots.

The next morning, Box was awakened by two warriors with spears and escorted to Chief Gumbo's conference room. Gumbo and Whiz were there.

Chief Gumbo said, "Box, we know a con man when we see one. We want no more of your bull that debt is happiness.

However, you extolled debt is happiness so much I have decided to let you enjoy some. This morning I am going to be a central banker and you are going to be the victimized government."

Box turned pale but managed to say, "No, I can't agree with that."

A warrior nudged Box in the ribs with the point of a spear.

"On second thought, I can agree with that."

Whiz said, "During the night, we incinerated the bonds you designed and substituted these. Here, have one."

Box read the bond and turned paler than before. The bond stated that J. Martindale Exeter Box would pay the bearer one million dollars at 10% interest.

Whiz said, "Would you like to sell your bond?"

Box looked at a spear under his nose and said, "Yes." Whiz handed a million dollars to Box and Box handed the bond to Whiz.

Whiz said, "Box, you have now borrowed $1,000,000.00 at 10% interest from Gumboland. At the end of a year you will owe us $1,100,000.00.

Box turned white as a sheet and was barely able to grasp the piece of paper chief Gumbo handed him. Gumbo said, "This is your receipt for the office space you bought from me. It came to exactly one million dollars."

"Didn't know I bought any," mumbled Box as the meanest looking of the two warriors took the million dollars from him.

"Wazzo is my IRS," chuckled Gumbo.

Box said, "I really don't need an office. I have a strong urge to return to the USA where the officials cooperate."

Gumbo said, "Not yet. I have your bond for a million dollars bearing interest at 10%. At the end of this year you will owe me $1,100,000.00. How do you propose to pay?"

"I'll put it in the mail the minute I get back to the United States."

Gumbo said, "I wouldn't trust a central banker at ten feet. You know and I know that governments are foolish for placing themselves under the thumb of central bankers. Central banks should never be permitted to create money. Creation of money should be a monopoly of a government's treasury department. Central bank functions should be a mere branch of the treasury department."

Box had never been lectured to before. He was accustomed to flim-flamming sympathetic senators on TV and sending them campaign contributions through carefully selected channels.

Gumbo said, "I'll make you an offer you can't refuse. I will buy back your office space and that will satisfy the principal of your debt and I will discount the interest to 5% provided you pay me now. $50,000.00, please."

Box wired for the money. It arrived within the hour. Box paid Gumbo and asked permission to leave.

Gumbo said, "You are an heir of Alexander Hamilton who favored for the United States a government by a few powerful men—an oligarchy. His great opponent, Thomas Jefferson, fought for a democracy and would have won had he been able to get into the Constitution his amendment to prevent the government from borrowing money. Hamilton won the battle from the grave. In 1913, a bribed United States Congress delivered the United States into the hands of internationally minded bankers. Today the Great Republic is an oligarchy controlling a democracy. It has the trappings of democracy but the actual power is exercised by a few powerful men—the majority owners of your central bank, the Federal Reserve system. You may go now."

No sooner had he arrived in the USA than a letter came from Gumboland. It read, "Discounted interest considered income. Remit $10,000.00 by the 10th of next month or severe penalties and interest will accrue. Signed: Wazzo, Commissioner of Gumboland Internal Revenue Service."

Second, a dialogue:
Paul and Sam

Time: Prior to 1913.

Characters: Two 10-year-old boys. Sam, honest but slow of wit, grew up to be Uncle Sam and took over the federal government. Paul, precocious. Even at ten years of age his hero is Meyer Amschel Rothschild, the smartest banker who ever lived until Paul came along. Grew up to be Paul Warburg, multimillionaire banker and father of the Federal Reserve system.

Sam: Look, Paul, I got a printing press for Christmas and I'm printing dollar bills.

Paul: You must not do that. Money comes from banks.

Sam: If money comes from banks, why do all dollar bills have UNITED STATES OF AMERICA on them?

Paul: Congress misleads the people by printing those words on all bank notes. Banks create and loan money. The United States of America collects taxes and fights other nations.

Sam: Oh.

(Paul was laughing on the inside. Sam was so stupid, ignorant and easy to hoodwink! Paul was only 10 but he already knew that bankers should be restricted to loaning money and never allowed to create it. No matter what the name or profession of the criminal, counterfeiting is counterfeiting.)

Sam: Okay, you be the banker and print some money for me.

(Paul prints some dollar bills, which Sam looks over.)

Sam: You are calling your dollars FEDERAL RESERVE NOTES.

Paul: That's fancier than calling them plain bank notes. Also, when you grow up to be Uncle Sam you will be spending a lot of my bank notes and I feel sure we will both want the public to think it is your money. FEDERAL RESERVE printed on my bank notes will sound like they are federal government money.

Sam: Sounds like a bunch of foolishness to me but okay, I'll go along. Gimme some bank notes, I want to buy some candy.

Paul: I'm a banker. I don't give money, I loan money. You've got to put up collateral.

Sam: What's collateral?

Paul: Farms, homes, real estate, valuable things that bankers like to foreclose. I'll tell you what I'll do. You print some bonds that will pay me 8% interest and I'll give you all the money you want in exchange for your bonds.

Sam: That sounds dumb. Why print two pieces of paper when one will do. I think I'll go ahead and print my own money which I will entitle UNITED STATES NOTES.

Paul: As your banker, I tell you that you must not create your own money. For your own good, I'll pay Congress to stop you.

Sam: You bankers certainly complicate money creation. I'm not going to ask why. Not even Einstein could make sense of it.

(Sam prints some bonds paying 8% interest.)

Sam: Here are some interest-bearing bonds for your money. Since we are using my printing press to print your currency which does not pay me any interest, I think you should pay me for the use of my press.

Paul: Okay, I'll pay you 2½¢ for each FEDERAL RESERVE NOTE I print. On top of that I'll give you candy free.

(But on a $20 bill, for example, Paul—by loaning it back—will receive 16¢ *every year* as profit. In his generosity he refunds 90% of "earnings.")

Sam: What a good deal, free candy! Okay, it's settled then.

(Sam thinks to himself: That Paul is one clever fellow. Any country sure would be lucky to have the benefit of his services.)

And third, a parable:

Once upon a time there was a congressman named Joe. In a dream he was visited by the Spirit of his Forefathers. The Spirit said, "I'm leaving you a priceless gift. You will see it when you awaken."

When Joe awoke he was amazed to find a goose in his bed. Thankful the goose hadn't relieved himself, or herself, Joe grabbed the goose and threw it out the door. Just in time! The goose squatted a bit and let go. Let go a golden egg! Joe charged out the door, pocketed the egg, kissed the goose, built it a pen, bought it the biggest bag of goose feed in town and went to see a gold assayer. "This egg is pure gold," said the assayer.

In all the excitement, Joe had not seen the envelope left on his dresser by the Spirit of his Forefathers. An ill wind arose and blew the envelope behind the dresser.

On the way home from the assayer, Joe met a man with shifty eyes who was walking with a rooster. "Biggest rooster I ever saw," said Joe.

"He's got to be big. He lays thirty pieces of silver at a time."

Joe said, "I've never understood farm problems but I thought hens laid eggs."

Shifty said, "I didn't say this rooster lays eggs, I said he lays thirty pieces of silver all at one time, plink, plink, plink."

"You aren't going to believe this, but I've got a goose that lays golden eggs. She just came to work this morning."

"Real gold?"

"Pure solid gold. Feel how heavy this one is. No wonder it goes klunk when she lays it."

Shifty inspected the egg and said, "You are in serious trouble. President Roosevelt just this morning signed the bill making it illegal for Americans to own gold."

In disbelief, "Even congressmen?"

"Especially congressmen. But I can save you provided you follow my instruction to the letter."

"How?"

"It so happens that I wrote the bill. I am a central banker and we central bankers always get special privileges from gullible governments. It is okay for me to own gold. I will do you the great favor of taking from you the goose that lays the golden eggs. In return, I'll slip these thirty pieces of silver into your pocket while nobody is watching. And, on top of that, I'll give you my giant rooster."

So the deal was done. Every morning after that the banker got a golden egg. Joe is still waiting for the rooster to come through with more silver. Only a congressman could believe that roosters lay anything. (If we want to make a double-entendre out of that, we can say that roosters do to hens what congressmen do to citizens.)

The banker built an enormous mansion on top of a big hill. Joe goes up there every two years, hat in hand, and pleads for contributions. Shifty gives him thirty pieces of silver from time to time as a reminder of who owns who.

It was only the other day that Joe found the envelope that was hidden behind his dresser. Inside was a document, "This is your Constitution speaking to you. You are hereby empowered to create the medium of exchange for the United States, her national currency. You will have this power as long as you keep the goose that lays the golden eggs. Whatever you do, never give away your power over America's currency to a central bank, especially one named 'The Federal Reserve System.'"

110-U9. *At this point we interpose a verity from* THE NATIONAL EDUCATOR, *Fullerton, California.*

You may not be aware that our lawmakers have given a priority rating to interest debt so that payment of interest is the first charge against the budget, currently 14 percent of the *entire* budget. That means that taxpayers have to pay many billions out of their earnings, while the banks collect the billions on securities bought with checkbook dollars created as ledger entries. This is such a scandal it is no wonder that the late Professor Henry Simons said, "It is difficult to conceive of a worse system than the current one." In the same vein noted author Eric Butler wrote that, "Modern governments and the powers that control them represent the anti-Christ, and their financial and economic policies must be challenged by all Christians." [Most non-Christians are also good people, Eric, so please count us in too—and that includes atheists like myself.]

110-V9. And if you can handle one more asseveration, it comes from Robert Hemphill, who served for eight years as credit manager of the Federal Reserve Bank of Atlanta.

He observed: "If the banks create ample synthetic money, we are prosperous; if not, we starve. We are absolutely without a permanent monetary system. When one gets a complete grasp upon the picture, the tragic absurdity of our hopeless position is almost incredible, but there it is. It (debt money) is the most important subject intelligent persons can investigate and reflect upon. It is so important that our present civilization may collapse unless it is widely understood and the defects remedied very soon."

The rub is that so few of the policy makers have any sense of this truth themselves.

110-W9.
A Short History on the Debt System of Finance
by James P. Fitzgerald, THE NATIONAL EDUCATOR

Students of history will recall the year 1694 as a red letter year in the history of the West, the year that King William the

Third of England agreed to let William Paterson and his friends form a bank called the Bank of England. The agreement was that Paterson would collect from public subscribers the sum of 1,200,000 pounds sterling and lend the total to the King at eight percent to help finance the war with France.

In turn, the bank received the astounding privilege of printing currency notes to the amount of the loan. This agreement sealed the bank's right to create money, a right historically belonging to government alone. Having secured the sovereign right to create money the bank naturally acquired all the prestige and power belonging to unlimited wealth.

This was the beginning of the so-called debt system of finance which has throttled every nation in the West. This debt system changed the nature of banks which had always been exclusively "lenders of money" to "creators of money." Admittedly this change was accomplished with the greatest secrecy and carried out with the cleverest propaganda that money could buy.

Some of that money bought ready cooperation from the professional economists as noted by the authors of *Money—The Decisive Factor.*

"It may well be asked why generations of professional economists were content to talk about everything under the sun . . . but to keep silent about the one thing that really mattered, the exploitation of money for profit. They presented the puzzling spectacle of a body of men devoted to the pursuit of knowledge who appeared to be determined to look in every direction except the right one."

This blindness does not puzzle students of economic history who are familiar with the taboo put in place by the money power: "The money system is not to be discussed." That is why it is very rare to find a bank confessing outright in its literature that bank loans are money that never existed until entered on the bank ledger as a deposit. Incidentally, entering bank loans as deposits is part of the policy of concealing the creation of money.

The results of this diabolical debt system can be seen in the economic distress and serious labor, production and distribution problems which plague every nation in the West. The widespread unemployment breeds untold domestic and civil evils including broken marriages, alcohol abuse, and rebellious street gangs, the product of a disintegrating social order.

Our most urgent task is to spend the time necessary to educate ourselves on money, and especially on the importance of debt-free money.

It will take a real hat trick to correct this habit. Wright Patman concluded: "One of the unwritten political commandments of Washington is: 'Thou shalt not get involved in a controversy with the banking industry.' " We shall see.

110-X9. *Has any nation refused the bankers' bribes?* Yes! Guernsey.

Guernsey is an English Channel island that uses their own notes instead of bankers' notes. Columnist William Raspberry reported in the January 4, 1992 edition of the *Arizona Republic* that Ken Bohnsack, Chairman of Sovereignty, said "The Guernsey Experiment" was introduced 174 years ago to restore that English Channel island's crumbling infrastructure and deteriorating economy. It has worked all these years, without inflation. Bohnsack quotes a recent visitor to Guernsey:

"It is a fascinating little island. There are about 60,000 permanent residents. The average family owns 3.3 cars, their unemployment rate is zero, their standard of living is high and there is no public debt."

Hooray for Guernsey.

William Howle's extraordinary insight into his subject concludes #110 in fine fashion. Thank you, Colonel Bill, for the material in R9, S9, T9, and X9.

Sherlock Holmes said: "We see but we do not observe."

Philosophy Nuggets is a picture puzzle painted in words.
I have supplied the pieces.
It is now up to you to put them together. Good luck.

■ ■ ■

111. *December 19, 1989*

Is the buying of America by Japan, Inc. as good for us long-term as it is short-term? (Yes, but with the proviso given near the end of this Nugget). Should we allow them the same freedoms as we allow the English, the Dutch, and other brands of capitalists? That depends on how unfettered we want our form of capitalism to be. If left unchecked, they could succeed in peace where they failed in war; that is, acquire dominance over global trade, industry, and who knows what else. If we don't want that to happen—and I'm not saying we shouldn't—then we must come to terms with our most basic beliefs about freedom and free enterprise. The awful truth is that when confronted with cultures that, if left to nature, might outshine us at our own game, we tend to renege on applying those basic beliefs. I raised this delicate point in Nuggets #45 and #74 from an opposite perspective. I realize it is painful to face up to, but why do you think there is apprehension over a united Germany, for example? We're concerned that they will rise again to dominate (this time economically) over a boundless area. These are real fears and are why I abhor nationalism and yearn for a single, fully assimilated world society, of which America is an aspiring microcosm.

Where does Japan get all its money? They create it by borrowing from their banks at low interest rates (my concept of no interest would prove even more dynamic) using as collateral assets that are, because of supply and demand, increasing in value at a rate commensurate to their ability to produce and save. Why is saving so important? If instead of consuming all that is produced, the surplus is sold instead, that money can then be used to buy land, stocks, or T-bills. And why do they save so much? The severe limitations of space in Japan actually turns out to be an advantage for them in an ironic sort of way. Much like England and Holland—two other densely popu-lated countries that have equally vast investments in the U.S., they physically lack the room to accommodate the large array of products that we have in America. It is of necessity that a small kitchen be more efficient than a large kitchen. They save because they are forced to (unless they were willing to work fewer hours) and the surplus capital thus generated finds its way to the friendliest foreign shores, America topping the list. So you can see why these nations invest their vast surpluses abroad, they just don't have room for much expansion at home.

Will this bubble eventually collapse or can their growth continue at an accelerating pace? As long as their supply of talented people holds out and is kept busy producing, inno-vating, and managing, their growth can sustain itself. Opening factories in America is and will continue to be a gold mine for them. It is all a form of leveraging their know-how, the same principle as franchising. It doesn't matter if the money to finance these ventures is based on assets that we consider over-valued; as long as the supply of well-trained workers is ample and everyone is kept working *productively*, success will come, assuming there is a market for the products.

Far be it for me (with no degrees in economics) to second-guess the learned men in our Federal Reserve, but I only wish they would come to understand this secret of Japan's success and emulate it. You can't have too much money (or credit) *as long* as there is capacity to absorb it in the form of sufficient and capable manpower.

Resentment against Japan is not lessened when we are confronted by successful Japanese who can be every bit as arrogant as a Berliner or a New Yorker (excuse the generalization but this is true to a large degree). While such abrasive attitudes are a natural turn-off to the rest of us (if they were smart they would at least have the decency to be hypocritical!). I prefer to swallow my pride and not hold this against them, but only so long as they can produce in a superior way that justifies this distasteful behavior without relieving me of equal rights or being reduced to a state of slavery.

P.S. Only the top tier of Japan's elite are getting super-rich from all this. Most just hang in there and plug away earning a modest return.

112.   *December 28, 1989*

The following is my solution to the drug problem, and as a bonus, the answer to the problems of crime, homelessness, and the underprivileged as well, not to mention relief for taxpayers now supporting welfare programs and expensive and inhumane prison facilities that so often harden, not soften, the antisocial traits of their charges. I have stated it before, most notably in Nugget #103, and am now repeating myself with different wording.

But first, let us look to history for answers to our current situation. The world's greatest all-time drug problem has to be China's experience in dealing with the unwanted opium trade which lasted over 200 years into the mid-20th century. Through behavior that would be unacceptable in today's climate, England defeated China twice in what we know as the opium wars.

In an effort to rid his country of this foreign scourge, China's Emperor failed to stem what was to be the greatest transfer of wealth from one country to another that the world had ever seen. In what was not her finest hour, Britannia kept open by force the exchange of China's silver and riches for opium supplied by the British owned East India Co. The opium was grown in India and Burma, both British colonies at the time, in poppy fields that extended as far as the eye could see.

This infamous trade was not stopped until Mao Tse-tung came to power. It took Mao 10 years, but he ended the demand by simply executing on the spot anyone and everyone who had anything to do with opium. And guess what? It worked. Now Mao is gone and drugs are back! You sometimes have to wonder who are the good guys and who are the bad guys? (You will notice that curtailing demand lowers the price of the drug, while disrupting only the supply raises it. Higher prices generate a higher incidence of crime.)

Now, obviously, we are not going to shoot people on the spot; but we could separate them on the spot from the rest of us, by isolating them in what is my answer to the prison shortage. Inexpensive work camps (as many as it takes, as President Bush might say) secured only by fencing and sensors, could offer dormitories, excellent food, a social life with the opposite sex, and the most important ingredient of all, meaningful jobs that actually produce for profit. These practical, low cost camps (closed military bases would be ideal) would best be run by private enterprise (thus *adding* to the tax base as it should, not drawing from it). Homeless, unemployed, and volunteers would all be welcome and would be *paid* more, but otherwise be treated equally. It is unrealistic not to believe that most would experience an improvement in the quality of their lives.

The key element that would clear our streets of drug offenders and other lawbreakers alike would be *extraordinarily long* and indefinite sentences for repeat offenders, who need to be *separated* from the law-abiding, as opposed to punishing for its own sake. Separation imposed with a disciplined lifestyle is its own punishment and curiously its own reward as well (if you can't find your niche in life). Those admitted on a voluntary basis would of course be free to leave at will, so long as they not be a burden on society once on their own. As for finding politicians who will back these changes, it takes great courage to deviate sharply from the safe and orthodox path, especially for the ones who must accept final responsibility. Such leaders are rare, but the time is at hand for someone to step forward. Dante Alighieri, the great Italian writer, said, "The hottest places in hell are reserved for those who in time of great moral crisis maintain their neutrality."

"I found my niche in life but I couldn't keep up the payments."

113. *Completed in July, 1990*

I am a friend of the Jews as well as all nationalities, but it bothers me when offense is taken, where none is intended, when trying to discuss sensitive issues with someone—*anyone*, simply because elements are included which may be potentially embarrassing or uncomplimentary, even when based upon historical facts, albeit with evidence that is circumstantial. Open discussion suffers when one must always be on guard as to what he says, lest he offend. I can understand victims being supersensitive for a time, but how long should we expect this kind of reaction to last? While questioning motives is a proper function, knowing when to be satisfied is equally important.

Let me offer an example: Beginning in 1880 and especially from 1903 to 1907, the Jews in Russia suffered greatly (you have no doubt heard of the pogroms). But from the time the communists took power in 1917, and until Stalin captured total control for himself, the number of Jews in the movement's top ranks was disproportionately high. This does not surprise me. To a people who had been maligned and made history's scapegoats, communist ideology promised to change the very nature of man from that of a barbarian into a cooperative human being. This must have seemed to be the panacea they were looking for. The intent was good, but the reality proved nothing more than wishful thinking. Meanwhile the Bolshevik communists came down hard on those who opposed them, so hard, in fact, that untold millions were massacred (mostly the intelligentsia). Had the formerly oppressed Jews now become the oppressors (at least those in a position to be)? Placing blame is pointless. That is to say, a few of us such as Genghis Khan (Jenghiz Khan) are capable of abominations without *any* rationale, but *almost* all of us, given the opportunity, are capable of horrendous excesses in the name of what we believe to be righteous goals. Even Hitler believed his cause to be noble and correct (although the logic in his thinking has always eluded me). Had the communist dream evolved as planned, who is to say it would not have been worth it; much like enduring purgatory before entering heaven?

It is said that he who controls the present controls the past. But if we are to *learn* from history, it must be presented accurately, and written with objective stoicism rather than subjective emotionalism. Attempts to remake it to suit our prejudices do much harm.

What is evident here is that wrongs beget greater wrongs, and hate begets greater hate, which can lead to extreme situations. For every door unlocked and opened to the past, there is likewise one opened for us to the future, with the words "Knowledge, use with caution" written on it. There is a Hebrew expression: *tikun olam* (to repair the world), which describes perfectly what it is I want to do. The path to salvation is a long and dark one with no shortcuts. Those who take it must light the way for others to follow, until gradually the whole world is redeemed. (Any similarity to scripture is coincidental.) Leonard Read, who founded the Foundation for Economic Education, once said, "All of the darkness in the world cannot overcome the light shed by a single candle."

114. *January 13, 1990*

While there are exceptions, the happier life will not usually be the one in which perfection is sought, but the one whose client aspires only to the upper comfort zone of his talents. The Greeks too believed that happiness was related to the degree to which you fulfill your capacities. But it is equally important not to overreach yourself. What long-term reward does perfection offer when it is accompanied by undue stress and followed by early burnout? The sum total output from that individual is bound to be less. A car will last longer and eventually go farther at 50 mph than it will at 90 mph. The trip may not be as exhilarating, but the arriving will be more certain in the end.

115.   *January 14, 1990*

The National Association for the Advancement of Colored People is valid, while the National Association for the Advancement of White People is not. How so, you ask? Because we have had a de facto NAAWP from the beginning. The NAACP is merely making an effort to redress grievances and to seek equality. There exists no need for an NAAWP.

However, "Affirmative Action" is not the answer either. That is not equality, it is the seeking of the same unjustified privilege that it was meant to counter, and invites a backlash that to some people justifies the existence of a NAAWP.

116.   *January 24, 1990*

Is the institution of marriage suitable for everyone? Should it be detached from the grip of civil law that regulates it? Would children in many cases be better off if raised by professionals trained for the purpose, in communal living and learning facilities? I believe no, yes, and yes.

This would *not* be for everyone, of course. But for the disenchanted who believe there must be (at least for them) better ways of conducting their lives, whether this means in an atmosphere of polygamy, free love, or association only with their intellectual equals (which offers the best chance for making lasting friendships), accommodation should be permitted. People in conflict with their own culture don't always know why they are, they just know they must escape from it in their quest for something better.

History has not shown much success for such groups where the geography has permitted conquest by foreign incursions. But some remote islands and enclaves have had degrees of

**"During last month's visitation with mother I made a Freudian slip —
I meant to say 'Pass the hotcross buns,' but what I said was ...
'You ruined my life, you bitch!'"**

success when allowed to do their own thing without outside interference. The best example is America itself, whose isolation from the rest of the world permitted unprecedented development. Today, of course, changing circumstances have made isolationism a hindrance to progress; world trade is now the name of the game.

While ultimately I favor a single world totally assimilated, I recognize in the meantime that along the road toward this final goal, there should be groups allowed to form that share compatible philosophies, so long as they are positive. The time has come to take the bull by the horns. Terrorist groups that use violence and other wackos who preach hate and bigotry are unacceptable and should not be tolerated. When we speak of freedom, we should not mean freedom to do harm. It seems we are afraid to take bold stands anymore. I for one am getting tired of pussyfooting and head-in-the-sand evenhandedness.

Are we so fearful of making mistakes that we are compromising our ability to make responsible decisions?

In one case it may become necessary to isolate a particular group against their will; I am referring to the victims of AIDS. If a cure is not found before it threatens to get out of control, a general quarantine may be the only alternative, whether we like it or not. You will behave, or you will be damned.

117. *January 28, 1990*

I find that the last hurdle on the road to personal development that even otherwise highly accomplished and intelligent people must surmount is overcoming enmity towards others who have injured or disappointed them. Before we rush to judgment, consider first that there are always reasons for people's actions whether we understand them or not. Instead of

"Robert, in view of your feud with the choir director who is having a bypass, do you really think it's the best time to include 'I'll be glad when you're dead you rascal you' in Sunday's program?"

"I've learned to tolerate the opinions of people who
have no business having them."

meeting others only 45% of the way, while basking in self-satisfaction over the good deal we may have pulled off, and risking hostility when the other fellow doesn't see it our way, or when he is coerced into seeing it our way (not a situation that fosters goodwill), it would be better to go 55%, and if that still doesn't satisfy them, amicably terminate the relationship. He who so acts will only make enemies with those who are unreasonable to an extreme, and in that case he should have no regrets, for at least he tried.

Virtually all wars could be averted if all parties were willing to go more than half way; forget wrongs done to ancestors; and be able to bend with the wind.

Whosoever can do those things will know peace with himself, and peace with the world.

The War Prayer

*a highly sardonic essay
by Mark Twain*

"O Lord, our God, help us to tear their soldiers to bloody shreds with our shells . . . help us to lay waste their humble homes with a hurricane of fire . . . help us to turn them out roofless with their little children to wander unfriended the wastes of their desolated land in rags and hunger and thirst . . . We ask it, in the spirit of love."

118.   *February 17, 1990*

All of the world's religions were created by philosophers for the purpose of persuading people to lead a moral life. This used to be best accomplished by offering the reward of the carrot and the consequences of the stick in the form of a fable, to be interpreted literally by purists, and as allegory for the more sophisticated. Now comes a new era, where fantasy is found wanting altogether, and a force called reason is replacing it. It is what I call enlightened common sense, from which comes enlightened self-interest. In referring to a movement, we sometimes say that at the right moment its time will have come. Well, that time is now; the vanguard is forming. I invite those who agree to step up and be counted. Obsolete dogma and fiction are out, reason and logic are coming in. Solutions now in the making will eventually create that mystic place called heaven, and lo and behold, it will be right here on earth where the Bible says it all began as the garden of paradise. I have news for you: The garden of paradise will reappear as a result of economic abundance, and its location will be the entire planet Earth. All we need to do is make it through the next few decades.

119. *February 17, 1990*

The winds of change at the moment are blowing capitalism's way. And yet I do not think that pure capitalism is the final answer. While it does seem to produce the greatest overall benefits, it can be cruel and demanding. Capitalism may be best for now, while the world is still developing but once that task is completed, then what? The need for harsh solutions will diminish as we become a "kinder, gentler nation," to quote our leader. (First the house must be built; after that is accomplished we can relax in the living room and enjoy TV.) But now is now, and when is when. There is yet time before we must cross that bridge.

120. *February 18, 1990 and February 27, 1992*

The best board game is the one with the simplest rules, while at the same time being of sufficient difficulty so as to tax the outer limits of the human mind. Both chess and checkers fill the latter requirement, but only checkers can claim the former.

Milo Valdez, longtime checkers booster from Denver, has this to say about his favorite game: In life, as in the game of checkers, you win with the mind, blending classroom with practical experience. It is a fact that all manner of good qualities accrue to one's account from interest (pun intended), when mental deposits are invested in the Grand Old Game.

In the early history of our country, checkers was the only means of recreation our founding fathers had, yet they became great thinkers. Luminaries such as Lincoln, Franklin, and Edgar Allan Poe were but a few.

There are also modern day evangelists who preach the gospel of the King of Games, such as millionaire Charles Walker of Petal, Mississippi, who is listed in the *Guinness Book of World Records*. Mr. Walker is also founder of The International

Checker Hall of Fame, which has become the checkerplayers' Mecca.

Interested? It's your move.

121.   *March 9, 1990*
In Defense of a Beleaguered Japan

Allow me to state more clearly what I have previously alluded to concerning our trade deficit with Japan. Needless to say, our deficits allow them the means with which to buy our real estate and businesses as well as our bonds. However, I do not think an equal balance of trade is a realistic expectation on our part. They could and should be importing more of our food and raw materials (which would be to their benefit as well), but even with that we can use many more of their products, mostly high tech, than they can use of ours, thanks to their superior industriousness. The situation is much the same as between us and some of the less developed countries (LDCs) where *we* show a trade surplus. Of course we don't complain about *that!*

It is England, not Japan, who has the biggest share of investments in the U.S. And tiny Holland, which no doubt will come as a surprise to most Americans, is a strong third. Yet I hear no great outcry, or even a whimper, against these two countries. Why is Japan singled out for our criticism? I see two reasons: First is the alarming *rate* of growth of their investments here. And second, they are different from us Occidentals—they are Orientals with different customs, traditions, and values from our own. The English and the Dutch we understand; they are like us. But, we ask, can we trust Japan? If they come to own our country will they want to enslave us? Should we not have reason to fear a culture whose students have a slogan: 4 you pass, 5 you fail, referring to the number of hours of sleep one gets in a night (an extra hour of sleep means an hour less you can devote to study). Now that's so commendable that it's

"It's time to assign blame.
Whom do we have available?"

scary. But I would be more scared if they came from Mars instead of from a different location here on Earth. By that I mean we are all brothers under the skin. As our cultures intermingle (a process we should encourage) assimilation will occur and trust will follow.

Ask yourself this question, would you rather live in a world of Bangladeshes, who take much and offer almost nothing, or a world of Japans, who create prosperity for themselves and all those they touch? The U.S. has proven it has no desire to enslave those it conquered in war. Now it is Japan's turn to convince us of the same thing in peace. (See #110-U6 for a very important caveat.)

I am opposed to tariffs or other trade barriers. If they overwhelm us with exports we want because they are better and/or cheaper than what we can make for ourselves, and if they buy into our national holdings, so be it. We invented a name for that over 200 years ago, it is called capitalism. Or would you prefer "free enterprise"? Are we now to reject these terms and what they mean just because the shoe is on the other foot? If we wish to seek relief, we should become aware of and find remedy for the fact that too many of us are not pulling our own weight. Problems are less when people are trying to invest in your country than when they are not.

Those in the world with superior work habits should be encouraged and emulated, not chastened and penalized. I believe the work ethic is the single most important virtue anyone can have. Without it we would die and all other virtues would become moot; with it we prosper in proportion to the degree that it is applied, and Japan is proving this in no uncertain terms.

The more productive in the world will become the wealthiest, but no need to fear, there will still be plenty to go around for those willing to put forth their best effort, even if they're not in the highest bracket. Dr. W. Edwards Deming, the still-active 90-year-old American mastermind behind Japan's economic success, says that you stand no chance of catching a man who's running faster than you are unless you try harder.

If we want their products more than they want ours, that's *our* problem. How can it be unfair if they choose not to *buy* as much from us as we buy from them? I would not like it if I were coerced into buying something I didn't especially want. Our country is hurting, but the real villains are not who they seem to be. We are suffering from an acute case of misinformation on many fronts. This is but one.

We must all share the planet, we must all discover and learn about and from each other. If we can do that, mistrust will change into harmony, and strife will turn into happiness for all mankind.

Blame the Japanese *

by George Dawson

When the crooks are running rampant,
and the judges are too lax,
when letters from the IRS
demand some extra tax,
when your son is quitting college,
and your daughter's getting D's,
Just do what Iacocca does—
and curse the Japanese.

When your taxes keep on rising,
while your bankbook starts to shrink,
when pollution clouds your city,
so the air begins to stink,
when the temperature is falling,
and your pipes are sure to freeze,
call upon your congressman
to bash the Japanese.

When everyone around you
is complaining of the news,
and some condemn the Arabs
while others blast the Jews,
stiffen up your lip, my son,
and never bend your knees—
just be a true American,
and blame the Japanese.

---

* From the *New York Times,* January 29, 1992, by George
Dawson, Emeritus Professor of Economics at Empire State
College of the State University of New York

So much for the respondent's case; but the plaintiff also has valid points which need to be looked at. The larger problem is one of escalating *exploitative* capitalism feeding itself on a global scale and heading out of control, until the demands of a future purgation bring on a transmutation.

But more to the point—the Japanese are playing the game according to old rules still in vogue. The foremost example of this is passing the tax buck. Here's how it works:

The headquarter offices of foreign firms regularly overcharge their American subsidiaries so their U.S. operations show a very low profit. This transfers the real profits back to the company's "home" country, and lets the company avoid paying a fair tax on their U.S. business. Each year, foreign companies use this accounting gimmick to chisel the U.S. Treasury and American taxpayers out of hundreds of millions of tax dollars. The Japanese are very good at loopholes and self-interest; but as yet they understand nothing about that wave of the future which will advantage everyone: *enlightened* self-interest.

122.   *March 12, 1990*

My wish to pay at least $9 per hour to all workers who perform their jobs adequately will only be possible under conditions of full employment. I define that term to include not only the currently unemployed, but also everyone else excepting only students, those *severely* handicapped, and retirees who are *at least* 55 years old. Just because a person can afford to loaf is not an acceptable reason for doing so.

There is a good reason for requiring everyone to work. Aside from what can be argued is the moral imperative against parasitism, full employment is necessary to augment the pool of additional compensation which will result from an enlarged economy, that the working poor (who will no longer be poor) will receive.

At present we are paying for welfare (entitlements) and receiving nothing in return except the ills of crime from idle hands. This money would be *much* better spent in helping to make up the difference in pay to $9 per hour and getting back tangible benefits from the product of new labor, the availability of which would be guaranteed and its acceptance required in the same manner as it was during World War II (when we all had to work).

You are justified in asking: What kind of jobs would they do? I do not have the answer to that at this point, but I have no doubt that answers can be found. My motto would be: No permanent free lunches. Barry Asmus, a senior economist for the National Center for Policy Analysis, says that opportunity elevators are far more effective than safety nets. Now that is common sense. Were I president, I would like to make Asmus my economic czar, and he would be my very first appointee.

Once this matter is settled, the next item on the agenda to tackle will be the expensive problem of national health care, for which there is currently *no satisfactory solution* simply because it is unaffordable. To solve our many problems will require all of us to pitch in.

I seek radical changes in many areas but, let's face it, they're not going to come easily or soon. What to do? As I write this, Lithuania is shedding its shackles, so is Haiti, so is Chile, so is Nicaragua—and this is only Monday. The world is crying for answers and direction. Is the time for action at hand? Are the seeds of the ultimate morality to grow first in foreign soil? Maybe.

Enlightened self-interest based on enlightened common sense is not a religion, but a practical guide to the conduct of people and the management of their affairs. The need is there, the time is now; who shall go first? Whoever it be, let us begin. Remember: The secret of getting ahead is getting started.

123.   *March 21, 1990*

Conscience is what causes one to do the right thing even though he has the opportunity to do wrong and *get away with it*. It is of greater advantage to have a conscience in a near-perfect world (which would be the reason that it *is* near perfect) than in an imperfect one, although it would obviously benefit society in all cases.

To the unthinking, conscience comes as a result of external indoctrination and habit. To those of us who choose to be amoral intellectually (keeping an open mind), yet behave morally in practice (because its a good idea) conscience will develop internally, and will direct us to choose the preferred course of action when faced with alternatives. This will result from an understanding of enlightened self-interest, which will also develop into habit, and allow us to act reflexively to situations both old and new.

You may ask if there is a *difference* between morality that comes from indoctrination and that which comes from understanding. I believe very strongly that there is. With the former, disillusionment or disinformation can cause one to change course in midstream. But if you really understand the underlying reasons for your behavior, you cannot be led astray. This is the new morality which I hope to popularize. I see it replacing the old "morality by indoctrination" as promoted by your favorite church. The church had its day and served its purpose. Now it is time to move on to a more sophisticated morality.

124.   *March 30, 1990*

And what about euthanasia? Even if doubt exists in determining the proper course to follow in all other controversies, here is *one* over which there should be *no* doubt. Euthanasia is proper and should be for the most part left in the hands of the doctors (in consultation with the family) who in years past quietly provided this service passively, allowing nature to take its course (they are the logical ones who are in the best position to decide).

The abuses that will occur—and there *will be* some—are far outweighed by the desirability of termination when indicated. It seems the courts have too often decided that being sensible is inhumane and that society and family can bear the high costs of keeping the hopelessly ill and suffering alive by whatever means. They are wrong on both counts. Is it any wonder that some doctors have become cynical and more interested in making money when they can expect a lawsuit as reward for their good intentions? We can hardly expect their initial idealism to survive the harsh shock of realizing that their concept of good medicine may not be the same as that of a hostile lawyer's. And even if their defense is successful, it will have cost them a bundle. It's too bad that some of the judges who try these cases could not have been former doctors (or in the case of street crimes, former policemen). If they had they might have a more

"I got out of private practice when I found out I could make three times as much money doing urine tests for the government, and without the risk of a malpractice suit!"

realistic outlook on life. Under such conditions the common sense approach to death and healing is precluded. (Maybe it's time for judges to specialize as other disciplines are doing.) If allowed the luxury of *responsible* self-regulation without the sword of Damocles dangling over their heads, the medical professionals would again come to be regarded as they were not all that long ago: practitioners of the noblest of all human endeavors.

That the cost of health care is skyrocketing is the inevitable result of the unprecedented expansion of knowledge, refinement of newer techniques, and development of expensive new equipment together with the specialists who must operate and maintain it. Nor does it help that 20¢ out of every health dollar goes for administration (in Canada, it's 8¢). A former federal health minister, Monique Begin, once compared health care insurance in Canada and the U.S. by saying Canada is like a bed covered by a blanket while the U.S. is like one covered by a patchwork quilt with some of the patches missing. Also, to protect themselves in case of lawsuits, physicians practice "defensive medicine" and order unnecessary tests. False remedies should be avoided, e.g., nurses' salaries should not have to subsidize increased costs to patients.

This will sound cruel, but at this point in time, state-of-the-art care should only go to those who can afford it, or who can afford insurance that will pay for it (except where such care is used to advance medical knowledge).

I will agree that this is not right, that it is not the way it should have to be, but as John F. Kennedy once said, "Life is not fair" (but it should be society's *goal* to make it fair). In the meantime, however, we should avoid the trap of socialized medicine by whatever name you wish to call it. The good parts of Canada's health care system that I just paid tribute to notwithstanding, we need to remember that Socialism just doesn't work, history has proven this time and time again. When will

"Sorry, Mr. Quixote, but you're not covered for windmills."

we learn the lesson? A broken leg will heal very slowly in a welfare state (think that over).

Someday everyone will receive whatever care they need. That day is not here yet, nor should it be prematurely forced upon us. Until we provide the means for the poor to pay their own way, and this is the secret, they will just have to suffer. If there were to be full health coverage for everyone today, it would be paid for by only 30 percent of the population. The *real* solution here, as it is with all the other social ills we and the world are facing, should *begin* by exposing the hidden powers and the system of usury on created money that they control. Ernst Wynder, President of the American Health Foundation pointed to an ideal time when he said, "It should be the function of medicine to have people die young as late as possible." That too shall come to pass.

On a related but less obvious matter, I am pro-choice on abortion. The Catholic Church's views on many of these issues is right out of the dark ages. But then what else might we expect of an institution that took nearly 400 years to admit their premise was wrong when they found Galileo guilty of heresy for contending that the earth revolved about the sun and not the other way around. And if you think that's too incredible to top, they admitted last week to having performed two exorcisms, not in 1589, but in 1989, and not in some remote corner of the globe, mind you, but in New York state! You need not accuse *me* of ridiculing the Church, I don't have to; they are doing a good job of that by themselves, I am simply stating the facts. While you're thinking about this, you might ask your priest what the miracle of transubstantiation is (see glossary). If you're a true believer, you should at least know what you're expected to believe. Yet another surprise that you probably haven't heard about is that the practice of dentistry stagnated for a thousand years because the Church forbad invasive body procedures. On the other hand, to give the devil his due (forgive me, Father) they also forbad interest on money, and I strongly favor that prohibition. But the rigid thinking that ancient dogma begets is seldom consistent with modern realities. *Riddle:* When is any act a sin? *Answer:* When the Pope says it is. (Wasn't it Harry Truman who, on another matter, suggested that he's not giving them hell, he's just telling the truth and they think it's hell?)

"So we were wrong about Galileo ... that <u>WAS</u> an exception, wasn't it?"

331

Not surprisingly, I am also in favor of equal rights for women and gays. (Most women would rather watch men do the dishes than watch them dance naked.) As for sanctioning gay marriages, an area, by the way, that is outside the sphere to which moral judgments apply, my solution is simple: Do away with heterosexual marriages instead, and let all people live their private lives as they see fit, as long as all concerned are exercising free will, and the responsibilities of parenting are respected. (By this I mainly mean financial responsibility, since I favor the rearing of children by professionals where the parents are unwilling or unsuited to perform that task themselves.)

In bygone days women and men each had their separate roles to fill and marriage was useful. But today each of us is an individual largely self-sufficient and independent, which is as it should be.

You will notice that my views run the gamut from right to left, and while none of them by themselves are original (since all possible positions have already been taken on all possible subjects by someone or other), I think the particular *mix* of views that I support *is* unique, and, I would like to believe, on target.

125.   *March 30, 1990*

Flag burning, the very words are enough to raise some people's blood pressure. But this is one area where I am out of step with many of my fellow citizens (although much less so as far as the rest of the world is concerned). Symbolism does not move me. To me a flag is nothing more than a piece of cloth, and it seems quite silly to make it out to be any more than that. The thought of a constitutional amendment prohibiting its so-called desecration seems to be at the very least a case of overkill, and a trivial waste of time unworthy of serious concern. Our energies should be directed to matters of importance instead of chasing lesser demons.

"Gee, sir, I'd sure like to arrest you, but I don't think it's actually <u>ILLEGAL</u> to burn a Social Security card."

I am somewhat disappointed with President Bush for invariably siding with what he perceives to be the majority viewpoint. You will have to admit it has done wonders for his ratings, but is it unlike waiting to see which way the crowd is moving, jumping in front, and hollering "follow me"? I call that following, not leading.

"I don't think it matters what you're against, as long as you're sincere."

126. *Rewritten April 7, 1991*

As for gun control, I would like to speak for both sides. First, I think that in a more perfect world, the use of firearms would best be limited to those of constituted authority, and bona fide collectors, who could claim legitimate reasons for having them.

In the meantime, however, it becomes a necessary evil to allow those at risk the means to protect themselves, *even though* proliferation preordains that accidents *will happen*. When we consider that there are nearly as many firearms in America as there are automobiles, and 60 firearms for every criminal, gun control measures miss the mark (at the present time). Given the above, it makes a lot more sense from a practical standpoint to contain the violent criminal minority than it does the tools they misuse.

December 1993 addendum: Our politicians tell us they want to disarm the criminals (well, who doesn't?) but it is through their own inept policies (including those of omission) that the criminals are thriving to begin with. The real purpose behind gun control is to disarm potential resistors when the time comes to declare martial law (which will all be for our own good, of course).

127.   *April 17, 1990*

I think the reason our society is overly permissive to troublemakers on the bottom of the totem pole is that the same laws that govern them were formulated to protect troublemakers on the top of the totem pole, allowing *them* the freedom to go their *own* merry way. Could this be a self-serving shadow cast by Mafia influence, which I believe has permeated our whole society to a much greater degree than is commonly imagined? Friedrich Nietzsche once wrote that the gravest threat to a society's survival is its unwillingness to control its criminals. Rather than implementing real and immediate solutions (like those that I have previously outlined) to a crime problem that is a national scandal, the attitude of the elite who make the rules seems to be: I can afford to live in a secure complex; how others manage to cope is not my problem, they can fend for themselves. In other words: Let the general welfare be damned, just don't rain on *my* parade, and oh yes, please don't put me in the same prison with the rabble if *I* finally happen to get caught doing wrong, thank you!

128.   *April 17, 1990*

The down side of the women's liberation movement is in casting aside old values somewhat indiscriminately, all in the name of emancipation. What a minority of its advocates all too often do—and I strongly support *most* of their aims—is to

335

throw out the baby with the bath water. They don't seem to realize that not all of the old restraints are without merit, that smoking and drinking may go hand in hand with being liberated, but are not in anyone's best interests, and that the sexual revolution is accompanied by risks such as AIDS, newer strains of venereal diseases that can be difficult to cure, and, of course, unwanted pregnancy.

When we rebel against the past, some overkill is probably inevitable initially, but hopefully will be followed by mellowing and maturing. The social forces that represent the mass body of opinion are merely a consensus of the moment. Those who participate in the struggle for liberation must constantly fight reactionaries who resist change, but the temptation to overreact should be resisted in order to promote maximum credibility among reasonable people along the way. One sturdy lass was seen driving a jeep with a sticker that shouted out to all who saw: A WOMAN WITHOUT A MAN IS LIKE A FISH WITHOUT A BICYCLE.

129. *April 25, 1990*

Why is Russia now collapsing after it had become the second greatest power in the world? Hold it right there: They may have been number two in military might, but beyond that they were stretched very thin. I think what is finally doing them in is the aftermath of Reagan's eight year, three-fold military budget increase. While it was merely a strain on the financial back of America, it became a backbreaker for Russia. Their economy simply could not support the demands put on it to stay militarily competitive with the U.S. These mounting pressures exacerbated their internal problems, and they are now forced into an all-out effort to hold together their crumbling empire.

Thank you Ronald Reagan, and thank you President Bush, for your cool and even-handed approach in dealing with Gorbachev during this critical period. While our hearts go out to the Lithuanians, we must keep a proper perspective of the bigger picture, taking care not to back the Russians into a corner from which they cannot escape without a modicum of grace. Allow me to fast forward this writing by 13 months and read this profound statement (for that time) by President Bush: "The moral dimension of American policy requires us to chart a moral course through a world of lesser evils. That is the real world, not black and white. Very few moral absolutes."

Communism as we know it is on its way out, the result of economic failure brought on by a lack of individual incentive. Henceforth it will appear in a mutated form that allows an accommodation with all the other forces in the world that compete for people's allegiance. Likewise must others respond to the clarion call for unity through compromise and above all, through understanding.

130.   *April 30, 1990*

I am of the sad opinion that the enlightened self-interest that I advocate, and the enlightened common sense upon which it is based, are probably beyond the grasp of most to truly appreciate, at least to the point of actually incorporating into the way they live their lives. This is similar to my own inability to appreciate art and classical as well as rock music.

Primate Speech Lab

"He still has trouble conjugating verbs, but so far he's
written three hit rock songs!"

Give me instead an AM radio station that plays big band swing music, and that is all the entertainment I need.

Mark Twain once said at a music recital, "It's not nearly as bad as it sounds."

131.   *May 8, 1990*

If more petty felons went to jail, the mafia would lose them as customers for drugs, deals, and loans which they would not be able to pay back. Think about it—who stands to gain the most from our rampant crime problem? And who has the political clout to tip the scales of justice in the criminal's favor? And if weakened laws and permissive attitudes are good for the goose, do they not benefit the gander also?

132.   *May 9, 1990*

If you live in Hawaii, you can expect to live two years longer than the rest of us. Virtually everyone who holds a job there, or who is retired or disabled has all their medical bills paid for them through a single universal health insurance plan. (But, curiously, this is not so for the mentally ill. The Hawaii State Mental Hospital is literally a Third World hospital.) Would this work in the other states? No, I'm afraid not. The reality of it is that its very high cost is being subsidized by proportionally large numbers of monied tourists, to a degree that other states cannot match, thanks to a favorable combination of climate, geography, and vacation atmosphere (visitors from Japan account for 43% of tourist spending). By milking these willing visitors through high prices, plus an abundance from crops, courtesy of mother nature, the thriving economy can afford this service for its citizens.

How can places not as blessed enhance the quality of life of their residents? Answer: Make the most of whatever assets they do have. If still not sufficient to support full employment, relocate. Obviously not all places have the conditions necessary to support life equally well. Japan, for example, has pitifully little in the way of natural resources, so they invested in education, which allowed them to make things others could not, utilizing a sea of highly trained technicians. This is how they found success. As a rule the most educated will be the most prosperous. The challenge is to help the *least* prosperous become self-sufficient *without* subsidies, in their own environment if need be, and encouraged to advance as far as they can without the handicap of discrimination.

133.   *May 11, 1990*

Why am I so opposed to interest? Let me give you an example of the distortions it can and does cause in the economy. This illustrates how interest perverts our values, and makes stupidity a virtue. Let's say you need a new vacuum cleaner. For $70 you can get a plastic job that might last an average of four years, or you can buy a lightweight Royal that should last over 30 years, for $500 plus occasional maintenance. Assuming you can afford the Royal in the first place, after 30 years, either choice would have cost you about the same, but the better unit would have allowed you the benefit of enjoying superior performance and versatility for all that time, hence it *should* be the better deal. But wait, that would be the case only if there was no interest. Could it somehow be that the inferior machine might be the smarter buy? (Never mind that your rugs won't be as clean.)

Let's figure it out. If the real annual interest rate (nominal rate less inflation) is 4%, and the buyer invested the difference of $430 at that rate (the disadvantage of buying the better unit would be even greater if the purchase were financed) his interest return alone would be enough to pay for a new inexpensive unit once every four years. Think of that—you buy the first one for $70, and after that get free vacuum cleaners forever plus a permanent bank account of $430, all for a $500 investment, and in constant 1990 dollars—remember—we are discounting inflation by basing our premise on the *real* interest rate. (I have never heard anyone advance this clear and logical argument *against* interest before.) Hence when we *are* offered a choice, the right choice is negated by external factors. Clearly, the requirement of paying interest compels industry and individuals alike to tilt their actions in favor of short-term gains merely to pay the interest on their loans.

I will admit that few examples can illustrate my point as well as the above which vividly exemplifies how the principle of enlightened common sense is violated. Interest influences just about every major transaction made to some degree, but in an artificial and negative way. I regard this distortion as *one* of the causes of our flight from quality, and of our attraction to cheap, shoddy, and inferior products of all kinds. The majority of people cannot afford quality, interest being one factor. This is unfortunate, buying quality (without going to an extreme) should nearly always be the *more* desired, not the less desired option.

To sum up, I am suggesting that interest is detrimental to, and interferes with, the process of applying common sense to decisions we make every day of our lives. At the end of this book I suggest that if the world's major wrongs are corrected, the minor problems will solve themselves, that if the tree is diseased, so too must be the fruit that it bears. If interest were done away with, inflation's days would be numbered too. Interest is a contagious disease; enlightened common sense and its application is the cure.

134.   *May 21, 1990*

What is the psychology at work that will cause a person to turn over his life's savings piecemeal to a con artist? Why does he want to give all, sometimes even mortgaging his house to satisfy the hypnotic urge to give until there is nothing left—only then to grasp the reality of what is happening after it is too late? Only by living through the situation can it be appreciated. As the end approaches, the victim labors over ways to help the culprit to the nth degree. He will *voluntarily* do whatever it takes, but interspersed periods of doubt plague him more frequently. Then, as he begins to awaken, and determines that the bleeding *must* stop, a phone call from his guest is all that it takes to again give in. Finally the spell is broken, and he emerges poorer, but wiser.

It's all right to believe people, just don't take their word for it.
— GIVOTANGI

I have posed questions, but I have no answers; the questions are rhetorical, the facts are real.

But that suggests yet another question: Can the same phenomenon also apply to a body as large as Congress? Apparently so. As evidence I submit the following items:

1. The S&L decay was apparent for close to a decade before the roof fell in all at once (the same fate that befell communism). Why does the deer freeze in the middle of the road when staring down headlights of a speeding car that is about to do him in?

2. Crime is out of control, many criminals should be separated from the rest of us for a *very* long and indefinite period of time. Why don't we address this problem head on, and do whatever it takes to solve it? Few things are as important as public safety.

3. Dissect the inner workings of the Federal Reserve system with the aim of exposing its shareholders and what may amount to trillions in profits (fat chance of pulling this lid off) in what has to be the best kept secret of all time. Most books

"I'd be happy to have you audit my return if you let me audit the government's books on the S&L bailout."

about the Fed are intentional smokescreens "exposing" only what is already documented. Through invisible wholesale skimming, is it any wonder why every year it becomes harder to make ends meet for the average working man, when the opposite should be the case?

4. Why can't we bring ourselves to overhaul, simplify, and reduce the *entire* income tax code to one page?

5. Farm subsidies and price controls defy all levels of common sense. As for price controls; you can't cure dysentery with adhesive tape. Each layer of government programs is put in place to try to water down the damage caused by other federal programs. Why can't we break free from this madness?

Solutions for *major* wrongs like these are so difficult to effectuate that I believe they can only come if we change to an absolute monarchy, and are lucky enough to be led by a benevolent monarch with the power to make the necessary fundamental changes. But if the right reforms are put in place (to learn the key one read on) electing a monarch need be only a one-time event. Risky, very. It is also antithetical to the aims of our nation's wise and farsighted founders. But we have reached the point where that risk must be taken, as the patient's life is now in danger. We should hope that after this one time, we will never again need to take the risk of placing total power in the hands of a single individual. What went wrong? Special interest groups and the monied power structure have, with the passage of time, come to achieve de facto control over our lives, much like the con man had over his victim. This destructive tidal wave can now only be stemmed by a concentration of power the likes of which we usually see only in wartime. Once underway, the excision must occur swiftly. It serves no purpose to cut off a dog's tail one inch at a time. The adversary must be

"Oh, great — I kill myself, and <u>THEN</u> they reform the tax laws!"

caught off guard and denied time to react in any major way (Churchill once said there was nothing more exhilarating than to be shot at without effect).

This will indeed be a high risk venture. But risking your *life* is no big deal; risking the loss of your freedom *is*.

The American Revolution is to be played out once more for the last time. May the benevolent side win.

And if our drama does unfold accordingly, what is to prevent future reoccurrences of abuses? Listen to this: Money spawns power. Power accumulated over generations usually takes improper liberties and more often than not engenders outright corruption. *Put limits* on *inherited* wealth and you limit *inherited* power. This includes closing the door on that granddaddy of all loopholes—the tax-exempt foundations. If we can all begin the race with equal opportunity and run it on a nearly level field, success will depend on ability, not on privilege, permitting *meaningful* competition. This should make the crucial difference, and give the forces of enlightened common sense a fighting chance to prevail, a chance that they do not now have.

135.   *June 2, 1990*

How much government regulation should we have in our lives? My answer is: different amounts for different people. That is to say, the least amount of regulation necessary to keep people in line. Some need to be led by a stronger hand than others; for these, greater monitoring is appropriate.

A good preschool teacher, if given enough time to spend with and get to know a child, can tell with unerring accuracy the direction that a three-year-old is likely to take in life. As I have said before, it would be so nice, and make life so much easier, if we were all born equal, but of course we're not.

Ed Crane, president of the Cato Institute, has said that civilization is maturing, and it is doing so at precisely the rate at which the counterproductivity of discrete instances of coercive government intervention is recognized.

While I agree with that, I must add that troublemakers and others without visible means of support should be perpetually monitored (but not unduly harassed), provided with jobs if they can't find their own, and required to work but paid at least a *living wage* (for most jobs). Although I regard $9 per hour as a living wage, I would *not* make it a minimum wage. For that, it would require that the job be of at least a normal amount of stress, effort, and importance. Easy jobs paying less would be reserved for those who can afford to live on lower pay. There is more crime today because there are more poor people. If paid adequately they would no longer be poor. Not commonly known is the fact that for every 1% rise in unemployment, the number of homeless will increase by 11%. Fewer poor means not only less crime and its related costs, including less welfare, it also means more hope, respect, happiness, and let's not forget added GNP. These benefits would extend beyond an inner circle, reaching out to affect everyone, like ripples from a stone cast in the water.

Talk about spin-offs from space technology, that's nothing compared to the social spin-offs from having adequately paid jobs. Therein lies the real nuts and bolts of progress. It would be interesting to calculate the cost/benefit ratio to society of paying a living wage while making sure all the intangibles on *both* sides of the equation are factored in. If you include quality of life, which in turn impacts on our children to the extent that ⅓ cannot cope at school because there are too many problems to cope with at home, I already know what the preferred choice will be.

In conclusion, it is just common sense to make use of bank, social security, and IRS records, in the monitoring and pursuit of those who abuse freedom while at the same time expanding the freedom (by eliminating the harassment of excessive regulation) of those of proven integrity. These principles should apply also to corporations and their officers. The days of corporate indifference to the world beyond their own narrow interests are numbered.

As it stands now, the good guys are at a competitive disadvantage when the bad guys can cut corners and get away with it. By the time these unsound shortcuts catch up with the perpetrators, they all too often have moved on. That will not do. By undertaking corrective measures here, we can plant the seeds of benevolent capitalism, replacing the weeds of exploitative capitalism.

AUTHOR'S NOTE: When I wrote Nugget #3 back in February, 1985, alluding to the evils of exploitative capitalism while suggesting an easy transition to benevolent capitalism, I had no idea what the key to that change would be. But alas, with #135, it has just rolled off my pen—some five years later—and it seems so obvious to me now, that I have to wonder why it wasn't always so. There are times when we know we're right, the correct path revealing itself only as we progress one step at a time, making sure of our footing as we go.

"As I see it, we either dump our ethics committee
or file for Chapter 11."

136. *June 5, 1990*

Without reviewing the myriad second-tier opinions that I have offered herein, I *would* like to reemphasize the more salient recommendations for getting society back on track to permanent progress:

1. Limit inheritance to $500,000 per person. This will in time eliminate inherited power as well as oligarchies and put a premium on ability and effort as the true road to success.

2. Require everyone who is even the least bit able, to work (this is the real soul food), excepting only students, and retirees over 55 if they so choose, while reminding them that retirement in idleness is like practicing to be dead, and that doesn't require practice. The pay scale for any job of normal stress, effort, and complexity should start at $9 per hour in 1990 dollars.

3. Eliminate giving or receiving all interest on money. Life annuities will provide sufficient income for retirement when that time comes.

4. Put prisoners to work 45 hours per week, at productive, income producing jobs, with all but the hard-core housed in inexpensive camps (as many as it takes), with dormitories, excellent food, a social life, strict discipline, and very good treatment, but with life terms for unreformed and repeat offenders.

5. Equal treatment for all without considering circumstances is obsolete (what's safe for a good driver can be unsafe for a mediocre driver). Give less freedom to the bad guys; more freedom to the good guys. This alone will provide a strong incentive to behave.

6. Phase out almost all subsidies, especially for farming.

7. Pull out all the stops on genetic engineering—proceed full speed ahead. Here lies the best hope for improving man without waiting for the evolutionary process that would take eons.

You might call the foregoing my shopping list. And what do you think my chances are of leaving the store with any two in my basket? We both know: slim, and none. To enact these features would require the U.S. to collapse totally, like an alcoholic who must bottom out first before he finds the resolve to exorcise the devil that doesn't want him to reform. We may or may not come to that point.

But wait—why does it have to be the U.S.? Are there not other countries that have already hit bottom? Throw a dart at a map of eastern Europe and you can't miss hitting one, and what about Russia itself? Opportunities to sell my elixir abound. But I am not selling snake oil. It is instead a tonic to cure a disease that up to now has always been with us. No matter what the system of government, as time goes by, a few will gain advantage over their contemporaries. What invariably follows then is the immorality of exploitation. Well, unfortunately, religious faith is not enough to ensure morality.

Paradoxically, you can best appreciate the meaning of what I happen to call enlightened self-interest by first becoming amoral, which is the essence of open-mindedness, devoid of all prejudice, and unintimidated by religious injunction. It is *then* that you have true freedom of choice to decide whether to take the high road or the low road. Remember, a man convinced against his will, is of the same opinion still. Would you like to know what made Humphrey Bogart so popular? He would begin by taking a neutral (amoral) stance and gradually become the patriot. We subconsciously identified with this because it was so sensible. The uncommon man will choose morality as a way of life (while holding on to amorality as a belief) by virtue of understanding the underlying reasons for doing so.

The majority suffer from mental myopia and will choose the low road because of it. When the gap between the ideal and the reality is too great, all values, all incentives, all that is sensible,

"A federal study released today revealed the existence of three heretofore unknown disadvantaged minority groups . . ."

becomes warped, and spot repairs will not hold up. Only a complete overhaul will bring lasting relief.

NOTE: The above list differs from the summary given in #56, which gives the major points that are of a general nature. Although some appear on both lists, the items here are specifically those believed necessary to implement if we are to reverse the declining standard of living that the middle class and especially the lower class and minorities are experiencing. These are major and radical changes intended to rejuvenate the populace. Some would even find that if they shared their cake, part of what they give up would come back to them, along with a piece of pie, that's the way it works. They have never been taught about the delayed but long-lasting residual benefits of *enlightened* self-interest.

137.   *June 23, 1990*

I believe that the soul of a country is best revealed by the games its people play and have the most loyalty for. America's favorites are physical games like baseball and football. Baseball, because you may be behind 7 to 0, and in the last half of the final inning, score 8 runs to win the game. We love the excitement of the possibility of a spectacular finish. We also take delight in the brute force and excitement of the long pass and explosive runs provided in football. In plain words, we Americans are thrill-seekers and risk-takers (characteristics that made *America* great).

What is Russia's favorite game? What else but chess, the contemplative thinking game. Their national character is mimicked in the complexity of intrigue found in this board game. Communism has been played out much according to concepts found in the maneuvers underlying chess (characteristics that made *Russia* great).

But the greatest of *all* games is none of the above, and is virtually unknown outside of its region. In my youth I frequented the chess club in Philadelphia, looking to play checkers. We would rile the chessophiles present by relegating their game to third place following checkers, which in turn took second place to a game called GO. Nor did it hurt our case to have a member skilled in all three to postulate it. The fact that they *were* riled and not smug gave further evidence to the possibility

"If the Nobel Prize ain't fixed, how come nobody
ever wins it for playing <u>FOOTBALL</u>?"

of our contention being true. GO was invented by the Chinese, but like other foreign pearls has been adopted and dominated by the crafty Japanese. The object of this game, whose hallmark is subtlety, is to gain more territory than your opponent (appropriate, isn't it?). Attempts to secure islands of territory can be frustrated if your opponent can secure an even larger territory of which yours is but a part—in which case yours will have to be forfeited.

Does all this not sound like the ideal *game plan* needed to fulfill their national aspirations? It's downright eerie.

What brought this subject to mind is when I found out that Japan is planting its seeds of influence globally from Peru to Guam and points beyond, all in strategic locations, and wherever the chance for success *appears* to be worth the effort. I instantly identified the techniques they're using with strategies employed by master GO players: Occupy key points first, consolidate gains later, but be forever careful not to bite off more than you can chew (characteristics that *make Japan* great).

Does it not appear that Japan has attained what Russia could not, namely, Marx's higher stage of truth which he called the Synthesis (why hasn't this been noticed before?) through a blend of raw capitalism (in this case the Thesis) and an authoritative totocracy (the Antithesis), where a mere suggestion from the finance ministry (that invisible entity that is the real seat of power in Japan) becomes tantamount to marching orders for the troops? (They all work for the national good.) Why don't we call the resulting product a captotocracy? (A country or body governed through the judicious use of capital by a reclusive, elitist group steering the ship of state from behind the scenes.) And don't knock it, whatever you want to call it, it's working better than anything heretofore.

These are a people to be reckoned with. If you are good at foreign languages, I suggest this would be an ideal time in our history to take up Japanese; you might find it quite useful in the years ahead.

NOTE: The principle of Marx's Synthesis theory was stated some 2½ centuries earlier by another philosopher, Francis Bacon, who said, "When one of the factions is extinguished, the remainder subdivideth." Both men died at the age of 65.

138. *June 25, 1990*

This book is directed to those searching for *meaningful* answers about people and the affairs of man. Let us face the fact that if we're to be saved by a politician—whose ilk has persisted in peddling doublethink and evasion, and whose interest in government has been largely mercenary—it will be a one-in-ten-million long shot (I think it was Will Rogers who said, "An honest politician is one who when he's bought, stays bought"). For instance, a true leader in the mold of Gorbachev would have difficulty getting elected in America, because the real solutions he would have to propose would be too traumatic

"I know I'm behind in the polls, but I'm counting on late-breaking voter apathy."

to be accepted (does this sound somewhat like what happened to Barry Goldwater)? What, then, is left? Certainly something more than Irish diplomacy (the ability to tell a man to go to hell, and make him look forward to the trip).

As for the present two-party system, it's strictly Tweedledum and Tweedledee. Nearly all proposed reforms address peripheral issues. They just aren't getting it. Would they "get" it if we changed the message? Limit politicians to two terms: one in office, one in jail. When moral decay sets in in a society, the society will not long endure. De Toqueville believed that America became great because America was good, and that when America ceased to be good, America would cease to be great. We need independent thinkers to give us direction, so that we know where the pressure points are. If enough people press hard enough in the right places long enough, there *will* be consequences. If your quest ends here, you should feel well satisfied.

One of the penalties for refusing to participate in politics is that you end up being governed by your inferiors. — PLATO

139. *July 11, 1990*

We can all make more money out of peace than we can out of war—even the munition makers. So . . . I say, TO HELL WITH WAR!
— SMEDLEY D. BUTLER, 1881-1940: MAJOR GENERAL,
UNITED STATES MARINE CORPS

Is war becoming obsolete? Yes, gradually and among the major players, it is, partly because it has become too terrible, and partly because we're starting to wise up. In reflecting upon our human history, we can find peaceful peoples only in remote corners of the globe. And I am talking about *very* remote—deep-in-the-jungles remote. You might want to credit these people with an inherently peaceful nature. Wrong. It is because they must live life on the edge.

To exist in a marginal environment, sustaining oneself consumes every waking hour. There is no time or surplus wealth to invest in the art of warfare. We are now within 100 years of filling up the globe (while leaving barely enough natural earth to sustain ourselves). This comes just in time, I would say, to learn the disincentives of the destructive power of modern weapons and the antiproductive nature of coercion from a long-term point of view.

In spite of this, threats from countries of less than superpower status could be with us for some time to come. In my view this justifies the need for a world (U.N.) police force *gradually* assuming the ability to spot renegade nations that are up to no good, and nip trouble in the bud by taking *preemptive* measures that will enforce the peace.

It is difficult to appreciate the short span of time that man has been on the scene, and the advances made thus far—advances that will grow exponentially henceforth. The obsolescence of warfare is but one more step in this journey.

When I wrote the above 2½ years ago, I made a structural error that I now wish to correct. Smedley Butler was right, of course, but that doesn't mean it is yet so or that inevitably it has to be so. I have a tendency to mix up the ideal with the actual reality, and I have committed this sin elsewhere in this book also.

The world police force that I envision would be for the benefit of the world's peoples, whereas presently I have to wonder if it is not answerable instead to a group who confuse having gold in their vaults with being happy.

Think about this: The military is looking for new enemies. After all, there are hundreds of billions to be made in these sham wars that we somehow keep getting mixed up in. Did not President Eisenhower warn us against the military/industrial complex? President Kennedy was going to cease and desist waging war—is this why he was killed?

My optimism is premature to say the least, the hand has yet to be played out.

140.   *July 23, 1990*

By what reasoning do I place a greater value on free thought than on spiritual admonishments? Aside from the primary reason of credibility, any belief system that advocates virtue based on faith is fine if its vaccine "takes," but look out if it doesn't! The subject will have nothing to fall back on, whereas the freethinker is dependent only on his own logic, which will keep pace with his personal development come what may. While morality benefits everyone regardless of the reasons for it, those reasons must meet evermore rigid standards as civilization continues to mature. British social critic C.P. Snow wrote, "Civilization is hideously fragile and there's not much between us and the horrors beneath, just about a coat of varnish."

I submit the following three stages of very broad and very general evolutionary growth. Most of us fall into one of these three groups.

1. The basest person never thinks of the need for any values.

2. The conscientious person does, usually turning to conventional theism as an answer. From a variety of religious sects, most will select the one they were brought up in; others of greater discernment will shop around first, but still end up choosing a standard brand off the shelf.

3. In the third stage, the subject dares to question the old order. As a freethinker, he or she is not satisfied with misguided faith alone, and seeks understanding through reason, which is the ultimate weapon against not only ignorance, but against also what we know that ain't so. It is legitimate to dream of greatness, but not to believe in imaginary messiahs.

141.   *July 24, 1990*

How to Discipline Children, or
The Junior Ten Commandments

1. Let *no* infringement pass without being addressed.

2. Take remedial action on the spot (for less serious misdeeds) often by stopping in your tracks and summoning the child to you in a pleasant but firm manner before your admonition.

3. Harbor no anger in manner or tone of voice.

4. Explain the reason for doing right. (Tell them it's because it *very* probably is in your best long-term self-interest to do so.)

5. Explain the reason for disciplining. (We must learn that our actions have consequences—negative as well as positive.)

6. Explain why you are the one passing judgment. (I am much older than you and have therefore had time to gain experience and knowledge that you do not yet have, but which I can teach you).

7. Be firm, consistent, and caring.

8. You may or may not choose to invoke religious injunctions consistent with your own beliefs.

9. As the child develops, let him know that you respect his views, even though they may differ from your own, and encourage him or her to express themselves. However, he needs to know that you have the final say.

10. When a person is wrong and won't admit it, they always get angry. So see to it that neither party ever goes to bed angry.

142.   *August 3, 1990*

Civil laws, like religious laws, are meant to control our behavior for our own good in spite of ourselves. While violating civil or criminal laws can bring us punishment in the form of real physical sanctions, enforcement of religious law depends upon psychological sanctions such as suffering the loss of heaven and the pains of hell, or remorse that would come from offending our particular God and those close to us. Notice that while both secular and religious laws serve to rein in antisocial tendencies, the main incentives to do so are based on fear and vengeance, which are negative emotions.

Isn't it time we shift the emphasis to the positive side? Yes, the concept of heaven *is* one such attempt, but even that falls short of ideal by being based on fancy instead of reason. From the secular side, instead of waiting for a criminal to harden (regardless of age) via numerous round trips through revolving prison doors, let us keep him segregated early on for very long and indefinite periods of time in *nonpunitive* work camps previously described. Then, as with the rest of us, reward future merit with the fruits of achievement if and as it occurs, while all the time "confining him to base." Call this "positive coercion."

The ratio of good people to bad people is about 100 to one. In big cities today the 100 are uncomfortable. If common sense was the law, the one would be uncomfortable. Therefore, I would like to see the laws referred to above eventually replaced with what I call the law of common sense (at the present time it would be more accurate to call it uncommon sense). But once it becomes embedded in our genes—I think acquired traits *can* be passed down at times through our genes—restraints upon our conduct will come from an internal appreciation of *enlightened self-interest,* and not from external mandates, be they secular or spiritual. There is no reason why future man cannot be his own master, and still live the moral life.

I *do* believe such a day is coming.
I *do* believe the journey will be long.
Let us begin.

143.   *August 19, 1990*

In the final analysis, most relationships are based on trust—
or the lack of it. From individuals to countries, the degree of
this attribute determines our behavior and guides our actions.
It is when people and cultures fail to interrelate or to learn of
the other's ways that trust becomes tentative, danger of hostil-
ities the greatest, and fear of the unknown adversary pervasive.
The early stage of the trusting process is especially critical, and
a misstep by either party, particularly when emotions are
included in the mix, can be disastrous.

Unfortunately, the willingness to take the initiative in selectively trusting others (although we can be fooled at times)
requires a level of mental development that most of the world's
inhabitants (along with many of their leaders) do not have yet.
In addition, befriending takes considerable courage (it is dangerous to be sincere with insincere people) because you risk
exposure to the vulnerability associated with being first to show
trust (or first to do anything). If this results in being rebuffed
or betrayed, maturity and tenacity should save us from discour-
agement. We can then continue with the business of building
bridges of understanding among all peoples.

144.   *August 22, 1990*

When one hears about the Savings and Loan Associations'
collapse, his first question should be: How is it possible to lose
$500 billion? That's more than World War II cost us! That is
the $64 question, and I see two reasons for it happening, the
second of which is the herd instinct brought on by peer
pressure. The voice that tells us, never mind how unsound a

"You must be kidding!"

deal appears to be, everyone else is doing it (making loans willy-nilly). We must do the same or we'll be left in their dust and lose business. Besides, we're insured aren't we? So why worry? (Accountability is missing here.)

But it is the first reason I want to talk about. A mentality of greed (high payoff commensurate with high risk) is replacing sound judgment. I see it manifested in such moral pollution as the burgeoning states lotteries mania, and other false prospects of revenue enhancements such as proposals for building Atlantic City clones in various cities. I call it false because it is fool's gold; they are bending to the current fashion. Real gold would be in creating value via producing, constructing, innovating. But let's back up; how *did* greed adversely affect our lending institutions? By the George Steinbrenner syndrome—trying to produce returns that exceeded what was possible through the means employed, and without making allowances for an economic downturn, thus bringing on wholesale failures. (And now the inevitable backlash is changing to the other extreme.)

What might have been merely a venial sin of a smaller magnitude became a mortal sin when misdirected funding on a massive scale resulted in negative value instead of positive value that *worthy* projects would have yielded. In investing, as in anything, there is no substitute for competence secured by *appropriate* incentives. And that includes disincentives for incompetence as well.

145.   *August 26, 1990*

There is something wrong here. There is something wrong when we dare not come to the aid of a neighbor for fear that we may get sued as a result. There is something wrong when the professor advises his journalism student against ghostwriting a book because of potential legal complications. There is something wrong when I can no longer buy a simple newspaper such as the *Wall Street Journal* or the *New York Times* from vending machines at a mall because the distributor could not afford the liability insurance premiums now required by the lessor. There is something wrong when I face a law suit brought against *me* by a trespasser or even worse by a burglar who gets hurt on my property, even when it's due to his own wrongdoing. There is something wrong when benign amusement rides must close because the insurance is too expensive. There is something wrong when the IRS says *you* owe *them* more money because you paid the lawyers 75% too much to settle an estate thus inflating that deduction, even though that is what the lawyers *charged* you. And let's not even talk about the "defensive medicine" doctors are forced to practice.

The above examples are *not* hypothetical. They are all based on true stories told to or experienced by me in the last twelve months. How many more stories are there like these?

What would be my solution? Field cadres of no-nonsense judges working no-nonsense hours, who are experienced in

"You have to have a positive attitude, sir — Just think of all the hundreds and hundreds of dollars that we let you KEEP!"

binding arbitration, and empowered to invoke heavy sanctions against the plaintiff *and his attorneys* in cases lost that are obviously devoid of merit, with double sanctions if lost again on appeal. Judges on the appellate level should be selected for their demonstrated abundance of common sense aided by guidelines, not inflexible rules, and monitored to ensure that usage of common sense is always paramount in their decisions.

It is my contention that with every new generation, the top achievers in any given field of endeavor tend to be a little better than the top achievers they are replacing. If this is indeed the case, might we not be safe in endowing our better judges with more discretionary powers than we were willing to in the past? Decentralization becomes more desirable under such circumstances, whereas once there were so few wise men that they had to express the rules as definitive law for others to do or die, but not to reason why. Today we can commit discretionary authority to a sizable number, and trust in their good judgment, or common sense. Every great truth can be revealed as a lesson from history.

The defeat of the Spanish armada in 1588 was in no small part due to the English first attacking and sinking the Spanish flagship. Once the commanding Admiral was eliminated, the remainder of the leaderless Spanish fleet was no match for the small English fishing boats whose entrepreneurial owners were accustomed to applying common sense to more than just fishing. What remained of the Invincible Armada after the English were through with them was destroyed by storm and tempest. Spain was never a major power after that, and all because the Spanish valued blind obedience to authority to the exclusion of a greater discipline: the application of common sense by *many* ordinary citizens. Curiously, the English seemed to have lost this good sense two centuries later when their inept land army came up against the superior tactics utilized by the Americans, who won their war for independence.

Following a capable leader is wise; maximizing the capabilities of *all* through the use of common sense is even wiser.

146. *September 16, 1990*

Do workable innovations exist that we are not taking advantage of?

Somewhere in Indiana there is a breakthrough in the education of schoolchildren. Divided into very small groups in classes with changing seating patterns, kids of varying aptitudes can discuss the lesson at hand with their mates, thus teaching each other. When I excitedly divulged this great find to a first grade teacher friend here in Florida, she calmly informed me that its called peer tutoring, that she finds it very effective, and that she's been doing it for years. If they can foist a disaster like "new math" on the whole country, how come they haven't discovered something that really works? Is it because most administrators are failed teachers who don't really understand teaching, and because they're unhappy at teaching, go into administration? Aha—so that's why they're put in charge! It's a way of getting rid of them! As an aside, teaching 40 children in a single class 50 years ago, must certainly have been easier than *trying* to teach half that number in most of today's public schools, where discipline, respect, and desire to learn are all too often lacking.

Let's look at waste disposal. Nashville, Tennessee, has this marvelous technique for converting rubbish into steam and coolant for all of their larger downtown buildings including the capitol, except for one. Imagine that, what was a liability becomes an asset. And various cities around the country have their own versions. But obviously none of them can work. If they did, *surely* such worthwhile endeavors would be made a national priority, anyone can see that, can't they?

Energy fuels: Most vehicles in Brazil run on alcohol; is this alternative feasible for us? Can we really make liquefied or compressed natural gas for the gasoline equivalent price of 70¢ per gallon as they claim? Please, let us *know* if this is real.

Can juvenile delinquents be rehabilitated? Sam Ferrainola *is* doing just that in Concordville, Pennsylvania. At only half the usual cost of incarceration, he is changing our residue population into respectable citizens, not only salvaging past and future wasted lives, but sparing the rest of us from becoming crime *victims* as well.

And from Baldwin, Illinois, comes an EPA-approved method for burning old tires and leaving clean air while generating electricity. How about that!

But even more encouraging: According to the engineering firm of Booth-Graham-and-Nunez (BGN), solutions to our problems already exist. They developed a system of processing municipal solid waste 20 years ago, which has been continually upgraded to current state-of-the-art technology. Although not a cure-all, it does address a major portion of our waste disposal problem. Burying waste in landfills does not mean we've solved the problem. We have just created bigger ones for future generations. Besides, once filled, the property does not provide an ideal site for future land development.

The BGN municipal waste processing system actually consists of many integrated subsystems. Everything is processed mechanically or chemically in a contained environment. It is designed to meet current and future EPA standards. All manual sorting is eliminated. You can readily appreciate the advantages of just this one improvement when it is realized that at garbage transfer stations they even have people hand sorting plastic materials. And what are they sorting? Pop and milk bottles and similar items, which amount to only 14 to 15 percent of the total plastics in the waste stream. The balance is lost to the landfill. A better solution is to go after all the plastics and reduce them to ethanes, the original material from which plastics are made.

Were I the president, my *first* priority would be to seek out all of these promising people with their promising ideas, choose the best ideas, try them out, and when found workable, run with them. The process would start one minute after the high noon inaugural ceremony. Let's find the courage to take stock of, to reevaluate the whole of our situation, to challenge entrenched orthodoxies, to ask why we have so many problems and why it is that they're getting worse. Certainly the legal philosophy of the past two decades of applying penalties rather than rewards to environmental problems has retarded the implementation of many solutions. Neither does catering to special interest groups help the cause. When the day comes that all decisions and appointees are made and selected on merit alone, progress will surely follow.

We need not abandon conservative values in embracing

revolutionary changes. *Fear* of change is the *real enemy.* Change that improves the lot of mankind, not just ourselves, is the *true friend* of *all.*

147.

Fact Sheet on Taxes, Spending, Government Waste, and The Deficit

Taxes

Taxes collected this year will eat up 19.6% of America's gross national product (GNP), the measure of all goods and services we produce. That's the fourth highest level in peacetime history.

"The only two times taxes soared above 20% of the GNP, in 1969 and 1981, the economy paid a heavy price: Recessions occurred the following years." — DONALD LAMBRO

"The surest way to kill a recovery is to raise taxes. That will stifle everything from investment and personal savings to consumer spending. It will clamp down on growth. It will invite a recession. There is no quicker way to kill prosperity than to raise taxes." — CANDIDATE GEORGE BUSH

"Federal taxes in 1989 consumed 19.2% of our GNP and are expected to consume 19.6% in the current fiscal year. In only five years since the turn of the century has the tax burden been higher. The tax-and-spend crowd loves to blame the deficit on 'the Reagan tax cuts.' They conveniently forget Congress has passed 14 separate tax increases—that's right, 14 since 1982." — ED FUELNER

Government Spending

"The federal government has no shortage of cash; it has a surplus of programs." — WILLIAM MURCHISON

"Various studies show that since World War II every dollar of legislative higher taxes has been matched by $1.28 to $1.58 in higher spending."

> – OHIO UNIVERSITY ECONOMIST RICHARD VEDDER,
> AND LOWELL GALLOWAY

"In the decade from 1979 to 1989 federal revenues increased by $528 billion or 114%. Spending, however, grew by 127%. Americans have let government grow out of hand because we have allowed special interest groups to elect politicians who repay them with spending programs funded by our tax dollars."

> – PAUL CRAIG ROBERTS

"Indeed, if Congress could limit the rate at which it increases spending to less than 4% annually, there wouldn't be a deficit at all by fiscal 1993. A study done for Congress' own Joint Economic Committee indicates that for every dollar taxes have been increased since 1949, spending has gone up by $1.48."

> – ED FUELNER

"Each year, taxpayers transfer billions of dollars to farmers whose average equity is one million dollars."

> – PATRICK BUCHANAN

Government Waste

"The place to start saving is found in the General Accounting Office's (GAO) estimate that $180 billion of the federal budget is lost annually to waste, fraud and abuse."

> – ALAN KEYES

"Charles Bowsher, the Comptroller General who heads Congress' watchdog agency, the General Accounting Office, says waste, fraud, abuse and mismanagement total between $100 and $200 billion."

> – DONALD LAMBRO

Baloo

**"Cut taxes, decrease spending, and balance the budget?
You must have me mixed up with someone else."**

The Deficit

"As much as $100 billion may have to be slashed from the budget to reach the $64 billion deficit target in the fiscal year beginning October 1, 1990."

— White House Budget Director Richard Darman

"Planned outlays this year are $1.2 trillion—about $125 billion more than we have on hand. Since 1954 the federal budget has been in deficit 30 times." — William Murchison

"The deficit, as a percentage of gross national product, has fallen steadily since 1985 (when it was 5.4%) to an estimated 2.2% for 1990. With the latest revised 'the sky is falling' estimates, the deficit would still be only 2.6% of the GNP in 1990, and 1.5% in 1991. We have had deficits in this range many times before. They are serious but not catastrophic, and certainly not justification for raising taxes and jeopardizing the economy." — Martin Anderson

"That is why President Bush and Congressional leaders are now playing with economic dynamite. Not only would a $30 billion tax increase generate a likely $40 billion or more in spending, it would kill all capital expansion, send the stock market off at least 10 to 15 percent and push the deficit way up, not down." — Warren Brooks

Raising taxes is not the answer. We have no "budget crisis," we have a "spending crisis." Numerous studies have shown that not only do tax increases not decrease the deficit, they actually *increase the deficit!* So the way to reach a balanced federal budget is not to increase taxes but to cut spending. Less federal government spending means more consumer dollars, lower interest rates, more jobs and economic growth. Economic growth means more federal revenues and a lower budget deficit.

"We interrupt this soap opera to bring you an even steamier report from Congress."

Why don't the politicians in Congress simply implement the Grace Commission recommendations for eliminating waste? That's an easy one to answer—it's because their nests are feathered with the campaign dollars of special interest groups who expect and get handouts (pork barrel spending) in return for lining pockets. This "buddy system" is so pervasive that resisting it is akin to resist being sucked into a jet engine: The closer you get the harder it is not to give in.

How many on every level begin their service with honor and good intentions, only to lose them along the way because so very few appreciate the slower but superior rewards of *enlightened* self-interest, or whatever name *you* want to call it.

148.   *October 2, 1990*

Since the disintegration of communism, traffic accidents have soared in those countries. It's as if they lack the good sense to determine which rules are in their best interests and which are not. In the meantime they mindlessly drive through red lights in a newfound euphoria of freedom that they have not yet learned to cope with.

I like to compare this to those who lose their moral anchors after rejecting the religion of their fathers along with accompanying elements thereof, some of which *are* obsolete but most are not, and some of which will always be valid.

Like the liberated communist, the liberated theist must learn a new value system to live by, and when he does, he may have to assume responsibility for becoming his own master.

The new morality that I advocate resolves this question through reliance on our own ability to think freely, and from this develop understanding through what I call enlightened common sense. This will not happen overnight, nor—at least initially—with large masses of converts. But eventually? That is something else again.

149.   *October 15, 1990*

They say we are a nation governed by laws, not men, implying this to be the better way. Let's examine that premise. If it is laws we are to obey, who makes them? If you answer that moral laws come from God or from Him through his prophets or assigns, you are entitled to your opinion. However, I believe *all* laws have a *secular* purpose, and that they originated from men, most of whom were well-intentioned. What makes our Constitution so special, is that those who wrote it were themselves so special, not just because of their intellect, but because they endured their baptism by fire. When the times demand greatness, great people will appear.

It was therefore desirable in bygone days for a brilliant individual or a select few of uncommon talent to chronicle their insights so that such wisdom could be passed on for posterity in the form of laws and rules, whether they be the Ten Commandments or the first ten amendments to the U.S. Constitution. This was the method of choice then for perpetuating values to live by. But times can change. I think today we should consider allowing individual states and localities more autonomy in deciding their own affairs for the same reason that today we allow athletes more freedom to call the shots during a game; it is because they are better than their predecessors of a generation ago were. They play better and they think smarter. And because of it they don't have to rely as much on the dictates of others, thus expanding their scope.

One reason for our mounting and pervasive problems is the ineffectiveness of an imperial congress (that lacks the time and expertise to perform their jobs as formulated). Add to this a bureaucracy that interferes endlessly in the affairs of businesses. I advocate *greatly* expanded freedom from regulation and paperwork for individuals and firms who have a record of fair play and honesty. As for those who do not, *greater restrictions*

and monitoring need to be applied to a degree appropriate. An additional benefit to this dual approach is the powerful built-in incentives it provides. Then one and all would have good reasons to behave.

Until diversity eventually consolidates into a uniformity of excellence (which would happen only because inferior choices will have all fallen by the wayside), *decentralization* should be the preferred strategy. The time should come when we'll be left with that proverbial but so far elusive utopia that we call "the best of all possible worlds." If that can ever take hold, the world will be blessed and be one. Amen.

150.   *October 18, 1990*

If I were to rule the world, I would *not* subordinate my personal desires to the greater cause demanded by my new calling, for you see, my own desires *are* those which would benefit my constituency. The only reason absolute power corrupts absolutely is because the monarch's private wants *differ* from those of his subjects. When all checks and balances are removed, no man can for long resist indulging his whims, however well-intentioned he was when his reign began. A happy outcome, then, can *only* result if all concerned are in harmony.

To be master in a world without other people is to have an empty victory and a hollow existence. Once this is realized, it becomes clear why our own happiness is *best* served by promoting the happiness of others. The satisfaction that some derive from exploiting others must of necessity, by its very nature, be less fulfilling than that which comes to those with the courage to trust others, and have the good fortune for them to prove deserving of it. (Reward is not without risk, but if at first you don't succeed, try, try again. The harder the conflict, the more glorious the triumph when it comes.)

Now you may truly understand what I mean by *enlightened* self-interest.

151. *October 20, 1990*

People who suffer major tragedies in their lives, especially in mid-life, are the very ones most likely to join fringe movements in their subsequent search for acceptance and belonging. But why must they look for answers outside of mainstream beliefs? I guess it's due to the credibility gap. They correctly sense that the old ways, being inherently flawed, do not always work. Of course they're right, and the worse conditions get, the more personal tragedies there are. So they experiment with the exotic, and convince themselves that they are "saved," or otherwise better off than before. Whether true or not, if this results in *lasting* constructive behavior, I say "wonderful!" But if not, beware, the influence of cults can be pernicious.

To those looking for lasting answers who can face reality without illusions and with open minds, I suggest you look no further than this book. Recognition of the disease is the point where the cure beings, and the legacy you leave to your children if you can help them gain understanding, will never be tainted by disillusionment later on.

Just remember, in the long run, for those who want and

can *accept* the truth (that's the key), frankness will prove superior to all but the most innocuous deceptions. Neither will it be easy to accept the truth when you've believed a lie all your life.

152.

October 29, 1990

The Supreme Court—Who's Kidding Who?

The theory is that their sole duty is to interpret the meaning of the Constitution as it applies to the case before them, without tainting their decisions with their personal inclinations. What surprises me is not that they so often do not do this, but that any of them can fool themselves into believing that they *do*. It is easy to interpret cases that are unambiguous, but how many are? The easy ones never make it this far.

Truth had been supposed to be revealed by God. Since Rousseau and Tom Paine, truth has been supposed to be revealed by reason. Whereas the medium of God was one's conscience if one was a Protestant, and God's vicar on earth if

"It never ceases to amaze me that we've been able to interpret a 6000-word Constitution into briefs of 100,000,000 words."

one was a Roman Catholic, the medium of reason in the American commonwealth has been supposed to be the courts. Like the priests of the ancient cults who were ready to say what God or the oracle revealed, the American courts are supposed to be ready to say what the Constitution and reason reveal through them to the human mind at large. If five of the nine judges agree on the revelation, that makes it binding.

Decisions more often than not *do* reflect personal beliefs— and I think with all of the new situations that arise in today's world, they *should*. That is why only the best minds with the greatest capacity for applying *common sense* to their judgments should be selected for this supreme calling.

153.   *November 4, 1990 and February 27, 1992*

These are not accusations. (Let's not ask for trouble.) However, the temptation to pose certain questions *is* hard to resist. Is mishandling of the economy through actions taken by the Federal Reserve more than mere ineptness? Could it be intentional just to create profit opportunities? If there's one inviolate economic law, it's that recoveries need money; but where is it? Never underestimate the ability of Washington to perceive the opposite of what is actually happening and to conjure up the data to support its perception. Can any sensible person really believe that higher unemployment is good because it's supposed to result in lower inflation? Alan Greenspan seems to think so! Would Greenspan know it if he's being used? Why was Paul Volcker forced out as Fed chairman? Was it because his "good guy" white hat was the only one he was willing to wear? Was he too good for his *own* good? Or was it simply that his talents were needed elsewhere? Treasury secretary Nicholas Brady said regarding the economy, that he sees robins on the lawn. I think what he may be seeing is their droppings on his spectacles. This is the corollary of Bismarck's insight that nothing is confirmed

"The trouble is not with your set — the government economists you have just heard actually do not make any sense."

until it is officially denied. In a January 1991 writing titled "Stand Still Little Lambs, To Be Shorn," the highly respected American Institute for Economic Research said that the politicians and money managers in Western Civilization have systematically embezzled by the inflating process the surplus product of all who produce. Too few fully understand the success of this process. In just five decades, our planners have taken $8,176,900,000,000 (trillion) from the savings of the Nation's "forgotten citizens," those who mistakenly relied upon the dollar and dollar-denominated assets for a store of value.

If there *are* powerful interests that are pulling strings from behind the scenes, rather than oppose them, I would prefer winning them over to occupy an even more exalted pedestal (no catcalls please, would you not act the same way were you in their shoes?). For jaded lives seeking new thrills, I can offer the ultimate and perpetual high: *enlightened* self-interest. It is the optimal life-style for *everyone*, including those who already enjoy high privilege, power, and wealth. (That's the beauty of it, one party would not have to sacrifice their happiness for another's. Life improves for everybody who understands *enlightened* self-interest.) But in all fairness, I would caution the well-to-do that, although their own emotional and financial well-being would improve in absolute terms, their position *relative* to others would moderate by virtue of the lower stratum narrowing the gap due to a low starting point. Such equality enhancement could be a blow to a few egos, but they would soon recover and bask in the same sunlight that would then be available to all.

Trading in your old egos for new understanding would be the deal of a lifetime. And what do I think the chances of that happening are? For the replacement generation, I have high hopes. As for most (but not all) of the elite who are currently in power and have been accustomed to privilege from birth, I will relate a parable that an old man tells to his great-grandson: A swan came to a broad stream and was about to swim across when he noticed a scorpion at the water's edge. As the swan approached, the scorpion asked the swan if he could ride on his back since he too wanted to cross over. The swan hesitated, saying, "Your sting is deadly, but if you promise not to harm me, I will let you ride on my back."

So it was agreed, and they proceeded to cross the stream. The swan felt secure knowing that if he were poisoned, they would both drown. But lo and behold, halfway across the scorpion did sting the swan with his venomous tail, and they *both* did indeed, drown.

The little boy could not understand this, and he said, "But grandpa, why did he do that?" And the old man said, "Because it is his nature." Sometimes we get caught up in forces too primal to control. (See habit, #89 and #123)

We hope destiny does not bring us to repeat the words of General William Tecumseh Sherman, but if it does . . . "War is a remedy that our enemy has chosen; let them have as much of it as they want." Or as military strategist Carl von Clausewitz wrote: "War therefore is an act of violence intended to compel our opponent to fulfil our will."

154.   *November 5, 1990*

Can man save himself from his baser instincts without sacrificing personal satisfaction, or is it even desirable for him to do so? For most, yes, for a few, perhaps not. Once you have reached your potential, the pleasures of the moment *do* assume a higher priority if for no other reason than, "Where can I go from here?" So you simply enjoy yourself while you can, however you can. When one balances short-term benefits against long-term benefits on life's scale (our subconscious is good at doing this task for us at propitious moments), it is only natural that the greater the weight your potential long-term advantages can account for, the greater your incentive to pass up *relatively* less rewarding transitory pleasures that are accompanied with risks

"If I had known I was going to live this long, I'd probably have taken better care of myself."

you do not wish to assume. H. Ross Perot says that when you go to the dentist you expect a little pain in return for a long-term benefit. But if your future holds little promise, so too do you have fewer reasons to resist the quicker, easier, short-term gratifications. A man without bread today can hardly concern himself with tomorrow's problems.

We are most enriched when our sights are set the highest they can be without overreaching our personal limits, *and* we be lucky enough to hit our target (see #110-GG). It is most fortuitous that the more we apply ourselves the luckier we seem to get. In the immortal words of Branch Rickey, the colorful manager of the old Brooklyn Dodgers, "Luck is the residue of design."

155.   *November 11, 1990*

As you have seen, I have covered many sensitive topics within these pages. And perhaps I should not try to stretch my luck. The safe play would be to let well enough alone at this point. Then again, does not the notion of a higher level of truth suggest that less than complete honesty is less than what you now want and expect from me? So, at the risk of alienating the same fair-minded people I wish to win over, I want to discuss the merits of vigilantism.

When good ideas are forged into the steel of unbending laws, without allowing them to be tempered by common sense, injustices can frequently occur which offset the good these laws normally provide. Should we allow the tyranny of unquestioned authority (laws and rules) to usurp the application of common sense? Would we not be much better off to *decentralize* authority (to a greater degree than we do now) all the way down to the policeman on the beat—but only after first upgrading his job with appropriate pay, respect, and authority? Higher quality applicants would then be attracted to that calling, and

"Don't be so hasty — you've got to work
for change **<u>WITHIN</u>** the system!"

the good ones would be likely to stay aboard longer without becoming discouraged. Atlanta mayor Maynard Jackson will tell you: If the cream does not rise to the top the crud will.

I am leading up to something here; I believe there are times when it is proper for people with uncommon common sense to act unilaterally. Fidel Castro may possibly be up to the level of the South American liberator, Simon Bolivar, whose profound remark I quoted in #26, and he wasted *no* time in ridding Cuba of entrenched mafia influence *overnight* when he first came to power. If Fidel could only learn to be less ideologically rigid in his thinking, he could be a leader of the first rank. His problem is that he is too far ahead of his time.

I am suggesting there are times when the vigilantes are *right.* The mafia *should* be neutralized, period. Saddam Hussein *should* be neutralized, one way or the other, period. Oliver North was a hero, not a villain, that should be clear. The trouble is, vigilante justice walks an extremely fine line. Even well-meaning prosecutors can and often do get carried away in zealous excesses; ask Michael Milken. It is so easy to come down on Leona Helmsley and it may turn out Imelda Marcos too (they make such easy targets), both of whom were naive enough to think that justice can always be had without the need to aggressively defend oneself. I too was initially prejudiced against these two personalities as a result of the barrage of one-sided publicity against them. The vigilante's no-nonsense approach will expeditiously hang the suspects—often whether they're guilty or not. Nevertheless, *sometimes* we need to bypass the bureaucracy and accept any resultant injustices as the lesser evil.

To sum up, I would say: Don't rush to judgment, but at the same time, don't equivocate endlessly. There is no perfect answer to all problems, and mistakes will be made. But to the degree we can be imbued with common sense (for this, no age is too early), and ultimately, *enlightened* (a higher level of) common sense, is the degree to which man will succeed. This remains our best hope.

156.   *November 25, 1990*

Should we place relative values on human lives? It's something to consider. Is the life of a healthy fetus more important than the life of its 25-year-old mother as the Catholic Church believes? I think not, in fact I think the opposite. (In fairness to the Church, when that rule was made, it was probably sensible at the time. My only complaint is their failure to keep pace with changing conditions. It is also worth noting that the Islamic religion is even less amenable to change. Being shackled to the past is not conducive to making progress. Just the fact that Christian Arabs invariably do better economically than Moslem Arabs should tell you something.) Is that same mother's life to be valued more than her 85-year-old grandparent (assuming no unusual circumstances exist)? Yes, I think it is. Is the life of an army general of greater value *to society* than that of the corporal? Obviously it is—all the more so if it's wartime.

So far I've picked the easy ones. What about Hitler's notions of race superiority? Do they have any validity at all? Careful, careful; the ice is getting pretty thin where I'm standing, but let's continue anyway. I would offer this distinction: Saddam Hussein is an evil man; Hitler did evil deeds. Saddam pursues only his own narrow self-interest, unfortunately it is not of the newer enlightened variety that I subscribe to (the difference being what day is to night). As a result, he faces an uncertain future at best. But even if he were to win (how that could happen I don't know) he would still be *less* well-off personally than he would be by following my proposed life-style, and this is without even considering how much better off the welfare of humanity at large could be. Saddam's brand of morality is not only obsolete, it is an insult to Islam. On the other hand, Hitler pursued *his* vision of greatness for the German people with Teutonic efficiency and a passionate loyalty to principles that he believed in but were warped to begin with. And again unfortunately, his gains were to have come at the expense of others, which is also the antithesis of enlightened self-interest. The Germans are collectively manic-depressive; they are either jumping off towers or climbing them.

But to return to the question of race superiority. Certainly genes *do* make a difference, but it is equally certain that to optimize the long-term happiness of everyone, each of us needs an environment conducive to realizing our full potential. Every person should be measured as an individual, not as a member of a particular group or race. And every individual deserves an equal shot at making his mark and a try for happiness. But please realize that those who achieve these goals will *not* be in proportion to their ethnic or racial numerical makeup. Look— that's just the way it is. What *nature* gives us or does not give us, cannot be altered by wishful thinking or by legislation. However, no one should despair; good guidance, good sense, and good science will someday bring freedom of the spirit to virtually all of us.

157. *December 3, 1990*

Which values are really the more important: material, or ethical? Ethical values are superior, but *only* after a certain threshold where minimum material needs are satisfied. The *main* reason our jails are occupied by a widely disproportionately greater number of poor people, is that basic needs rightly take priority over ethical niceties at that level. Such ethics are a luxury that the poor cannot afford. After all, the first law of nature is survival, and if the law of man becomes its first victim, so be it. Unless people can earn an honest living and look ahead to a good life, they will make a dishonest living and take their pleasures, however short-lived and destructive, where they find them. This mentality usually becomes habit-forming. Too bad for them, and too bad for us.

Here I will delve further into a solution touched upon earlier regarding the dilemma presented above, by asking this hypothetical question: If we were to take away nearly all the monies from almost all the many entitlement (read: welfare) and subsidy programs that now exist, and added that sum to the new value

"Be careful what you say in front of Nevelstrom —
he's some kind of ethics nut."

that would be created if all freeloaders (rich and poor alike) were put to work (especially those who *cannot now afford to work* lest their "benefits" be reduced too drastically), would it be enough to pay a living wage ($9 per hour in 1990 dollars) for any job with a *normal amount of stress, effort, and complexity?* My answer to this is an unequivocal YES. We *can* put an end to poverty without undue pain.

I will tell you how in a moment. First, would you agree with me that anyone in this day and age (at least in the U.S.) who wants to and can perform the kind of job mentioned above, deserves a wage sufficient to live decently on? You do. Now will you also agree that if this person cannot find such a job on his own, he be guaranteed one of his choice from those available, with the understanding it be at the convenience and location of the guaranteeing authority? This would not be un-like joining the Army. Also, should not anyone who is without a visible means of support or at least the prospect thereof, be *required* to accept the same *opportunity?* What seems to be harsh would be ultimately humane. What's that you say? Your constitutional rights are being violated? Pooh—here's your castor oil, take it.

It is difficult to exaggerate all the social benefits that would accrue from taking such actions. The energies of many police-men, social workers, prison workers, court workers, lawyers, could all be redirected into *productive* labor. *Of course* their lives would be disrupted, that's part of progress; spare me the need to argue *that* point. Additionally, GNP and revenues would rise, allowing taxes to be reduced. But most important of all, less crime means fewer victims, hence fewer cases of anguish and trauma for the innocent. Once a wholesome life-style is made affordable to all, the American disease of the disen-chanted, drug addiction, would show signs of decline, as would that universal Russian disease, alcoholism (cigarettes too).

"It's the media, Senator. They want to know if
you've ever used drugs."

And now, finally, you may ask me the big question. How can McDonald's et al, afford to pay my *living* wage (not a minimum wage) of $9 an hour in 1990 dollars, without making inflationary price hikes? Answer—through tax incentives powerful enough to allow them to do so, and replenished by sources already noted (value in—value out). Here is an instance where the government can really do some good. Understand, the government's task is merely to pull the trigger, to redistribute the rewards of increased output more sensibly by eliminating the bottom rung of the ladder; the extra gunpowder is made by putting *all* idle hands *to work* (that's *real* soul food). Just as you cannot fill a water bucket if outflow exceeds input; so you will not use it up as long as input exceeds outflow. No matter that you are using more than before, all parties can end up one way or another with an overall quality of life better than they had before. Isn't this what it's all about?

What really makes the equation dynamic are all the intangible benefits. Trust me, where I go wrong will be more than offset by where I am right.

158.   *December 2, 1990*

Between improvements in communications and faster package delivery services to even more places, it would seem to me the need for a concentration of high-rise office buildings in crowded urban areas will lessen in coming years. After all, why commute 30 miles to work each day and home again at night at a cost of 30¢ a mile and two hours of our time, if we no longer have to? Why live in one place and work in another, thus underutilizing both at twice the cost? If we work in a factory it's one thing, but an office is quite another. We could both live and work where we want to, not where circumstances dictate we have to.

159.   *December 6, 1990*

Wait till you read this! Mr. Norman Dodd, (deceased) former Director of the Committee to Investigate Tax Exempt Foundations, U.S. House of Representatives, obtained the following information from the minute books of the Carnegie Endowment for International Peace, founded in 1908.

During 1908, these minutes reported the following: The trustees of the Carnegie Endowment bring up a single question, namely if it is desirable to alter the life of an entire people, is there any means more efficient than war to getting that end? They discussed this question at a very high academic and scholarly level for a year and they came up with an answer. There are no known means more efficient than war, assuming the objective is altering the life of an entire people. That leads them to another question. How do we involve United States in a war? (This was in 1909.)

The trustees then answered the question of how to involve us in a war by saying we must control the diplomatic machinery of the United States. That brings up the question of how to secure that control and the answer is: We must control the State Department.

Now at that point, research discloses a relationship between the effort to control the State Department and an entity which the Carnegie Endowment set up, namely the Council of Learned Societies, and through that entity were cleared all of the high appointments in the State Department. They have continued to be cleared that way since then. (So stated on September 26, 1978.)

The above is an almost verbatim account from the December 1990 (#346) Bulletin of the Fort Collins, Colorado-based Committee to Restore the Constitution. Don't you find this interesting? And what do I think of it all? First, I think I would like to have been in on that year-long discussion. But since I wasn't, I believe if one is provoked into a war, it becomes acceptable, but to be the provocateur is probably unacceptable. I find Thoreau's aphorism given in #110-GG and its afterthought compelling, especially the last line which goes: If you seek moral ends, you must employ moral means. After all, what might have seemed sensible in 1909, could quite obviously look much different to us in 1990.

"That one? Oh, I got it in a war we're not allowed to talk about."

160. *December, 1990*

The incentive to misinvest capital from the point of view of our country's welfare has been brought to my attention by a very insightful person who eschews publicity and does not even like to be quoted. So to bring his message to a larger audience, I am forced to rewrite some of his ideas in my own words while adding more myself.

Michael Milken was not the cause for the proliferation and ultimate havoc rendered by junk bonds. Responsibility for that debacle lies with the authors of the tax code itself. Milken the superbroker, was merely a facilitator to the deed. The die was cast when tax incentives lured companies into borrowing money in preference to selling equity, which proves especially burdensome for emerging businesses in the face of today's high interest rates. (If you've read the first half of this book, you know what I think about interest.) And as for investors, thanks also to U.S. tax laws, there is no inducement to favor the risk of ownership over the *relative* safety of making loans. Only in America is this the case. I don't mind telling you, this won't hack it in the competitive world which is coming.

Japan is a different story. Until recently, their interest rates had at times been *below* the inflation rate. It *paid* to borrow in Japan. When individual Japanese put their money into savings accounts (which is the main source of industry financing there), it is more for reasons of safekeeping, as it should be. A society that allows profits of any significance on interest will only weaken itself, though it may not be obvious as to why and how. Even though their stock market plunged 42% from its apex on December 26, 1989 to its trough almost one year later, a late November, 1990, report from Tokyo's Mitsui Research Institute pointed out that new plant and equipment spending was up 16% over the previous year. What's their big secret? An efficient, skilled, productive labor force, of which there is a *chronic shortage.*

America should reduce the capital gains tax substantially, and eliminate it altogether on sales of assets held for longer than three years. This is nothing more than a tax in a person's ability to create *additional* wealth (such wealth benefits everybody) from savings on which he has already paid taxes. I say once is enough. There are better ways of securing revenue for the national good, as a complete reading of this work will suggest.

The ongoing collapse in junk bonds was at least triggered, if not caused, by an economic slump. This in turn was brought on by high interest rates and tight credit. If legitimate needs for money are not fulfilled, commerce will come to a standstill. Have we learned nothing from the great depression? As I suggested in #47, the gravest sin of all is to allow a situation where able men and women sit idle for want of financing. In such a situation, any action that will correct this stupidity is justified.

At the scene of the present crime we find the fingerprints of Alan Greenspan. This misfortune might never have happened under Paul Adolph Volcker, although he did hint at troubles to come when in 1985 he said: "We are in a real sense living on borrowed money and borrowed time." Volcker has an understanding of money like no other since the legendary elder J.P. Morgan himself.

To quote one of the better ideas of John Maynard Keynes: "Activity of production depends on the business man hoping for a reasonable profit. The margin which he requires as his necessary incentive to produce, may be a very small percentage of the total value of product. But take this away from him and the whole process stops."

161.   *December 30, 1990*
I do not agree with those who say that what others think does not matter. I believe in tempering my actions and even

my own personal behavior in an effort to accommodate the sensitivities of my neighbors (within reason, of course) even though at times this conflicts with my own views. And all the more so if the inconvenience for me is less distressing than the discomfort that could come to them by having *their* long held beliefs challenged.

However, do not for one moment assume I will not try to win them over. And how do I propose to do that?—through arguments that are fortiter in re (strong in the substance) with its complement suaviter in modo (smoothness in the style), and finally the piece de resistance: convincing through example. This means gaining first the respect, then the support, and finally the emulation of others. And all this can come by way of demonstrating through the practical consequences of our individual and collective actions the superior results that are to be had for the taking by practicing enlightened self-interest. It has certainly worked for me, and without ever having hurt another. Can anyone ask for more than that?

162. *December 30, 1990*

With the 21st century just one decade away, humanity has something to hope for that they never had before. Until now, science was not developed enough to consider this a possibility. I am talking about arresting the aging process indefinitely.

The desire for immortality has always intrigued humankind, as manifested in our religious beliefs and/or legends.

But now the time has come to put our faith in what we know rather than what we don't know but saw fit to create from our imagination in order to satisfy a wish.

Going to the moon, Mars, and beyond is glamorous stuff, I admit, but it is infinitely less important (*literally* speaking), than applying the same money towards medical research into aging.

And maybe it would all be in vain. But since we don't know what is or isn't possible, research at least affords us a chance that trying to lower your golf handicap does not. A slim chance is better than none at all.

You are now entitled to ask the final question. If we learn how to prevent aging, who gets to take advantage of it and who doesn't? That, dear friends, is the kind of dilemma I would love to be faced with.

163.   *February 2, 1991*
Gary Kasparov is the world chess champion. Gary Kasparov is also the head of the Moscow regional branch of the Democratic Party of Russia. In making the following points (all of which come from him), it becomes clear that his gift for insightful thought is not limited to chess.

The U.S. must make the right moves while communism is dying in the Soviet Union. If ever there was a time for America to base its Soviet policy on long-term strategy rather than short-term calculations, this is it.

Those of us who play chess know that *tactics not mated to strategy* lead to unintended consequences—to dictatorship instead of democracy; to new world wars instead of new world orders; to, in fact, the sacrifice of a strategic interest, the development of democracy across Soviet Eurasia, to the tactical convenience of Mikhail Gorbachev's tepid support in the Persian Gulf.

The U.S. needs to turn things right-side up again by adopting a strategy to manage the *demise* of communism, a strategy that has as its first principle the promotion of liberal democracy, a product that America is fitted to supply and that the Soviet peoples demand. Halfway measures or mere reforms are not enough, the people want genuine perestroika, of society, not of communism. Hard-liners react to all this by attempting to justify the imposition of martial law in the following ways:

First, use KGB thugs to perpetrate what is later called "ethnic violence." Second, use official propaganda organs to fan the flames of ill will (in Lithuania, the party press whips up the Russian minority against the Lithuanian majority). Third, stand by idly while a slaughter occurs (for six days last January, Soviet authorities in Azerbaijan permitted wholesale murder of Armenians by ultra-nationalist Azerbaijanis). Fourth, dispatch troops only after the killing is over and then use those troops to crush indigenous national-democratic forces. Fifth, make no effort to punish those who conducted this attack or that pogrom. And sixth, establish regimes of occupation or, in the case of Lithuania and Latvia, "national salvation committees" that justify their existence by promising, if that's the right word, to "restore order."

With a different face here and a changed circumstance there, this is how Stalin twisted steel in Czechoslovakia in 1948 and how Gorbachev turns the trick in 1991.

None of this surprises most Soviet citizens. What Mr. Gorbachev and the West call new thinking is old thinking to us. Force is still *prima ratio* in resolving political disputes, and state-organized robbery is still the engine of economic policy. Mr. Gorbachev's recent decree removing 50- and 100-ruble notes from circulation is no different from Stalin's forced "state loans." In the hoariest of Bolshevik traditions, the life savings (granted, at least it is not the lives) of millions of people are wiped out by a decision from above.

Less obviously, whatever little political capital the Soviet government managed to accumulate with the population since 1985 has also been destroyed. Not a shred of confidence remains in the government.

On Thursday the U.S. Senate passed a resolution, 99-0,

calling on the Bush administration to suspend all technology exchanges, review all economic aid proposals and withdraw support for Soviet membership in the International Monetary Fund, the General Agreement on Tariffs and Trade and the World Bank.

It's a start. But the problem with the Senate vote is identical with the problem of overall U.S. policy toward the Soviet Union. Both are reactive rather than proactive. Mr. Gorbachev acts, the U.S. protests; act, protest; act, protest; etc. The U.S. is constantly behind the curve of events because it has yet to identify its own interests in the outcome of these events and to develop a strategy to implement those interests.

If the Bush administration is serious about a new world order based on free trade and peaceful relations among sovereign states, then it must *become serious about democracy in the Baltic republics.* The political outcome in Lithuania, Latvia and Estonia will probably determine the fate of democracy elsewhere across the Soviet Union. For without democracy in the various countries of the Soviet Union, there will be no new world order, though there may be a new world war.

That's the bad news. The good news is that the course of events, if not impeded by the U.S. and other liberal democracies offering aid and comfort to Mr. Gorbachev, is leading toward the development of several national democracies from a fast-decaying union.

At this juncture, the U.S. is unquestionably at the helm and can steer events. Here's what it should do to promote democracy:

1. Cooperate closely with the various Soviet republics, placing special emphasis on developing economic relations with Russia. Instead of offering the anti-market central government most favored nation status and membership in the IMF, GATT and the World Bank, invite Russia and other

market-oriented republics to join the world financial community. In the case of the Baltic countries, confirm the legitimacy of their redeclarations of independence. *This course of action would embolden democrats throughout Soviet Eurasia,* while simultaneously restoring the good name of the U.S.

It is crucial to understand that after 74 years of dictatorship, many people in the Soviet Union have little conception of this thing called democracy. To an astonishing degree, they judge democracy by the extent of support offered to Soviet democrats by Western governments.

2. Recognize that the old black (Brezhnev) vs. white (democratic dissidents) paradigm for Soviet society is dated. Today, there is a powerful middle class of *nomenklaturshchiks* who expected Mr. Gorbachev to deliver stability and Western credits, not civil war and canceled loans. These managers, though necessary for the survival of the central regime, carry no brief for the current arrangements. If they and the emerging democratic leaderships in the republics were to join forces, there could be a new order with sufficient consent to avert civil war.

3. Promote human rights. Postponing the February U.S.—USSR summit is fine, but because of the war in the Baltics, not the war in the Gulf. Cancel plans to hold this year's Helsinki human rights conference in Moscow.

Thomas Carlyle once remarked that what really counts is the mights rather than the rights of man. If the Annus Mirabilis of 1990 taught us anything, it ought to have taught us that rights, too, have mights and that if American policy makers can summon the nerve to conduct policy according to a strategy that employs this country's political analog of the Patriot missile, then they may actually create a new world order.

(To repeat: This brilliant essay is the work of Gary Kasparov.)

164.   *February 12, 1991*
Division I . . . The Question:
What do we do about education?

There are two sides to every story

Peter M. Flanigan is chairman of the advisory board of the Center for Educational Innovation in New York City (among other endeavors). He tells us that while that city's Catholic schools do a far better job of educating disadvantaged inner-city students than do the public schools, even though these students' backgrounds are similar in every way, they are doing it at about half the cost. One has to ask why that is. Mr. Flanigan suggests an answer.

Among the most fundamental explanations of the achievements of the archdiocesan system is that it is based on educational choice. The principal has chosen to be at his or her school, and has chosen the school's educational program and faculty. Each teacher has chosen to work at that particular school. Each student has chosen to study there. Everyone involved in the enterprise has "bought into" it, has become involved by choice. In the zoned inner-city school, the principal is assigned to the school, the curriculum is determined in detail by the central bureaucracy, the teachers are assigned and finally the students are required by law to attend. Nobody has "bought into" such a school, nobody has made a choice. Every aspect of the school is dictated from above. The New York City school system is like the Soviet economy, where everything is also dictated from above, and both are failures.

So why should New Yorkers respond to the campaign to keep the 140 inner city Catholic schools open? Because the gap between what single-parent, minority, poverty-level families can pay for their children's education, and what it costs the archdiocese to provide it, has grown beyond the archdiocese's capacity to fill.

"Of course your son's teacher is incompetent and uncaring —
that's how we prepare these kids for LIFE!"

Unless those families get help with that tuition, either by contributions or vouchers, many of these schools will close. And if these schools close, all of their students will be returned to the public school system. They will add costs that the city cannot afford to meet. The work force able to function in today's world and available to the City's employers will shrink even further. A yardstick by which to measure the job being done by the public schools will be lost. And most important, many kids will lose their only opportunity to learn their way out of poverty and into the American dream.

Now for a rebuttal

Albert Shanker, President of the American Federation of Teachers, takes a different view of Mr. Flanigan's conclusions, which were based in large part on a study by the Brookings Institution. Could it be here that a political agenda is masquerading as objective research? (The following by Mr. Shanker is verbatim.)

The claim that Catholic and public schools are educating the same kind of youngsters but that Catholic schools are doing a much better job of it; that the reason is school choice; and that since the Brookings Institution study "proves" this, the way out of our educational crisis is to divert tax dollars from public to Catholic and other private schools. None of the above is true.

First, the data the Brookings study is based on show that public schools are educating far poorer youngsters than are Catholic schools, either in cities, suburbs or rural areas.

But what about the poor youngsters Catholic schools *are* educating? Do such schools do a better job than public schools, and is the reason school choice? Choice certainly is the reason—but not because the choice is being exercised by students or parents. It's because Catholic schools, unlike all but a handful of public schools, get to choose their students and exercise this choice to exclude low-achieving youngsters and those with discipline problems. At least that's what a nationwide survey of Catholic-school principals revealed—a survey, by the way, that was available to but ignored by the Brookings-study authors. Is doing a good job with highly motivated, achieving youngsters whose parent or parents may be poor but nevertheless are involved in their education, "proof" of the superiority of Catholic schools? Hardly. Public schools have done this for generations and continue to do so every day.

Still, you'd think that with a handpicked student body, Catholic schools would be doing a better job than public schools that have a similar student body. But according to the most recent research review of this issue, the difference in student achievement between Catholic and public schools is either trivial or nonexistent. Despite publicity to the contrary, there is nothing in the Brookings study that contradicts this finding.

I share Mr. Flanigan's respect for Catholic schools, and agree they have an important lesson to teach public schools about how to function without a huge bureaucracy. I also believe they have an important lesson to teach about the importance of standards and student discipline. I also support—that is, public-school choice—and believe it can be accomplished in a way that respects the public-school system's legal and moral responsibility to take all comers. But neither the evidence nor common sense supports the argument that the way to improve public schools, which the overwhelming majority of our kids depend on, is to bail out private schools with public dollars.

Another relevant comment

From Stanley S. Litow, Deputy Chancellor for Operations, New York City Public Schools

A significant omission in Mr. Flanigan's piece is that a hefty portion of the cost per pupil for Catholic schools in New York City is actually borne by the public-school system. This includes costs for food, transportation, remedial reading and math programs, and substance-abuse education. Our Bureau of Non-Public Schools, with about 300 employees, helps budget and deliver these extensive services not just to Catholic but to Jewish and nondenominational private schools. These costs artificially inflate our own costs per pupil (which is $500 less than the state average) and our administrative payroll, and partially account for the small administrative staff at the diocesan schools.

Our schools also bear enormous additional costs for the 120,000 youngsters in special-education classes, and average $15,000 per child. Most of these costs are mandated by the courts or by state and federal law. It should be obvious that the insignificant numbers of special education children in Catholic schools result from their specialized admissions criteria. Our schools are also the point of entry for non-English-speaking children in far greater numbers than in parochial schools. We also serve large numbers of homeless and foster-care children.

If you think education is expensive, try ignorance.

Division II . . . The Problem:

To understand why we foster mediocrity in education today, we first need to understand how it all began, and why. There are thousands of humane, caring people that work in schools, as teachers and aides and administrators, but the abstract logic of the institution overwhelms their individual contributions. The top disciplinary problems in American schools in 1940 before the liberals, integrationists and world improvers started correcting them were: talking out of turn, chewing gum, making noise, running the halls, cutting in line, dress code infractions and littering. Today, enroute to the new world disorder, they are: drug use, alcohol drinking, pregnancy, suicide, rape, robbery and assault.

When the term "New World Order" is used, all can agree that it is *meant* to connote one idea: a better life. To some that means egalitarianism, where any independent head that rises above the crowd is lopped off. The resulting wreckage left by this "dumbing down" process is what ails American education today, and hence what ails America today. Socialism/communism was and is a noble failure.

They say the road to hell is paved with good intentions; thus it was in 1902 that John D. Rockefeller said in his "Occasional Letter No. 1," the following: "In our dreams we have limitless resources and the people yield themselves with perfect docility to our moulding hands. The present educational conventions fade from our minds, and unhampered by tradition, we work our own good will upon a grateful and responsive rural folk. We shall not try to make these people or any of their children into philosophers or men of learning, or of science. We have not to raise up from among them authors, editors, poets or men of letters. We shall not search for embryo great artists, musicians, nor lawyers, doctors, preachers, politicians, statesmen of whom we now have ample supply . . . So we will organize our children into a little community and teach them to do in a perfect way the things their fathers and mothers are doing in an imperfect way, in the homes, in the shop and on the farm."

Being a man of action, Mr. Rockefeller set about to rebuild the educational system, using John Dewey's "progressive education" formula and the Lincoln School of Teachers College, Columbia University, as a model. By means of generous grants to increase the endowments of colleges around the nation, he gained a foothold for a voice in the policies and curriculums of these institutions, and later for influencing the character of scholarship and teaching.

After Mr. Rockefeller's retirement from the scene, his descendants, in league with other affluent internationalists, carried on the task he had started. In the course of events, the alliance of the International Financiers with the Communist Cause was accomplished, and the communists brought some ideas of their own into the remodeling of our education. These included:

Get control of the schools. Use them as conveyor belts for socialism and communist propaganda. Soften the curriculum. Get control of teachers' associations. Put the party line in text books, and encourage students to crusade for radical causes they are not yet fully qualified to understand and evaluate.

So it is that today we are saddled with this nefarious legacy.

Returning to the definition of New World Order; others might define it as elitism. Here the standard example is Fascism, which is another form of dictatorship that knows what's best for the people. But unlike a communist society that acclaims the *least* able, Fascism acclaims the *most* able (and incidentally, these people would just as soon have the world all to themselves.) Remember this distinction in case you're ever asked what the difference between the two is. Henry Ford leaned in this direction, and few people know that Hitler admired "Heinrich"—whose picture adorned his wall—more than any other man. (Of course, we cannot fault Henry for that.)

It is very easy for me to imply criticism of the above two versions of the New World Order, for I am blessed with the sagacity that comes from hindsight. Yet here we have two giants of industry, each with a certitude of finding Camelot; each looking for it in opposite directions . . . both of which were wrong. And the ultimate irony was that both were already *in* Camelot; both were helping to build it; and neither recognized it as such. In running a society according to either of these two principles, we find that one was meant to be noble but doesn't work; the other works but isn't noble. Shouldn't we have the third option which encompasses both?

So now it is time to suggest what New World Order *should* mean. And I will not keep you waiting for the answer; it is *liberty* and *justice* for *all* (that includes both the least able *and* the most able).

But isn't that what America was all about to begin with? Yes, but compared to the world at large, our team is still young and inexperienced, so it is not surprising if at times we drop the ball. But remember this; having somewhat more liberty and justice here than anywhere else has made us (in spite of our errors) the world's #1 success story. If we are to keep it that way, be advised that no document, not even the U.S. Constitution, can save us if we fail to mind the store. Do not be deceived by a guarantee. It is possible to be educated and not have freedom; but if you are kept in a state of ignorance, you are at greater risk of losing whatever freedoms you do have. Remember, times do not change; they are made to change.

As the day of reckoning draws near, a cloud from the right is drifting toward a void that had been left. Left has two meanings here, but the real significance is a call for liberty that is best summed up by the following maxim: "On the Starship Liberty there are no passengers. We are all crew."

— BUCKMINSTER FULLER PARAPHRASED

> They came first for the tax protesters,
> and I didn't speak up
> because I wasn't a tax protester.
> Then they came for the gun owners,
> and I didn't speak up
> because I owned no guns.
> Then they came for the home
> educators and I didn't speak up
> because I had no children.
> Then they came for me,
> and by that time—
> no one was left to speak up.

— A MODERN VERSION OF THE FAMOUS QUOTE
FROM PASTOR MARTIN NIEMOLLER

Unless you're willing to die for your cause, you will be less than completely effective in promoting it. — GIVOTANGI

Division III . . . The Answer:

Reprinted March 1992 (in condensed form) by permission from IMPRIMUS, *the monthly journal of Hillsdale College, Michigan*

Annual spending on education has increased over 300 percent in less than twenty years. Why, then, are America's schools in crises? Why have education task forces failed to achieve significant reform?

Polly Williams and J. Patrick Rooney say it's time to stop relying on more money, more task forces, more experts, and more bureaucrats; genuine reform can only be brought about by creating incentives for schools—and therefore students—to succeed, i.e., by introducing competition.

Polly Williams is America's leading advocate of parental choice in education. She has been successful in securing private school vouchers—the first in the nation—for inner city students in Milwaukee. To millions of American parents who want the freedom to decide what education is best for their children, Polly Williams has become a national symbol of hope, courage and determination. A six-term state representative in the Wisconsin legislature, she holds the record for the highest number of votes for reelection. In 1986, the figure was 94 percent. What follows are ideas expressed by Ms. Williams.

Historically, blacks have demanded equal opportunity education; what they've gotten instead is forced desegregation. What do blacks want? We want the same thing whites want. We want our kids educated in their own communities. Yet for the last decade and a half, forced busing in Milwaukee has thwarted this desire, and in the process cost taxpayers $335 million.

In the meantime, the public schools are failing to educate our children. Sixty percent of all Milwaukee ninth graders do not complete high school, and of the 40 percent who stay in the school and walk across the stage to receive their diplomas, only 10 percent can read. For what amounts to a 90 percent failure rate, we pay $600 million a year to support the Milwaukee public schools—that averages out to about $6000 per student. The educrats keep saying "You've got to give us more money, because it's tough to educate these inner city kids. They are poor, and they are raised by single mothers; we can't expect them to learn . . ."

Well, poor black children *do* share a major disadvantage. Unlike those whose parents can vote with their feet and enroll in good private schools, poor black children are forced to go to the school the government selects for them. It just isn't the same thing. The kids get to where they don't care, and then they won't even try to learn, but if we don't educate them we're going to incarcerate them. Wisconsin, for example, has eight new prisons on the drawing board, but no new schools. Children need basic academic skills and adults need to work, instead of giving them endless social programs. Blacks want to learn and to earn their way just like everybody else. We don't want welfare that just puts us back on the plantation—this time the government plantation.

I opposed forced desegregation from the start. I wanted what most parents want: for my children to be educated in their own community. At the time, there were about a dozen private schools in the inner city of Milwaukee. They were previously Catholic institutions that had been reorganized as private non-sectarian academies, and they were a wonderful alternative for low-income and minority students—predominantly blacks, but also Hispanics, Asians and whites. They allowed students to get a good education in their own neighborhoods with teachers who really believed in *them*, rather than the educrats' stereotypes. What's really impressive is that these private schools had a 98 percent graduation rate.

But they couldn't get by on the tuition they charged, and although successful, they were in danger of closing their doors. Meanwhile, the public schools were getting millions of our tax dollars whether they did a good job or not. So a few years ago, a small group banded together and approached the state legislature. We said: "Why not allow tax dollars to go to the schools that *are* working?" We didn't know that vouchers had already been defeated in every other state where they'd been proposed.

We didn't even call our proposal a voucher plan; we called it "parental empowerment" or "choice." Meetings were organized to discuss our proposal. We hoped to attract a few dozen people, but hundreds of enthusiastic parents began showing up and staying for sessions that ran on for hours. This shocked public school officials, especially since they couldn't get more than a few parents to any of *their* meetings.

People often fall into the habit of saying, "How do you get the poor involved in the education of their children? They just don't care, or they don't know enough to make 'intelligent' choices." But, in reality, if you give them a sense that they can make a difference in the lives of their children, if you give them some power, you'll find out that poor parents can care more than anyone. They don't take education for granted. They know that education is the only way out of poverty. And when you empower people and give them a sense of ownership, they become responsible, and they learn how to make decisions. And when they are treated with dignity and respect, they respond to it.

Choice empowers parents. It allows them to choose the best school for their children. Poor people are the same as rich people. They may not have much money, but they have the same desires and the same needs. And poor people make decisions all the time. They decide where they are going to live, what grocery store to buy from, where to shop for clothes—they decide everything, but all of a sudden, the educrats claim that they don't have enough sense to make a decision about the education of their children.

The teachers' unions, the NAACP, the bureaucracy, and the educational establishment didn't agree. In the name of protecting the poor, they all opposed choice. Everyone, that is, except the parents.

Well, to everyone's surprise, the parental empowerment bill—the first in the U.S.—*did* pass into law. Starting in the

1990-1991 school year, up to 1000 students could claim $2500 worth of tuition vouchers (a fraction, of course, of the per-student expense at public schools). This year, one private school had 600 applicants for 100 openings. Every private school in the inner city has a waiting list. Hundreds of low-income families want out of the public school system. Those who have succeeded in getting out are spreading the word: Their children, two to three grade levels behind in the public school, are now working at their grade levels. Once always absent, they are even refusing to stay home sick! A typical response is, "Please don't make me stay home—my teacher is expecting me." There are no gang problems and only a two percent drop out rate.

Sure, it's only one thousand in a city that has one hundred thousand students, and the educrats are fighting the bill in the state supreme court, but I think it's a real victory, and we've only just begun. If the poor people of Milwaukee can achieve something no other group in the nation has been able to do, then anything is possible.

J. Patrick Rooney has been in the health insurance industry for over three decades. He is chairman of the board of the Golden Rule Insurance Company, which is licensed in 49 states and which earns a premium income of almost $600 million annually. The company is generally considered the nation's largest writer of individual medical insurance, which is marketed by over 70,000 independent brokers. Mr. Rooney has gained national attention in the last year for establishing a $1.2 million fund for private education vouchers which enable hundreds of low-income parents in Indiana to send their children to the private schools of their choice. In two recent headline editorials, the *Wall Street Journal* hailed Mr. Rooney's efforts as a real "breakthrough in corporate support for educational choice."

[This is the sort of thing I had in mind when I spoke of benevolent capitalism.]

Advocates of choice in Indiana have worked hard to achieve meaningful education reform, but we just can't get an educational choice bill through the state legislature. (If you have ever worked with any government branch, you know that it is a lot easier to prevent something from happening than it is to get anything innovative done.)

The odds are clearly on the side of the bureaucrats, even though there is considerable evidence that choice, where it has been tried in states such as Minnesota and districts such as East Harlem, is a phenomenal success. We know that educational choice in Indiana might be realized someday, but, in the meantime, we are abandoning another generation of children who are not getting a decent education.

Recently, we at the Golden Rule Insurance Company decided to do something about education reform right now. In 1991, we created *private* vouchers; that is, as a company in the private sector, we offered to pay half of the tuition of any student who wanted to leave the public system and go to a private school. (Most of the non-public schools in Indianapolis charge $1600 or less—our cap was, therefore, $800.) This voucher program is for grade school children. We would have loved to extend it to the high school level, but we have limited resources, so it was a matter of priority.

The only criterion is financial need. If students qualify for the free or reduced cost lunch program in the public schools, then they qualify for our educational grant. This is purposely a very generous criterion. We do not impose academic requirements of any kind, and there is a "first come, first served" basis for awarding the vouchers. (When we began, we tried elaborate questionnaire forms but quickly abandoned them. We are a society that is accustomed to filling out too many forms that are of dubious value.) We make no attempt to decide which private schools are eligible. We are about the business of helping parents and students; hence they are free to choose any school that meets their needs.

The beauty of private vouchers is that they are so simple— no red tape, no need to depend on bureaucrats to administer them, no worries that the vouchers will be used later as a way for the government to claim that private schools are accepting federal or state subsidies. And they start working right away.

Golden Rule's private vouchers are a great success, much greater than we expected, in fact. We called a press conference to announce the start of the program only three weeks before the commencement of the 1991-92 school year. We stated very cautiously that we anticipated that only 100-200 students would want to be involved in this program. Well, within the first three days, Golden Rule had 621 requests for applications, and at the present time, we have distributed more than 2,000 applications.

A temporary obstacle is that most of the private schools already have full or near-full enrollments. But the response to our private voucher plan will inevitably lead to expansion, as it has created a whole new supply of potential students for private schools. In the first school term of this year, 705 students were awarded vouchers and there were 199 on the waiting list. (This list would have been larger, but many parents knew that the private schools were full.)

Why do we support private education through vouchers? There are three reasons. The first reason is that Golden Rule is interested in helping the disadvantaged, particularly the minority citizens of our country. Our vouchers are not awarded on the basis of race or ethnic background, they are color-blind, but since they go to mainly inner city residents, the natural effect is to help blacks, Hispanics and other minorities.

Sources such as the Hudson Institute's report, *Workforce 2000,* estimate that over the next decade, the work force will be very slowly growing older, more female, more minority, and more disadvantaged. Only 15 percent of the new entrants to the labor force during that period will be white males compared with 30 percent today. The demographic opportunity of the 1990s will be missed unless something is done now. The problems of minority unemployment, crime and dependency could be far worse than they are today.

The second reason for Golden Rule's interest in vouchers is very practical. New jobs in service industries will demand much higher skill levels than the jobs of today. Many companies are already forced to run remedial education programs for their employees. We can't put off educating people until the time they apply for work; that is the wrong time to fix the problem. But according to their own standardized tests, Indiana public schools are failing to teach adequate basic skills and are far behind the private schools in terms of overall student achievement. If for no other reason than this, competition is needed at the elementary and secondary school levels where the monopoly position of the public school has stifled innovation.

The third reason is linked to the second: It is vital to the public interest that students work hard and learn basic habits like punctuality and diligence. Yet, the Committee for Economic Development published a study several years ago arguing that one of the most important failures of the public schools is that they have failed to teach even a basic "work ethic."

Add drug abuse and violence to the list: Public schools have failed there too, resorting to metal detectors, locker searches and security guards. And despite all such efforts, many students do not learn to respect or heed authority. Lastly, there is the dropout rate in public institutions. In one Indianapolis high school, *80 percent* of the student body typically does not graduate.

The American Federation of Teachers (AFT) and the National Education Association (NEA) have recently begun a new media campaign to convince Americans that the public schools are doing every bit as well as the private schools. I don't think Americans will be convinced, simply because there is too much evidence to the contrary. Who, for example, has ever heard of a private school with metal detectors or with an 80 percent drop out rate?

In summary, with private vouchers, we have made a real and practical investment in the future of our own business as well as our society. Every business and charitable organization should start its own voucher program, for one or one thousand students, it doesn't matter. What *does* matter is that they will have taken a step toward helping others *as well as themselves.* [Does this not sound to you like the enlightened self-interest that I keep talking about?]

■ ■ ■

Maybe Mark Twain was right when he said: "Learning is way too important to be left in the hands of educators."

165.

By and large, I do not believe in foreign aid. The Marshall Plan after World War II was a quick fix for the rebuilding of Europe. Yet today we find Japan, a country totally devastated and given little economic aid, leading the pack.

Ostensibly, aid is to lend a helping hand, but in practice its diluted benefits are short-term or regressive. To be more effective, why not impress the world by bettering *ourselves?* With that accomplished, let the power of example work its chemistry on peoples' aspirations and watch what happens.

Only self-determination can make us the best that we can be. Do not fall for misdirected handouts that undermine the initiative of the grantee, and ultimately disappoint the grantor as well. The real intent of foreign aid is to keep the recipient in servitude, which is a bad idea unless maybe you're out to conquer the world. Foreign aid is aptly named; it is aid that is foreign to the notion that nations as well as individuals thrive best through self-help. Do we really believe, everyone considered, that we are "blessed" when unearned largess is dangled before us, strings and all? So says Samoht.

Franklin Roosevelt put his own slant on it in a 1936 speech: "I believe in individualism . . . up to the point where the individual starts to operate at the expense of the community."

166.   *from THE CONTENT OF OUR CHARACTER:*
A NEW VISION OF RACE IN AMERICA
(St. Martin's Press, 1990) by Shelby Steele

There is real anti-black sentiment in American life, but it is no longer as powerful as we *remember* it to be. Our memory makes us like the man who wears a heavy winter coat in springtime because he was frostbitten in winter. Every sharp spring breeze becomes a correlative for the enemy of frostbite so that he is still actually living in winter even as flowers bloom all around him. Not only do subjective correlatives cause us to reenact the past, they also rarely bring us to the power we seek through them because they are too much based on exaggeration. Worse, they cut us off from the present and its many opportunities by encouraging the sort of vision in which we look at the present only to confirm the past.

167.

First there are those who will not cheat for ANY price; and then there are those who WILL cheat for any price.
                                        — GIVOTANGI

In the permissive climate of today, the moral code seems to be that if you can get away with something, it's okay to do wrong, and wrong, and wrong. I see two reasons to refute this line of thinking, and this from an amoral iconoclast, no less! In case you're wondering, know that the ethos to which I subscribe correlates one's own interests with the interests of others for a true synergism. This doctrine is not consistent with taking advantage of people.

The negative reason for doing right is that sooner or later you might get caught, and if you did, how would you handle the punishment, and how might it affect your future? Of course, if you're one of the growing forgotten residual citizens for whom jail would be a step up, you will not find this argument compelling, nor should you.

But there *is* a more subtle and positive reason not to cheat. Doing right for its own sake can afford most of us a satisfaction that transcends practical considerations, and imbues us with an integrity that is cumulative. Whosoever can stake that claim will not likely deal or barter it away. Such a wealth of spirit (for the chosen) has value with which dollars cannot compete.

Some would call this view spiritual; I simply call it enlightened self-interest.

The greatest victories are yet to be won and the greatest deeds are yet to be done.
— THEODORE ROOSEVELT

168.

Why good cops are going bad: Are you familiar with the police seizure laws? They were passed to catch drug lords, but their abuse puts even average citizens at risk of becoming victims. Because seizures are so simple and lucrative, police forces around the country are pursuing them with ever-increasing ardor. Did you know that no more evidence is needed to seize your home than it once took to search it?

The laws governing how the seizure booty is split up varies from state to state. A typical state split for the balance (snitches get up to 25% off the top) might run 70% to the local police, with the DA's office, judge's chambers, and the Feds splitting the balance.

Did you know that at "forfeiture" hearings—which harken back to the days of the Spanish Inquisition—you are presumed guilty and have to prove your innocence?

Did you know that the *Federal Register*, which records in small type the new regulations of the federal bureaucracies, ran 67,715 pages last year? We might echo Winston Churchill when he said: "The length of this document defends it well against the risk of being read." You're responsible for following every one of those regulations. Because it was printed in the *Federal Register*, it has the weight of law. Many of these regulations have criminal penalties. You can not only lose your property for violating one of them, you can go to jail as well.

In the face of unprecedented temptation, is it any wonder that some lawmen have discovered a renegade's playground in seizures? If ever there was such a thing as legalized theft, this has to be it. Appropriating your assets if you're not poor no longer seems to require any more than a loose definition of "just cause." The basic question of fairness no longer seems to matter.

When injustices are perpetrated under the aegis of law you know that social degeneration is that much closer. We have not gone awry by accident. I think we are witnessing an intentional undermining of all sensible values as an excuse to take over our government using emergency laws. But not before the manipulators feel it's time.

One way to prepare a takeover was touched upon in the Oliver North hearings: Divide up the country into "more manageable" *regions*, each headed by an Army General. These one-star Generals answer to someone above them; if they're given orders to declare martial law they say "yes, sir," and overnight you have a de facto dictatorship.

Enter gun control, a fine idea if you're living in Belgium where you don't need guns, but make them illegal here and we will be left with no means to protect ourselves in these unfortunate times.

And another thing that's breaking our backs . . . a $4 trillion debt. Who do we owe it to? And more importantly, *why* do we owe it? Surely not for services rendered. Boiled down to its essence, who are the individuals holding most of the mortgage on our national homestead? We need answers, and what isn't kosher, repudiate—that's right, repudiate! Repudiate all debt said to be owed by citizens that is not founded in actual obligations to those who have loaned money to our banking system.

I think it is safe to say that it is the banking and financial institutions that ultimately control our lives today. We are at their mercy now and more so every day that goes by. The most powerful banking house of all time started with Mayer Amshel Bauer (later Rothschild), born 1743, and his five sons. Today this behemoth appears unstoppable. We shall see.

In his book, *The World Order,* Eustace Mullins attributes their success not to making loans to individuals, although that too could be profitable, but rather to nations, which is ever so much more profitable. Mullins goes on to say that the first precept of success in making government loans lies in "creating a demand," that is, by taking part in the creation of financial panics, depressions, famines, wars and revolutions. The overwhelming success of the Rothschilds lay in their willingness to do what had to be done. Someone once said that the wealth of Rothschild consists of the bankruptcy of nations.

In *The Empire of the City,* E.C. Knuth says, "The fact that the House of Rothschild made its money in the great crashes of history and the great wars of history, the very periods when others lost their money, is beyond question."

So there we have it. May good people receive the sacrament of liberty whether inside church or outside of church, so as to thwart these forces which by logical progression will overrun our freedoms if not stopped soon.

169.

The church can inspire good people to be better; it does not cause bad people to be worse (historical excesses notwithstanding) . . . so chalk up one for the church. But can we do better than that? If reason was the criterion for proper behavior instead of faith in God, might that be the way to advance the cause of good even further? Well, that's what this book is about, but you must search it out. I think there *was* a time when faith in the Lord caused the most good. But alas, no more. Today, many people are disillusioned with their faith, but aren't quite sure what to replace it with. There was a time when earning our way into heaven was the chief concern, but now we're more concerned with earning a living, period. And well we should be.

It's not the devil who has us in his grip, it's a coterie of international bankers who have covertly turned most of us into indentured servants in our own homes, and the shame of it is we don't even know who to blame it on. It is this sort of moral issue that should occupy our attention, and it is here that understanding through reason can help us where the church cannot.

While the Church has been losing the interest of its flock, the top financiers are gaining with interest of a different kind. By controlling our money, they are well on the way to controlling our lives. And then what will they do, take us from regulation to regimentation to tyranny?

If only they knew, there is an even more rewarding route to happiness than great wealth and power, and that is an understanding of enlightened self-interest. The old orthodoxy was to pursue an ignis fatuus, oblivious to shifting undercurrents that can bespeak of resplendent changes, if we can only survive the meantime.

170.

If you'd like to know what a world class economist thinks of things, try this from Dr. Kurt Richenbacker, Frankfurt, Germany.

The gross neglect of American economists to capital building is a consequence of their focus on statistics and correlations. This explains the astonishing complacency of most U.S. economists. "The forces that are presently depressing their economy—budget deficits, trade deficits, over-consumption, under-saving, under-investment, over-indebtedness, and collapsing asset price inflation—simply have no place in their customary business cycle models. This complete inability to waken up to the gravity of the present situation is the product of traditional American economics."

"The bizarre result of this simplistic short-term thinking is that virtually every single major affliction depressing the U.S. economy over the longer run is being ignored. It's like a doctor who knows no other illness than pneumonia and pronounces everyone who doesn't have it as healthy."

171.

Now, how many readers believe that a growing debt makes economic growth possible? You should know that while deficits are stimulative in the short run, they are depressive and destructive over the long run. It is not possible to maintain "infinite" debt, and those who believe it can perpetually be shuffled off as next year's problem, are suffering brain damage induced by economic disinformation. So forget about a Mexican standoff, ultimately there are no permanent stalemates—all debt will be resolved one way or another.

172.

*From the book PROPAGANDA
written in 1928 by Edward Bernays*

As civilization becomes more complex, and as the need for invisible government has been increasingly demonstrated, the technical means have been invented and developed by which public opinion may be regimented. With printing press and newspaper, the telephone, telegraph, radio and airplanes, ideas can be spread rapidly, and even instantaneously, across the whole of America. [Bernays had not yet seen how much better television, which was to follow, would do the job.]

The conscious and intelligent manipulation of organized habits and opinions of the masses is an important element in a democratic society. Those who manipulate this unseen mechanism of society constitute an invisible government which is the true ruling power in our country.

We are governed, our minds are moulded, our tastes formed, our ideas suggested, largely by men we have never heard of. What ever attitude one chooses to take toward this condition, it remains a fact that in almost every act of our daily lives, whether in the sphere of politics or business, our social conduct or our ethical thinking, we are dominated by a relatively small number of persons, a trifling fraction of our hundred and twenty million, who understand the mental processes and social patterns of the masses. It is they who pull the wires which control the public mind, and who harness old social forces and contrive new ways to bind and guide the world.

173. *December 17, 1992*

We have now come to the bottom line: The most elemental unit of humanity is not a family group as our politicians insist, it is the individual. And whether alone or in concert with others most individuals' inclinations are singular for their sameness— an impellment toward self-interest.

That can be good as well as bad, however. Generally, the shorter the time frame of the goal and the less concern there is for others, the less desirable the outcome will be. That is every-day garden variety self-interest, whereas to weigh the consequences of our actions and take aim on the future happiness of everyone is enlightened self-interest.

Now consider Albert Schweitzer and Mother Teresa; humanitarians extraordinaire. I believe they acted from their hearts and an ideological fervor that allowed them to live their convictions through sheer willfulness. Willfulness is defined as: governed by will *without regard to reason.* Personally, I prefer to answer the call of reason since I am not an altruist, but just someone who wants to help make the world a better place to live in, because doing so would be to my advantage. And if others are advantaged the same as I am, we might all be happier together than we are apart.

He who will not reason is a bigot, he who cannot is a fool; and he who dares not is a slave.

– WILLIAM DRUMMOND (1585-1649)

174. *January 26, 1993*

*The following is taken from a 1948
Canadian booklet written in French*

When Canada declared war against Germany in September, 1939, the whole country—from the government to the individual—had just gone through a 10-year money shortage. But overnight money was no longer lacking, not even for a minute, during the whole war.

Money came by the millions, by the billions, as much as was required. And this, in all the countries at war. Where did this money come from? Certainly not from the opening of new gold mines, since workers were directed not to gold mines but to the army and the war industries. Money came with one stroke of the pen, through the mere decision to create it.

During the war, our country was able to feed and clothe adequately, besides its civilian population, 750,000 soldiers who produced nothing. So why could not Canada feed and clothe all of its population, even better than during the war, when these 750,000 vigorous people came back to Canada, thus increasing our capacity to produce?

With so many workers absent during the war, Canada was nevertheless able to produce, besides consumer goods, cannons, shells, warships, tanks, military aircraft and several other deadly weapons. Why could not the same Canada, now without having to sustain this war production, and now having at its disposal 750,000 more workers, supply its population with enough food, clothes and houses?

Not a single warring government would have agreed to bring its soldiers back, or to shut down its ammunition factories, because of a money shortage. So how could these same governments have agreed to let hundreds of thousands of individuals and families suffer from hunger, lose their homes, their farms because of a mere shortage of money?

■ ■ ■

Givotangi's sad answer to that one is: There is more to be made by bankrupting the farmer for his assets, never mind the human toll, than by taxing his prosperity.

The leading author at exposing the Fed, Eustace Mullins, tells us that as early as 1923 William Jennings Bryan wrote in

Hearst's magazine: "The Federal Reserve Bank that should have been the farmer's greatest protection has become his greatest foe. The deflation of the farmer was a crime deliberately committed."

Those who control events know not of enlightened self-interest; but they will come to.

175.

In looking back on what was communism's whole purpose, heed the words of R.E. McMaster who wrote in *The Reaper,* "The goal of international communism is not to destroy Western international debt capitalism. The goal of international communism is to enslave mankind at the behest of Western international debt capitalism." Should you need to know but one thing about communism or the kind of world we're living in, this would be it.

But wait! There was a fly in the ointment in the person of Ronald Wilson Reagan. Being outside the conspiracy loop, this independent president pushed spending on the military to nearly $300 billion annually, and in the process broke the back of the Soviet Union, who could not keep up the pace. Could this be a reason they tried to stop Mr. Reagan? This time the patsy was John W. Hinkley, Jr., yet another of so many "lone" gunmen that had gone before. The time had come to make another coincidence and sell it to the public as such. What did someone want to "teach" President Reagan on that fateful day? (It was only by accident that the .22 caliber bullet hit him.) One cannot be blamed if he gets the feeling that the scenario of the high cabal was being applied again for purposes that we may never know.

I can now offer circumstantial evidence to support this notion. On May 5, 1977, in Los Angeles, there occurred an event which you may never have heard of. It was reported by a well-known journalist, Penn Jones, who published a privately circulated newsletter at the time entitled *Penn Jones: The Continuing Inquiry.*

On that day, two men were arrested and charged with attempted assassination of then President Jimmy Carter. One of the men had a blank pistol and 70 rounds of blank ammunition. But here is how we *know* this was meant to be a "message" . . . one man was named Raymond *Lee Harvey*, and the other's name was *Oswaldo* Ortiz!

Within days, Carter had cancelled a scheduled nationwide speech, secluded himself at Camp David, and was quoted as saying . . . "I've lost control of the government." He had gotten the message.

176.

Homosexuals in the military?

Here is a crackpot idea whose time should never have come. I believe in freedom of choice, but not in the military where discipline must be paramount, and countervailing influences kept in check. The most important part of discipline is morale, which could not help but suffer if the ban on gays is lifted. To give just one example: The blood supply in the military walks on two legs, your donor may or may not have AIDS. Is that something you want hanging over your head?

What I think is happening here is the purposeful undermining of the American fiber, a slow eroding of sensible values whose place is taken up by notions calculated to bring down America and set our people against each other.

I believe the purpose of a select group who have no national allegiances is to control the world by hook or by crook. Since the U.S. is the world's strongest bastion of liberty, you can say that we represent the last hurdle in their plans.

We are victims of the Chinese curse: "May you live in interesting times."

It was reported on August 21, 1993 that Barry Goldwater said it was dumb that gays be excluded from the military. Now I like Barry Goldwater. One must admire his forthright style. But in this case I think he's wrong. While his statement may be correct in theory, we must here deal with realities, and the reality is that such action would be counter to the military ethos. He further states that a person should be able to do as they damn please, or else they are not free. This is simply nonsense. To suddenly deviate from time-honored practices can be an unsettling action that should not be taken lightly. These days I cannot help but feel that a chaos mentality is being imposed on us from above.

Is the groundwork being prepared so that a national emergency can be declared followed by martial law? (All for our own good, of course!)

177.   *March 8, 1993*

If you dare believe it, left is right, but not all left is right. Nor is all left wrong. Since right is right, it follows that a competition here exists among those with the same or similar goals. And then there's America, whose undoing was her innocence. Or at least we will say "was," if the U.S. nuclear triad loses its sea leg. It seemingly has already lost its ground and air legs. We need to ask the real reasons why 12 admirals of the fleet may be disciplined over a peripheral issue like the Tailhook Scandal.

Things are about to get hot very fast from here on in, so buckle up, buckle down, and decide where you stand, and if you're willing to take a stand. I salute you.

The past is my heritage,
The present is my responsibility,
The future is my challenge.

178.

Wouldn't it be funny if: God and the Devil were meant to be interpreted figuratively instead of literally? If God means simply a force for good while the Devil represents a force for bad? Wouldn't it also be interesting if the usual order of God being the #1 most powerful force in the world was actually only the second most powerful (figuratively speaking, of course), and the devil at least *up to the present time*, was the *most* powerful force in the world?

It would sure explain a lot of things for me if all this were so.

I have an idea, why don't all of us with good intentions assume that all the above *is* so, so that as #2 we will just try harder. And if once we do come out on top, we'll ensure that we stay there by proving to the devil (bad people) that being good is the more rewarding. After all, that's the whole purpose for being good, it really *is* more rewarding, and not just for a privileged few, but for virtually *everyone* (including most of those former privileged few). But they must acknowledge the superiority of good of their own free will. In other words, they must repent and convert to good, so that the world will ever after be free of malignity.

179. *March 22, 1993*

All over the world, and especially here in America, free elections have been regarded as the best and fairest way to choose our leaders. It still might be that if all the players had equal opportunity to get their message across to the people, and if the litmus test for character was administered and revealed evenly to the public. J.P. Morgan was asked after he had retired what was the first quality he looked for when granting a loan. His answer: character. The news the establishment doesn't want you to hear simply doesn't get the coverage, the power structure sees to that. The power of persuasion through control of the media has gone from an art to a science, with the winner chosen well in advance of any election.

I now believe that Boris Yeltsin is a puppet of the world manipulators, and a recipient of their favors. One indication of this is watching who the media bias slants to. The conspirators now have such control here that most any stand they take is echoed en masse and is for the purpose of promoting their cause, and the more they gain control, the more predictable they become. But that should not impel us to oppose for its own sake. Where they take correct positions, we will support them, for in such case the good deeds will probably outweigh the bad intentions. When your adversary outsmarts himself, help him to continue doing so by going along with him.

However, the clincher came for me when I read a buried item that the censors apparently missed . . . Paul Volcker was advising the Yeltsin team in financial methodology—need I say more? When Volcker saved us from Carter's monetary meltdown, he was my hero, but what I didn't realize then was that it was all orchestrated. In the final analysis, even Paul is just a hired hand doing his job.

180.   *March 26, 1993*

The lead headline in the Daytona Beach Florida News-Journal for March 24, 1993 reads: "Police arrest cab driver for shooting his attacker." It should be obvious that the new ideology is against anyone who tries to defend himself. Under the guise of keeping guns out of the hands of criminals, "they" would disarm law abiding private citizens who represent potential resistance against the day when subjugation is forced upon us. If you doubt that such an extreme action could happen, take stock of what is going on all around the world. Would you not have doubted 30 years ago that things today would have deteriorated to the state they have?

My friends, there are forces in motion—man-made forces—which want to take over the world. I would have no objections to this if their aim is benevolence, but if it is to get "even," I object, although I do understand and can sympathize. And although I forgive them for acting like human beings have always acted, I fear in the process they will destroy themselves, and I don't want that to happen, as these are my people. Jefferson wrote: "Experience has shown that even under the best forms, those entrusted with power have, in time, and by slow operations, perverted it into tyranny."

Events are accelerating daily. Democracy is losing its underpinnings, and yet it remains to everyone's advantage that this not happen.

To prepare ourselves, we need above all to know the truth surrounding the manipulation of events. That accomplished, and with the cat now out of the bag, we can *all* proceed mutatis mutandis to right the world with malice toward none, and charity for all.

181.   *March 30, 1993*

Do I agree with the concept of "America first"? Yes and no, since to me it means two different things. I do equate the worth of a *productive* Mexican or Chinese or anyone else with their American counterparts. All peoples of the world deserve the same square deal. Of course in practice relatively few receive it. This is why I favor free trade, even though it leaves potholes in the road that should be repaired, not by tariffs, but by benevolent capitalism replacing exploitative capitalism everywhere. As to the other interpretation, I feel we should repair America before we try to fix the rest of the world. In this sense I am indeed an America firster. If we led by example, we would be making friends instead of enemies. The paper *Spotlight* (800-522-6292) said in its March 22, 1993 issue: "As far as foreign aid is concerned, are you aware that the foreign aid law, PL.-480 (started after World War II) has a section in it requiring that any country receiving foreign aid must receive the aid through American corporations that are based in that country? As a result, American corporations have changed their entire pattern of doing business, and they have received the 'foreign aid' dollars.

They pay no taxes and bank the money in foreign countries and become essentially foreign corporations living on U.S. taxpayer's dollars in those countries. This has been going on since the 1940s.

There's a lot more to the foreign aid-and-trade business than most Americans realize, and the media keeps it covered up."

182.   *April, 1993*

I thank the reader of this book for staying the course, and after coming this far with me, one more unorthodox view should not come as a surprise to you.

It is the cost of money, whether it is borrowed or comes out of savings, that inspires the contractor to staple the shingles to the roof instead of nailing them, or to use 2x4s instead of 2x6s, etc. If money held its value over time, if there were no inflation and no interest charges to consider, it would behoove the customer to appraise the value of quality realistically on its own merits without extraneous factors to muddy the waters.

I am suggesting that once the burden of interest and inflation is permanently lifted from our shoulders, and all the ancillary monetary gimmicks that accompany them are buried for all time, the violent up-and-down swings in all financial markets would indeed stabilize, and that this would be a permanent condition. In fact financial planning, complex estate planning, even the financial markets themselves along with the people it takes to run them, could in large part all be eliminated. There are tens of millions of people needlessly employed in make-work jobs. Now this in itself would be bad enough, but much of the work these people do actually hampers efficiency and is generally counterproductive, so millions more are given the task of straightening out this needless mess.

Here, then, is my proposal: To start with, Social Security should be mandatory, universal, and individual (each person insured as an individual only). It should be government-run, and provide retirement benefits in an amount sufficient to live on comfortably for one's lifetime between retirement day (as determined by the actuaries) and death. There will be no limits or penalty on the amount one can earn after they retire. Additional private insurance and other pension plans would be an option, although not necessary to effect a happy retirement.

Surprisingly, the savings gained by eliminating waste and clutter would allow a retirement financed solely by accumulated principal, with responsible accounting methods to determine when that will be, in the form of a life annuity administered through Social Security. What, you say, I don't get to live off my interest? No, interest is a cruel illusion and a fraud. If you think in terms of something for nothing, reflect for a moment upon where it has led us. Interest paid to one must come from the pocket of another. Is that your notion of sound financial management?

I also envision a world where all jobs (not hobbies) that smack of busywork (work that usually appears productive or of intrinsic value but actually only keeps one occupied), are replaced by useful work; and virtually all efforts at advantaging for special interests, such as the quirky federal income tax code, are eliminated. Whatever the task, and especially those of zero sum values, simplicity and not complexity should be the goal, using common sense as the final arbiter.

183.   *April, 1993*

I cannot say that the Jesse Helms of 1993 is the same Jesse Helms who on December 15, 1987, gave an electrifying speech before the Senate that was truly a revelation, but here in extracted form is some of what he said then:

This campaign against the American people—against traditional American culture and values—is systematic psychological warfare. It is orchestrated by a vast array of interests comprising not only the Eastern establishment but also the radical left. Among this group we find the Department of State, the Department of Commerce, the money center banks and multinational corporations, the media, the educational establishment, the entertainment industry, and the large tax-exempt foundations.

Mr. President, a careful examination of what is happening behind the scenes reveals that all of these interests are working in concert with the masters of the Kremlin in order to create what some refer to as a new world order. Private organizations such as the Council on Foreign Relations, the Royal Institute of International Affairs, the Trilateral Commission, the Dartmouth Conference, the Aspen Institute for Humanistic Studies, the Atlantic Institute, and the Bilderberger Group serve to disseminate and to coordinate the plans for this so-called new world order in powerful business, financial, academic, and official circles . . .

The psychological campaign that I am describing, as I have said, is the work of groups within the Eastern establishment, that amorphous amalgam of wealth and social connections whose power resides in its control over our financial system and over a large portion of our industrial sector. The principal instrument of this control over the American economy and money is the Federal Reserve system. The policies of the industrial sectors, primarily the multinational corporations, are influenced by the money center banks through debt financing and through the large blocks of stock controlled by the trust departments of the money center banks.

Anyone familiar with American history, and particularly American economic history, cannot fail to notice the control over the Department of State and the Central Intelligence Agency which Wall Street seems to exercise . . .

The influence of establishment insiders over our foreign policy has become a fact of life in our time. This pervasive influence runs contrary to the real long-term national security of our Nation. It is an influence which, if unchecked, could ultimately subvert our constitutional order.

The viewpoint of the establishment today is called globalism. Not so long ago, this viewpoint was called the "one-world" view by its critics. The phrase is no longer fashionable among sophisticates; yet, the phrase "one-world" is still apt because nothing has changed in the minds and actions of those promoting policies consistent with its fundamental tenets.

Mr. President, in the globalist point of view, nation-states and national boundaries do not count for anything. Political philosophies and political principles seem to become simply relative. Indeed, even constitutions are irrelevant to the exercise of power. Liberty and tyranny are viewed as neither necessarily good nor evil, and certainly not a component of policy.

In this point of view, the activities of international financial and industrial forces should be oriented to bringing this one-world design—with a convergence of the Soviet and American systems as its centerpiece—into being . . . All that matters to this club is the maximization of profits resulting from the practice of what can be described as finance capitalism, a system which rests upon the twin pillars of debt and monopoly. This isn't real capitalism. It is the road to economic concentration and to political slavery.

184. *May 9, 1993 (Mother's Day)*

Why is the conspiracy—as I will refer to those who would manipulate events—out to undo individualism, and hence freedom, in our country? Clearly, if they can subdue us as a nation, starting with the Randy Weavers in Idaho and the Branch Davidians in Texas, not to mention the law-abiding gun owners, on whatever pretexts they can think up, their ability to intimidate the rest of us becomes greatly enhanced.

But what's their aim? Simply, it is to take over. Why? Because this is what turns them on. They have not evolved to the higher ethic of enlightened self-interest, which generates happiness through mutual respect and cooperation, rather than through the subjugation and enslavement of others.

You might wonder why so many leaders who rail passionately against sin prove ineffectual once in power. Simple: They are hypocrites who worked harder than honest men to get their jobs, because they had incentives that only dishonesty could provide. To an honest man the hassle was not worth what the job paid. Too bad for society—what can we do about it now? Help Diogenes find his honest man, put that person in charge of *all* government hiring and firing, and earmark the villains for isolation early on, where they can never do harm again.

Is all this possible? I don't know, but I think so. And since the world is too far gone to be saved in any other way that has been tried, what other choice is there?

Worldwide, various competing power blocks with a common malintentioned bent are insidiously preparing the way for their versions of a new world order. Ironically, it will be left to the good atheists in league with the *good* churches to stem the evil tide and right the world (my criticism of the Church notwithstanding).

Have you noticed a subtle change away from Free China (Taiwan) and toward mainland China? The Chinese are fine people, but their present leadership is enigmatic. It remains to be seen whether tyranny or freedom will win out in that contained country. But the very thought of turning over Hong Kong to Red China—really, now, that *is* devolution.

The "Great counterattack" must be manned by those who have already found their Heaven, for with no unfulfilled wants to covet, they are beyond the sway of the tempters.

185.   *May 24, 1993*

I have recently become aware of a circumstance worthy of note. The rank and file members of an organization are not always privy to the ultimate aims and ambitions of its leaders.

What makes this arrangement ominous is that while you are attacking a movement on a strategic level, the followers whose hierarchy and agenda you are bemoaning are interpreting your criticisms on a tactical level, and to them your protestations come across as outrageous heresy. You will not find an objective audience here without first sorting out and agreeing on the facts. It is this divergence of understanding that gives meaning to the Tower of Babel parable.

So the battles rage on, combatants listening not to words; but responding instead to the emotions that are triggered by their utterance.

The prophet begins with a vision—Martin Luther King called it a dream—in which to attain Heaven we must first move Earth. That's the hard part, moving the masses inhabiting the Earth. If the vision is true, man will save himself and be free. But if along the way he should lose his vision by not being true to it, his fate will be to wish for eternal death.

186.   *May 31, 1993*

Now I would like your special attention, please. This is how I would approach the free trade vs. fair trade embranglement.

I call it "the Givotangi Parity Swap," and here's how it would work: Since there will always be inequalities in production costs, and since full employment should be the capstone in any answer to the problem, we need to bring together in a trading partnership localities that, because of their uncompetitively high production costs, cannot sell their wares through normal commercial channels. For example:

1. Japan's price for widgets is $4.00
2. Detroit's price for the same item is $10.00
3. Mexico sells gizmos for $2.50, while
4. Pittsburg's price for gizmos is $8.00

To satisfy its current needs let's say that Detroit requires 1,000 gizmos, which it can get from Mexico for $2,500. Mexico, on the other hand, needs widgets, which Detroit can supply for $10 apiece. But Mexico can buy the same widgets from Japan for $4 apiece, so it doesn't buy from Detroit. Now it so happens that Pittsburg has also been buying $3,200 worth of widgets at a time from Japan, but the gizmo factory in Pittsburg cannot compete with cheap imported Mexican gizmos, so is planning to shut down and lay off its 25 workers.

Now let us suppose for a moment that a central clearing house knew about and arranged for Detroit to buy its 1,000 gizmos from Pittsburg for $8,000, and Pittsburg was to buy 800 widgets from Detroit, also for $8,000. What would this have accomplished? The two U.S. factories, by remaining in production, would have continued supplying jobs and goods—even if those goods *are* more expensive—thus earning from each other the money to pay for them. The reality is that both the finances and morale of the people affected would be better than had they bought at a lower price only to watch their own jobs disappear and their families go on the dole (which drains the public coffers).

Presently, we are seduced by the misguided attraction of lower cost, only to ignore how the items in question will be paid for, especially when faced with retaliatory tariffs that make our own goods harder to sell. No matter how cheap a product may be, it is still too expensive if we cannot earn the money to pay for it with equal values of sales and exports. And that can only be done if someone wants our wares. Those wants can be satisfied through the right incentives.

Under the Givotangi Parity Swap, high cost producers worldwide would trade with *each other* through multi-member partnership exchanges that would not endanger their own productive capabilities. Swapping in specie makes better sense than artificially imposing quotas and pressuring acceptance of our wares on reluctant partners. Relationships are always better when they are voluntary and not coerced. And if they too are facing the same problem, a bilateral or multilateral swap becomes an arrangement to be desired, not spurned. The reason some may have higher costs might have more to do with safety and environmental expenses than with inefficiency per se. Such enterprises are assets to be encouraged, not abandoned.

The Givotangi Parity Swap is better than applying tariffs because it is a natural solution, not an artificial one. It therefore will produce a healthier outcome. It is user-friendly, it is fair and straightforward, and it is free of artificial preservatives. It is good for everyone.

To be sure, marginal survivors will not be transformed into first-place finishers, but aggregate wealth will improve considerably, and the least among us will walk that much taller.

187.   *June 14, 1993*

Once long ago there was an honest government
by John F. Bell, columnist for THE NATIONAL EDUCATOR

Suppose all our public officials, the officers of our corporations, and all our private citizens were completely honest. What would it mean? Believe it or not, this ideal state was approached closely enough to provide a very interesting demonstration of the benefits of eliminating corruption in government and society 200 years ago.

Napoleon Bonaparte provided us with that demonstration. He was an exceptional person because he had an exceptional mother. He may have had some exceptional genes also, but I am inclined to give Letitia, the mother of Napoleon, most of the credit for building and forming the remarkable character and personality that made such a profound impression in the age in which he lived. We have much to learn from the example he set before us. Today, we have serious problems. What is the source of those problems, what are the problems, and what must we do about them?

We have a four trillion dollar national debt and local and private debts that are almost as unreasonable. We have crime, drugs, alcohol, divorce, juvenile delinquency and teenage pregnancy problems; and we do not seem to be able to provide adequate medical care or to take care of our aged. Too many of us are just plain unhappy. We simply have not learned how to live, and we have forgotten how to run our government.

What did Napoleon have that we do not have? Our technological, industrialized economy is obviously capable of providing for every one of us handsomely, yet so many of us are in real need. Let's pinpoint the real cause of our distress. It is that we tolerate evil in our government and society. Napoleon

433

nearly eliminated the evil in the governments he set up after defeating the oppressors that he found nearly everywhere. He has been much vilified by his enemies and, therefore, much misunderstood. But he fought the most bloody of wars in defense of freedom and, though much suffering resulted from these struggles, the oppressed peoples understood very well that he was fighting for their freedom, and they joined his armies and fought and died for him.

Napoleon combined the purest of moral qualities with the most exceptional competence in his leadership. He was fierce in fighting for freedom, but compassionate and fair in dealing with those he had liberated. He understood the mighty force imbedded in man's yearning for freedom and he used it as no other leader ever has. He told his liberated people he would respect their freedom, their religion and their property rights. He was a military genius and a genius in political adminis-tration. When he set up a government, it functioned so well that the people benefited almost immediately. He selected local people based solely on their qualifications, of which he was an excellent judge, to administer governments. He seemed to be exceptionally competent in detecting any tendency to corrup-tion or dishonesty in possible selections. As a result, when he set up a government, corruption was essentially eliminated.

Therefore, we have in the liberated governments he set up, a magnificent demonstration of the almost unbelievable benefits of truly honest administrations. The people loved him for it, and he was the most popular man in Europe, while the English, controlled by the corrupt European bankers, were busy vilifying him with their powerful propaganda machine.

Today, we have a very powerful force available to us that can be used for good or ill. We do not appreciate this, but our enemies do, and they have seized control of it and are using it most effectively in advancing their evil schemes. This force is our magnificent television broadcast system with which we can talk to most of our population instantly and intimately. We do not understand this, but our enemy does, and he uses it with a devastating effect on all of us, especially our children.

We do not have to tolerate evil in our midst, but it will be there if we are so blind as to tolerate it. We have the franchise, but we are too lazy and indifferent to make effective use of it. There are plenty of honest and capable people available to us, but they will be crowded out if we do not make the organized effort necessary to find them and elect them. We need to learn that, under present conditions, no candidate who makes the commitments necessary to run on either of the major party tickets can be trusted. The potential benefits of the elimination of evil in our government and society are so great that, if they were really understood by the public, that organized effort could be mobilized. Of course, there will be powerful opposition. Imagine, if you can, reaction to giving up control of the Fed, that carefully structured system that manipulates resources for the benefit of those who have behind-the-scenes control of the banks. Benefits from the enormous productivity of our economy must be returned to the people, and our ingenuity applied toward reposing with the people the importance of directing their own destiny for all time to come.

188.   *June 21, 1993*

Billions for the bankers—debts for the people
The real story of the money-control over America
by Sheldon Emry — Box 5334, Phoenix, AZ

Americans, living in what is called the richest nation on earth, seem always to be short of money. Wives are working outside the home in unprecedented numbers, husbands hope for overtime hours to earn more, or take part-time jobs evenings

and weekends, children look for odd jobs for spending money, the family debt climbs higher, and psychologists say one of the biggest causes of family quarrels and breakups is "arguments over money." Much of this trouble can be traced to our present "debt-money" system.

In the early 1930s, bankers, the only source of new money and credit, deliberately refused loans to industries, stores and farms. Payments on existing loans were required however, and money rapidly disappeared from circulation. Goods were available to be purchased, jobs waiting to be done, but the lack of money brought the nation to a standstill. By this simple ploy

America was put in a "depression" and the bankers took possession of hundreds of thousands of farms, homes, and business properties. The people were told, "Times are hard" and "Money is short." Not understanding the system, they were cruelly robbed of their earnings, their savings, and their property.

Money for peace? No!
Money for war? Yes!

World War II ended the "depression." The same bankers who in the early '30s had no loans for peacetime houses, food and clothing, suddenly had unlimited billions to lend for Army barracks, K-rations and uniforms! A nation that in 1934 couldn't produce food for sale, suddenly could produce bombs to send free to Germany and Japan! (More on this riddle later.)

With the sudden increase in money, people were hired, farms sold their produce, factories went to two shifts, mines reopened, and "The Great Depression" was over! Some politicians were blamed for it and others took credit for ending it. The truth is the lack of money (caused by the bankers) brought on the depression, and adequate money ended it. The people were never told that simple truth and in this article we will endeavor to show how these same bankers who control our money and credit have used their control to plunder America and place us in bondage.

Since our money was handled both legally and illegally before 1913, we shall consider only the years following 1913, since from that year on, nearly all of our money has been created and issued by an illegal method that will eventually destroy the United States if it is not changed. Prior to 1913, America was a prosperous, powerful, and growing nation, at peace with its neighbors and the envy of the world. But, in December of 1913, Congress, with many members away for the Christmas holidays, passed what has since been known as the Federal Reserve Act.

This simple but terrible law completely removed from Congress the right to "create" money or to have any control over its "creation" (Article I of the U.S. Constitution reads: Congress shall have the Power to Coin Money and Regulate the Value Thereof), and gave that function to the Federal Reserve Corporation. This was done with appropriate fanfare and propaganda that this would "remove money from politics" (they didn't say "and therefore from the people's control") and prevent "Boom and Bust" from hurting our citizens. The people were not told then, and most still do not know today, that the Federal Reserve Corporation is a private corporation controlled by bankers and therefore is operated for the financial gain of the bankers over the people rather than for the good of the people. The word "federal" was used only to deceive the people.

More disastrous than Pearl Harbor

Since that "day of infamy," more disastrous to us than Pearl Harbor, the small group of "privileged" people who lend us "our" money have accrued to themselves all of the profits of printing our money—and more! Since 1913 they have "created" tens of billions of dollars in money and credit, which, as their own personal property, they then lend to our government and our people at interest. "The rich get richer and the poor get poorer" had become the secret policy of our national government. An example of the process of "creation" and its conversion to people's "debt" will aid our understanding.

They print it—
We borrow it and pay them interest

We shall start with the need for money. The federal government, having spent more than it has taken from its citizens in taxes, needs, for the sake of illustration, $1,000,000,000. Since it does not have the money and Congress has given away its authority to "create" it, the government must go to the "creators" for the $1 billion. But, the Federal Reserve, a private corporation, doesn't just give its money away! The bankers are willing to deliver $1,000,000,000 in money or credit to the federal government in exchange for the government's agreement to pay it back—with interest! So Congress authorizes the Treasury Department to print $1,000,000,000 in U.S. bonds, which are then delivered to the Federal Reserve bankers.

The Federal Reserve then pays the cost of printing the $1,000,000,000 (about $1,000) and makes the exchange. The government then uses the money to pay its obligations. What are the results of this fantastic transaction? Well, $1 billion in government bills are paid all right, but the government has now indebted the people to the bankers for $1 billion on which the people must pay interest! Tens of thousands of such transactions have taken place since 1913 so that by the 1980s, the U.S. government is indebted to the bankers for over $1 trillion on which the people pay over $100 billion a year in interest alone with no hope of ever paying off the principal. Supposedly our children and following generations will pay forever and forever!

And there's more

You say, "This is terrible!" Yes, it is, but we have shown only part of the sordid story. Under this unholy system, those United States bonds have now become "assets" of the banks in the Reserve system which they then use as "reserves" to "create" more "credit" to lend. Current "reserve" requirements allow them to use that $1 billion in bonds to "create" as much as $15 billion in new "credit" to lend to states, municipalities, to individuals and businesses. Added to the original $1 billion, they could have $16 billion of "created credit" out in loans paying them interest with their only cost being $1,000 for printing the original $1 billion! Since the U.S. Congress has issued only a token amount of Constitutional money since 1863 (over 100 years), in order for the people to have money to carry on trade and commerce they are forced to borrow the "created credit" of the monopoly bankers and pay them usury (interest!).

And there's still more

In addition to the vast wealth drawn to them through this almost unlimited usury, the bankers who control the money at the top are able to approve or disapprove large loans to large and successful corporations to the extent that refusal of a loan will bring about a reduction in the price that that Corporation's stock sells for on the market. After depressing the price, the bankers' agents buy large blocks of the stock, after which the sometimes multi-million dollar loan is approved, the stock rises, and is then sold for a profit. In this manner billions of dollars are made with which to buy more stock. This practice is so refined today that the Federal Reserve Board need only announce to the newspapers an increase or decrease in their "rediscount rate" to send stocks up and down as they wish. Using this method since 1913, the bankers and their agents have purchased secret or open control of almost every large corporation in America. Using that control, they then force the corporations to borrow huge sums from their banks so that corporation earnings are siphoned off in the form of interest to the banks. This leaves little as actual "profits" which can be paid as dividends and explains why the banks reap billions in interest from corporate loans. In effect, the bankers get the lion's share of the company profits.

The millions of working families of America are now indebted to the few thousand banking families for twice the assessed value of the entire United States. And these banking families obtained that debt against us for the cost of paper, ink, and bookkeeping!

The interest amount is never created

The only way new money (which is not true money, but is "credit" representing a debt), goes into circulation in America is when it is borrowed from bankers. When the state and people borrow large sums, we seem to prosper. However, the bankers "create" only the amount of the principal of each loan, never the extra amount needed to pay the interest. Therefore, the new money never equals the new debt added. The amounts needed to pay the interest on loans is not "created," and therefore does not exist!

Under this kind of a system, where new debt always exceeds the new money no matter how much or how little is borrowed, the total debt increasingly outstrips the amount of money available to pay the debt. The people can never, ever get out of debt!

An example will show the viciousness of this usury-debt system with its "built-in" shortage of money.

If $60,000 is borrowed, $255,931.20 must be paid back

When a citizen goes to a banker to borrow $60,000 to purchase a home or a farm, the bank clerk has the borrower agree to pay back the loan plus interest. At 14% interest for 30 years [this was written over a decade ago; today, in 1993, the rate would be about 8% total], the borrower must agree to pay $710.92 per month for a total of $255,931.20. The clerk then requires the citizen to assign to the banker the right of ownership of the property if the borrower does not make the required payments. The bank clerk then gives the borrower a $60,000 check or a $60,000 deposit slip crediting the borrower's checking account with $60,000.

The borrower then writes checks to the builder, subcontractors, etc., who in turn write checks. $60,000 of new "checkbook" money is thereby added to "money in circulation."

However, and this is the fatal flaw in a usury system, the only new money created and put into circulation is the amount of the loan, $60,000. The money to pay the interest is *not* created, and therefore was *not* added to "money in circulation."

Even so, this borrower (and those who follow him in ownership of the property) must earn and *take out of circulation* $255,931, almost $200,000 *more* than he put *in circulation* when he borrowed the original $60,000! (By the way, it is this interest which cheats all families out of nicer homes. It is not that they can't afford them; it is because the banker's usury forces them to pay for four homes to get one!)

Every new loan puts the same process in operation. Each borrower adds a small sum to the total money supply when he borrows, but the payments on the loan (because of interest) then deduct a much *larger* sum from the total money supply.

There is therefore no way all debtors can pay off the money lenders. As they pay the principal and interest, the money in circulation disappears. All they can do is struggle against each other, borrowing more and more from the money lenders each generation. The money lenders (bankers), who produce nothing of value, slowly, then more rapidly, gain a death grip on the land, buildings, and present and future earnings of the whole working population. Proverbs 22:7 has come to pass in America. The borrowers have become the servants of the lenders.

Small loans do the same thing

If you haven't quite grasped the impact of the above, let us consider a small auto loan for three years at 18% interest. Step 1: Citizen borrows $5,000 and pays it into circulation (it goes to the dealer, factory, miner, etc.) and signs a note agreeing to pay the banker $6,500. Step 2: Citizen pays $180 per month of his earnings to the banker. In three years he will take *out* of circulation $1,500 more than he put *in* circulation.

Every loan of "banker-created" money (credit) causes the same thing to happen. Since this has happened millions of times since 1913 (and continues today), you can see why America has gone from a prosperous, debt-free nation to a debt-ridden nation where practically every home, farm and business is paying usury-tribute to some banker. The usury-tribute to the bankers on personal, local, state and federal debt totals more than the combined earnings of 25% of the working people. Soon it will be 50% and continue up.

The cost to you?
Eventually, everything.

In 1910 the U.S. federal debt was only $1 billion, or $12.40 per citizen. State and local debts were practically nonexistent. By 1920, after only 6 years of Federal Reserve shenanigans, the federal debt had jumped to $24 billion, or $228 per person.

In 1960 the federal debt reached $284 billion, or $1,575 per citizen, and state and local debts were mushrooming.

By 1981 the federal debt passed $1 trillion and was growing exponentially as the bankers tripled the interest rates. State and local debts are now *more* than the federal debt, and with business and personal debts totalled over $6 trillion, three times the value of all land and buildings in America.

If we signed over to the money lenders all of America we would still owe them two more Americas (plus their usury, of course!)

However, they are too cunning to take title to everything. They will instead leave you with some "illusion of ownership" so you and your children will continue to work and pay the bankers more of your earnings on ever-increasing debts. The "establishment" has captured our people with their ungodly system of usury and debt as certainly as if they had marched in with a uniformed army.

Yes, it's political, too!

Democrat, Republican, and Independent voters who have wondered why politicians always spend more tax money than they take in should now see the reason. When they begin to study our "debt-money" system, they soon realize that these politicians are not the agents of the people but are the agents of the bankers, for whom they plan ways to place the people further in debt. It takes only a little imagination to see that if Congress had been "creating," and spending or issuing into circulation the necessary increase in the money supply, *there would be no national debt*, and the over $4 trillion of other debts would be practically nonexistent. Since there would be no *original* cost of money except printing, and no *continuing* costs such as interest, federal taxes would be almost nil. Money, once in circulation, would remain there and go on serving its purpose as a medium of exchange for generation after generation and century after century, just as coins do now, with *no* payments to the bankers whatever!

Mounting debts and wars

But instead of peace and debt-free prosperity, we have ever-mounting debt and periodic wars. We as a people are now ruled by a system of banker-owned Mammon that has usurped the mantle of government, disguised itself as our legitimate government, and set about to pauperize and control our people. It is now a centralized, all-powerful political apparatus whose main purposes are promoting war, spending the people's money, and propagandizing to perpetuate itself in power. Our two large political parties have become its servants, the various departments of government its spending agencies, and the Internal Revenue its collection agency.

Unknown to the people, it operates in close cooperation with similar apparatuses in other nations, which are also disguised as "governments." Some, we are told, are friends. Some, we are told, are enemies. "Enemies" are built up through international manipulations and used to frighten the American people into going billions of dollars more into debt to the bankers for "military preparedness," "foreign aid to stop communism," "minority rights," etc. Citizens, deliberately confused by brainwashing propaganda, watch helplessly while our politicians give our food, goods, and money to banker-controlled alien governments under the guise of "better relations" and "easing tensions." Our banker-controlled government takes our finest and bravest sons and sends them into foreign wars. When the "war" is over, we have gained nothing, but we are scores of billions of dollars more in debt to the bankers, which was the reason for the "war" in the first place!

And there's more

The profits from these massive debts have been used to erect a complete and almost hidden economic and political colossus over our nation. They keep telling us they are trying to do us "good," when in truth they work to bring harm and injury to our people. These would-be despots know it is easier to control and rob an ill, poorly educated and confused people than it is a healthy and intelligent population, so they deliberately prevent real cures for diseases, they degrade our educational systems, and they stir up social and racial unrest. For the same reason they favor drug use, alcohol, and crime. Everything which debilitates the minds and bodies of the people is secretly encouraged, as it makes the people less able to oppose them or even to understand what is being done to them. All that is honorable is being swept away, while they try to build their new, subservient man. Our new "rulers" are trying to change our whole racial, social, religious, and political order, but they will not change the debt-money economic system by which they rob and rule. Our people have become tenants and debt-slaves to the bankers and their agents in the land our fathers conquered. It is conquest through the most gigantic fraud and swindle in the history of mankind. And we remind you again: The key to their wealth and power over us is their ability to create "money" out of nothing and lend it to us at interest. If they had not been allowed to do that, they would never have gained secret control of our nation. How true Solomon's words are: "The rich ruleth over the poor, and the borrower is servant to the lender." (Proverbs 22:7)

Most of the owners of the largest banks in America are of Eastern European ancestry and connected with the Rothschild European banks.

The idea of debt-free and interest-free money scares the bankers. Their propagandists will immediately cry, "printing press money," and warn that it would soon be "worthless" and would "cause inflation."

The truth is their immense usury charges on their "created" credit (our debt) is the real cause of "inflation." All prices on all industry, trade and labor must be raised periodically to pay the ever-increasing usury charges. That is the usual cause of higher prices, and the money-changers spend millions in propaganda to keep you from realizing it.

The money-creators (bankers) know that if we ever tried a constitutional issue of debt-free, interest-free currency, the benefits would be apparent immediately. That they must prevent. Abraham Lincoln was the last president to issue such debt-free and interest-free currency (in 1863) and he was assassinated shortly thereafter.

No banker's plunder

Under a constitutional system no private banks would exist to rob the people. Government banks under the control of the people's representatives would issue and control all money and credit. They would issue not only actual currency, but could lend limited credit at no interest for the purchase of capital goods, such as homes. A $60,000 loan would require only $60,000 repayment, not $255,931, as it is now. Everyone who supplied materials and labor for the home would get paid just as they do today, but the bankers would *not* get $195,931 in usury, and that is why they ridicule and destroy anyone suggesting government (citizens') money without interest and without debt.

History tells us of debt-free and interest-free money issued by governments. The American colonies did it in the 1700s and their wealth soon rivaled England and brought restrictions from Parliament, which led to the Revolutionary War. Abraham Lincoln did it in 1863 to help finance the Civil War. Several Arab nations issue interest-free loans to their citizens today. The Saracen Empire forbad interest on money for 1,000 years, and its wealth outshone even Saxon Europe. Mandarin China issued its own money, interest-free and debt-free, and historians and collectors of art today consider those centuries to be China's time of greatest wealth, culture and peace.

Germany issued debt-free and interest-free money from 1935 on, accounting for its startling rise from the Depression to a world power in 5 years. Germany financed its entire government and war operation from 1935 to 1945 without gold and without debt, and it took the whole capitalist and communist world to destroy the German power over Europe and bring Europe back under the heel of the bankers. Such history of money does not even appear in the textbooks of public (government) schools today.

It is as ridiculous for a nation to say to its citizens, "You must consume less because we are short of money," as it would be for an airline to say "Our planes are flying, but we can't take you because we are short of tickets."

Stable money

If we are to have stable money, it would not be under the control of a privately owned corporation whose individual owners benefit by causing the money amount and value to fluctuate and the people to go into debt.

Under the present debt-usury system, the extra burden of usury forces workers and businesses to demand more money for the work and goods to pay their ever-increasing debts and taxes. This increase in prices and wages is called inflation. Bankers, politicians and "economists" blame it on everything but the real cause, which is the usury levied on money and debt by the bankers. This "inflation" benefits the money lenders, since it wipes out savings of one generation so they cannot finance or help the next generation, who must then borrow from the money lenders, and pay a large part of their life's labor to the usurer.

With an adequate supply of interest-free money, little borrowing would be required and prices would be established by people and goods, not by debts and usury.

A debt-free America

With debt-free and interest-free money, there would be no high and confiscatory taxation, our homes would be mortgage-free with no $10,000-a-year payments to the bankers, nor would they get $1,000 to $2,500 per year from every automobile on our roads. We would need no "easy payment" plans, "revolving" charge accounts, loans to pay medical or hospital bills, loans to pay taxes, loans to pay for burials, loans to pay loans, nor any of the thousand and one usury-bearing loans which now suck the life-blood of American families. There would be no unemployment, divorces caused by debt, destitute old people, or mounting crime, and even the so-called "deprived" classes would be deprived of neither job nor money to buy the necessities of life.

Criminals would not become politicians, nor would politicians become criminals in the pay of the money lenders. Our officials, at all government levels, would be working for the people instead of devising means to spend more money to place us further in debt to the bankers. We would get out of the entangling foreign alliances that have engulfed us in four major wars and scores of minor wars since the Federal Reserve Act was passed, alliances which are now used to prevent America from preparing her own defense in the face of mounting danger from alien powers.

A debt-free America would mean mothers would not have to work outside the home. With mother at home, juvenile delinquency would decrease rapidly. The elimination of the usury and debt would be the equivalent of a 50% raise in the purchasing power of every worker. With this cancellation of all debts, the return to the people of all the property and wealth the parasitic bankers and their quasi-legal agents have stolen by usury and fraud, and the ending of their theft of $300 billion (or more) every year from the people, America would be prosperous and powerful beyond the wildest dreams of its citizens today. And we would be at peace! (For a Bible example of cancellation of debts to money lenders and restoration of property and money to the people, read Nehemiah 5:1-13.)

Why you haven't known

We realize this small and necessarily incomplete article on money may be charged with oversimplification. Some may say that if it is that simple the people would have known about it, and it could not have happened. But this money lenders' consPIRACY is as old as Babylon, and even in America it dates far back before the year 1913. Actually, 1913 may be considered the year in which their previous plans came to fruition, and the way opened for complete economic conquest of our people. The consPIRACY is old enough in America so that its agents have been, for many years, in positions such as newspaper publishers, editors, columnists, church ministers, university presidents, professors, textbook writers, labor union leaders, movie makers, radio and TV commentators, politicians from school board members to U.S. presidents, and many others.

Controlled news and information

These agents control the information available to our people. They manipulate public opinion, elect whom they will locally and nationally, and never expose the crooked money system. They promote school bonds, municipal bonds, expensive and detrimental farm programs, "urban renewal," foreign aid, and many other schemes which will put the people more into debt to the bankers. Thoughtful citizens wonder why billions are spent on one program and billions on another which may duplicate it or even nullify it, such as paying some farmers not to raise crops, while at the same time building dams or canals to irrigate more farm land. Crazy or stupid? Neither. The goal is more debt. Thousands of government-sponsored ways to waste money go on continually. Most make no sense, but they are never exposed for what they really are, builders of "billions for the bankers and debts for the people."

So-called "economic experts" write syndicated columns in hundreds of newspapers, craftily designed to prevent the people from learning the simple truth about our money system. Commentators on radio and TV, preachers, educators, and politicians blame the people as wasteful, lazy, or spendthrift, and blame the workers and consumers for the increase in debts and the inflation of prices, when they know the cause is the debt-money system itself. Our people are literally drowned in charges and counter-charges designed to confuse them and keep them from understanding the unconstitutional and evil money-system that is so efficiently and silently robbing the farmers, the workers and the businessmen of the fruits of their labors and of their freedoms.

When some few patriotic people or organizations who know the truth begin to expose them or try to stop any of their mad schemes, they are ridiculed and smeared as "right-wing extremists," "super-patriots," "ultra-rightists," "bigots," "racists," even "fascists" and "anti-semites." Any name is used which will cause them to shut up or will at least stop other people from listening to the warning they are giving. Articles and books such as you are now reading are kept out of schools, libraries, and book stores.

Some, who are especially vocal in their exposure of the treason against our people, are harassed by government agencies such as the EPA, OSHA, the IRS, and others, causing them financial loss or bankruptcy. Using the above methods, they

"Above all else — control the media."

have been completely successful in preventing most Americans from learning the things you have read here. However, in spite of their control of information, they realize many citizens are learning the truth. Therefore, to prevent violence or armed resistance to their plunder of America, they plan to register all firearms and eventually to disarm all citizens. They have to eliminate most guns, except those in the hands of their government police and army.

Tell the people

The "almost" hidden conspirators in politics, religion, education, entertainment, and the news media are working for a banker-owned United States in a banker-owned world under a banker-owned World Government!

Our generation has not suffered under the "yoke" as the coming generations will. Usury and taxes will continue to take a larger and larger part of the annual earnings of the people and put them into the pockets of the bankers and their political Agents. Increasing "government regulations" will prevent citizen protest and opposition to their control. Is it possible that your grandchildren will own neither home nor car, but will live in "government-owned" apartments and ride to work in "government-owned" buses (both paying usury to the bankers), and be allowed to keep just enough of their earnings to buy a minimum of food and clothing while their Rulers wallow in luxury? In Asia and eastern Europe it is called communism; in America it is called democracy and capitalism.

America will not shake off her banker-controlled dictatorship as long as the people are ignorant of the hidden controllers. International financiers, who control most of the governments of the nations, and most sources of information, seem to have us completely within their grasp. They are afraid of only one thing: an awakened patriotic citizenry, armed with the truth.

Audit the Federal Reserve system

The Federal Reserve has never been audited by the government since it took over our money and credit in 1913. In 1975 a bill, H.R. 4316, to require an audit was introduced in Congress.

During the April, 1975 hearings, this author submitted a statement favoring the audit, as did many others. Due to pressure from the money controllers, it was not passed. No audit of the Fed has ever been made.

Why haven't they told you?

Why haven't they told you about this scandal, the greatest fraud in history which has caused Americans and others to spill oceans of blood, pay trillions of dollars interest on fraudulent loans and burden themselves with unnecessary taxes?

When the credit/debt bubble is pricked by the bankers they will foreclose on America. Then, they will own it all. There may be a "managed chaos"—riots and terrorism—to alarm the people with the fear of anarchy as the bankers prepare to impose a dictatorship on America as the "solution" for the problems they, themselves, have created.

Only an educated people will be able to resist the lies of the bankers' stooges. This is why it is important for you to know the truth about how the bankers make billions for themselves and bring debts to the people.

■ ■ ■

Don McAlvany, editor of the *McAlvany Intelligence Advisor,* reported in *The Fatima Crusader* Spring issue, that it should be obvious to any thinking person that our press lies, manipulates and distorts the truth. He goes on to tell us that John Swinton, editor of the *New York Times,* said at a dinner of the American Press Association in 1914: "There is no such thing as an independent press in America. . . . Not a man among you dares to utter his honest opinion. . . . You know beforehand that it would never appear in print. It is the [means by which the newsman earns his sustenance] (his salary). We are the tools and the vassals of the rich behind the scenes. We are marionettes. These men pull the strings and we dance. Our time, our talents, our lives, and our capacities are all the property of these men; we are intellectual prostitutes."

Remember that quote the next time you watch CBS, NBC, ABC, or CNN.

The usurper is slave to self-interest, unaware that the greatest rewards are found in <u>ENLIGHTENED</u> self-interest.

189.   *June 28, 1993*

Taken from THE BENT (Winter '93 issue),
an organ of the Engineering Society Tau Beta Pi

One of the biggest puzzles of economics in a scientific age is the peculiar frequency with which money systems become unstable and ultimately collapse. To the engineer, trained in the science of getting things right, chronic breakdown is a signal that there is a serious flaw in the system's design. The engineer ignores such a signal at his or her peril. The repetition of disaster is totally unacceptable.

For instance, suppose that a bridge was designed and built in 1913. It collapsed seven years later. When it was rebuilt, the original blueprints were used. No study was done concerning the cause of the collapse, nor were any structural corrections made.

In 1929, the bridge collapsed again. It was rebuilt, again with no study and no changes. The bridge collapsed in 1958 and again in 1962. Both times it was rebuilt according to the old blueprints. It collapsed in 1973 and was rebuilt to the original specifications.

In the early 1980s it fell again. It is trembling and shaking right now! Yet despite this long history of chronic failure, the bridge repairmen are in their hard hats, with the same old tattered blueprints in hand, waiting for the next terrible crash. They are ready to put the pieces back just where they were, then stand back and hope for the best.

The engineers on a project with this track record would have been seeking alternative employment in another field after the crash of 1929. They wouldn't have been allowed to remain professional engineers, because professional engineers are required to be right. At the very least they are required to find their mistakes—preferably before a disaster—and correct them.

Of course, the bridge is a thinly veiled allusion to the successive economic disasters the country has suffered since the founding of the Federal Reserve in 1913. The economy is now in the midst of the seventh major recession/depression in almost 80 years. These are events which the Federal Reserve system was supposed to prevent. Yet, once again, there is uncertainty about the direction of the economy and what measures should be taken to forestall another major financial collapse.

What would an engineer do?

To the engineer, chronic instability of any system raises the all-important question: Why? Specifically, in the case of the money system:

- Why are recessionary cycles appearing at more frequent intervals?

- Why does the purchasing power of the dollar decline over time?

- Why is debt—of both the private and public sectors— growing exponentially?

There are as many answers to these questions as there are schools of economic thought. It is this inconsistency, this lack of agreement among those who are supposed to know, that disturbs the professional engineer.

Economists have been studying the problem of economic instability for decades, and by now they ought to know exactly what is going wrong and thus be able to correct the problem permanently. Yet when one studies economics, it becomes clear that every school of economic thought is based on a different set of hypotheses.

But money is governed by certain mathematical principles. This is obvious, given the fact that all monetary transactions are various forms of addition, subtraction, multiplication, and division. Therefore, it ought to be possible to define the cause of inflation and depression in mathematical terms and then use this analysis to construct a stable, inflationless money system. This approach is essentially the application of the problem-solving methodology taught in every engineering college throughout the country. It is not mysterious, the only mystery is why economists can't agree over the effects of what basically is simple arithmetic! Is it because solutions that are valid in the ideal world differ from those solutions that are valid in the real world?

One thing is for sure, the real world is crying out for monetary reform. The engineering community is equipped to respond. The question is: Will it?

190.   *August 3, 1993*

Reprint from a monthly BULLETIN
by Lt. Col. Archibald E. Roberts
P.O. Box 986, Ft. Collins, CO 80522

Americans are an endangered species

American citizens have failed to understand or even recognize the fact that gross changes have been gradually and illicitly brought about in the political and sociological climate of this land.

It is evident, however, that a subtle and perilous change has occurred in America. Within the past two or three generations the civilization of our forefathers has come under sophisticated assault. The structures of freedom erected at such great cost in blood, sweat and treasure are crumbling. Our God is blasphemed, our lineage reviled, and our Constitution dismantled.

Our destiny has turned to dust.

Americans have been reduced to economic serfs in the land that once was theirs. A secret government of monetary power, employing perverted mass media and the coercive authority of a captured bureaucratic civil service, is forcing us into a New World Order of so-called "Liberty, Equality, Fraternity."

To liquidate this threat to life and property Americans must first accept the fact that the frame of reference upon which they erroneously rely to preserve the Republic no longer exists.

Gone is the Constitution, and its protective covenants. Gone are the courts, and their shield to personal freedom. Gone is representative government, and the sovereignty of the individual. Gone is the U.S. dollar, and its authority in the market place. All have been surreptitiously phased out of the society to usher in a totalitarian one-world autocracy of the financial "elite."

There is, however, a practical and attainable solution to the state of national emergency. Conscientious men and women can successfully energize state power to expose the covert transfer of state and federal sovereignty to private interests. The law involved is the fundamental law of principal. Actions of an agent are not binding upon the principal if those actions are not authorized by the principal. Constitutionally, departments of government are agents of the state . . . which created them by constitutional compact.

The mission of informed citizens, therefore, is to activate the sovereign powers of the state to expose and neutralize interlocking subversion in government departments and restore control of government to the people. Remember that any government which gets so big that it can give you anything you want will also be so big that it can take everything you've got!

America need not become a land of "yesterday's people." All it takes to regain the freedoms lost is the courage to face today's political reality, and to implement successful techniques and procedures to reverse the mindless march toward the new feudalism.

191. *August 5, 1993*

"But whose New World Order will we be subject to?"

Presenting a secular catechism on the final struggle:

Q: We know the world is messed up. Is this an accident or is it intentional?

A: It can only be intentional.

Q: What is the purpose of this?

A: To gain world control.

Q: Why would anyone want that?

A: It is a natural consequence of being human.

Q: Do you regard lording it over others' as natural?

A: For a few; no. But for most; yes.

Q: Who are these people who would control us?

A: Most, but not all, of the super, super wealthy, being mainly the heirs to financial fortunes passed down largely intact and through tax-exempt foundations.

Q: If you win the battle, will you punish these people?

A: I would grant overwhelming—but short of total— amnesty. Their main punishment would be isolation with their own kind. They would be sent to Limbo.

Q: Do you believe in the supernatural?

A: No. 100% no.

Q: Then you don't believe in destiny or fate?

A: I didn't say that. I think we have free will, but I also think there are forces of an imponderable nature that we will someday come to understand that now offer us direction. Accepting it is up to us.

Q: Do you believe these forces are extraterrestrial?

A: No.

Q: What do you think the final outcome will be?

A: I think the forces for good, i.e., bringing happiness to people through sensible policies, will win out in the end, but there are no guarantees that it will.

Q: How will this come about?

A: I do not know. The manipulators have the upper hand, and are gaining momentum daily. If Mother Liberty is to have her last child, it will most likely be by cesarean section.

Q: When might this be?

A: I have no way of knowing, but I would like to make a guess; as early as the summer of '95, but more likely in 1997.

Q: What will happen then?

A: Take heed—people will call for a man on a white horse, and there are a lot of guys out there with brown horses and whitewash.

192.   *August 8, 1993*

What is your preference: inflation, hyperinflation, another recession, or worst of all—depression? Sorry, no other choices are available. When the present stock market bubble bursts and our economic house of cards implodes, I expect a full blown case of depression. This will come as a surprise, as the rise in the price of gold since March, '93, suggests quite the opposite, i.e., a coming period of inflation. But I think the manipulators are setting us up for the *final* coup de grace: a depression so deep that values, instead of inflating, will collapse. Assets will be bought up at pennies on the dollar for those with cash, and there won't be many of them around what with all the debt the world is saddled with.

The conspirators (the ones to whom most of that debt is owed) expect first to "legally" steal the assets of us the people; and then unceremoniously strip us of our liberty in accordance with their version of the New World Order.

While this remains *their* vision of the future, I am not so sure that intervention on the side of right by unseen forces might not come to our rescue, if only we will have the courage to involve ourselves when that time comes.

As Dick Cheney said: "It is easy to take liberty for granted, when you have never had it taken from you."

193.   *August 13, 1993*

Open Letter:
U.S. regulating the life out of the little guy

Editor:

My wife and I are small business owners. I am probably the biggest flag waver who ever lived, to the point of crying when I see our flag go by in a parade.

However, I am disenchanted with our system, due to federal laws, state laws, county laws, and city laws, Republicans, Democrats, plutocrats and autocrats.

Through these laws I am compelled to pay business tax, sales tax, school tax, vehicle tax, gas tax, water tax, utility tax, federal tax, state tax, county tax, city tax, cigarette tax, liquor tax, excise tax, unemployment tax and Social Security tax.

I am required by law to obtain a business license, car license, driver's license, insurance license, liquor license, hunting license, fishing license, not to mention marriage license and dog license.

I am regulated as to whom I may hire or fire. My speech, opinions, and even my thinking are regulated by government as to political correctness.

I am also expected to contribute to every society and organization in the country which the genius of man is capable of bringing to life, including United Way, March of Dimes, Salvation Army, Boy Scouts, Cub Scouts, YWCA, Christmas Seals, Easter Seals, Boy's Ranch, WEAVE, MADD, and Little League. Also, peace officers associations and fire fighters associations.

For my own safety I am required to carry health insurance, life insurance, property insurance, flood insurance, liability insurance, car insurance, business insurance, disability insurance, professional insurance, credit insurance, and unemployment insurance.

My business is so governed, I'm beginning to wonder who owns it.

Simply because I refuse to donate to something or other, I am boycotted, talked about, lied about, held up, held down, and robbed until I am totally stripped of my human dignity.

I am inspected, expected, suspected, disrespected, dejected, rejected, examined, informed, noticed, audited, inquired, summoned, fined, commanded, and compelled until I provide an inexhaustible supply of money for every known need, desire and hope of the human race.

George Orwell was right. Only his timetable was off.

194. *September, 1993*

Read it and weep . . .
How our economic system was designed to fail

Are you tired of the deficit? Get used to it because it cannot go away under our present economic system. It is the primary source of "new debt money" which keeps our economy stumbling along. New debt money? Every dollar in existence has to be *borrowed* into existence and when that dollar which has been *borrowed* into existence, has been repaid, it *disappears.* Sound confusing? It's not. It's very simple to have prosperity in America; we have to borrow more and more money. Then, when you begin to prosper and pay that money back, the money disappears and precipitates a slump. Therefore the only way to continue to prosper is continue to borrow more and more and more new debt money into existence. Which is exactly what is occurring in this nation. It's not a complicated system. It's very simple. The truth is hidden from you by the claim that it is complicated; too complicated for you to understand. But you can understand it after you read this book, *Read It and Weep,* for you surely will as you begin to understand the perfidy of those you have chosen and trusted to lead you and to protect you.

Another item of some interest to the average American citizen may be that the Federal Reserve system is a privately owned bank. It is *not* a federal agency as so many American citizens believe. And the primary controlling interest of the Fed, as it's often called, is not even by American citizens? Yet this privately owned, for profit (Oh boy, for profit indeed!) bank controls the entire monetary policy of this nation. That's what the Department of the Treasury says: "The Fed has the responsibility for determining United States monetary policy." Control of our national monetary policy by a private, for profit bank. Sound interesting? You haven't heard anything yet! Wait til we discuss the new Constitution with you. It's your nation, right? Maybe not anymore.

This book, READ IT AND WEEP, can be purchased from Loyalist Publishing, Palisade, CO 81526, 303-464-0521.

195. *September, 1993*

U.S. military globalists' tool

Internationalists want the president and Congress out of the "loop" when decisions are made to spill American blood.

Reprinted from THE SPOTLIGHT, by James P. Tucker, Jr.

The world army, long a vision of proponents of turning the United Nations into a global government, has arrived, creeping in on little cat's feet.

The UN army's main forces are called NATO, but it is backed up by troops of what had been the American military, with UN blue helmets stashed by quartermasters to be issued at the moment of call-up.

State Department officials point out the significance of procedures globalists are using to intervene in the former Yugoslavia:

UN Secretary General Boutros Boutros-Ghali calls for intervention, NATO prepares a list of bombing targets, and, to set an important precedent without awakening American patriotism, then asks the UN's permission to do what it was told to do.

Note the absence, they said, of any role for President Bill Clinton or Congress in this decision to potentially spill American blood.

Campaign promise

Clinton had urged action earlier and had called for a UN "rapid deployment force," the current euphemism for a world army, during his 1992 campaign without drawing much attention to the issue.

In a skilled move to condition the public mind, the administration gave its Bilderberg group-Trilateral Commission collaborator, *The Washington Post*, a "scoop" on August 5. Clinton and *Post* executives belong to the Trilateral Commission and

Bilderberg group, secret organizations with overlapping leadership and a common world agenda.

The *Post* reported a classified final draft of Presidential Decision Directive 13, which "endorses the United Nations as ersatz world policeman and commits Washington to support multinational peacemaking and peacekeeping operations politically, morally and financially."

The "directive would formalize the president's acceptance of UN command over U.S. troops, a significant milestone," the *Post* reported.

The precedent for American soldiers fighting under a foreign commander came in Somalia, where U.S. troops are commanded by a Turkish general under a UN flag.

However, ambitions of Clinton and State Department officials ran into some resistance from patriots in the Pentagon and certain politicians, these government sources said.

Career military officers wanted American sovereignty preserved and the president to retain his constitutional role of commander in chief. Pragmatic globalists wanted language "to keep the right wing under control."

Thus, the directive said the United States would not "earmark" U.S. units for UN service. While it endorses placing American soldiers under foreign UN officers, any American commander involved is to maintain separate reporting channels to higher U.S. officials and even to refuse UN orders they consider illegal, or "militarily imprudent and unsound."

Don't be fooled

"Those words are supposed to pacify you American patriots, but you would be a fool to take them seriously," one official said as the other nodded agreement, both speaking on condition of job-saving anonymity.

"In the first place, there is no need to publicly 'earmark'

American units when the NATO forces have already become the UN's standing army, as demonstrated by Bosnia. It is on orders of and with permission of Boutros-Ghali that NATO is intervening there," he said.

"Besides, backing up the standing UN army are many American standby units," said the other. "All officers and enlisted men know, and are told, that they could be assigned to UN forces anywhere in the world. It doesn't take long to put on a blue helmet."

And Clinton's instructions to any U.S. commanders involved in a UN operation to maintain separate reporting channels to Washington and even disobey UN orders?

"Don't take it seriously," the first official replied. "First of all, most UN commanders will be European and American 'shavetails' (lieutenants) who will give them no problem. Senior officers are political or they would be junior officers, and they know this is just rhetoric to diminish American objections."

"Here is another piece of the manipulation of the public mind," the other said, pointing to a *New York Times* editorial of August 9 criticizing Clinton for approaching the subject of a world army too cautiously.

The *Times*, like *The Washington Post, Los Angeles Times* and the major establishment media, has executives participating in the secret deliberations of Bilderbergers and the Trilateralists on condition they maintain blackout secrecy.

UN charter cited

The UN charter calls on "members to commit forces . . . for a standby army," and Clinton held back, the *Times* editorial complained.

"Brilliant, isn't it?" the first State Department official said. "Clinton is cast, by this editorial, as the president who protects American sovereignty when he is actually surrendering sovereignty."

"Those words about reporting separately and disobeying orders will be no obstacle to the UN army," the other said. "If they ever become inconvenient, they can simply be struck out. These directives remain classified and secret until the government decides to use *The Post* or other papers as a propaganda tool, then they are selectively leaked."

This surrender of sovereignty is taking place with no apparent protest from American leaders, all of whom have sworn to defend the constitution.

But, before the latest directive was leaked to the *Post*, Rep. Barbara Vucanovich (R-Nev.) placed into the *Congressional Record* a resolution by the National Society of the Daughters of the American Revolution objecting to the surrender of sovereignty in Somalia.

Placing the GIs under UN control in Somalia is part of a "plan to turn all of our military forces over to the United Nations and not replace them, leaving the United States entirely without a national defense," the D.A.R. said.

Few Americans listened.

196.   *October 1993*

Here's more from *Read It and Weep:*

The Solution
by Frederick Soddy, M.A. F.R.S.
1921 Nobel Prize winner

The most sinister and anti-social feature about bank deposit money is that *it has no existence.* The banks owe the public for a total amount of money which does not exist. In buying and selling, implemented by cheque transaction, there is a mere change in the party to whom the money is owed by the banks. As the one depositor's account is debited, the other's is credited and the banks can go on owing for it all the time.

The whole profit of the issuance of money has provided the capital of the great banking business as it exists today. Starting with nothing whatever of their own, *they have got the whole world into their debt irredeemable, by a trick.* This money comes into existence every time the banks "lend" and disappears every time the debt is repaid to them, so that if industry tries to repay, the money of the nation disappears. This is what makes prosperity so 'dangerous' as it destroys money just when it is most needed and precipitates a slump. There is nothing left now for us but to ever get deeper and deeper into debt to the banking system in order to provide the increasing amounts of money the nation requires for its expansion and growth. *An honest money system is the only alternative!*

■ ■ ■

To begin with, you have to realize that we, the citizens of America, are at war. This is *not* an undeclared war, except that the average American citizen does not realize that a war is ongoing. Those who are fighting to destroy America and everything she stands for have made their intentions clear and, just as in any war, there have been casualties. Millions of them. These casualties, however, are just as likely to occur on *your* street corner or in *your* family as they are to happen in Concord, Vietnam, Flanders or Pearl Harbor. Why? Because this is truly *the* World War, as in New World Order. Ultimately, the question is whether the average man can be free. We must win back the freedoms we have lost here in America. Freedom is like a disease; once it breaks out, it is very difficult to control. The freedom disease of the world is in America. That is why the "control" of this disease had to start here. Why would we be so surprised at that? Why would we be so surprised that they do not stand up and declare that they are going to take away our freedom? By its very nature this type of movement, to suppress freedom, must be hidden *until it achieves the majority of its goals.* We are very close here in America to the point where the iron fist comes out of the velvet glove. How do these men win the control of America and her people? The best, most easily obtained control of human beings is through economics. *That* is our problem. An honest money system is the answer.

Buy the Fed!

This is the *automatic* solution. Under the original law setting up the Federal Reserve, our government has the legal right to purchase the outstanding stock of the Fed at any time (see #35). The cost of this purchase is for the amount of the paid-in capital at the time of the repurchase of the 12 Reserve banks, just 550 million dollars. (The paid-in capital could be as much as or even more than 550 million dollars or as little as 135 million dollars. There is bound to be more than a small argument about this. But the amount *doesn't matter!*)

Remember, for that paid-in capital of 550 million dollars, the Fed has the "right" to loan out trillions of dollars. Of course, the only way you can accomplish that feat, loan out trillions of dollars on the basis of a total paid-in capital of 550 million dollars, is to be privileged to create debt from "nothing." Understanding this brings us back to one of the most basic reasons for the formation of the Fed; to saddle the American government with a debt of nonexistent money. By definition, this is unpayable. If it does not exist, it cannot be rounded up and paid. However, the secret to understanding this is in the statement of *nonexistent money.* If it does not exist—*it does not exist!* Not as money and certainly not as debt.

This is why you hear it referred to as fraud. Fraud which *cannot* be committed without the knowledge and assistance of the government.

Having the government purchase the outstanding stock of the Fed accomplishes three things:

1. It puts the power to issue money back with Congress *which is where the Constitution says it belongs.*

2. It turns off the spigot of funds from the public treasury to the pockets of those who have demonstrated, in their own words, their wish to subvert this nation and our Constitution.

3. It pays off the major portion of our national debt. The Fed holds well over 90% of our national debt and when the government buys the Fed, the government holds its own debt *thus canceling the debt.* This is what I meant by if it does not exist, it does not exist. Our national debt *is* an illusion; nothing more.

Just that easily America would be virtually debt free and back to prosperity. *Within one year* most of our problems would disappear. On the other hand, if you keep doing what you have been doing, expect to continue to get what you have been getting.

197.   *March 24, 1991*

Have you ever wondered why once-great societies go into decline? Do you suppose it could come from misplaced priorities that the unenlightened majority fall victim to? I think they perceive their future happiness to be something it is not. Accomplishments cannot be sustained solely of their own momentum. They must be nurtured and maintained on a continuing basis. Fun and games can be pleasing diversions, but they won't keep the house in repair.

The secret is to labor at the task you do best, provided it is useful or productive. It will probably also be the activity you like doing the most. With luck like that who would ever want to make changes? You will already have achieved your most important goal.

But there's more to it than that. You will also need to learn the art of pacing yourself, eating right, and how to manage your most valuable resource—time—to maximum advantage (this includes resting). I seldom watch TV. The radio is much better. Every half hour, news highlights and summaries break up the music that can be enjoyed while simultaneously permitting me to read the *Wall Street Journal, Insight* magazine, and a few choice newsletters that took several years to uncover. TV makes you a captive audience, forced to watch more of what you don't want to see than what you do. Could we find a similitude here with George Bernard Shaw's comment that the media is unable to distinguish between a bicycle accident and the collapse of civilization? But reading allows additional selectivity (you can read or reread just the parts that interest you) to choices of the printed word that you have already identified as generally worthwhile, thus providing enormous efficiencies of time. The results of all this are summed up in #110-T4a and T4b.

I would like to wish the same fortune for everyone, which is not unlike the way fairy tales of yesteryear often ended, proclaiming, after the principals survived their final obstacle, the ultimate uplift (on which note this treatise comes to a prophetic end): ". . . and they lived happily *ever after.*"

Those who bring sunshine to the lives of others cannot keep it from themselves.
— SIR JAMES BARRIE

The facts are from others, the philosophy is my own, the mix becomes the gel that promotes coherence.
— SAMOHT GIVOTANGI

Epilogue

The new morality that *Philosophy Nuggets* espouses (among many other things) is not a religion, but a more sophisticated value system meant to *replace* religion by culling out the deadwood of fantasy, and filling that void with the kind of reasoning by which *modern* man has the potential to be elevated.

An observation: You can find yourself on the wrong side of history today, but gain vindication tomorrow. When you know you're right even while under attack from various quarters, just hang in there long enough, and if you *are* right, sooner or later the world will come knocking at your door.

The motivation: I have assembled truisms from others and added them to my own inventory of beliefs in an effort to arrive at conclusions that I can only hope will someday benefit all (including myself) by freeing us from the illusion that *real* happiness can come at the expense of others.

A final word: If allowed but one thought to leave with the readers of this work, it would be that if we can correct the major wrongs of this world, the multitude of minor problems that surround us will begin to correct themselves. If the tree is diseased, so too must be the fruit that it bears.

I am proceeding as though on a mission—a mission to save the world. I call it Mission: Impossible. Whether it turns out to be that or not, only time will tell. As Frank Sinatra sings: "Everyone knows an ant can't move a rubbertree plant . . . oops, there goes another rubbertree plant."

■ ■ ■

Glossary
*denotes a term original to this work

allegorical: having hidden spiritual meaning that transcends the literal sense of a sacred text (#110-D8)

altruism: unselfish regard for or devotion to the welfare of others

amoral: being outside or beyond the moral order or a particular code of morals

analog: something that is analogous or similar to something else

annus mirabilis: wonderful year (#163)

benevolent capitalism: see #97, #135

captotocracy*: a country or body governed through the judicious use of capital by a reclusive, elitest group steering the ship of state from behind the scenes (#137)

cognitive dissonance: psychological conflict resulting from incongruous beliefs and attitudes held simultaneously (110-W3)

compendious 1a: marked by brief expression of a comprehensive matter **b:** full in scope yet concise in treatment

dogma: a point of view or tenet put forth as authoritative *without* adequate grounds. Adequate grounds meaning reasonable, which in turn means possessing *sound judgment.*

dogma vs. certitude explained and clarified as well as defined: as to the degree of belief in my own ideas, it is one of certitude as distinguished from dogma. Certitude may emphasize a faith in something not needing or not capable of proof, but justified by reason.

enlightened common sense: see #65

enlightened self-interest: see #65

enlightener*: one with less specific knowledge than a teacher, but who views a broader horizon combined with the ability to draw conclusions (#110-N4)

eupraxophist: one who demonstrates wisdom, good sense, and correct actions in their conduct

minigram*: a short written expression of thought

nomenklaturshchiks: ruling class (#163)

prima ratio: the first reason (#163)

prophet 1. one gifted with more than ordinary moral insight **2.** an effective or leading spokesman for a cause, doctrine, or group

rentier \ron-tyā\: a person who receives a fixed income from investments. (As used in this work it means interest income only) (#22, #27)

star move: in the game of checkers, a star move is the *only* move that *forces* a win or a draw (as the case may be). It is not uncommon for upwards of a dozen *consecutive* star moves to be necessary in a single game before we can get to "checker heaven." Life is no different. (#110-D5)

totocracy*: a totalitarian state that does not appear on the surface as such (#137)

transmute: implies transforming into a higher element or thing (#110-S4)

transubstantiation: the miraculous change by which according to Roman Catholic and Eastern Orthodox dogma the eucharistic elements at their consecration become the body and blood of Christ while keeping only the appearances of bread and wine.

The term came into ecclesiastical use in the Berengarian controversy of the 11th century. The belief was laid down by the Council of Trent. Please understand that this is not meant to be merely symbolic. The claim is that the bread and wine are literally changed into the body and blood of Christ via a miracle. I infer from this that another miracle retains the perceived properties of bread and wine (which of course is all it is). (#124)

Criticisms

'Tis rare that genius comes to earth
    to beautify the mind;
inventive skill is not a trait
    that burdens human kind.

How few, alas, can e'er excel
    in letters or in art;
appreciation doesn't dwell
    in every human heart.

In fact we're mostly commonplace,
    but few are really wise;
Yet nature ne'er designed the
    man who could not criticize.

– W.H. WILSON, SAVANNAH, N.Y.

■ ■ ■

To fill a small place that one is well fitted for is a greater honor than to have filled a high place poorly.

I do not have the raw intelligence required to rule the world of tomorrow. What I bring to the table is wisdom— enough to enable us to survive the meantime. Having intelligence means you understand what Michael Kinsley and William F. Buckley are saying; having wisdom means you understand Charlie Brown and Linus.

One does not start out with wisdom; it is acquired over time, and even then comes only to a few.

– GIVOTANGI

The Woeful Double Game

(duplicity by another name could best be called a double game)

Oh world of today, where incompetents play,
    why are your wars not the same anymore?
What once could be fathomed no longer makes sense,
    could it be that I am becoming more dense?

In fact it's so different that one cannot tell
    who's ready for heaven, and who's slated for hell
Without looking too hard you can sense the aim;
    to make knavery part of their own double game.

We like to pretend that we're fighting Saddam
    but we dare not succeed any more than in Nam
Cause the ultimate rulers do not empathize
    they just give the orders of who lives or dies

So we shoot down a jet to make it look serious
    and mow down boy soldiers so totally wearious
Well it's all for the sake of appearance you see
    to let the far right make us slaves without shame
By producing these wars for their own double game.

               – SAMOHT GIVOTANGI

The All-Time Best
Comic Strip Episode

PEANUTS ®   by Charles Schulz

Reprinted by permission of UFS, Inc.

Poems

A poetic prayer

Index of Quotables

*We quote some of the best statements
and one-liners from a broad spectrum of personalities*

Cartoons

Index

A

abdication, 64
abduction, 120
ability, 106, 344
  lack of, 121
  success dependent on, 344
  unequal, 70
abortion
  author pro-choice, 330
  Catholic Church's views
    on, 330
  post-birth, 165
absolute power, former Soviet
  Union, advantages of, 123
abuses, reoccurrences of, 344
acceptance, 218
  search for, 372
accountability, poor, 196
achievement, 235–36, 470
  (See also student achievement)
achievers
  outnumbered, 284
  preferring conservatism,
  284
  rewards for, 119
  self-made, 170
  top, 361
ACLU, 73
action
  and reaction, 83
  reasons for, 317
  result of unconscious
  factors, 274
  without knowledge, 256

administrators, as failed
  teachers, 362–63
adult, value of life, 380
adversary, 227, 423
advice, bad, 268
Aesop, 60
affirmative action, 89, 315
afflictions, 233
affluence
  growing, 160
  in U.S., 173
Afghanistan, atrocities, 86
Africa, 247
  mineral wealth, 84
Afro-Americans, opportunities for, 122
aged. See elders
aging
  arresting indefinitely, 389
  medical research into,
  389–90
agricultural
  base, erosion of, in
    Roman empire, 150
  commodities, price
    supports, 342
aid, apportioning, 260
AIDS, 336
  and military blood
    supply, 420
  patients, isolation, 317
  virus, 260
air, 256
alcohol, 336
  abuse, 307

Empire of the City, The, 413
employer, not wanting to
  know about irregularities,
  280
employment
    See also wages, living
  full, 383–84
      excepting students,
        the severely disabled
        and retirees, 325
      intangible benefits of,
        384
empowering people, 404
Emry, Sheldon, 435–54
emulation, 389
encounters, 255
encyclical "Quadragesimo
  Anno," 105–6
*Encyclopedia Brittanica,
  The,* 245
end
    justifying means, 75
    of the world. *See*
      eschatology
ending, 213
Ends of Power, The, 46
enemies, 424, 472
    built through international
      manipulations, 445
enemy, our own worst, 190
energy, alternative, 191
engineers, 213
England,
    1765 debt-to-income
      ratio, 179
    Bank of, 306
      investments in U.S.,
        321

opium wars, 310–11
right to create money,
  305–6
densely populated, 309
English language, 88
enlightened
    common sense, 22, 174,
      177
    also called God's law,
      110
    and moralism, 159
    and reason, 319
    and success, 380
    and thinking freely,
      369
    basis of enlightened
      self-interest, 326
    beyond the grasp of
      most, 337
    high level insight, 108
person, 280
self-interest, 60, 63, 140
    aiming at everyone's
      happiness, 417
    amoral, 199
    and discipline, 151
    and Givotangi Parity
      Swap, 284
    and morality, 107
    and religion and vice,
      217
    and star moves, 209
    antithesis of, 381
    appreciating by first
      becoming amoral,
      348
    based on enlightened
      common sense, 326

equality
before the law, 197
seeking, 315
equities, 90
equivocating, 380
escape, 216
eschatology, 243
estate planning, 425
Estonia, 392. *See also* Baltic
republics
ethanes, 364
ethical values superior to
material after basic needs
satisfied, 382
ethics, 107
higher, rewards of, 213
eugenics, 280
euphoria, from purchases,
195
European Community, 166
European unity, 182
euthanasia, 327–30
abuses, 328
desirability of, 328
handled by doctors,
327–28
proper, 327
evenhandedness, 316
evil
and good, 222
eliminating in
Napoleonic govern-
ments, 434
ignoring, 234
refusal to recognize, 277
tolerating, 433, 435
evolution, 238

evolutionary growth, stages
of, 355
exaggeration, 410
example
convincing through, 389
leading by, 424
power of, 199, 409
setting an, 61
excellence, uniformity of, 371
excesses
accommodation of, 160
avoiding, 203
Executive Order #11490,
231, 243
exercise, 230–31
exhilaration of being shot at,
344
exorcisms, recent, 331
exotic, the, 372
expansionary periods, 117
expectations, unrealistic, 153
expediency, 198
experience, 147
experimental
communities. *See* work
camps
proving areas for radical
new policies, 154
expert at everything, 175
experts, 18
intimidation by, 215
exploitation, 63, 94
immorality of, 348
exploitative capitalism, 60,
75, 82, 117, 175, 184, 424
See also capitalism
escalating, 325

Hall of Fame, baseball, 196
Hamilton, Alexander, 242,
  296–98, 300
handicapped. *See* disabled, the
handicrafts, private solo, 97
happily ever after, 471
happiness, 23, 60, 143, 195,
  255
    at expense of others, 281
    best served by promoting
      others', 372
    by helping others be
      happy, 219, 282–83
    for all, 323
    maximizing for all feeling
      beings, 239
    real, 473
    versus health, 183
happy people, 273
harassment, 207, 451
hardship, 220
    building character, 183
    ennobling ourselves
      without, 183
harmony, 323
    need for, 237
Harvey, Raymond Lee, 420
Harvey, W.H., 276
hate, 62, 270, 316
Hawaii, 338
headlights, overrunning, 200
health, versus happiness, 183
health care
    administration cost, 329
    affordable, 269
    cost of, 329
    insurance, 118
      Canada, 329

    single universal plan,
      338
    U.S., 329
    national, currently
      unaffordable, 326
    problems, 433
    state-of-the-art, 329
    unaffordable, 269
Hearst's magazine, 418–19
heart
    attack, 230
    satisfying, 224
heaven, 60, 218, 414, 429
    on earth, 238, 283, 319
    or hell, 357
heirs, and interest, 216
Helms, Jesse, 427–28
Helms, Richard, 29, 46–47
Helmsley, Leona, 379–80
helping others to help
    themselves, 164
Hemphill, Robert, 305
Henry, James, 260
Henry I, King of England, 92
herd instinct, 358
hereafter, the, 67
heritage, 181
Hewitt, Ed, 246
Hicks, Stephen R.C., 212
high
    greatest, 23
    place, filling poorly, 477
Hill, Anita, 239
Hinkley, John W., Jr., 419
Hippocrates, 205
hiring
    and firing regulations,
      462

man
  being his own master,
    357
  in the street, 119
  nature of. *See* human
    nature
  new subservient, 445
  on a white horse. *See*
    benevolent monarch
managers, American, lack of,
  269
Mandarin China, interest-
  free, debt-free money, 447
mandates, external, 357
mankind, improvement, 110
Mao Tse-tung, 182
  eradicating opium trade,
    311
Marchetti, Victor, 29
Marcos, Imelda, 379–80
market
  economics, 228
  economy. *See* free trade
  forces, 153
marriage
  broken, 307
  deregulating, 315
  formerly useful, 332
  gay, sanctioning, 332
  group. *See* group marriage
  heterosexual, abolishing,
    332
Mars, trip to, 183
Marshall Plan, 409
martial law, 391, 421
  resistors, 335
Marx, Karl, 68, 75, 82, 102,
  351–52

  communism usher, 128
Marxists, 14
Mass, 231
masses, the, 281
  achievers fooling the, 284
  manipulating, 416
mass movements, 180
mass transit, 258
master plan, 258
master/slave relationship.
  See slavery
materialism, 163
Mayor's Housing Program,
  New York City, 185
McAlvany, Don, 453
McBride, Joe, 40
McCloy, John J., 60
McCracken, Paul, 271
McFadden, Louis T., 286
McMaster, R.E., 419
McNamara, Robert, 108
meaningful wage, 155
meanness, 225
media
  campaign against
    American people, 427
  control of the, 422–23,
    453–54, 458
  to increase debt,
    450–51
  influenced by big money,
    288
  intellectual prostitutes,
    454
  marionettes, 454
  tools of the rich, 454
medical
  care. *See* health care

nations
bankruptcy of, 413–14
irrelevant, 428
rebirth of, 233
NATO, 464, 466
forces as UN standing
army, 466
natural resources, 72
nature
taking its course, 328
versus nurture, 211, 218
naval nuclear forces, U.S.,
421
Nazi Germany, interest-free,
debt-free money, 447
near-utopia, 132
necessities of life, 247
need, real, 433
negative options in economics, 117
Nehemiah 5:1-13, 449
neighbor
aiding, 360
accommodating sensitivi-
ties of, 389
Ness, Elliot, 114
neutron bomb, 139
New Deal, 198
new debt money, 463
New England states, 185
"new math," 362
new towns. *See* work camps
New World Order, 15, 46,
74, 226, 392–93, 427, 429,
458, 461
better life, 398
defined, 399–400
whose?, 459

World War ongoing, 468
New York City, 174
possible bankruptcy, 185
Public Schools, 394–97
Bureau of Non-Public
Schools, 397
subway system, 207
New York Colony system,
295
New York Times, The, 45,
264, 324, 360, 466
New Yorkers, arrogance, 310
New Zealand, 51–52
newspapers as propaganda
tools, 467
Nicaragua, 326
Niemoller, Martin, 401
Nietzsche, Friedrich, 335
nirvana, 203
Nixon, Richard, President,
U.S., 231, 243
and CIA, 34, 46
no-debt, 179
nomenklaturshchiks, 393
nonexistent money. *See*
money, debt of nonexistent
nonsense, 214
/sense, 268
North, Gary, 260–61, 263,
266
North, Oliver, 243, 379, 412
Notes to Myself, 210
nurses' salaries, 329
nurture vs. nature, 211, 218

O

"Occasional Letter No. 1,"
398

self-fulfillment, 124
self-help, 410
self-interest, 417
    enlightened. *See* enlight-
        ened self-interest
    groups, 64
    long-term, 142–43
    narrow, 381
    short-term benefits, 124,
        143
    unenlightened, 248
self-preservation, 240
self-protection with guns, 334
self-reliance, 150
self-respect through work
    ethic, 149
self-sufficiency, 198, 332
    "Give a man a fish,"
        163–64
    in relocation centers, 123
    without subsidies, 339
self-supporting relocation
    centers, 123
selling, to yourself, 230
Senate Finance Committee,
    261
senators' address and phone,
    58
Seneca, 179
sense/nonsense, 268
sensible, being, rewards of,
    194
sentences, prison, longer, 164
separation from society,
    punishment and rewards
    of, 312
settlements, 148
sex, 176–77

engaging in, discussing,
    69
    illicit, compared to drugs,
        177
sexes, battle of the, 273
sexual
    desires, determined
        by brain chemistry,
        240
    harassment, 272
    revolution, 336
sexually transmitted diseases,
    176–77, 336
Shakespeare, William, 219
shame, 90, 255
Shanker, Albert, 395–97
shape, being in, unnecessary,
    230
Shaw, Clay, 53–54
Shaw, George Bernard, 120,
    471
Sherman, William Tecumseh,
    376
Shifty, parable, 303
short-term
    gratifications. *See*
        pleasures, transitory
        /long-term benefits,
        balancing, 377
silver, 303–4
Simons, Henry, 305
simplicity, financial, 425–26
simplification, 209
sin, 331, 429
    venial and mortal, 360
    forgiving, 60
Sinatra, Frank, 473
sincerity, 358

T

U.S. *(continued)*
    1990 debt-to-income
       ratio, 179
    armed intrusions, 285
    Banking and Currency
       Commission, 286
    Bonds, etc., interest on,
       290
    dividing country under
       generals, 412–13
    dollar, 458
    government, barred from
       borrowing money, 290
    military commanders,
       disobeying UN orders,
       465–66
    monetary policy, 463
    most debt of any nation,
       296
    notes, 241
       versus Federal Reserve
         notes, 288
    once great, 148
    Postal Service, 206
    potential, 77
    promoting democracy in
       Soviet republics, 392
    salvaging, 149
    Senate, protest against
       Soviets, 391–92
    Soviet policy, long-term
       strategy, 390
    subversion, 470
    total collapse, 348
ultra-rightists, 451
unalignment, 119
Uncle Sam, 301
uncommon sense, 357

under-investment, 415
under-saving, 415
underclass, 143, 162, 207,
    217. *See also* poor, the
underground economy, 72
underprivileged. *See* poor, the
understanding, versus
    knowledge, 181
unearned income, 90
unemployables, 131
unemployed
    the, work camps for, 311
    people, relocation centers,
       122
unemployment, 95, 101, 179,
    216, 242, 291
    civil evils of, 307
    former bank employees,
       250
    prohibiting, 325
    relation to inflation, 374
unfairness, 94
unhappiness, 433
unions, 75, 186, 269
    excesses, 131
    membership, 224
uniqueness, of author's views,
    332
United Nations. *See* U.N.
United Parcel Service, 206
unity
    by choice, 13
    through compromise and
       understanding, 337
untruths, benefits of
    believing, 225
USSR, terminology, 15
usury, 90

The future begins TODAY

Nugget Shavings . . .

A defective money system assures a defective economy.

The real purpose of the Fed is to expedite the creation of debt.

Some people give meaning to their lives by redistributing other people's money. Welcome to the decade of altruism…or socialism by installments.

LIBERTYGRAM:
Dear Patriot: Get *Philosophy Nuggets*…sheds light; draws blood; expands mind…read at once, time is short.   – Samoht

If what grabs you most is our fancy footwork with words—look again, you've missed the main point.

Our collective sixth sense tells us that buy-buy today means bye-bye tomorrow.

You might say insider Professor Carroll Quigley was somewhat talking out of school when he spoke of the financial elite thus: The objective is nothing less than a world system of financial control in private hands, able to dominate the government of each country and the economy of the world as a whole.

In order to develop a genuine sense of "right" conduct, a person must be free to engage in the "wrong" conduct.

Join Samoht's think-a-thon. All able-minded persons accepted.

Judge not the soldiers in the trenches. Orders do not come from them, or from their generals for that matter. Orders come from the money kings who wend their will through the political system which they control.

There is no one who has a rational and morally sound answer to why government should pay interest on borrowed money when it could issue the money interest-free.

We are in epochal history now.

Give that special someone the gift of enlightenment!

Order Form

Please send _____ copies of *Philosophy Nuggets* @ $25.00 each _____

Florida residents, please add $1.50 tax per book _____

Shipping and handling $2.50

Total _____

Good-faith money-back guarantee!

NAME *(please print)* _____

ADDRESS _____

CITY _____

STATE _____ ZIP _____

Please make check payable to The Givotangi Company

Mail this page (or a copy of this form) to:

THE GIVOTANGI COMPANY
P.O. BOX 120
DAYTONA BEACH, FL 32115
USA